Structures of Judicial Decision Making from Legal Formalism to Critical Theory

Structures of Judicial Decision Making from Legal Formalism to Critical Theory

REVISED SECOND EDITION

Roy L. Brooks

WARREN DISTINGUISHED PROFESSOR OF LAW
UNIVERSITY OF SAN DIEGO

CAROLINA ACADEMIC PRESS
Durham, North Carolina

Library of Congress Cataloging-in-Publication Data

Brooks, Roy L. (Roy Lavon), 1950-
Structures of judicial decision making from legal formalism to critical
theory / by Roy L. Brooks.-- 2nd ed.
  p.   cm.
Includes bibliographical references and index.
ISBN 1-59460-123-2 (alk. paper)
1. Judicial process--United States. 2. Formalities (Law) 3. Critical theory.
I. Title.

KF380.B76 2005
347.73'12--dc22

2005001765

Carolina Academic Press
700 Kent Street
Durham, NC 27701
Telephone (919) 489-7486
Fax (919) 493-5668
www.cap-press.com

For Carl A. Auerbach
and
In Memory of
Paul C. Wohlmuth

Summary of Contents

PART 2
CRITICAL PROCESS

CONTENTS

TABLE OF CASES

Table of Secondary Authorities

A Handbook to Literature 6th ed., C. Hugh Holman and William Harmon, eds., New York: McMillan, 1992.

A History of American Life: The Quest for Social Justice, 1898–1914, vol. Xi, Arthur M. Schlesinger and Dixon Ryan Fox, eds., New York: The MacMillan Company, 1931.

Abraham Lincoln: Speeches and Writings 1859–1865, Don E. Fehrenbacher, ed., 1989.

Abraham Lincoln: Speeches and Writings 1859-1865: Speeches, Letters, and Miscellaneous Writings, Presidential Messages and Proclamations, Don E. Fehrenbacher, ed., New York: Literary Classics of the United States, 1989.

Adamson, Walter L., Hegemony and Revolution: A Study of Antonio Gramsci's Political and Cultural Theory, Berkeley: University of California Press, 1980.

Agassiz, Louis, "Evolution and Permanence of Type," Atlantic Monthly, 33 (1874): 95.

Aldisert, Ruggero J., Logic for Lawyers: A Guide to Clear Legal Thinking, New York: C. Boardman Company, 1989.

Alexander, Lawrence, and Michael Bayles, Hercules of Proteus? The Many Theses of Ronald Dworkin, Social Theory and Practice 5 (1980): 267.

American Legal Realism, William W. Fischer, III, Morton J. Horwitz, Thomas A. Reed, eds., New York: Oxford University Press, 1993.

Anderson, Jerry L., Law School Enters the Matrix: Teaching Critical Legal Studies, Journal of Legal Education 54 (2004): 201.

Anderson, Perry, The Antinomies of Antonio Gramsci, New Left Review 100 (1976): 5.

Antonio Gramsci, James Martin, ed., New York: Routledge, 2001.

Appiah, Kwame Anthony, Thinking It Through: An Introduction to Contemporary Philosophy, New York: Oxford University Press, 2003.

Ascheri, Mario, and John Minor, Wisdom Lecture on Civil Law: A Turning Point in the Civil Law Tradition: From Ius Commune to Code Napoleon, Tulane Law Review 70 (1996): 1041.

Ashmore, Harry S., Hearts and Minds: The Anatomy of Racism from Roosevelt to Reagan, New York: McGraw-Hill, 1982.

Atwood, Barbara Ann, Child Custody Jurisdiction and Territoriality, Ohio State Law Journal 52 (1991): 369.

Auerbach, Carl A., The Relation of Legal Systems to Social Change, Wisconsin Law Review 1980 (1980): 1227.

Austin, John, The Province of Jurisprudence Determined, London: John Murray, 1832.

Balkin, Jack M. and Sanford Levinson, Understanding the Constitutional Revolution, Virginia Law Review 87 (2001): 1045.

Ball, Terrance, and Richard Dagger, Political Ideologies and Their Democratic Ideal, New York: Harper Collins, 1991.

Banks, Sandy, When Racial Bias Emerges, Despite Our Best Efforts, Los Angeles Times, 9/19/00, p. E1.

Barlett, Donald L., and James B. Steele, "Big Money Politics: Who Gets Hurt," Time 2/7/00, p. 38.

Bartlett, Katherine T., Feminist Legal Methods, Harvard Law Review 103 (1990): 829.

Bass, Jack, Unlikely Heroes, New York: Simon and Schuster, 1981.

Bator, Paul M., The Judicial Universe of Judge Richard Posner, University of Chicago Law Review 52 (1985): 1146.

Beauvoir, Simon de, The Second Sex, New York: Knopf, 1974.

Beermann, Jack M., The Supreme Court's Narrow View on Civil Rights, Supreme Court Review 1993 (1993): 199 (civil rights law).

Bell, Derrick A., A Question of Credentials, Harvard Law Record, 9/17/82, p. 14.

_____, And We Are Not Saved, New York: Basic Books, 1979.

_____, Brown v. Board of Education and the Interest-Convergence Dilemma, Harvard Law Review 93 (1980): 518.

_____, Faces from the Bottom of the Well: The Permanence of Racism, New York: Basic Books, 1992.

_____, Race, Racism and American Law 4th ed., New York: Aspen Law and Business, 2000, 1st, 2nd, 3rd ed., Boston: Little, Brown and Company, 1973, 1980, 1992.

Bentham, Jeremy, An Introduction to the Principles of Morals and Legislation, New York: Hafner Publishing Company, 1948.

Berlin, Isaiah, "Equality," in Introduction to Great Books 2nd Series, Chicago: The Great Books Foundation, 1990.

_____, Four Essays on Liberty, New York: Oxford University Press, 1969.

Bickel, Alexander M., The Least Dangerous Branch: The Supreme Court at the Bar of Politics, Indianapolis: Bobbs-Nerrill, 1962.

_____, The Morality of Consent, New Haven: Yale University Press, 1975.

Biden, Joseph, On Judicial Imperialism, Congressional Record, vol. 146, no. 99, 106th Congress, July 26, 2000.

Bishpan, George Tucker, The Principles of Equity: A Treatise on the System of Justice Administered by the Courts of Chancery, New York: The Banks Law Publishing Co., 1917.

Bittler, Boris I., Interpreting the Constitution: Is the Intent of the Framers Controlling? If Not, What is?, Harvard Journal of Law and Public Policy 19 (1995): 9.

Black, Charles, The Lawfulness of the Segregation Decisions, Yale Law Journal 69 (1960): 421.

Black, Henry C., Black's Law Dictionary 4th ed., St. Paul: West Publishing Co. 1968.

Blackman, Rodney, J., Procedural Natural Law, Durham: Carolina Academic Press, 1999.

Blackstone, William, Commentaries on the Laws of England, vol. I, Oxford: Clarendon Press, 1765. Special Edition for the Legal Classic Library, Birmingham, Ala., 1983.

_____, Commentaries on the Laws of England, vol. III, Oxford: Clarendon Press, 1768. Special Edition for the Legal Classic Library, Birmingham, Ala., 1983.

Bocock, Robert, Hegemony and Socialist Strategy: Towards a Radical Democratic Politics, London: Verso, 1985.

Bodenheimer, Edgar, Jurisprudence: The Philosophy and Method of the Law, Cambridge: Harvard University Press, 1962.

Bond, Horace Mann, Negro Education in Alabama: A Study in Cotton and Steel, New York: Octagon Books, 1969, originally published in 1939.

_____, The Education of the Negro in the American Social Order, New York: Octagon Books, 1966, originally published in 1934.

Boot, Max, Rule of Law: Law Professors v. The Supreme Court, Wall Street Journal, 8/13/01, p. A13.

Bork, Robert H., The Tempting of America, New York: Free Press, 1990.

Brennan, William J., Jr., Speech at the Text and Teaching Symposium, Georgetown University, Washington, D.C., 10/12/85.

Brigham, John, The Constitution of the Interests: Beyond the Politics of Rights, New York: New York University Press, 1996.

Brooks, Roy L., Civil Procedure: Cases and Materials for Policy Analysis, San Diego: Western Academic Press, 1995.

_____, Critical Procedure, Durham: Carolina Academic Press, 1998.

_____, Integration or Separation? A Strategy for Racial Equality, Cambridge: Harvard University Press, 1996.

_____, Rethinking the American Race Problem, Berkeley: University of California Press, 1990.

_____, Civil Rights Symposium-Racial Subordination Through Formal Equal Opportunity, San Diego Law Review 25 (1988): 879.

_____, Rule 10b-5 in the Balance: An Analysis of the Supreme Court's Policy Perspective, Hastings Law Journal 32 (1980): 403.

_____, What About Souter's Human Resume, New York Times, 8/1/90, p. A11.

Brooks, Roy L., Gilbert P. Carrasco, and Michael Selmi, Civil Rights Litigation: Cases and Perspectives 2d ed., Durham: Carolina Academic Press, 2000.

Buckley, William F., Jr., Up From Liberalism, New York: Arlington House, 1959.

Bugliosi, Vincent, The Betrayal of America: How the Supreme Court Undermined the Constitution and Chose Our President, New York: Nation's Books, 2001.

Cain, Patricia A., Same Sex Couples and the Federal Tax Laws, Law and Sexuality 1 (1991): 97.

Calmes, Jackie, and Edward P. Foldessy, Florida Revisited: In Election Review, Bush Wins Without Supreme Court Help—Still, Majority of State Voters Would Have Picked Gore But for Poor Ballot Design, Wall Street Journal, 11/12/01, p. A1.

Cardozo, Benjamin N., The Growth of the Law, New Haven: Yale University Press, 1924.

_____, The Nature of the Judicial Process, New Haven: Yale University Press, 1921.

Case, Mary Ann, Disaggregating Gender from Sex and Sexual Orientation: The Effeminate Man in the Law and Feminist Jurisprudence, Yale Law Journal 105 (1995): 1.

Chang, Robert S., Toward an Asian American Legal Scholarship: Critical Race Theory, Post-Structuralism, and Narrative Space, California Law Review 81 (1993): 1241.

Chayes, Abraham, The Role of the Judge in Public Law Litigation, Harvard Law Review 89 (1976): 1281.

Cheever, Susan, Twiggy: A Stick Figure, New York Times Magazine, November 24, 1996, p. 74.

Chomsky, Carol, Unlocking the Mysteries of Holy Trinity: Spirit, Letter, and History in Statutory Interpretation, Columbia Law Review 100 (2000): 901.

Chomsky, Norm, Hegemony or Survival: America's Quest for Global Dominance, New York: Henry Holt and Company, 2003.

Clark, Kenneth B., "The Social Scientists, the Brown Decision, and Contemporary Confusion," Argument: The Complete Oral Argument Before the Supreme Court in Brown v. Board of Education of Topeka, 1952–1955, Leon Friedman, ed., New York: Chelsea House Publishers, 1969.

Cohen, Julia E., Lochner in Cyberspace: The New Economic Orthodoxy of 'Rights Management,' Michigan Law Review 97 (1998): 462.

Cole, David, Strategies of Difference: Litigating for Women's Rights in a Man's World, Law and Inequality: A Journal of Theory and Practice 2 (1984): 33.

Collected Papers of Charles Sanders Peirce, Charles Hartshorne, Paul Weiss, and Arthur Burks, eds., Cambridge: Harvard University Press, 1931–1966.

Conn, Peter, Pearl S. Buck: A Cultural Biography, New York: Cambridge University Press, 1996.

Connolly, Peter, The Ancient City: Life in Classical Athens and Rome, Oxford: Oxford University Press, 1998.

Cook, Walter, Wheeler, Cases and Materials on Equity, 4th ed., St. Paul: West Publishing Co., 1948.

Coolidge, David Orgon, Voters Finally Get a Say on Same-Sex Marriage, Wall Street Journal, 11/02/98, p. A34.

Coon, Arthur I., and John B. Oakley, The Federal Rules in State Courts: A Survey of State Court Systems of Civil Procedure, Washington Law Review 61 (1986): 1367.

Cornelius, Janet Duitsman, When I Can Read My Title Clear: Literacy and Religion in the Antebellum South, Columbia: University of South Carolina Press, 1991.

Crenshaw, Kimberle W., Race, Reform, and Retrenchment: Transformation and Legitimation in Antidiscrimination Law, Harvard Law Review, 101 (1988): 1331.

Critical Race Theory Perspectives on the Social Studies : the Profession, Policies, and Curriculum, Gloria Ladson-Billings, ed., Greenwich, Conn.: Information Age Pub., 2003.

Critical Race Theory: The Cutting Edge 2d ed., Richard Delgado and Jean Stefanic, eds., Philadelphia: Temple University Press, 2000.

Critical Race Theory: The Key Writings that Formed the Movement, Kimberle Williams Crenshaw, Neil Golanda, Garry Peller, and Kendall Thomas, eds., New York: New Press, 1995.

Critical White Studies: Looking Behind the Mirror, Richard Delgado and Jean Stefanic, eds., Philadelphia: Temple University Press, 1997.

Crossroads, Directions, and a New Critical Race Theory, Francisco Valdes, Jerome Mc-Cristal Culp, Angela P.Harris, and Francisco Valdez, eds., Philadelphia: Temple University Press, 2002.

Cruse, Harold, The Crisis of the Negro Intellectual: From Its Origins to the Present, New York: William Morrow & Co., 1967.

Cultural and Literary Critiques of the Concepts of "Race," E. Nathaniel Gates, ed., New York: Garland Publishers, 1997.

Cushman, Robert Eugene, The Social and Economic Interpretation of the Fourteenth Amendment, Michigan Law Review 20 (1922): 737.

Dalton, Harlan, The Clouded Prism, Harvard Civil Rights-Civil Liberties Law Review 22 (1987): 335.

Deerlin, Van, Drawing the Battle Lines Anew on Same-Sex Marriage, San Diego Union-Tribune, 10/28/98, p. B9.

Decter, Midge, An Old Wife's Tale: My Seven Decades in Love and War, New York: Harper Collins Publishers, 2001.

DeFuniak, William, Handbook on Modern Equity, New York: Little Brown & Co., 1956.

Delgado, Richard, Alternative Dispute Resolution, Conflict as Pathology: An Essay for Trina Grillo, Minnesota Law Review 91 (1997): 1391.

_____, Crossroads and Blind Alleys: A Critical Examination of Recent Writings About Race, Texas Law Review 82 (2004): 212.

_____, Derrick Bell's Toolkit—Fit to Dismantle That Famous House?, New York University Law Review 75 (2000): 283.

_____, Fairness and Formality: Minimizing the Risk of Prejudice in Alternative Dispute Resolution, Wisconsin Law Review 1985 (1985): 1359.

_____, Richard, Mindset and Metaphor, Harvard Law Review 103, (1990): 1872.

_____, The Ethereal Scholars: Does Critical Legal Studies Have What Minorities Want?, Harvard Civil Rights-Civil Liberties Law Review 22 (1987): 301.

_____, The Imperial Scholar: Reflections on a Review of Civil Rights Literature University of Pennsylvania Law review 132 (1984): 561.

_____, When a Story is Just a Story: Does a Voice Really Matter? Virginia Law review 76 (1990): 95

Delgado, Richard, and Jean Stefancic, Critical Race Theory, New York: New York University, 2001.

Deliberative Democracy, John Elster, ed., Cambridge: Cambridge University Press, 1998.

Dershowitz, Alan M., Supreme Injustice: How the High Court Highjacked Election 2000, New York: Oxford University Press, 2001.

De Tocqueville, Alexis, Democracy in America, George Lawrence, trans., J.P Mayer, ed., New York: Doubleday, Anchor Books, 1969.

Developments in the Law-The Path of Civil Litigation, Harvard Law Review 113 (2000): 1851.

Dewey, John, Reconstruction in Philosophy, Boston: Beacon Press, 1948.

Diggins, John Patrick, Max Weber: Politics and the Spirit of Tragedy, New York: Basic Books, 1996.

Dillon, Sara, Looking for the Progressive Empire: Where is the European Union's Foreign Policy? Connecticut Journal of International Law 19 (2004): 275.

DuBois, W.E.B., Black Reconstruction in America, New York: Atheneum, 1992, reprint of 1935 edition.

_____, "Does the Negro Need Separate Schools?", Journal of Negro Education, 4 (1935): 328.

DuBois, W.E.B., and Augustus Gill, The Common School and Negro American, New York: Russell and Russell, 1969, originally published in 1911.

Dusky, Lorraine, Still Unequal: The Shameful Truth About Women and Justice in America, New York: Crown, 1996.

Duxbury, Neil, Faith in Reason: The Process Tradition in American Jurisprudence, Cardozo Law Review 15 (1993): 601.

_____, Patterns of American Jurisprudence, New York: Oxford University Press, 1995.

Dworkin, Ronald, In Praise of Theory, Arizona State Law Journal 29 (1997): 353.

_____, Law's Empire, Cambridge: Belknap Press, 1986.

_____, Taking Rights Seriously, Cambridge: Harvard University Press, 1977.

_____, The Model of Rules, University of Chicago Law Review 35 (1967): 14.

Dyson, Michael E., Race Rules: Navigating the Color Line, Reading: Addison-Wesley Publishing Company, 1996.

Eisenberg, Melvin A., The Nature of the Common Law, Cambridge: Harvard University Press, 1988.

Ely, John H., Democracy and Distrust: A Theory of Judicial Review, Cambridge: Harvard University Press, 1980.

Epstein, Richard A., The Price of a Judge's Hubris, Wall Street Journal, 6/9/00, p. A18.

Eskridge, William N., Jr., Gaylaw: Challenging the Apartheid of the Closet, Cambridge: Harvard University Press, 1999.

_____, Reneging on History? The Court/Congress/President Civil Rights Game, California Law Review 79 (1991): 613.

_____, Textualism, the Unknown Ideal?, Michigan Law Review 96 (1998): 1509.

_____, The New Textualism, UCLA Law Review 37 (1991): 621.

Eskridge, William N., Jr., and Gary Peller, The New Public Law Movement: Moderation as a Postmodern Cultural Form, Michigan Law Review 89 (1991): 707.

Eskridge, William N., Jr., and Philip P. Frickey, Legislation Scholarship and Pedagogy in the Post-Legal Process Era, University of Pittsburgh Law Review 48 (1987): 691.

_____, The Making of the Legal Process, Harvard Law Review 107 (1994): 2031.

Fajer, Marc A., Can Two Real Men Eat Quiche Together? Storytelling, Gender-Role Stereotypes, and Legal Protection for Lesbians and Gay Men, University of Miami Law Review 46 (1992): 511.

Fallon, Richard H., Jr., Reflections on the Hart and Wechsler Paradigm, Vanderbilt Law Review 47 (1994): 953.

Farber, Daniel A., and Philip P. Frickey, In the Shadow of the Legislature: The Common Law in the Age of the New Public Law, Michigan Law Review 89 (1991): 875.

Farber, Daniel A., and Suzanna Sherry, Beyond All Reason: The Radical Assault on Truth in American Law, New York: Oxford University Press, 1997.

Farber, Daniel, Symposium Contribution, The Ages of American Formalism, Northwestern University Law Review 90 (1995): 89.

Feagin, Joe R., Racist America: Roots, Current Realities, and Future Reparations, New York: Routledge, 2000.

Feeley, Malcolm M., and Edward L. Rubin, Judicial Policy Making and the Modern State: How the Courts Reformed America's Prisons, Cambridge: Cambridge University Press, 1998.

Feminist Legal Theory II: Positioning Feminist Theory Within the Law, vol. 2, Frances E. Olsen, ed., New York: New York University Press, 1995.

Fish, Stanley, Doing What Comes Naturally, Durham: Duke University Press, 1989.

Fiss, Owen M., History of the Supreme Court of the United States, 1888–1910, vol. 8, New York: Macmillan, 1993.

Flagg, Barbara J., Fashioning A Title VII Remedy for Transparently White Subjective Decisionmaking, Yale Law Journal 104 (1995): 2009.

_____, Was Blind, But Now I See: White Race Consciousness and the Law, New York: New York University Press, 1998.

Foucault, Michael, Madness and Civilization: A History of Insanity in the Age of Reason, Richard Howard trans., New York: Vintage Books, 1973.

America, New York: Metropolitan Books/Henry Holt and Company, 2004.

Frank, Jerome, Are Judges Human?, University of Pennsylvania Law Review 80 (1931): 17.

_____, Law and the Modern Mind, New York: Tudor Publishing, Co., 1936.

_____, What Courts Do In Fact, Illinois Law Review 26 (1932): 645.

Frank, Thomas, What's The Matter with Kansas: How Conservatives Won the Heart of Frankfurter, Felix, Some Reflections on the Reading of Statutes, Columbia Law Review 47 (1947): 527.

_____, The Task of Administrative Law, University of Pennsylvania Law Review 75 (1927): 614.

Franklin, John Hope, Reconstruction: After the Civil War, Chicago: University of Chicago Press, 1961.

Fredrickson, George M., Reflections on the Comparative History and Sociology of Racism, Racial Classification and History, E. Nathaniel Gates ed., New York: Garland Publications, 1997.

Freeman, Alan, Book Review, Race and Class: The Dilemma of Liberal Reform, Yale Law Journal 90 (1980): 1880.

_____, Legitimizing Racial Discrimination Through Antidiscrimination Laws, Minnesota Law Review 62 (1978): 209.

Frickey, Philip P., Congressional Intent, Practical Reasoning, and the Dynamic Nature of Federal Indian Law, California Law Review 78 (1990): 1137.

_____, Revisiting the Revival of Theory in Statutory Interpretation: A Lecture in Honor of Irving Younger, Minnesota Law Review 84 (1999): 199.

Friedman, Lawrence M., A History of American Law, New York: Simon & Schuster, 1973.

Friendly, Henry, The Courts and Social Policy: Substance and Procedure, University of Miami Law Review 33 (1978): 21.

Fuller, Lon L., American Legal Realism, University of Pennsylvania Law Review 82 (1934): 429.

_____, Positivism and Fidelity to Law—A Reply to Professor Hart, Harvard Law Review 71 (1958): 630.

_____, Positivism and the Separation of Law and Morals, Harvard Law Review 71 (1958): 593.

_____, The Forms and Limits of Adjudication, Harvard Law Review 92 (1978): 353.

Garrett, Elizabeth, Who Directs Direct Democracy?, The University of Chicago Law School Round Table 4 (1997): 17.

Garvey, Stephen, Book Review: Did Making Over the Prisons Require Making Up the Law?, Cornell Law Review 84 (1999): 1476.

Gates, Henry Louis, Jr., and Nellie Y. McKay, The Norton Anthology: African American Literature, gen. eds., New York: W.W. Norton and Company, 1997.

Gillman, Howard, The Constitution Besieged: The Rise and Demise of Lochner Era Police Powers Jurisprudence, Durham: Duke University Press, 1993.

Gilmore, Grant, The Ages of American Law, New Haven: Yale University Press, 1977.

Goldberg, Carey, First Gay Couples Join in Civil Unions: Cheers, Boos at Vermont Ceremonies, San Diego Union Tribune, 7/2/00, p. 1.

Gordon, Robert W., New Developments in Legal Theory, in The Politics of Law: A Progressive Critique, David Kairys, ed., New York: Pantheon Books, 1982.

Gordon, Robert W., Unfreezing Legal Reality: Critical Approaches to Law, Florida State University Law Review 15 (1987): 195.

Graham, Howard J., The "Conspiracy Theory" of the Fourteenth Amendment, Yale Law Journal 47 (1938): 371.

Gramsci, Antonio, Pre-Prison Writings, Richard Bellamy, ed. Virginia Cox, trans., New York : Cambridge University Press, 1994.

Grana, Sheryl J., and Jane C. Allenbruger, The Social Context of Law, Upper Saddle River: Prentice-Hall, Inc., 1999.

Greenhouse, Linda, High Court Appears Diminished in Process, San Diego Union-Tribune, 12/14/00, p. A24.

_____, Rehnquist Asks Limit to Automatic Appeals, New York Times, Section 1 (Main), 9/16/84 p. 27.

Greenwalt, Kent, Variation on Some Themes of a 'Disporting Gazelle' and His Friends: Statutory Interpretation as Seen by Jerome Frank and Felix Frankfurter, Columbia Law Review 100 (2000): 176.

Grillo, Trina, The Mediation Alternative: Process Dangers for Women, Yale Law Journal 100 (1991): 1545.

Guinier, Lani, The Triumph of Tokenism: The Voting Rights Act and the Theory of Black Electoral Success, Michigan Law Review 89 (1991): 1077.

Gutman, Amy, and Dennis Thompson, Democracy and Disagreement, Cambridge: Harvard University Press, 1993.

Habermas, Jurgen, Between Facts and Norms, Cambridge: MIT Press, 1992.

Hacker, Andrew, Two Nations: Black and White, Separate, Hostile, Unequal, New York: Ballantine Books, 1995.

Harmony, Michael A., Harmony or Hegemony? The American Military Role in the Pursuit of Justice, Connecticut Journal of International Law 19 (2004): 231.

Harris, Angela P., Race and Essentialism in Feminist Legal Theory, Stanford Law Review 42 (1990): 581.

Harris, Cheryl, Whiteness as Property, Harvard Law Review 106 (1993): 1707.

Hart, Henry M., Jr., The Relations Between State and Federal Law, Columbia Law Review 54 (1954): 489.

_____, The Supreme Court, 1958 Term-Forward: The Time Chart of the Justices, Harvard law Review 73 (1959): 84.

Hart, Henry M., Jr., and Albert M. Sacks, The Legal Process: Basic Problems in the Making and Application of Law, William N. Eskridge, Jr. and Philip P. Frickey, eds., New York: Foundation Press, 1994.

Hart, H.L.A., Essays on Bentham, Oxford: Claredon Press, 1982.

_____, Law in the Perspective of Philosophy: 1776–1976, New York University Law Review 51 (1976): 538.

_____, Positivism and the Seperation of Law and Morals, Harvard Law Review 71 (1958): 593.

_____, The Concept of Law, Oxford: Oxford University Press, 1961.

Hart, Jeffrey, Smiling Through the Cultural Catastrophe, New Haven: Yale University Press, 2001.

Hasnas, John, Back to the Future: From Critical Legal Studies Forward to Legal Realism, or How Not to Miss the Point of the Indeterminacy Argument, Duke Law Journal 45 (1995) 84.

Heyman, Michael, The Chief Justice, Racial Desegregation, and the Friendly Critics, California Law Review 49 (1961): 104.

Holmes, Oliver Wendell, The Common Law, Mark DeWolfe Howe, ed., Cambridge: Harvard University Press, 1963.

_____, The Path of the Law, Harvard Law Review 10 (1897): 457.

_____, The Theory of Legal Interpretation, Harvard Law Review 12 (1899): 417.

Homosexuality: Opposing Viewpoints, Mary E. Williams, ed., San Diego: Greenhaven Press, 1999.

Hora, Peggy Fulton, William G. Schma, and John T.A. Rosenthal, Therapeutic Jurisprudence and the Drug Treatment Court Movement: Revolutionizing the Criminal Justice System's Response to Drug Abuse and Crime in America, Notre Dame Law Review 74 (1999): 439.

Horowitz, Morton J., History and Theory, Yale Law Journal 96 (1987): 1825.

_____, The Transformation of American Law, 1870–1960, Cambridge: Harvard University Press, 1977.

_____, The Transformation of American Law: 1870–1960: The Crisis of Legal Orthodoxy, New York: Oxford University Press, 1992.

_____, The Warren Court and the Pursuit of Justice, New York: Hill and Wang, 1998.

Hull, N.E.H., Roscoe Pound, and Karl Llewellyn: Searching for an American Jurisprudence, Chicago: University of Chicago Press, 1997.

Hunt, Alan, The Big Fear: Law Confronts Postmodernism, McGill Law Journal 35 (1990): 507.

Ideology and Power in the Age of Jackson, Edwin C. Rozwene, ed., New York: Anchor Books, 1964.

Jackman, Mary, and Marie Crane, Some of My Best Friends Are Black...Interracial Friendship and Whites' Racial Attitudes, Public Opinion Quarterly 50 (1985).

Jackson, Vicki C., Federalism and the Uses and Limits of Law: Printz and Principle?, Harvard Law Review 111 (1998): 2180.

James, William, Pragmatism and Other Writings, Giles Gunn, ed., New York: Penguin Books, 2000.

Jamieson, Kathleen Hall, Beyond the Double Bind: Women and Leadership, New York: Oxford University Press, 1995.

Johnson, Haynes, The Best of Times: America in the Clinton Years, New York: Harcourt, 2001.

Johnson, Kevin, Roll Over Beethoven: A Critical Examination of Recent Writings About Race, Texas Law Review 82 (2004): 717.

Johnson, Paul, A History of the American People, New York: Harper Collins, 1997.

Kalman, Laura, Legal Realism at Yale, 1927–1960, Chapel Hill: University of North Carolina Press, 1986.

Kaufman, Andrew L., Cardozo, Cambridge: Harvard University Press, 1998.

Kearns, John T., Deductive Logic: A Programmed Introduction, New York: New Century, 1969.

Kearns, John T., Deductive Logic: A Programmed Instruction, Albany: State University of New York Press, 1969.

Kelman, Laura, Review Essay, Eating Spaghetti with a Spoon, Stanford Law Review 49 (1997): 1547.

Kennedy, David, Critical Theory, Structuralism and Contemporary Legal Scholarship, New England Law Review 21 (1986): 209.

Kennedy, Duncan, A Critique of Adjudication {fin de siècle}, Cambridge: Harvard University Press, 1997.

_____, From the Will Theory to the Principle of Private Autonomy: Lon Fuller's 'Consideration and Form,' Columbia Law Review 100 (2000): 94.

_____, The Structure of Blackstone Commentaries, Buffalo Law Review 28 (1979): 205.

Kennedy, Randall L., Nigger, New York: Pantheon Books, 2001.

Kennedy, Randall L., Racial Critiques of Legal Academia, Harvard Law Review 102 (1989): 1745.

Kincheloe, Joe L., and Shirley R. Steinberg, "Addressing the Crisis of Whiteness: Reconfiguring White Identity in a Pedagogy of Whiteness," in White Reign: Deploying Whiteness in America, Joe L. Kincheloe, Shirley R. Steinberg, Nelson M. Rodriguez and Ronald E. Chennault, eds., New York: St. Martin's Griffin, 1998.

Kirkpatrick, David D., A Black Author Hurls That Word As a Challenge, New York Times, 12/1/01, p. A15.

Klarman, Michael J., Brown, Originalism, and Constitutional Theory: A Response to Professor McConnell, Virginia Law Review 81 (1995): 1881.

Klinkner, Philip A., and Roger M. Smith, The Unsteady March: The Rise and Decline of Racial Equality in America, Chicago: University of Chicago Press, 1999.

Kluger, Richard, Simple Justice, New York: Alfred A. Knopf, 1976.

Koh, Harold H., Two Cheers for Feminist Procedure, University of Cincinnati Law Review 61 (1993):1201.

Kornhauser, Marjorie E., The Rhetoric of the Anti-Progressive Tax Movement: A Typical Male Reaction, Michigan Law Review 86 (1987): 465.

Kovel, Joel, White Racism: A Psychohistory, New York: Vintage Books, 1970.

Kozyris, John, The Conflicts Provisions of the ALI's Complex Litigation Project: A Glass Half Full?, Louisiana Law Review 54 (1994): 953.

Krieger, Linda Hamilton, Content of Our Categories: A Cognitive Bias Approach to Discrimination and Equal Employment Opportunity, Stanford Law Review 47 (1995): 1161.

Kroger, John R., Supreme Court Equity, 1789–1835, and the History of American Judging, Houston Law Review 34 (1998): 1425.

Krotoszynski, Ronald J., Jr., The New Legal Process: Games People Play and the Quest for Legitimate Judicial Decision Making, Washington University Law Quarterly 77 (1999): 993.

Kunhardt, Philip B., Jr., Philip B. Kunhardt III, and Peter W. Kunhardt, The American President, New York: Riverhead Books, 1999.

Kurland, Philip B., The Privileges or Immunities Clause: "Its Hour Come Round at Last?," Washington University Law Quarterly 1972 (1972): 405.

Kutler, Stanley I., Privilege and Creative Destruction: The Charles River Bridge Case, Baltimore: The Johns Hopkins University Press, 1971.

La France, Marianne, The Schemas and Schemes in Sex Discrimination, Brooklyn Law Review 65 (1999): 1063.

Landis, James M., The Administrative Process, New Haven: Yale University Press, 1938.

Law, Sylvia A., Homosexuality and the Social Meaning of Gender, Wisconsin Law Review 1998 (1998): 187.

Lawrence, Charles, Symposium: Race and Remedy in a Multicultural Society: Forward: "Race, Multiculturalism, and the Jurisprudence of Transformation", Stanford Law Review 47 (1995): 819.

_____, The Id, the Ego, and Equal Protection: Reckoning with Unconscious Racism, Stanford Law Review 39 (1987): 317.

Lawrence, Charles, and Mari Matsuda, We Won't Go Back: Making the Case for Affirmative Action, New York: Houghton Mifflin Co., 1997.

Lazarus, Richard J., and Claudia M. Newman, City of Chicago v. Environmental Defense Fund: Searching for Plain Meaning in Unambiguous Ambiguity, New York University Environmental Law Journal 4 (1995): 1.

Leiter, Brian, Rethinking Legal Realism: Toward a Naturalized Jurisprudence, Texas Law Review 76 (1997): 267.

_____, Review Essay: "Positivism, Formalism, Realism," Columbia Law Review 99(1998): 1138.

Leo, John, On Society: Pain in the Heartland, US. News and World Report, Sept. 6, 2004.

Lessig, Lawrence, Understanding Changed Readings: Fidelity and Theory, Stanford Law Review 47 (1995): 395.

Levin, Shana, Social Psychology Evidence on Race and Racism, Chapter 3, p.2 in A Report of the AGRA Panel on Racial Dynamics in Colleges and Universities, Mitchell Chang, Daria Witt, James Jones, Kenji Hakuta, eds., Stanford: Center for the Comparative Studies on Race and Ethnicity, 1999.

Levinson, Daniel J., with Judy D. Levinson, The Seasons of a Woman's Life, New York: Knopf, 1996.

Levy, Leonard, Original Intent and the Framers' Constitution, New York: MacMillan, 1988.

Lewan, Todd, and Dolores Barclay, Oral History Found True: Hundreds of Blacks Were Cheated of Land, San Diego Union Tribune, 12/2/01, p. A 25.

Litowitz, Douglas, Gramsci, Hegemony, and the Law, Brigham Young University Law Review, 2000 (2000): 515.

_____, Postmodern Philosophy and Law, Lawrence: University Press of Kansas, 1997.

Littleton, Christine A., Reconstructing Sexual Equality, California Law Review 75 (1987): 1297.

Livingston, Michael A., Symposium—"Radical Scholars, Conservation Field: Putting 'Critical Tax Scholarship' in Perspective" North Carolina Law Review 76 (1998): 1791, citing William A. Klein and Joseph Bankman, Federal Taxation 11th ed., New York: Aspen Law and Business, 1997.

Llewellyn, Karl, Some Realism About Realism—Responding to Dean Pound, Harvard Law Review 44 (1931): 1222.

_____, The Bramble Bush: Some Lectures on Law and Its Study, Birmingham: The Legal Classics Library, Special Edition, 1986.

Loffreda, Beth, Losing Matt Shepard: Life and Politics in the Aftermath of Anti-Gay Murder, New York: Columbia University Press, 2000.

Lopez, Ian F. Haney, White by Law: The Legal Construction of Race, New York: New York University Press, 1996.

_____, Institutional Racism: Judicial Conduct and a New Theory of Racial Discrimination, Yale Law Journal 109 (2000): 1717.

_____, "The Social Construction of Race: Some Observations on Illusion, Fabrication, and Choice, "Harvard Civil Rights—Civil Liberties Law Review 29 (1994) 1.

Lopez, Steve, "To Be Young and Gay in Wyoming," Time, 10/26/98, 38.

Love, Jean L., Legal Formalism from the Perspective of a Reasonable Law Professor, Harvard Journal of Law and Public Policy 18 (1993): 627.

Lyotard, Jean Francois, Postmodern Condition: A Report on Knowledge, Geoff Bennington and Brian Massumi, trans., Minneapolis: University of Minnesota Press, 1984.

MacKinnon, Catharine A., "Feminism, Marxism, Method, and the State: An Agenda for Theory," Signs: Journal of Women in Culture and Society 7 (1982): 515.

_____, Feminism, Marxism, Method, and the State: Toward Feminist Jurisprudence, Signs 8 (1984): 635.

_____, Feminism Unmodified: Discourses on Life and Law, Cambridge: Harvard University Press, 1987.

_____, Sex Equality, New York: Foundation Press, 2001.

Macia-Lees, Frances E., Patricia Sharpe, and Colleen Ballerino Cohen, The Postmodernist Turn in Anthropology: Cautions from a Feminist Perspective, Signs 15 (1989): 7.

Malcom X, The Ballot or the Bullet (April 3, 1964), Malcom X Speaks: Selected Speeches and Statements, George Breitman, ed., New York: Grove Weidenfeld, 1990.

Manning, John, Textualism as a Nondelegation Doctrine, Columbia Law Review 97 (1997): 673.

Margo, Robert A., Race and Schooling in the South, 1880–1950: An Economic History, Chicago: University of Chicago Press, 1990.

Marshall, Thurgood, Teacher Salary Cases, The Negro Handbood 1946–1947, Florence Murray, ed., New York: A. A. Wynn, 1947.

Martin, Michael, Legal Realism: American and Scandinavian, New York: Peter Lang Publishing, Inc., 1997.

Marxists Internet Achieve, http://www.marxists.org/archive/marx/txindex.htm.

Mashaw, Jerry L., Textualism, Constitutionalism, and the Interpretation of Federal Statutes, William & Mary Law Review 32 (1991): 827.

Matsuda, Mari, Looking to the Bottom: Critical Legal Studies and Reparations, Harvard Civil Rights—Civil Liberties Law Review 22 (1987): 323.

_____, Public Responses to Racist Speech: Considering the Victims' Story, Michigan Law Review 87 (1989): 2320.

_____, Charles R. Lawrence III, Richard Delgado, and Kimberle Williams Crenshaw, Words that Wound: Critical Race Theory, Assaultive Speech, and the First Amendment: New Perspectives on Law, Culture Society, Boulder: West View Press, 1993.

Max Weber on Law in Economy and Society, Edward Shils and Max Rheinstein, trans., Max Rheinstein, ed., Cambridge: Harvard University Press, 1954.

McConnell, Michael W., Originalism and The Desegregation Decisions, Virginia Law Review 81 (1995): 947.

_____, The Originalist Case For Brown v. Board of Education, Harvard Journal of Law and Public Policy 19 (1996): 457.

McCullough, David, John Adams, New York: Simon and Schuster, 2001.

McDonald, Jeff, Shop Owner Fights Judge's Ruling in Ethnic Slur Case: Clerk Receiving Jobless Benefits, San Diego Union-Tribune, 9/17/01, p. B1.

McDowell, Gary L., Equity and the Constitution: The Supreme Court, Equitable Relief and Public Policy, Chicago: University of Chicago Press, 1982.

McIntosh, Peggy, White Privilege and Male Privilege: a Personal Account of Coming to See Correspondences Through Work in Women's Studies, Critical White Studies: Looking Behind the Mirror, Richard Delgado and Jean Stefarcic, eds., Philadelphia: Temple University Press, 1997.

McIntyre, Lisa J., Law in the Sociological Enterprise: A Reconstruction, Boulder: Westview Press, Inc., 1994.

McLean, Edward B, Law and Civilization: The Legal Thought of Roscoe Pound, Lanhan: University Press of America, 1992.

McPherson, James M., For Cause and Comrades: Why Men Fought in the Civil War, New York: Oxford University Press, 1997.

Meckler, Laura, Ad Takes Swipe at 'Diversity,' San Diego Union-Tribune, 9/19/00, p. A9.

Meier, August, and Elliot Rudwick, Black History and the Historical Profession, 1915–1980, Urbana: University of Illinois Press, 1986.

Menand, Louis, The Metaphysical Club: A Story of Ideas in America, New York, Farrar, Straus and Giroux, 2001.

Menkel-Meadow, Carrie, Portia in a Different Voice: Speculations on a Woman's Lawyering Process, Berkeley Women's Law Journal 1 (1985): 39.

Michelman, Frank I., The Supreme Court and Litigation Access Fees, Duke Law Journal 1973(1973): 1153.

Mill, John Stuart, On Liberty, Elizabeth Rappaport, ed., Indianapolis: Hackett, 1978.

Minda, Gary, Postmodern Legal Movements: Law and Jurisprudence at Century's End, New York: New York University Press, 1995.

Moir, Anne, and David Jessel, Brain Sex: The Real Difference Between Men and Women, New York: Dell Publishing, 1991.

Moore, Andrew, G.T., II, Tribute to Daniel L. Herrmamm, Chief Administrator of Justice, Delaware Journal of Corporate Law ID (1986): 367.

Moore, Michael S., Educating Oneself in Public: Critical Essays in Jurisprudence, New York: Oxford University Press, 2000.

Moran, Beverly I., and William Whitford, A Black Critique of the Internal Revenue Code, Wisconsin Law Review 1996(1996): 751.

Murdoch, Joyce, and Deb Price, Courting Justice: Gay Men and Lesbians v. The Supreme Court, New York: Basic Books, 2001.

Myrdal, Gunner, An American Dilemma: The Negro Problem and Modern Democracy, New York: Harper and Brothers, 1944.

New Developments in Legal Theory, in The Politics of Law: A Progressive Critique, David Kairys, ed., New York: Pantheon Books, 1982.

Newman, Jon O., Between Legal Realism and Neutral Principles: The Legitimacy of Institutional Values, California Law Review 72 (1984): 200.

New Yorker's Attitudes Toward Cops Shifting, San Diego Union Tribune, 3/5/00, p. A12.

Nolan, Virginia E., and Edmund Ursin, Dean Leon Green and Enterprise (No-Fault) Liability: Origins, Strategies, and Prospects, Wayne Law Review 47(2001): 91.

Nolan, Virginia E., and Edmund Ursin, The Revitalization of Hazardous Activity Strict Liability, North Carolina Law Review 65 (1984): 257.

Noonan, Peggy, When Character Was King, New York: Viking, 2001.

Novak, William J., The People's Welfare, Chapel Hill: University of North Carolina Press, 1996.

Noyes, John E., American Hegemony, U.S. Political Leadership, and General International Law, Connecticut Journal of International Law 19 (2004): 293.

Patterson, Edwin W., Jurisprudence: Men and Ideas of Law, Brooklyn: Foundation Press, 1953.

Paul, Arnold M. Conservative Crisis and the Rule of Law, New York: Harper & Row, 1969.

Paul, Julius, The Legal Realism of Jerome N. Frank: A Study of Fact-Skepticism and the Judicial Process, The Hague: Martinus Nijhoff, 1959.

Pegoraro, Rob, U.S. Settlement Leaves Microsoft More Entrenched, washingtonpost.com, 11/9/01.

Peirce, Charles Sanders, Fraser's The Works of George Berkeley, in Writings of Charles S. Peirce: A Chronological Edition, Peirce Edition Project, vol. 2, Bloomington: Indiana University Press, 1982.

Peller, Gary, Neutral Principles in 1950s, University of Michigan Journal of Law Reform 21 (1988): 561.

Perry, Michael, The Constitution in the Courts: Law or Politics?, New York: Oxford University Press, 1994.

Persaud, Randolph B., Shades of American Hegemony: the Primitive, the Enlightened, and the Benevolent, Connecticut Journal of International Law 19 (2004): 263.

Phillips, Kevin, Arrogant Capital: Washington, Wall Street, and the Frustration of American Politics, Boston: Little, Brown and Company, 1994.

Phillips, Michael J., The Progressiveness of the Lochner Court, Denver Law Review 75 (1998): 453.

Plissner, Martin, Majority of Voters Should Pick the President, San Diego Union Tribune, 11/18/01, p. G4.

Pollack, Louis, Racial Discrimination and Judicial Integrity: A Reply to Professor Wechsler, University of Pennsylvania Law Review 108 (1959): 1.

Posner, Richard A., 1997 Oliver Wendell Holmes Lectures: The Problematics of Moral Theory, Harvard Law Review 111 (1997): 1637.

_____, Breaking the Deadlock: The 2000 Election, the Constitution, and the Courts, Princeton: Princeton University Press, 2001.

_____, "Pragmatic Adjudication," The Revival of Pragmatism: New Essays on Social Thought, Law, and Culture, Morris Dickstein, ed., Durham: Duke University Press, 1998.

_____, The Meaning of Judicial Restraint, Indiana Law Journal 59 (1983): 1.

_____, The Problematics of Moral and Legal Theory, Cambridge: The Belknap Press of Harvard University Press, 1999.

_____, The Problems of Jurisprudence, Cambridge: Harvard University Press, 1990.

Pound, Roscoe, A Survey of Social Interests, Harvard Law Review 57 (1944): 1.

_____, Common Law Legislation, Harvard Law Review 21 (1908): 382.

_____, Do We Need a Philosophy of Law?, Columbia Law Review 5 (1905): 339.

_____, Jurisprudence, St. Paul: West Publishing Co., 1959.

_____, Law and Morals, Chapel Hill: University of North Carolina Press, 1924.

_____, Liberty of Contract, Yale Law Journal 18 (1908): 454.

_____, Mechanical Jurisprudence, Columbia Law Review 8 (1908): 605.

_____, Outlines of Lectures on Jurisprudence 5th ed., Cambridge: Harvard University Press, 1943.

_____, "Roscoe Pound," in Julius Rosenthal Foundation, My Philosophy of Law: Credos of Sixteen American Scholars, Boston: Boston Law Book Co., 1941.

_____, Spurious Interpretation, Columbia Law Review 7 (1907): 379.

_____, The Call for a Realistic Jurisprudence, Harvard Law Review 44 (1931): 697.

_____, The New Deal in the Courts: A Changing Ideal of Justice, New York Times, 9/9/34, p. 83.

_____, The Scope and Purpose or Sociological Jurisprudence, Harvard Law Review 24 (1911): 591, and Harvard Law Review 25 (1912): 489.

_____, The Theory of Judicial Decision, Harvard Law Review 36 (1923): 940.

Powell, John A., An Agenda for the Post-Civil Rights Era, University of San Francisco Law Review 29 (1995): 889.

Prison Notebooks: Antonio Gramsci, Joseph A. Buttigieg, ed., Joseph A. Buttigieg and Antonio Callari, trans., New York: Columbia University Press, 1996.

Purcell, Edward, The Crisis of Democratic Theory: Scientific Naturalism and the Problem of Value, Lexington: University Press of Kentucky, 1973.

Race Relations: "Examining White Privilege and Whiteness Studies," wysiwyg://5/http://racerelations.ab...actions/library/weekly/aa060200a.htm, 9/6/00.

Raspberry, William, Evidence Here That Race Still Matters, San Diego Union-Tribune, 3/4/00, p. B10.

Rawls, John, A Theory of Justice, Cambridge: Harvard University Press, 1971.

Raz, Joseph, Symposium: The Works of Joseph Raz: Facing Up: A Reply, Southern California Law Review 62 (1989) 1153.

_____, The Concept of a Legal System 2d ed., Oxford: Oxford University Press, 1980.

Rehnquist, William H., Observation: The Notion of a Living Constitution, Texas Law Review 54 (1976): 693.

_____, The American Constitutional Experience: Remarks of the Chief Justices, Louisiana Law Review 54 (1994): 1161.

Rhode, Deborah L., Justice and Gender, Cambridge: Harvard University Press, 1989.

_____, Feminist Critical Theories, Stanford Law Review 42 (1990): 617.

Rodriguez, Daniel B., Review Essay, The Substance of the New Legal Process, California Law Review 77 (1989): 919.

Rogat, Yosal, Legal Realism, The Encyclopedia of Philosophy vol. 4, Paul Edwards, ed., New York, The Macmillan Publishing Company and The Free Press, 1967.

Rorty, Richard, "Pragmatism as Romantic Polytheism," The Review of Pragmatism: New Essays on Social Thought, Law, and Culture, Morris Dickstein, ed., Durham: Duke University Press, 1998.

_____, The Linguistic Turn, Chicago: University of Chicago Press, 1967.

Rosen, Jeffrey, Overcoming Posner, Yale Law Journal 105 (1995): 581.

_____, The Next Court, New York Times Magazine, 10/22/00, p. 76.

Rowe, Gary D., Lochner Revisionism Revisited, Law and Social Inquiry 24 (1999): 221.

Rustad, Michael and Thomas Koenig, The Supreme Court and Junk Social Science: Selective Distortions in Amicus Briefs, North Carolina Law Review 72 (1993): 91.

Sacks, Albert, The Supreme Court, 1953 Term Forward, Harvard Law Review 68 (1954): 96.

Scalia, Antonin, A Matter of Interpretation: Federal Courts and the Law, Princeton: Princeton University Press, 1997.

_____, Originalism: The Lesser Evil, University of Cincinnati Law Review 57 (1989): 849.

_____, The Rule of Law as a Law of Rules, University of Chicago Law Review 56 (1989): 1175.

Schauer, Frederick, Formalism, Yale Law Journal 97 (1988):509.

_____, Is the Common Law Law?, California Law Review 77 (1989):455.

_____, Playing By the Rules: A Philosophical Examination of Rule-Based Decision Making in Law and in Life, New York: Oxford University Press, 1991.

_____, Statutory Construction and the Coordinating Function of Plain Meaning, Supreme Court Review 1990 (1990): 231.

Schlegel, John Henry, American Legal Realism and Empirical Social Science, Durham: The University of North Carolina Press, 1995.

Schmitt, Richard B., A Breakup Primer for Microsoft?, Wall Street Journal, 6/6/00, p. B1.

Shea, Christopher, White Men Can't Contextualize, Linguafranca: The Review of Academic Life, (2001).

Sherwin, Richard K., When Law Goes Pop: The Vanishing Line Between Law and Popular Culture, Chicago: University of Chicago Press, 2000.

Slater, Robert, Microsoft Rebooted: How Bill Gates and Steve Ballmer Reinvented Their Company, New York: Penguin Books, 2004.

Simon, Dan, A Psychological Model of Judicial Decision Making, Rutgers Law Journal 30 (1995): 1.

Simons, Kenneth W., The Logic of Equality Norms, Boston University Law Review 80 (2000): 693.

Smith, Robert C., Racism in the Post-Civil Rights Era, Albany: State University of New York, 1995.

Sneyd, Ross, Vermont House Passes Gay-Rights Legislation Allowing 'Civil Union,' The News and Observer, 3/17/00, p. A10.

Sommers, Christina Hoff, Who Stole Feminism: How Women Have Betrayed Women, New York: Simon and Schuster, 1994.

Sowell, Thomas, The Quest for Cosmic Justice, New York: Free Press, 1999.

Spencer, Herbert, Social Statics: or, The Conditions Essential to Human Happiness Specified, and the First of Them Developed, London: Chapman, 1851.

Stacy, Helen M., Postmodernism and Law: Jurisprudence in a Fragmenting World, Burlington, VT: Ashgate Publishing Company, Ltd, 2001.

Steele, Shelby, The Content of His Character, The New Republic, 3/1/99, p. 31.

Stephan, Walter G., Blacks and Brown: The Effects of School Desegregation on Black Students, (prepared for the United States Department of Education, National Institute of Education), 1983.

Stephenson, Gloria: Deconstruction, in Women's Studies Encyclopedia: Views from the Sciences, Vol. 1, Helen Tierney, ed., New York: Peter Bedrock Books, 1991.

Story, Joseph, Commentaries on Equity Jurisprudence, London: Stevens and Haynes, 1884. Special Edition for the Legal Classic Library, Birmingham, Ala., 1988.

Stromberg, Roland N., European Intellectual History Since 1789, New York: Meredith Publishing Company, 1968.

Summers, Robert, Institutionalism and American Legal Theory, Ithaca: Cornell University Press, 1982.

———, On Identifying and Reconstructing a General Theory—Some Thoughts Prompted by Professor Moore's Critique, Cornell Law Review 69 (1984): 1014.

Sunstein, Cass R., Designing Democracy, New York: Oxford University Press, 2001.

———, Justice Scalia's Democratic Formalism, Yale Law Journal 107 (1997): 529.

———, Lochner's Legacy, Columbia Law Review 87 (1987): 873.

———, The Partial Constitution, Cambridge: Harvard University Press, 1993.

Swisher, Kara, Behind the Blustering Over the Microsoft Settlement, Wall Street Journal, 12/3/01, p. B1.

Symposium—"Formalism and Statutory Interpretation," Chicago Law Review 66 (1999) 636-698.

Symposium—"The Future of Intersectionality in Critical Race Feminism," Journal of Contemporary Legal Issues II (2001): 667–936.

Tanner, Deborah, You Just Don't Understand: Women and Men in Conversation, New York: Ballantine Books, 1990.

Taxing America, Karen B. Brown, and Mary Louise Fellows, eds., New York: New York University Press, 1996.

Tepker, Harry F., Jr., Writing the Law of Work on Nero's Pillars: The 1998–99 Term of the U.S. Supreme Court, The Labor Lawyer 15 (1999): 181.

Terzian, Philip, Media's Vote Tally is in: President Bush is President, San Diego Union Tribune, 12/2/01, p. G4.

The African American Book of Values, Steven Barboza, ed., New York: Doubleday, 1998.

The American Heritage College Dictionary, 4th edition, New York: Houghton Mifflin Co., 2004.

The Black Aesthetic, Addison Gayle, Jr., ed., Garden City: Doubleday, 1972.

The Communist Manifesto: New Interpretations, Mark Cowling, ed., New York: NYU Press, 1998 (includes, in full, The Manifesto of the Communist Party, written by Marx and Frederick Engels, Terrell Carver, trans., first published in 1848).

The Federalist, or The New Constitution, London: J.M. Dent and Sons Ltd., 1948.

The Federalist Papers in Modern Language Indexed for Today's Political Issues, Mary E. Webster, ed., Bellevue: Merril Press, 1999.

The Latino/a Condition: A Critical Reader, Richard Delgado and Jean Stefancic, eds., New York: New York University Press, 1998.

The Politics of Law: A Progressive Critique, 3d ed., David Kairys, ed., New York: Basic Books, 1998.

The Republic of Plato, F.M. Cornford, trans., New York: Oxford University Press, 1945.

The Vote: Bush, Gore and the Supreme Court, Cass R. Sunstein and Richard Epstein, eds., Chicago: University of Chicago Press, 2001.

The Works of Aristotle, vol. III, Great Books of the Western World, vol. 9, Robert Maynard Hutchins ed., Chicago: Encyclopedia Britannica, 1952.

Thernstrom, Stephan, and Abigain Thernstrom, America in Black and White: One Nation, Indivisible, New York: Simon & Schuster, 1997.

Thomas, Clarence, Harvard Journal of Law and the Public Policy 12 (1989): 63.

Top N.J. Cops Knew Minorities Targeted, San Diego Union-Tribune, 10/13/00, p. A7.

Tribe, Laurence, American Constitutional Law 2d ed., Mineola: Foundation Press, 1988.

Trubek, David, Max Weber on Law and the Rise of Capitalism, Wisconsin Law Review 1972 (1972): 720.

Unger, Roberto, The Critical Legal Studies Movement, Harvard Law Review 96 (1983): 565.

Ursin, Edmund, Judicial Creativity and Tort Law, George Washington Law Review 49 (1981): 229.

Valdes, Francisco, Forward: Latina/o Ethnicities, Critical Race Theory, and Post-Identity Politics in Postmodern Legal Culture: From Practices to Possibilities, La Raza Law Journal 9 (1996): 1.

Valdes, Francisco, Queers, Sissies, Dykes, and Tomboys: Deconstructing the Conflation of "Sex," "Gender," and "Sexual Orientation" in Euro-American Law and Society, California Law Review 83 (1995): 1.

Valdez, Francisco, Theorizing Outcrit Theories: Coalitional Method and Comparative Jurisprudential Experience—Racecrits, Queercrits and Latcrits, University of Miami Law Review 53 (1999): 1265.

Valian, Virginia, The Cognitive Bases of Gender Bias, Brooklyn Law Review 65 (1999): 1037.

Volkomer, Walter E., The Passionate Liberal: The Political and Legal Ideas of Jerome Frank, The Hague: Martinus Nijhoff, 1970.

Wachtel, Paul L., Race in the Mind of America: Breaking the Vicious Circle Between Blacks and Whites, New York: Routledge, 1999.

Wall Street Journal, 9/5/91, p. A15.

Warren, Charles, The Progressiveness of the Supreme Court, Columbia Law Review 13 (1913): 294.

Warren, Earl, A Bulwark to the State Police Power—The United States Supreme Court, Columbia Law Review 13 (1913): 667.

Wechsler, Herbert, Toward Neutral Principles of Constitutional Law, Harvard Law Review 73 (1959): 1.

Weinrib, Ernest J., Legal Formalism, On the Imminent Rationality of Law, Yale Law Journal 97 (1988): 949.

Weisberg, Richard H., Judicial Discretion, or the Self on the Shelf, Cardoza Law Review 10 (1988): 105.

Weisberg, Robert, The Calabresian Judicial Artist: Statutes and the New Legal Process, Stanford Law Review 35 (1983): 213.

West, Robin, Feminism, Critical Social Theory and Law, University of Chicago Legal Forum 1989 (1989): 59.

_____, Jurisprudence and Gender, University of Chicago Law Review 55 (1988): 1.

_____, Relativism, Objectivity, and Law, Yale Law Journal 99 (1990): 1473.

Wetlaufer, Gerald B., Systems of Belief in Modern American Law: A View from the Century's End, American University Law Review 49 (1999): 1.

White, Edward, From Sociological Jurisprudence to Realism: Jurisprudence and Social Change in Early Twentieth-Century America, Virginia Law Review 58 (1972): 999.

White, Morton, Social Thought in America: The Revolt Against Formalism, Boston: Beacon Press, 1957.

Wiecek, William M., Liberty Under Law—The Supreme Court in American Life, Baltimore: John Hopkins University Press, 1988.

Wigdor, David, Roscoe Pound: Philosopher of Law, Westport: Greenwood Press, 1974.

Wigfield, Mark, A Primer on the Microsoft Antitrust Case Settlement, WSJ.com, 11/15/01.

Wildman, Stephanie M., Privilege Revealed-How Invisible Preference Undermines America, New York: New York University Press, 1996.

Willhelm, Sidney, Book Review, The Supreme Court: A Citadel for White Supremacy, Michigan Law Review 79 (1981): 847.

Williams, Gwyn, Gramsci's Conxept of "Egomania," Journal of History of Ideas 21 (1960): 586.

Williams, Patricia, Alchemy of Race and Rights, Cambridge: Harvard University Press, 1991.

_____, Alchemical Notes: Reconstructing Ideals from Deconstructed Rights, Harvard Civil Rights-Civil Liberties Law Review 22 (1987): 401.

Wilson, James Q., The Morality of Formalism, UCLA Law Review 33 (1985): 431.

Woloch, Nancy, Muller v. Oregon: A Brief History with Documents, Boston: Bedford Books, 1996.

Woodard, Calvin, Reality and Social Reform: The Transition from Laissez-Faire to the Welfare State, Yale Law Journal 72 (1962): 286.

Wright, Chauncey, The Philosophy of Herbert Spencer, North American Review 100 (1865): 436.

_____, The Winds and the Weather, Atlantic Monthly 1 (1858): 273.

Yoo, John Choon, Who Measures the Chancellor's Foot? The Inherent Remedial Authority of the Federal Courts, California Law Review 84 (1996): 1121.

Yoshino, Kenji, Assimilationist Bias in Equal Protection: The Visibility Presumption and the case of Don't Ask, Don't Tell, Yale Law Review Journal 108 (1998): 485.

Young, Jr., Benjamin L., Justice Scalia's History Tradition: The Chief Nightmare in Professor Tribe's Anxiety Closet, Virginia Law Review 78 (1992): 581.

Zlotnick, David M., Justice Scalia and His Critics: An Exploration of Scalia's Fidelity to His Constitutional Methodology, Emory Law Review 48 (1999): 1377.

PREFACE

There are any number of ways of finding a solution to any given legal problem. Some judges search for solutions syllogistically, often exaggerating the transparency of text (legal formalism, Chapter 1), while others purport to seek solutions through close, logical readings of authoritative text (Scalian textualism, Chapter 2). Still other judges look for answers in the social ends of law, largely determined by the judge's personal sense of justice (legal realism, Chapter 3), by well-defined community needs (sociological jurisprudence, Chapter 4) or by existing governmental or social arrangements (legal process, Chapter 5).

Sometimes these traditional judicial methods fail to see life beyond their individual structures, effectively leaving scores of Americans without a judicial means of resolving their social problems. These Americans have two choices: forget about finding judicial answers to their pressing problems; or, refusing to accept what might be called "juridical subordination," search for new judicial approaches. This book pursues the latter course. One of the book's major objectives is to create a process of judicial decision making that speaks to the needs and norms of millions of Americans. The objective here is to move the judiciary in the same direction as millions of citizens whose values are legitimate yet effectively outside the scope and concern of traditional judicial theories ("critical process," Chapters 8–12).

Another objective of this book is to construct or redesign several intellectual structures that not only deepen our understanding of traditional process, but also help to create critical process. These structures render fascinating juxtapositions that shed new light on familiar judicial theories and light the way for new theories. There is something in this book for both the "traditionalist" and the "criticalist."

In Section A of this Preface, I shall overview these structures and indicate the order in which topics are presented in the book. Section B closes out the Preface with a discussion of one of the intellectual structures employed in the book. This discussion appears here rather than in the body of the book because it is less juridical than the other structures. Taken as a whole, these intellectual frameworks attempt not only to strengthen the chain of our jurisprudential knowledge, but also to add links to it.

A. Overview

1. Juridical and Politico-Economic Structures

The first juridical structure presented in the book is very basic. It views judicial decision making as a linear movement from Point A (the dispositive issue of a case) to Point B (the judge's reasoning and, hence, the most important part of the process) to Point C (the judgment, or decision, in the case). Intended for the uninitiated, this very simple way of looking at judicial decision making is broached in the Introduction.

The Introduction also launches a second and more probing juridical structure. This structure views each judicial model as an expression of either the "logical method" (Part 1, Section A) or the "policy method" (Part 1, Section B). As its name implies, the logical method is judicial reasoning committed to a logical reading and application of authoritative text. Here, the judge sees her institutional role as maintaining a level of consistency with prior rules. In contrast, a judge proceeding under the policy method envisions her institutional duty in consequentialist terms. She is self-consciously attuned to the results of her decisions, and, as presented in this book, engages policy on multiple levels: "policy-making"; "policy-discovery";[1] and "policy-vindication." A new definition of judicial "policy-making" is forged from this reconceptualization of the judicial policy-formulation function (Introduction, Section C). Taken together, the logical method and policy method describe the actual and, arguably, permissible range of judicial decision making in Anglo-American law (Introduction, Sections A & B).

Viewing traditional process through the prism of the policy method creates possibilities for critical process. Critical process is structured as the latest, but undoubtedly not the last, articulation of the policy method. Those familiar with critical theory will instantly recognize the significance of this exercise. Critical theory is transformed from a theory of legal criticism, its current state, into a theory of judicial decision making, something judges can actually use in finding effective answers to problems that impact upon the lives of people of color, women, and homosexuals (collectively called "outsiders" in critical theory).

---

1. I am indebted to my colleague Walter Raushenbush for suggesting this term in lieu of the potentially misleading "policy-crafting."

Critical process should also prove useful to mainstream democratic theorists, who seek to find better ways for us to live our democratic lives. Although
they have largely ignored critical theory,[2] transforming critical theory into judicial theory should clarify its democratic message and potential beyond mere
protest.

A third juridical structure presented in this book is the most complex, and
ambitious. It synthesizes traditional process into three increasingly assertive levels of judicial analysis: "Level 1," or judicial positivism; "Level 2," or judicial
pragmatism; and "Level 3," or judicial nominalism (Part 1, Section C). While
critical process translates into the policy method quite effortlessly, it does not
find easy expression among the traditional levels of judicial analysis. Critical
process fits, if at all, somewhere between Levels 2 and 3. Although not a perfect fit, critical process reveals interesting insights into its purpose, its value,
and its operation when viewed within this structure (Part 2, Section B).

The use of philosophical methods in this book requires some explanation
in light of the on-going debate between legal philosophers and legal theorists.
Glimpses of that debate appear in the pages of this book.[3] Some legal philosophers believe that any discussion of legal theory (including judicial theory)
that does not delve deeply into underlying philosophical method is not to be
taken seriously. Following the lead of the legendary legal philosopher H.L.A.
Hart, whose ambition was to reshape legal philosophy in the image of academic philosophy, these legal scholars are essentially "doing philosophy"
within the context of the law. Not surprisingly, they do not take seriously legal
theories that, in their view, lack philosophical pedigree. Included in this group
of "second-rank" theories are legal realism and critical theory. However, as we
shall see, there is some difference of opinion among legal philosophers as to
whether legal realism is completely devoid of philosophical method.

Legal theorists take issue with this view of what counts as important legal
theory. They criticize legal philosophers for taking such a narrow view, one
that would have us dismiss or discount the writings of such influential legal
theorists as Lon Fuller and Judge Richard Posner. Indeed, it is said that Hart
himself, who debated Fuller in the pages of the *Harvard Law Review* in 1958,

---

2. See, e.g., Cass R. Sunstein, *Designing Democracy* (New York: Oxford University Press,
2001); Amy Gutmann & Dennis Thompson, Democracy and Disagreement (Cambridge:
Harvard University Press, 1997); Cass R. Sunstein, *The Partial Constitution* (Cambridge:
Harvard University Press, 1993); *Deliberative Democracy*, Jon Elster, ed. (Cambridge: Cam-
bridge University Press, 1998); Jurgen Habermas, *Between Facts and Norms* (Cambridge:
MIT Press, 1992).

3. See, e.g., Chapter 3, Section B2, infra, & Chapter 7, Section B3, infra.

did not take Fuller seriously as a legal philosopher. Similarly, some books written by legal philosophers scarcely mention Judge Posner, arguably our greatest scholarly jurist since Justice Oliver Wendell Holmes. Rather, legal theorists argue that theory about law can stand on its own, that it can and should be judged on its own terms. For them, the test for good legal theory is the extent to which it brings fresh thinking to the table.

Other legal theorists—critical theorists—also take strong exception to the legal philosophers' narrow view of legal theory. They argue that to try to pigeonhole twenty-first century life experiences into nineteenth or even twentieth century conceptualizations is rather perverse. Legal theory, they argue, should be useful; it should be empowering.

While this book discusses philosophical methods underlying several judicial techniques, it does not necessarily subscribe to the notion that good legal theory must have deep philosophical roots, or that legal theory devoid of philosophical method is "junk theory." This book takes the view that any theory about law or legal institutions is worth our time and effort if it is "good" theory, which is to say it is *descriptively accurate or prescriptively sound*. Thus, legal realism, critical process (or critical theory), Judge Posner, and certainly Lon Fuller should be taken seriously because they yield "good" legal theory. Legal realism, for example, is descriptively accurate in cases like *Brown v. Board of Education*, the Supreme Court's historic 1954 decision that overturned state school segregation statutes. Similarly, critical process should be studied because it is descriptively accurate in a whole range of cases. Critical process has value even though some legal scholars might not find it prescriptively sound.

A fourth and final intellectual structure that helps increase our understanding of traditional process and critical process is politico-economic rather than juridical. It attempts to distinguish between "progressive" and "nonprogressive" judicial decision making. As this framework is nonjuridical, it is presented in the last section of this Preface (Section B) rather than in the book's chapters where it would not keep good company with the more technical discussion of jurisprudence.

2. Structure of the Book

The Introduction attempts to establish a baseline for a technical study of the structure of judicial decision making: a judge's movement from dispositive issue (Point A) to judgment (Point C) through either the logical method, the policy method or both (Point B). After discussing the historical roots of both judicial methods, the Introduction ends with a reconceptualization of the policy method. Here an attempt is made to identify and classify the several levels at which judges actually engage policy.

Part 1 (Traditional Process) is written in three sections. Section A (Logical Method) and Section B (Policy Method) discuss the five traditional judicial models mentioned at the beginning of the Preface. Legal formalism (Chapter 1) and Justice Scalia's brand of textualism (Chapter 2) are presented as individual expressions (or attempted expressions) of the logical method. Legal realism (Chapter 3), sociological jurisprudence (Chapter 4), and legal process (Chapter 5) are organized under the policy method. As a basis for comparison, each traditional judicial model is applied to *Brown v. Board of Education*. This discussion should prove useful not only in sharpening our understanding of the differences among the individual traditional judicial models, but also in crystallizing our appreciation of the differences—great differences— between traditional process and critical process. Finally, Section C (A Philosophical Synthesis) concludes Part 1 with an attempt to synthesize the five traditional judicial models into three levels of judicial analysis: Level 1/judicial positivism; Level 2/judicial pragmatism; and Level 3/judicial nominalism (Chapter 7). This intellectual structure builds upon a prior discussion of philosophical presuppositions that give conceptual shape to traditional judicial analysis (Chapter 6).

Part 2 (Critical Process) is divided into two sections. The first, Section A, is a detailed discussion of critical theory, focusing on its central message, "anti-objectivism" (Chapter 8), and its operational elements, the "subordination question" and the "internal critique" (Chapter 9). The second section, Section B, transforms critical theory from its current state as a theory of legal criticism into a theory of outsider-oriented judicial decision making. Critical theory is thus transformed into critical process. Reflecting the intellectual diversity among critical theorists, this unique process of judicial decision making is fashioned into three "equality models," termed "symmetrical," "asymmetrical," and "hybrid." Once critical process is constructed, its institutional legitimacy is discussed (Chapter 10). Then, as a way of illustrating the judicial potential of critical process beyond civil rights, the birthplace of critical theory, critical process is applied to a routine legal problem in civil procedure (Chapter 11). Finally, critical process, like traditional process, is applied to *Brown v. Board of Education* (Chapter 12). This discussion highlights the value and uniqueness of critical process, including the failure of traditional process to meet the needs of outsiders.

These applications of critical process are by no means intended to be definitive. They are at best tentative and illustrative of the type of discourse and rigorous analysis one can expect to find when applying critical process.

B. The Meaning and Means of Progress

The judge's movement from Point A to Point C (Introduction), the logical/policy method dichotomy (Part 1, Sections A & B), and the levels of judicial analysis (Part 1, Section C) offer juridical frameworks for understanding the two judicial processes presented in this book—traditional process and critical process. In the remaining pages of this Preface, I shall discuss another conceptual scheme that is less technical than the others. It is based on the distinction between "progressive" and "nonprogressive" judicial decision making.

This distinction is implicit in each judicial model discussed in this book. Indeed, each judicial theory is typically classified as one or the other. Legal formalism (Chapter 1) and Scalian textualism (Chapter 2) are frequently described as "nonprogressive" judicial models whereas legal realism (Chapter 3) is usually characterized as "progressive." Similarly, sociological jurisprudence (Chapter 4) is often seen as "progressive" and legal process (Chapter 5) as "nonprogressive." Finally, criticalists routinely describe their work as "progressive."

In American society, the term "progressive" implicitly leans toward the political left. But this characterization begs many questions, such as: What form of liberalism does progressivism take? Is conservatism necessarily nonprogressive? Is it possible that Scalian textualism can be conservative yet both progressive and nonprogressive, or that sociological jurisprudence can be progressive in a way that is different from legal realism?

The chart appearing on the backside of the book's front cover is an attempt to provide a response to these and similar questions. It estimates the politico-economic implications of each judicial model discussed in the book. A more detailed discussion of the chart follows.

As used in this book, the word "progressive" describes a government whose laws, policies, or practices seek to move society forward socially, economically, politically, culturally or spiritually. "Progressive" suggests a journeying forward, a gradual betterment, a changing from old to new, continual improvements, social evolution. The ultimate goal is to create an increasingly enlightened government—one that is wiser and kinder in its treatment of its citizens. While this is but a working definition, it will suffice for present purposes.

A government can attempt to achieve progressive outcomes through many politico-economic strategies. For example, a government can pursue such outcomes through Lockean principles—free markets and protection of "natural rights," which John Locke defined as "life, liberty, and property"—or, in other words, through what Thomas Jefferson called "an empire of liberty"—a belief in "the people, in their ability to elevate themselves in society."[4] This politico-economic strategy describes a noninterventionist government, what we have come to know as *classical liberalism*.[5] The term "noninterventionist" is a bit of a misnomer, however, because government intervention is in fact welcomed to the extent that it protects fundamental rights or lays the groundwork for private enterprise. But, clearly, there is a distrust of government, a sense that the government's power and importance must be minimized, lest it threaten fundamental rights and inhibit free markets. This *minimalist* mindset is exhibited in Lochnerian jurisprudence (legal formalism).[6]

Another means of achieving progressive outcomes is through *welfare liberalism*, sometimes referred to as the "welfare state" or Benthamite utilitarianism.[7] This strategy calls for a *maximalist* government, which can be defined as a government that intervenes in economic markets or social arrangements to rescue the individual from poverty, illness, ignorance, or inequality.[8] "The first duty of a State," President Franklin Roosevelt insisted, "is to promote the welfare of the citizens of that State. It is no longer sufficient to protect them from invasion, from lawless and criminal acts, from injustice and persecution,

---

4. Philip B. Kunhardt, Jr., Philip B. Kunhardt III, and Peter W. Kunhardt, *The American President* (New York: Riverhead Books, 1999), pp. 259–60. See also ibid. at pp. 262–70; Terrance Ball and Richard Dagger, *Political Ideologies and Their Democratic Ideal* (New York: Harper Collins, 1991), pp. 60–61.

5. See, e.g., Ball and Dagger, *Political Ideologies and Their Democratic Ideal*, supra note 4, at pp. 59–61.

6. See Chapter 1, Section B, infra.

7. "Natural rights" for Jeremy Bentham was "nonsense, nothing counting except the practical." Roland N. Stromberg, *European Intellectual History Since 1789* (New York: Meredith Publishing Company, 1968), p. 53. Sweeping away tradition, and "requiring laws and institutions to justify themselves on the practical grounds of welfare achieved," utilitarianism "assumed that the sum of individual happiness is the social optimum....The Benthamite principle of social welfare as the sum total of units of individual happiness...was the driving force behind a series of liberal acts [that] culminat[ed] in the great political Reform Bill of 1832, [bringing] to Great Britain the equivalent of the French Revolution, by peaceful means." Ibid. at pp. 52–53. The lack of commitment to traditions and the desire for experimentation should be contrasted with Burkean conservatism discussed shortly. In addition, Bentham's utility principle should be compared and contrasted with laissez-faire. Both were closely related in that they sought to get rid of special privilege and inequalities, but they were not "necessarily logically linked." Ibid. at p. 53. "Bentham's instincts were in part to be a more active, positive reformer than the laissez-faire credo indicated." Ibid. at p. 52. See also Ball and Dagger, *Political Ideologies and Their Democratic Ideal*, supra note 4, at pp. 96–97.

8. See Ball and Dagger, *Political Ideologies and Their Democratic Ideal*, supra note 4, at p. 75. See also ibid. at pp. 74–78.

but the State must protect them, so far as lies in its power, from disease, from ignorance, from physical injury, and from old-age want."[9] Thus, the individual is rescued not just from society, but also from himself. Such inequalities warrant the ministrations of the government, maximalists argue, because they are socially constructed.[10]

---

9. *The American President*, supra note 4, at p. 192.

10. This argument is a modification of what Isaiah Berlin calls the "idealized model" of egalitarian thought, which offers an alternative, albeit more aggressive, ground on which to justify welfare liberalism:

> ...[S]o long as there are differences between men, some degree of inequality may occur; and that there is no kind of inequality against which, in principle, a pure egalitarian may not be moved to protest, simply on the ground that he sees no reason for tolerating it, no argument which seems to him more powerful than the argument for equality itself—equality which he regards not merely as an end in itself, but as *the* end, the principal goal of human life. I do not suppose that extreme equality of this type—the maximum similarity of a body of all but indiscernible human beings—has ever been consciously put forward as an ideal by any serious thinker. But if we ask what kinds of equality have in fact been demanded, we shall see, I think, that they are specific modifications of this absolute ideal, and it therefore possesses the central importance of an ideal limit or idealized model at the heart of all egalitarian thought.

Isaiah Berlin, "Equality," in *Introduction to Great Books* 2nd Series (Chicago: The Great Books Foundation, 1990), p. 107. Classical liberals, on the other hand, hold to a very different view of equality:

> ...There are those who believe that natural human characteristics either cannot or should not be altered and that all that is necessary is equality of political and judicial rights. Provided that there exists equality before the law, such normal democratic principles as that of one man, one vote, some form of government arrived at by consent (actual or understood) between the members of the society, or at any rate the majority of them, and finally, a certain minimum of liberties—commonly called civil liberties—deemed necessary in order to enable men freely to exercise the legal and political rights entailed by this degree of equality, then, according to this view, no interference in other regions of activity (say, the economic) should be permitted....If it is complained that in a society where a large degree of political and legal equality is ensured, the strong and the clever and the ambitious may succeed in enriching themselves, or acquiring political power, 'at the expense of' —that is to say, in such a way as to keep these goods from—other members of the society, and that this leads to patent inequalities, liberals of this school reply that this is the price for ensuring political and legal equality, and that the only method of preventing economic or social inequalities is by reducing the degree of political liberty or legal equality between men....[W]e are told, with considerable empirical evidence, that to count men for one and only one in every respect whatever is impracticable, that the full degree of, let us say, legal and political equality often results in economic and other forms of inequality, given the different endowments

Clearly, classical liberalism and welfare liberalism hold contrasting views regarding the proper relationship between the individual and the state. While classical liberals see government as a threat to individual freedom and prosperity, welfare liberals see government as an enabler of individual freedom and prosperity. While classical liberals fundamentally believe it is not the government's business to take care of the downtrodden or to undermine self-reliance in any other way, welfare liberals fundamentally believe the government should be involved in solving people's problems. Thus, the distinction comes to this: small government and civil liberties versus big government and civil liberties.[11]

Several judicial theories embrace welfare liberalism. Legal realism encourages judicial initiation of maximalist laws and policies.[12] In a slightly different approach, sociological jurisprudence supports welfare liberalism created through legislative initiatives rather than by judicial decision making.[13] Finally, critical process prescribes a judicial process that is totally committed to welfare liberalism as a judicially initiated strategy.[14] The similarity between critical process and legal realism is quite apparent.[15]

---

of men, and that only in an absolutely uniform, robot-like society, which no one wants, can this be effectively prevented. Those who believe this commonly maintain that the only inequality which should be avoided is an inequality based on characteristics which the individual cannot alter—unequal treatment based, for instance, on birth, or color, which human beings cannot alter at will. Given that all human beings start off with equal rights to acquire and hold property, to associate with each other in whatever ways they wish, to say whatever they will, and all the other traditional objectives of liberalism, and with no special rights or privileges attached to birth, color, and other physically unalterable characteristics, then even though some human beings, by skill or luck or natural endowment, do manage to acquire property or power of ascendancy which enables them to control the lives of others, or to acquire objects which the others are not in a position to acquire, then, since there is nothing in the constitution of the society that actually forbids such acquisitiveness, the principle of equality has not been infringed. Ibid. at pp. 107–9.

11. Thomas Jefferson, Andrew Jackson, Calvin Coolidge, and Ronald Reagan are among our classical liberal presidents, while Theodore Roosevelt and Franklin Roosevelt are among our welfare-liberal presidents. Obviously, party affiliation does not necessarily determine one's politico-economic stance. See *The American President*, supra note 4, at pp. 260–61, 277.

12. See Chapter 3, Sections B & C, infra.

13. See Chapter 4, Sections B, C, & D2, infra.

14. See Part 2, infra.

15. See, e.g., Richard Delgado and Jean Stefanic, *Critical Race Theory: An Introduction* (New York: New York University, 2001) pp. 1–11, 150.

Sometimes governments attempt to achieve progressive outcomes through conservative means, specifically *individual conservatism* and *Burkean conservatism*. Like classical liberalism, both forms of conservatism are minimalist strategies. Individual conservatism, sometimes called *Reagan conservatism* after former President Ronald Reagan, envisions a government that seeks to reduce its size and scope so as to free individuals to maximize personal wealth and happiness through self-reliance, honesty, and idealism.[16] With its emphasis on unregulated capitalism, individual accountability, and distrust of government, this strategy is functionally indistinguishable from classical liberalism. Indeed, President Reagan's administration received classical liberals with open arms.[17] Legal formalism certainly has a Reagan ring to it.[18]

Bearing the name of the philosopher Edmund Burke, Burkean conservatism is not nonprogressive as is often supposed. As Roland Stromberg points out, Burke "was certainly not opposed to change, if properly carried out, and his own career, that of a person of humble birth, consisted of one passionate crusade after another.... Burke may well be viewed as the founder of a real science of social reform, rather than as a hidebound conservative."[19] Change for Burke is properly executed if it is done in an orderly fashion with due deference to a society's traditions. A severe critic of the French Revolution, Burke believed government's role was to "make[] ordered liberty possible by preventing people from doing just about anything they happen to desire."[20] Thus, unlike Reagan conservatives or classical liberals, Burkean conservatives do not regard government as a threat to liberty. This does not, however, make them maximalists. Indeed, Burkean conservatives maintain a basic indisposition toward large government. Yet, they are more concerned with social and political stability than

---

16. See Peggy Noonan, *When Character Was King* (New York: Viking, 2001) (discussion Reagan conservatism).

17. See, e.g., Midge Decter, *An Old Wife's Tale: My Seven Decades in Love and War* (New York: HarperCollins Publishers, 2001) (wife of famous neoconservative Norman Podhoretz discussing their conversion from liberalism to neoconservatism in the wake of the 1960s and the warm embrace with which President Reagan and his friends greeted them and other political converts).

18. See Chapter 1, Sections C & D, infra. Again, this describes a minimalist government, not a noninterventionist government. It was, for example, the Reagan and Bush governments, Haynes Johnson argues, that laid the groundwork for the rugged dot-com individualism of the booming 1990s by investing in scientific research. See Haynes Johnson, *The Best of Times: America in the Clinton Years* (New York: Harcourt, 2001).

19. Stromberg, *European Intellectual History Since 1789*, supra note 7, at pp. 16–17.

20. Ball and Dagger, *Political Ideologies and Their Democratic Ideal*, supra note 4, at pp. 96. See also ibid. at p. 97.

with providing opportunities for personal profit or unfettered liberty.[21] Also, unlike welfare liberals, Burkean conservatives are reformers, not innovators. They seek to move society forward in a safe and orderly manner.[22] Overall, Burkean conservatism describes the politico-economic implications of legal process.[23]

Our final judicial model, Scalian textualism, is also unquestionably conservative, but in more than one way. Justice Scalia's statutory textualism seems progressive in a Reagan-conservative way—he sees government as a threat to individual liberty.[24] Justice Scalia's constitutional textualism is, however, more difficult to locate. On the one hand, Justice Scalia champions the "Dead Constitution." This is a belief in constitutional text frozen in time (1791 to be precise); a belief that the future lies in the past; a belief that our best days are behind us.[25] The desire for the good old days is the essence of *classical conservatism*.[26] It demonstrates an unmistakable preference for a nonprogressive government—a kind of extreme minimalism when compared with other minimalist judicial models.

On the other hand, Justice Scalia justifies his constitutionalism not only on the basis of his belief in devolution, but also on the basis of his desire to protect liberty.[27] This would suggest classical liberalism or Reagan conservatism and, hence, a progressive characterization of Justice Scalia's constitutional textualism. A close call, but Justice Scalia's sense of devolution seems to dominate his constitutional textualism.[28]

---

21. Indeed, Samuel Coleridge, a conservative who "built on Burke's foundations in England" and whose "influence flowed down through the nineteenth century as a strong philosophic source of British enlightened Toryism,...believed in government regulation of manufacturers, government aid to education, the duty of the state to enhance the moral and intellectual capabilities of its citizens in all sorts of positive ways." Stromberg, *European Intellectual History Since 1789*, supra note 7, at p. 46. "British and European conservatism has been an enemy of laissez-faire." Ibid. British Prime Minister Margatet Thatcher is most responsible for bringing individual, or Reagan, conservatism to England in the 1970s and 1980s, so much so that individual conservatism is sometimes called "Thatcher conservatism" as well as Reagan conservatism. See, e.g., Ball and Dagger, *Political Ideologies and Their Democratic Ideal*, supra note 4, at pp. 94.

22. See, e.g., Ball and Dagger, *Political Ideologies and Their Democratic Ideal*, supra note 4, at p. 97.

23. See Chapter 5, infra.

24. See Chapter 2, Section C, infra.

25. See Chapter 2, Section D, infra.

26. See, e.g., Ball and Dagger, *Political Ideologies and Their Democratic Ideal*, supra note 4, at pp. 91–92.

27. See Chapter 2, Section D, infra.

28. See ibid.

With this understanding of the politico-economic implications of each judicial model, summarized on the backside of the front cover of this book, we now move to a more technical, juridical discussion of jurisprudence.

ACKNOWLEDGMENTS

A book of this nature is impossible to write without considerable help from others. Paul Wohlmuth, who died suddenly in November of 2001, spent countless hours discussing almost every detail of the book with me. I shall miss his unique blend of intellectual range, worldly experience, open-mindedness, and friendship. I am also indebted to Carl A. Auerbach, Walter Raushenbush, Bernard H. Siegan, Hubert Kim, Jon Bialecki, Diana Krause-Leemon, Elizabeth A. Savage, Abby Snyder, and Helen Irza. Valuable research was provided by Virginia Barnes, Christine Stencil, Katy Pasieta, Watson Branch, Dan Lickel, and Jason Lindsay. An army of other students took care of the grubby details like proofreading and construction of the table of cases and secondary authorities. They are: Melanie J. Acorn, Ankush Agarwal, Stephenie M. Alexander, Amy M. Bamberg, Lori S. Batra, Jennifer E. Foster, Frances A. Goldfarb, Laura S. Gormican, Charlotte L. Hasse, Salem Naim Moukarim, Alexander Papaefthimiou, Anne Richardson, Shauna N. Roitenberg, Edward J. Sackman, Anahita M. Sahba, Jennifer A. Salem, Eve Scott, Celeste L. Toy, Michelle K. Webb, Claire C. Weglarz, Michael P. Zech, and Bryan McKeldin Ziegler.

I could not have completed this book without the assistance of my ever-reliable secretary, Roanne Shamsky. Finally, I would like to thank my dean, Daniel Rodriguez, for his solid support, and the University of San Diego for providing financial resources without which the book could not have been written.

Structures of Judicial Decision Making from Legal Formalism to Critical Theory

INTRODUCTION

The material presented in this Introduction is essential to an understanding of the book. It begins with the basic structure of Anglo-American judicial decision making, and traces the antecedents of this structure to the beginning of Western civilization. Moving to a more ambitious goal, the Introduction provides a fresh analysis of the judicial policy-formulation function, one that is more nuanced than the conventional conceptualization. Included in this analysis is a new definition of the term "policy-making." Several landmark cases in public law are reread in light of this new framework. Having offered a different way to conceptualize the judicial policy-formulation function, the Introduction ends with a discussion of its institutional legitimacy.

A. The Structure of Process

In the most basic terms, the process of judicial decision making proceeds along three points: A, B, and C. Point A is the starting point of the process, Point C is the end point, and Point B is the technique by which the judge moves from Point A to Point C. Point A begins the process with the statement of the dispositive issue of the case. Point C ends the process with the judgment, or decision, in the case. Point B is the method or process of reasoning by which the judge reaches the judgment. Typically, Point B begins with a construction of the controlling rule of law and ends with a statement of the "holding." The "holding" is the "law of the case," the legal proposition for which the case stands—but for "X" the case would have been decided the other way, "X" being the holding. All judicial decision making is structured in this fashion. Only the content of the points changes from case to case.

For legal scholars (whether law professors, judges, or practitioners), Point B is the most important and complex part of the judicial process. It is important because it sets forth the judge's reasoning in the case. It is complex because judges employ different methods of reasoning, different ways of moving from Point A to Point C. Some judges profess to be rule-oriented in their journey to the judgment, while others openly admit to being policy-oriented. Thus, the former can be said to follow the "logical method" of judicial reasoning whereas the latter can be said to follow the "policy method."

Taken together, the logical method and the policy method describe the actual and, arguably, the permissible scope of the judicial function in Anglo-American law. Judges can and have always decided cases using both methods. This range of judicial inquiry is deeply rooted in Western civilization.

B. Western Tradition

Though attacked by some as an unwholesome judicial method,[1] the policy method's legitimacy ultimately rests on its importance to the administration of justice. As we shall see in this subsection, the policy method, historically viewed, is deemed to be a necessary component of our legal system, a system committed to achieving justice. Thus viewed, the legitimacy issue seems settled. What remains subject to serious debate, however, is the question concerning the *proper mix* of law and policy needed to achieve justice in a given case. Too much policy kills law; too much law kills justice.

The Western tradition in law, a vast and rich area of study, is in large part the story of law and equity, the latter being the historical antecedent of policy. Given the cloud of suspicion hanging over the policy method, our focus will center primarily on equity. Let us begin, though, with a brief account of law (or *lex*), the thing equity is not.

Law is a system of rules of conduct prescribed by a legitimate authority — the legislature by a statute, the citizens by a constitution, and a judge by the holding in a case — binding on those to whom it applies. Thus, law is by nature positive; that is, it is actually enacted by the proper authority.[2] It is a regime of extant rights. Blackstone divided law into two kinds: "the *lex non scripto*, the unwritten, or common law; and the *lex scripto*, the written, or statute law."[3] Constitutional law is usually deemed to be of the latter type even though constitutional provisions require judicial interpretation.

In contrast, equity is not law but rather what law aspires to be — "the spirit and habit of fairness, justness, and right dealing which would regulate the in-

---

1. See Part 1, Section A, infra.
2. See, e.g., William Blackstone, *Commentaries on the Laws of England*, vol. I (Oxford: The Clarendon Press, 1765, Special Edition for the Legal Classic Library, Birmingham, Ala.: 1983), pp. 70–71.
3. Ibid. at p. 63.

tercourse of men with men."[4] This concept of equity can operate in two distinct ways—one *corrective* and the other *interpretive*. As a corrective measure, equity acts as a counterweight to law, a system of rules. As an interpretive tool, equity aids in the construction and application of the extant law to novel situations. Both forms of equity can be traced back to the very beginning of Western civilization.

Corrective and interpretive equity can be found in the writings of Greek scholars. The Greeks saw equity (what Aristotle called τὸ ἐπιεικες) as a "rectification of law where...[law] is defective owing to its universality."[5] As Aristotle further explained: "all law is universal but about some things it is not possible to make a universal statement which shall be correct."[6] It is not possible for law to cover all legal problems, not at least without succumbing to procrustean reasoning. Aristotle not only saw equity as a way to compensate for defects in the law, but also as a device to aid in statutory construction and application. "When law speaks universally," Aristotle said, "and a case arises on it which is not covered by the universal statement, then it is right, where the legislator fails us and has erred by oversimplicity, to correct the omission, to say what the legislator himself would have said had he been present, and would have put into his law if he had known."[7]

Aristotle, in fact, saw law and equity as distinct components of a legal system, each necessary for the administration of justice. Thus, equity did not replace law, it complemented law. Law and equity were seen as separate rooms in the house of justice. They were deemed to be essential features of any legal system committed to justice.[8]

The Romans were heavily influenced by the Greeks. Like the latter, the Romans viewed equity as an important ingredient in the administration of justice. Equity jurisdiction was exercised by the *Praetor*, who was nevertheless bound to follow the law if justly applied. Otherwise, the *Praetor* was empow-

---

4. Henry C. Black, *Black's Law Dictionary* 4th ed. (St. Paul: West Publishing Co., 1968), pp. 634–35.

5. "The Works of Aristotle," vol. III, in *Great Books of the Western World*, vol. 9, Robert Maynard Hutchins, ed., W. D. Ross, trans.(Chicago: Encyclopedia Britannica, 1952), p. 386 (*Nicomachean Ethics*, Book V. 10. 25; 1137b).

6. Ibid. at p. 385 (*Nocomachean Ethics*, Book V. 10. 5.; 1137b).

7. "The Works of Aristotle," supra note 5, at p. 386 (*Nicomachean Ethics*, Bk. V. 10.15-20; 1137b).

8. For further discussion, see e.g., Joseph Story, *Commentaries on Equity Jurisprudence* (London: Stevens and Haynes, 1884, Special Edition for the Legal Classic Library, 1988), pp. 3–4; Edgar Bodenheimer, *Jurisprudence: The Philosophy and Method of the Law* (Cambridge, Mass.: Harvard University Press, 1962), pp. 3–20.

ered to do justice where justice should be done.[9] But perhaps even more than the Greeks, the Romans used equity "to correct and measure the interpretation of the written and positive code."[10] Referring to the interpretative aspect of equity in the Roman legal system, Justice Story said: "When a right was founded in the expressed words of the law, the actions grounded on it were denominated *Actiones Directae*; where they arose upon a benignant extension of the words of the law to cases, not within the terms, but within what we should call the equity of the law, they were denominated *Actiones Utiles*."[11]

Both parts of the Aristotelian conception of equity—corrective and interpretive—appeared in England centuries later. At first, equity was administered by the king himself. Persons who felt they had not received justice in a court of law petitioned directly to the king. Gradually, the king appointed his secretary, the Chancellor, to entertain the burgeoning number of equity petitions. The Chancellor established the "Court of Chancery" (or "Court of Equity") to decide equitable claims, while the common law courts continued to hear legal claims. Between the reigns of Edward I and Edward IV, the Chancery Court grew and eventually created its own system of rules and procedure.[12]

In the early years, equitable decision making was based upon the unbridled discretion of the king, who had little knowledge of specific rules of law or procedure. The Chancellor would later exercise similar equitable decision-making authority. These decision makers did not hesitate to correct, mitigate or interpret the law, or to rewrite documents on the basis of their personal sense of fairness and good conscience.[13]

The case of *Kentish v. Newman* illustrates the unrestrained use of corrective equity by the Court of Equity. Under the terms of a marriage agreement, any money belonging to the wife at her death was to go to her brothers and sisters. At the time of the wife's death, the judge refused to enforce the agreement and,

---

9. See Story, *Commentaries on Equity Jurisprudence*, supra note 8, at p. 4.

10. Ibid.

11. Ibid. at p. 4, n.2 (citing sources). For an interesting discussion of what classic life was like in Greece and Rome, see Peter Connolly, *The Ancient City: Life in Classical Athens and Rome* (Oxford: Oxford University Press, 1998).

12. See, e.g., William DeFuniak, *Handbook on Modern Equity* (New York: Little Brown & Co., 1956), pp. 1–5; George Tucker Bishpan, *The Principles of Equity: A Treatise on the System of Justice Administered by the Courts of Chancery* (New York: The Banks Law Publishing Co., 1917), pp. 1–10; Walter Wheeler Cook, *Cases and Materials on Equity* 4th ed. (St. Paul: West Publishing Co., 1948), pp. 1–4.

13. See, e.g., Bodenheimer, *Jurisprudence*, supra note 8, at p. 11 n.11; William Blackstone, *Commentaries on the Laws of England*, vol. III (Oxford: The Clarendon Press, 1768, Special Edition for the Legal Classic Library, Birmingham, Ala.: 1983), p. 429.

instead, gave the money to the decedent's children. The judge added to the text of the marriage agreement the phrase "without issue," thus fundamentally changing the meaning and scope of the agreement. Citing the laws of nature as authority, the judge felt it could legally rewrite the marriage agreement to achieve justice.[14]

Legal scholars were by no means in agreement as to the legitimacy of such unbridled use of corrective equity. St. Germain, for example, argued strongly that "[i]n some cases, it is necessary to leave the words of the law, and to follow what reason and justice requireth, and to that intent equity is ordained."[15] But most English scholars and informed citizens alike did not approve of judges exercising absolute discretion, even in the name of corrective equity. Typical of the views of most scholars of the day was John Selden's ridicule of corrective equity:

> For law we have a measure, and know what to trust to.... Equity is according to the conscience of him that is chancellor; and as that is larger or narrower, so is equity: 'Tis all one as if they should make the standard for the measure of the chancellor's foot. What an uncertain measure would this be! One chancellor has a long foot, another a short foot. It is the same thing with the chancellor's conscience.'[16]

Blackstone more fully addressed the dangers of corrective equity. He warned that:

> Equity thus depending, essentially, upon the particular circumstances of each individual case, there can be no established rules and fixed precepts of equity laid down, without destroying its very essence, and reducing it to a positive law. And, on the other hand, the liberty of considering all cases in an equitable light must not be indulged too far, lest thereby we destroy all law, and leave the decision of every question entirely in the breast of the judge.[17]

In response to these concerns, the Chancellor took steps to rein in equity, essentially limiting its corrective feature. The Chancellor, *inter alia*, limited

---

14. 24 Eng. Rep. 368 (1713). See John R. Kroger, "Supreme Court Equity, 1789–1835, and the History of American Judging," *Houston Law Review* 34 (1998): 1425, 1434.

15. Story, *Commentaries on Equity Jurisprudence*, supra note 8, at p. 7 (sources cited therein).

16. Blackstone, *Commentaries* vol. III, supra note 13, at p. 432 (quoting John Selden). See Theodore Plunckett, *A Concise History of the Common Law* 5th ed. (New York: Little Brown & Co., 1956), pp. 702–3.

17. Blackstone, *Commentaries* vol. I, supra note 2, at pp. 61–62.

the types of cases subject to equitable review, standardized equity procedure, and established a set of "common maxims" under which the Court of Equity had to operate.[18] One maxim, in particular, was considered to be the first and most important: "equity follows the law." This seemingly unambiguous maxim was clouded by several other maxims that gave the Court of Equity permission to ignore the law as much as to follow it. For example, if the law provided a remedy that afforded slow, inefficient, and incomplete relief, the Court of Equity was allowed to disregard the legal remedy and supply its own. This was the gist of the equitable maxim, "equity acts if there is no adequate remedy of law."[19] Likewise, as Justice Story has observed, "There are cases in which equity will control the legal title of an heir...when it would be deemed absolute at law; and in which, therefore, so far from following the law, it openly abandons it."[20]

However contraposed these "common maxims" may have been, they arose from a common source—the English culture. They resonated with the English people, representing the community's expectations, its customs, and its values. Thus, it is not difficult to understand how the English legal system could have provided, on the one hand, that "[w]here a rule, either of the common law or the statute law, is direct, and governs the case with all its circumstances, or the particular point, a court of equity is as much bound by it, as a court of law,"[21] yet, on the other hand, permit a judge to dip into the community's culture or custom to fashion his own rules of decision where the matter before him was neither completely nor adequately covered by law. But even here, the judge was not so independent that he could ignore culture, the raw material of the law.[22] The intent of the maxims, and, indeed, the whole effort to curtail corrective equity, was to have the judge efface himself, but not so much that he would become as passive as a potted plant.[23]

---

18. See, e.g., Cook, *Cases and Materials on Equity*, supra note 12, at pp. 1–4; Blackstone, *Commentaries* vol. I, supra note 2, at p. 992, vol. III, supra note 13, at pp. 429–32.

19. See, e.g., *Boyce v. Grundy*, Pet (U.S.) 210, 7 L.Ed. 655 (1830).

20. Story, *Commentaries on Equity Jurisprudence*, supra note 8, at p. 41.

21. Ibid. at p. 40.

22. For Blackstone, law is "fixed and established by custom, which custom is evidenced by judicial decisions; and therefore can never be departed from by any modern judge without breach of his oath and the law." Blackstone, *Commentaries*, vol. I, supra note 2, at pp. 70–71.

23. For a more detailed discussion of the equitable maxims, see, e.g., ibid. at pp. 40–41 (citing cases); DeFuniak, *Handbook on Modern Equity*, supra note 12, at pp. 56–82. Blackstone himself did not accept the notion that customs can conflict. "Customs ought to be

Unlike corrective equity, interpretive equity received greater support from English judges and scholars.[24] Delineating in careful sequence five principles of statutory construction, Blackstone began: "Words are generally to be understood in their usual and most known signification;…as their general and popular use."[25] Blackstone maintained, however, that times arise when a judge "must a little deviate from the received sense" of the words in a statute or, by extension, constitution or judge-made law. One such time is "where the words bear either none, or a very absurd signification, if literally understood."[26] To illustrate this principle, Blackstone referred to the following rule of law: "Whoever drew blood in the streets should be punished with the utmost severity."[27] Applying this law to a doctor "who opened the vein" of a person who fell ill in the street would be absurd, Blackstone observed. The policy behind the law was to deter outbreaks of public violence, not to punish doctors for saving lives.[28]

Similarly, "when the words are dubious" they must be ignored and the judge must consider "the reason and spirit of it; or the cause which moved the legislator to enact it."[29] Blackstone cited as an example a law that gave "those who staid" on board a ship during a storm "all property therein," including the ship itself.[30] This law, Blackstone argued, should not apply to a person who was the only one to remain on board solely because he was too sick to jump ship with the rest of the crew. "Now here all the learned agree," Blackstone continued, "that the sick man is not within the reason of the law; for the reason of making it was to give encouragement to such as should venture their lives to save the vessel."[31]

Referring to the principles of statutory construction collectively, Blackstone concluded, "From this method of interpreting laws arises what we call 'equity,' [the means by which a judge can arrive at] the true meaning of [the] law."[32] This describes the fundamental relationship between law and interpretive equity.

---

certain…[they] must be consistent…which is to say [the notion] of contradictory customs is absurd." Blackstone, *Commentaries* vol. I, supra note 2, at p. 78.

24. The ensuing discussion is strikingly relevant to the various approaches to statutory construction put forth by Justice Scalia, Justice Frankfurter, and various scholars discussed in Chapters 2, 4, and 5, infra.

25. Blackstone, *Commentaries* vol. I, supra note 2, at p. 59.

26. Ibid. at p. 60.

27. Ibid.

28. Ibid.

29. Ibid. at p. 61.

30. Ibid.

31. Ibid.

32. Ibid. (emphasis in original).

The English legal system was transported to America by the British colonists. Once again, equity's place in the legal system became a point of contention, particularly after the war of independence. At the Constitutional Convention, Thomas Jefferson and other anti-Federalists opposed giving the new judiciary equitable powers, particularly corrective authority. Echoing the concerns of Blackstone, they argued that decisions based on equity were too arbitrary and, thereby, threatened the stability of the legal system. Anti-Federalists also feared corrective equity would give the federal judiciary substantial powers that could be used in tandem with Congress' powers to usurp states' rights.[33]

In contrast, the Federalists defended corrective equity, using some of the same arguments Aristotle had once employed. For example, in *Federalists 80* and *83*, Alexander Hamilton argued that corrective equity was necessary to deal with unfairness or hardships that might result from the application of general rules of law, including situations not covered by existing rules. He saw equity as an "exception" to law; a device to be used only in "extraordinary cases." Equity, Hamilton maintained, brought a measure of flexibility and, hence, justice to America's fledgling legal system.[34]

Although the Federalists won the constitutional debate—Article III of the Constitution grants the Supreme Court authority to decide (i.e., exercise jurisdiction over) matters involving both "law and equity"[35]—that did not end the matter. The young judiciary struggled with the conflicting ideals of judicial assertiveness and judicial restraint not only in equity cases but in law cases as well. Whether dealing with law or equity, American judges faced the same challenges. The legal system was too young to have developed an extensive set of precedents, but, as Grant Gilmore has noted, American judges were reluctant to defer to English precedents. After having fought a war (soon to fight another) against England, using its precedents would be bad form. More importantly, the conditions in rapidly changing America were not the same as in England. Law and equity had to be adapted to the exigencies of a young and vibrant nation.[36]

---

33. See, e.g., John Choon Yoo, "Who Measures the Chancellor's Foot? The Inherent Remedial Authority of the Federal Courts," *California Law Review* 84 (1996): 1121, 1152, 1154; Gary L. McDowell, *Equity and the Constitution: The Supreme Court, Equitable Relief and Public Policy* (Chicago: University of Chicago Press, 1982), p. 6.

34. See "Federalist 80" and "Federalist 83," in *The Federalist, or The New Constitution* (London: J.M. Dent and Sons, Ltd., 1948), pp. 423–36. See also, *The Federalist Papers in Modern Language Indexed for Today's Political Issues*, Mary E. Webster, ed.(Bellevue, WA: Merril Press, 1999), pp. 324, 342.

35. See U.S. Const., Art. III, Sec. 2.

36. See Grant Gilmore, *The Ages of American Law* (New Haven: Yale University Press, 1977), pp. 21–25.

Eventually, law and equity were merged into a single court in the American legal system. Today, most states and the entire federal judiciary have merged law and equity.[37] Delaware has retained the old English system, and Louisiana has chosen the equally ancient Napoleonic Code.[38] The merger of law and equity permits a judge to apply both sets of rules to a single case, rather than transferring cases back-and-forth between courts of law and courts of equity.

This has not, however, settled the historic debate regarding law and equity. Questions concerning the use of equity are debated today with the same intensity as in the days of Blackstone and St. Germain. Witness, for example, the controversy surrounding the Supreme Court's opinion involving the historic 2000 Presidential Election, *Bush v. Gore.*[39] This controversial opinion is struc-

---

37. See, e.g., F.R.Civ.P., Rule 1 ("These rules govern the procedure in the United States district courts in all suits of a civil nature whether cognizable as cases at law or in equity…"). See generally John B. Oakley and Arthur I. Coon, "The Federal Rules in State Courts: A Survey of State Court Systems of Civil Pocedure," *Washington Law Review* 61 (1986) 1367.

38. For a discussion of the Delaware and Louisiana legal systems, see, e.g., Andrew G.T. Moore, II, "Tribute to Daniel L. Herrmann, Chief Administrator of Justice," *Delaware Journal of Corporate Law* 10 (1986): 367, 369; Mario Ascheri, "John Minor Wisdom Lecture on Civil Law: A Turning point in the Civil Law Tradition: From *Ius Commune* to Code Napoleon," *Tulane Law Review* 70 (1996): 1041, 1043.

39. 531 U.S. 98 (2001). This controversial case stopped the recount in the 2000 Presidential Election. The common view among legal scholars is that this case is "quite demonstrably the worst Supreme Court decision in history….*Dred Scott* was, by comparison, a brilliantly reasoned and logically coherent decision." Max Boot, "Rule of Law: Law Professors v. the Supreme Court," Wall Street Journal, 8/13/01, p. A13. See Alan M. Dershowitz, *Supreme Injustice: How the High Court Hijacked Election 2000* (New York: Oxford University Press, 2001); *The Vote: Bush, Gore and the Supreme Court*, Cass R. Sunstein and Richard A. Epstein, eds. (Chicago: University of Chicago Press, 2001); Vincent Bugliosi, *The Betrayal of America: How the Supreme Court Undermined the Constitution and Chose Our President* (New York: Nation's Books, 2001); Linda Greenhouse, *High Court Appears Diminished in Process*, San Diego Union-Tribune, 12/14/00, at p. A24. For a partial defense of the Court's opinion, see Richard A. Posner, *Breaking the Deadlock: The 2000 Election, the Constitution, and the Courts* (Princeton, N.J.: Princeton University Press, 2001). A recount of some of the disputed Florida ballots (the "undervotes," which are ballots that registered no presidential preference, and the "overvotes," ballots that registered two votes for one candidate, or votes for multiple candidates) by the New York Times, The Wall Street Journal, the Washington Post, and CNN several months after the election revealed that Bush won Florida and, hence, the 2000 Presidential Election. On this basis it could be argued that the Supreme Court did not decide the election. On the other hand, it was also revealed that a statewide recount to determine the "intent" of voters would have given Florida and, hence, the election to Gore. See, e.g., Philip Terzian, "Media's Vote Tally is in: President Bush is President," San Diego Union-Tribune, 12/2/01, p. G4; Martin Plissner, "Majority of Vot-

turally indistinguishable from the opinion in *Kentish v. Newman*, supra. Both opinions disregarded applicable law in light of what the judge or justices believed were dire consequences. The only difference between the cases, outside of their factual patterns and the applicable law, is the lexicon we use to analyze them. Instead of "equity," the word "policy" is employed to describe *Bush v. Gore's* consequentialism.[40] Indeed, the term "policy" is used today to capture the consequentialism and sometimes the compassion of equity, as we shall see next.[41]

C. Policy and Judicial Policy-Formulation

The term "policy," or "public policies," plays a critical role in judicial reasoning. This section will attempt to clearly define this important term, and then try to explain the multiple ways in which judges actually engage policy today. This discussion will set the stage for a more sophisticated treatment of both judicial methods—the policy method and the logical method—in subsequent chapters of the book.

---

ers Should Pick the President," San Diego Union-Tribune, 11/18/01, p. G4. See generally, Jackie Calmes and Edward P. Foldessy, "Florida Revisited: In Election Review, Bush Wins Without Supreme Court Help—Still, Majority of State Voters Would Have Picked Gore But for Poor Ballot Design," Wall Street Journal, 11/12/01, p. A1. The media's vote tally does not, of course, excuse or justify the fact that by stopping the electoral process, the Supreme Court made a major inroad on a political matter that Congress, through statutes, and the people, through the Constitution, have reserved for themselves. The Supreme Court "has not...embraced the general proposition that a wrong may be done if it can be undone," *Stanley v. Illinois*, 405 U.S. 645, 647 (1972), nor should we. For a more detailed discussion of *Bush v. Gore*, see Chapter 7, Section B3, infra.

40. See sources in note 39, supra.

41. It might be useful to pause for a moment to consider this question: What exactly is the debate regarding law and equity (or policy) really about? Historically, the debate was at times about the legitimacy of equity in a system of laws. Yet, even here the debate was mainly about corrective equity; interpretive equity was largely accepted, as we have seen. Today, the legitimacy question is, as a practical matter, dead. Equity, including Hamilton's notion of corrective equity, is firmly codified in the Constitution and other national and state laws. As a theoretical matter, the legitimacy question should remain a dead issue because, as our discussion of Western tradition clearly demonstrates, equity is an essential feature of any legal system committed to justice. It is, along with law, the *sine qua non* of the American legal system. Thus, the legitimacy question cannot be taken seriously today. However, what can and *must* be subject to serious debate today is the proper-mix question. How much law, how much policy (equity) is needed to do justice in a given case? Again, too much policy kills law; too much law kills justice.

1. Definition of Policy

The policy method is all about policy, and the logical method is decidedly against policy. However, the term "policy" is not well-defined, although not for a lack of trying. Legal scholars have, in fact, made numerous attempts to define the term policy, and such related concepts as "principles," "rules," and "standards."[42] No one's work on the subject has drawn more attention from American legal scholars—treated with both criticism and encomium—than that of Ronald Dworkin.

Dworkin's thinking about the term policy seems heavily influenced by the work of Henry Hart and Albert Sacks, the leading proponents of the legal process model of judicial decision making.[43] Like Hart and Sacks, Dworkin attempts to define policies in contradistinction to "principles," and does so in a fashion similar to Hart and Sacks.[44] Dworkin writes:

> I call a 'policy' that kind of standard that sets out a goal to be reached, generally an improvement in some economic, political, or social feature of the community (though some goals are negative, in that they stipulate that some present feature is to be protected from adverse change). I call a 'principle' a standard that is to be observed, not because it will advance or secure an economic, political, or social situation deemed desirable, but because it is a requirement of justice or fairness or some other dimension of morality. Thus the standard that automobile accidents are to be decreased is a policy, and the standard that no man may profit by his own wrong a principle.[45]

Thus, for Dworkin, policies are social, political or economic goals, while principles are standards of justice, fairness or morality.

This distinction between policies and principles underpins Dworkin's vision of the judicial process. Judges are permitted to make decisions outside established rules on the basis of principles but not policies, Dworkin argues. The ju-

---

42. For a classic treatment of the problem, see Henry M. Hart, Jr. and Albert M. Sacks, *The Legal Process: Basic Problems in the Making and Application of Law*, William N. Eskridge, Jr. and Philip P. Frickey, eds. (New York: Foundation Press, 1994), pp. 141–43.

43. See Chapter 5, infra.

44. Regarding Hart and Sacks' discussion of policies and principles, see Hart and Sacks, *Legal Process*, supra note 42, at pp. 141–43.

45. Ronald Dworkin, *Taking Rights Seriously* (Cambridge, Mass.: Harvard University Press, 1977), p. 22.

diciary should not simply be used as an instrument of society in the achievement of particular policy goals or in providing an efficient means to the achievement of those goals. Instead, the judge's role in our liberal, democratic state is to ensure that a community treats its members in a principled, ethical manner.[46]

Dworkin's distinction between policies and principles collapses, however, in situations where policies, so defined, can easily be converted into principles, so defined. For example, John Rawls' difference principle—to wit, an action is acceptable if it makes the most disadvantaged as well off as is possible—may be taken as a political or economic goal as well as a standard of fairness or justice.[47] Securing racial or gender equality can be viewed as a wise or desirable social, political or economic goal as well as a requirement of fairness or justice.[48]

In this book, the term "policy" is used to refer to a community's values, its culture or expectations, whether they be social, political, economic (Dworkin's "policies"), ethical or moral (Dworkin's "principles"). A policy, to borrow from Justice Oliver Wendell Holmes, is the embodiment of a community's experience through many years, but also it is the "felt necessities of the time, the prevalent moral and political theories,...even the prejudices which judges share with their fellow-men."[49] A policy is what Justice Benjamin Cardozo referred to as "the *mores* of [the] day."[50] Whether avowed or unconscious, a policy is the stuff of which a rule (a standard of behavior) is made. It gives purpose, meaning, structure, coherence, and direction to a

---

46. See ibid.; Ronald Dworkin, *Law's Empire* (Cambridge, Mass.: Belknap Press, 1986). See generally Alan Hunt, *Reading Dworkin Critically* (New York: St. Martin's Press, 1992).

47. See John Rawls, *A Theory of Justice* (Cambridge, Mass.: Harvard University Press, 1971), p. 303. See, e.g., Edmund Ursin, "Judicial Creativity and Tort Law," *George Washington Law Review* 49 (1981): 229, 235; "Jurisprudence Symposium," *Georgia Law Review* 11 (1979): 969; Henry Friendly, "The Courts and Social Policy: Substance and Procedure," *University of Miami Law Review* 33 (1978): 21, 27; Lawrence Alexander and Michael Bayles, "Hercules or Proteus? The Many Theses of Ronald Dworkin," Social Theory and Practice, 5 (1980): 267, 287.

48. See Dworkin, *Taking Rights Seriously*, supra note 45, at pp. 22–23. For a more detailed discussion of Dworkin's views, see, e.g., Dworkin, *Law's Empire*, supra note 46; Ronald Dworkin, "Seven Critics," *Georgia Law Review* 11 (1977): 1207; Ronald Dworkin, "The Model of Rules," *University of Chicago Law Review* 35 (1967): 14, 22–23; Ronald Dworkin, et al., "Assisted Suicide: The Philosophers' Brief," *The New York Review of Books*, 3/27/97, p. 41. See generally Hunt, *Reading Dworkin Critically*, supra note 46.

49. Oliver Wendell Holmes, *The Common Law*, Mark DeWolfe Howe, ed. (Cambridge: Harvard University Press, 1963), p. 5.

50. Benjamin N. Cardozo, *The Nature of the Judicial Process* (New Haven: Yale University Press, 1921), p. 152 (emphasis in original).

rule, especially when the rule is carefully conceived.[51] A policy, in short, is a community norm. Let us now consider how judges actually engage policy under the policy method.

2. Judicial Policy-Formulation

Judges proceeding under the policy method engage policy in different ways. Some "make" policy (*policy-making*), others "discover" policy (what can be called *policy-discovery*), and still others "vindicate" policy (what can be called *policy-vindication*). Each is a distinctly different exercise of the judicial policy-formulation function. Each operates at a different level of judicial activism. And each is rooted in the traditional uses of equity in Western civilization: policy-making and policy-discovery in corrective equity; and policy-vindication in interpretive equity.[52]

Conventionally understood, policy-making occurs when the judge renders a decision based on her own personal policies. For example, Judge Newman of the Second Circuit Court of Appeals writes that policy-making is when "the judge simply selects the result that best comports with personal values."[53] Chief Judge Richard Posner of the Seventh Circuit Court of Appeals suggests that policy-making occurs when a judge "brings *his* own policy preferences to bear in order to decide the case at hand."[54] Ronald Dworkin defines policy-making as "judges actually decid[ing] cases according to their own political or moral tastes."[55] John Hart Ely asserts that policy-making occurs when judges, "consciously or unconsciously,…slip their personal values into their legal reasoning."[56] Fred Schauer argues that policy-making arises when judicial discretion is "unfettered," i.e., "largely unconstrained by forces external to…[the judge's] own decision-making preferences."[57] Malcolm Feeley and Edward Rubin de-

---

51. Sometimes a policy is no broader than the rule itself. See, e.g., 28 U.S.C. § 1391, (federal venue rules).

52. See discussion in Section B, supra.

53. Jon O. Newman, "Between Legal Realism and Neutral Principles: The Legitimacy of Institutional Values," *California Law Review* 72 (1984): 200, 203.

54. Richard A. Posner, "The Meaning of Judicial Restraint," *Indiana Law Journal* 59 (1983): 1, 9 (emphasis in original).

55. Ronald Dworkin, *Taking Rights Seriously*, supra note 45, at p. 3.

56. John Hart Ely, *Democracy and Distrust: A Theory of Judicial Review* (Cambridge: Harvard University Press, 1980), p. 44.

57. Frederick Schauer, *Playing By the Rules: A Philosophical Examination of Rule-Based Decision Making in Law and in Life* (New York: Oxford University Press, 1991), p. 191.

fine policy-making as "the process by which officials exercise power on the basis of *their* judgment that their actions will produce socially desirable results."[58]

This concept of policy-making—the advancement of a judge's private policy—is problematic for at least two reasons. First, it infuses a judicial policy with the notion of it being apart from something that is public. This ignores the judge's public commitments both within and outside the judiciary. The judicial process is so collaborative, especially at the appellate level, that it is simply incorrect to label a judge's policy preference as "private." The corporateness of judicial decision making cannot be overstated. A policy may enter the judicial process as the idea of a single judge, but as it works its way through the process, winning acceptance or modification from other judges, it exits the process fully dressed as an institutional policy, a corporate norm. In addition to the corporateness of judicial decision making, the publicness of a judicial policy is reflected in the judge's personal connection to a community. Judges are so acculturated that it must be conceded that their policies are held in common with *some* community in the country.[59]

Second, what if the policy the judge "makes up" is shared by the community affected by her judgment? What if the value is, in fact, the community's value? Is she not, then, affirming rather than creating policy? Affirming a community norm is quite different from disregarding it. If a judge's opinion favors a policy that is in sync with community expectations, no one would complain, and, in fact, most would say he is doing what he is supposed to be doing: following rather than leading.

To fully understand policy-making, we must first understand policy-discovery. The latter occurs when the judge *discovers* public policies—community expectations or extant social interests—that have yet to be expressed or implemented through the enactment of a rule of law, legislative, constitutional or judicial. These policies are buried in the culture and await discovery by the judge or legislature. They are to this extent *unarticulated* public policies. Policy-discovery can be analogized to opening a refrigerator door. The door is closed, but inside, representing culture, is a piece of pie. The pie exists even

---

58. Malcolm M. Feeley and Edward L. Rubin, *Judicial Policy Making and the Modern State: How the Courts Reformed America's Prisons* (Cambridge, England: Cambridge University Press, 1998), p. 5 (emphasis added).

59. "In examining [Supreme Court] nominees' qualifications, the [judiciary] committee must also consider their experience with people: whether they have a genuine feel for the human condition, and whether they have first-hand rather than mostly vicarious familiarity with the ebb and flow of life." Roy L. Brooks, "What About Souter's Human Resume," New York Times, 8/1/90, p. A11.

though we cannot see it through the refrigerator door. It is revealed to us, in a legal context, only when the court or legislature opens the refrigerator door.[60] In our society, courts and legislatures function as door openers.

Lon Fuller constructed a story about a catcher's mitt, a baseball glove, to illustrate unarticulated public policies, the policies that policy-discovery discovers. The story is intended to demonstrate that a "principle or standard" (i.e., policy) implied in a claim of right need not have been articulated prior to the expression of the claim itself. Here, the best-player public policy—a policy that taps into the nation's well-established competitive spirit—predates the boy's claim that he has a right to use the catcher's mitt even though the policy itself had never been articulated in an existing claim:

> If one boy says to another, 'Give me that catcher's mitt,' and answers the question, 'Why?' by saying, 'Because I am the best catcher on the team,' he asserts a [policy] by which the equipment of the team ought to be apportioned in accordance with ability to use it. He necessarily implies that, were the respective abilities of the two boys reversed, the mitt should remain where it is. But he does not, by necessary implication, assert that the [policy] by which he supports his claim is an established one. Indeed, up to the time this claim was made, the right to be catcher might depend, not on ability, but on ownership of the catcher's mitt. In that event the claim based upon the new [policy] of ability might, in effect, propose a revolution in the organization of the team. At the same time, this claim does necessarily imply a [policy] which can give meaning to the demand that like cases be given like treatment.[61]

With this understanding, the distinction between policy-making and policy-discovery becomes quite clear. Policy-making occurs when the judge advances a policy that does not sit well with the community to which it is applied. The judge, in other words, imposes a norm on a community before it is ready or willing to accept the norm. In contrast, policy-discovery is when the judge effectuates a policy the community has already accepted even though the policy has not been "established"—that is, officially effectuated through legitimate rules. If the decision maker in the catcher's mitt story had advanced the best-player policy in spite of the fact that the community was not ready for it or was

---

60. This seems to be what Blackstone meant when he defined positive law as "fixed and established by custom, which custom is evidenced by judicial decisions." See note 22, supra.

61. Lon L. Fuller, "The Forms and Limits of Adjudication," *Harvard Law Review* 92 (1978): 353, 368.

otherwise adverse to it, she would have acted as a policy-maker and not as a policy-discoverer. If she had acted paternalistically, was too far ahead of her times or was simply trying to anticipate the direction in which her community was moving, she would have acted as a policy-maker, not as a policy-discoverer.

Similarly, the Warren Court was an "activist" Court in civil rights cases not because the justices "made up" their policies (again, judges are too acculturated to have "radical" views on anything), but because they favored national values that were out of step with southern values during the 1950s and 1960s.[62] The Supreme Court during the Lochner Era[63] was similarly "activist" not because it "made up" conservative policies, but because it imposed those values on a progressive-minded country. And when some members of Congress in 2000 accused the Rehnquist Court of "judicial imperialism," their real complaint was not that the justices had "made up" the policy of federalism they had used to strike down socially progressive federal statutes, it was that the justices were out of step with current American society, a society that had grown wary of legislative gridlock and wanted Congress to resolve pressing social problems.[64] Whether liberal or conservative, judicial policy-making is

---

62. See, e.g., *Brown v. Board of Education*, 347 U.S. 483 (1954) (overturning the South's segregated way of life in the context of public schools); *Brown v. Board of Education*, 349 U.S. 294 (1955) (ordering the desegregation of public schools "with all deliberate speed"); *Cooper v. Aaron*, 358 U.S. 1 (1958) (holding that the governor and legislature of Arkansas were bound by the holding in the Brown cases, despite violent white opposition to such rulings); *Green v. County School Board of New Kent County, Virginia*, 391 U.S. 430, 441 (1968) (school board's "freedom of choice" desegregation plan "cannot be accepted as a sufficient step to 'effectuate a transition' to a unitary system" mandated by *Brown*).

63. See Chapter 1, infra.

64. See, e.g., Joseph Biden, "On Judicial Imperialism," *Congressional Record*, vol. 146, no. 99 (daily edition) (106th Congress, July 26, 2000); Harry F. Tepker, Jr., "Writing the Law of Work on Nero's Pillars: The 1998–99 Term of the U.S. Supreme Court," *The Labor Lawyer* 15 (1999): 181 (cases and articles collected therein). See also, *United States v. Morrison*, 529 U.S. 598(2000) (overturning the enforcement portion of the Violence Against Women Act authorizing a private right of action for any victim of a gender-motivated violent crime); *Alden v. Maine*, 527 U.S. 706 (1999) (private suit for damages under the Fair Labor Standards Act against nonconsenting states in their own courts violates state sovereign immunity), where Justice Souter argued in dissent that "[t]he resemblance of today's state sovereign immunity to the *Lochner* era's industrial due process is striking." Ibid. at 814 (Souter, J., dissenting); *United States v. Lopez*, 514 U.S. 549 (1995) (federal statute prohibiting knowing possession of firearms in or near schools held unconstitutional), was one of the first cases to give some hint of what looks like a return to legal formalism. For an excellent discussion of the Supreme Court's "constitutional revolution," see Jack M. Balkin and Sanford Levinson, "Understanding the Constitutional Revolution," *Virginia Law Review* 87 (2001): 1045.

manifested when a court moves in a direction opposite the direction in which a community is moving.

The question of how judges ascertain existing community norms is a question in search of a good answer.[65] Short of community polling,[66] judges have a variety of sources from which to gauge community sentiment, including: the parties' briefs and oral arguments;[67] norms addressed in similar cases, treatises, law review articles, monographs, newspaper editorials, popular magazines, and TV news programs;[68] everyday conversation;[69] and, of course, the views of members of the bar and bar associations as well as other judges in multi-member courts.[70] Judges are not social idiots—they know the society in which they live.[71] The important point to remember is this: policy-oriented judges tend to look outward (i.e., towards the community) rather than inward in their search for what might be termed "actionable norms," even when such norms collide.[72]

---

65. See, e.g., Carl A. Auerbach, "A Revival of Some Ancient Learning: A Critique of Eisenberg's *The Nature of the Common Law*," *Minnesota Law Review* 75 (1991): 539, 545–54, criticizing the views on the subject expressed in Melvin Eisenberg, *The Nature of the Common Law* (Cambridge: Harvard University Press, 1988); Ernest Nagel, "Reflections on *The Nature of the Judicial Process*," *Cardozo Law Review* 1 (1979): 55, 59–60, criticizing Justice Cardozo's views published in Cardozo's seminal work, Cardozo, *The Nature of the Judicial Process*, supra note 50, at p. 151.

66. See, e.g., Auerbach, "A Revival of Some Ancient Learning," supra note 65, at pp. 543–44 (discussing polling suggestions made as far back as the 1950s).

67. The "Brandeis Brief," packed with social science data as well as legal argument, was first used in *Muller v. Oregon*, 208 U.S. 412 (1908). See Nancy Woloch, *Muller v. Oregon: A Brief History with Documents* (1996). Perhaps its most famous use was in *Brown v. Board of Education*, 347 U.S. 483 , 493 n. 11 (1954).

68. See Auerbach, A Revival of Some Ancient Learning," supra note 65, at p. 542.

69. See ibid. at p. 544.

70. See ibid. at pp. 542, 545. Indeed, several Justices in *Bush v. Gore*, 531 U.S. 98 (2001), warned the majority Justices that the latter's decision in the case would bring discredit to the Court. Justice Stevens emphatically stated: "Although we may never know with complete certainty the identity of the winner of this year's Presidential election, the identity of the loser is perfectly clear. It is the Nation's confidence in the judge as an impartial guardian of the rule of law." Ibid. at pp. 128–29 (Stevens, J., with whom Justices Ginsburg and Breyer join, dissenting). In similar fashion, Justice Souter advised that the Court "should not have reviewed…this case," that it should have allowed the state of Florida to follow the course "indicated by the opinions of its own Supreme Court." Ibid. at p. 129. (Souter, J., with whom Justice Breyer joins, dissenting).

71. If not, they should not be sitting on the bench in judgment of others. See supra note 59.

72. The judge chooses the norm that has the strongest community support, or the one he thinks is "waxing while the other is waning." See, e.g., Eisenberg, *The Nature of the Common Law*, supra note 65, at p. 19.

An "actionable norm," or "actionable policy"—in other words, one that is ripe for judicial action—is that which has garnered substantial community support, something approaching majority support.[73] The substantial-community-support requirement gives policy-discovery its democratic fiber.[74]

Nonetheless, policy-discovery, like policy-making, constitutes "judicial activism." This term has several meanings,[75] but in the context of our current discussion it primarily arises from the fact that neither form of policy-formulation is directly tethered to authoritative text. Policy-discovery is, however, less activist, more self-effacing than policy-making, and, to that extent, is a lesser form of judicial activism. This point can be illustrated by comparing the Supreme Court's reasoning in *Griswold v. Connecticut*[76] with its reasoning in *Roe v. Wade*,[77] two "activist" opinions.

In 1965, the Court in *Griswold* overturned a Connecticut statute forbidding the use of contraceptives by married couples. The Court's reasoning was not activist in the sense that it sought to impose alien norms on the people of

---

73. For example, Holmes required substantial community support in cases wherein the judicial policy-formulation function was limited to policy-discovery; namely, cases arising in the context of *lex scripto*, or the written law. See, e.g., *Lochner v. New York*, 198 U.S. 45, 76 (1905) (Holmes, J., dissenting) (arguing that the Court should give effect to "the natural outcome of a dominant [community] opinion"). Holmes placed no such restriction on the judge in the context of *lex non scripto*. As Auerbach notes, "Nothing in Holmes' writings on the common law indicates that he would require common law judges to ascertain whether...policies have substantial popular support before using them to reach their decisions." Auerbach, "A Revival of Some Ancient Learning," supra note 65, at p. 551. This attitude, of course, sets the stage for policy-making in common law cases. Like Holmes, Judge Posner also seems to require substantial community support for discovered policies in the context of the written law, see Richard A. Posner, *The Problematics of Moral and Legal Theory* (Cambridge: Harvard University Press, 1999), p. 249 (arguing a court should not effectuate "a social policy that is deeply offensive to the vast majority of...[American] citizens"), but not in the context of the unwritten law, see note 107, infra.

74. This is not to suggest that judges should not be permitted to take stances against unjust majorities. A more detailed discussion of this point appears later in this section.

75. In addition to policy-formulation, judicial activism can mean, *inter alia*, deviation from the traditional judicial role in our adversary system in which the lawyer is said to be "active" (e.g., responsible for prosecuting civil cases) and the judge is said to be "reactive" or "passive" (e.g., doesn't intervene in the prosecution of civil litigation by, for example, questioning witnesses or raising issues *sua sponte*). For a more detailed discussion, *see generally* Roy L. Brooks, *Civil Procedure: Cases and Materials for Policy Analysis* (San Diego: Western Academic Press, 1995), pp. 3–1 to 3–23.

76. 381 U.S. 479 (1965).

77. 410 U.S. 113 (1973).

Connecticut or the nation as a whole. Indeed, as Morton Horwitz has said, "[b]y the time the Connecticut birth control law was challenged, public attitudes toward contraception had undergone a 180-degree change from early in the twentieth century," thus prompting Justice Stewart to characterize the anti-contraception law as an "uncommonly silly law."[78] Instead, the Court's analysis was activist because it sought to constitutionalize (i.e., "rulify") an unarticulated norm, even though the nation had already accepted the norm. In fact, *Griswold* involved double activism: policy-discovery (discovering the unarticulated, pre-existing policy of privacy in the context of contraception) plus law-making (finding a home in the Constitution for the privacy value, thereby transforming it from a community norm into a legally actionable right). On the latter point, Justice Douglas believed that the Court's prior interpretations of the Fourteenth and Fifth Amendments had created "penumbral rights of 'privacy and repose'"; that a "zone of privacy has been created by several fundamental constitutional guarantees."[79]

When we push forward to 1973 to the Supreme Court's most famous abortion case, *Roe v. Wade*, we see the Court engaged in policy-making, a more aggressive form of judicial activism than policy-discovery. In *Roe*, the Court arguably extended the privacy value, which had by then been constitutionalized, however shakily, in *Griswold*, into uncharted waters. The Court took the privacy value from contraception to abortion before public attitudes had similarly evolved. Hence, the Court went too far too fast. It did not efface itself by deferring to the privacy expectations of a substantial portion of American society.

Taken together, then, *Griswold* and *Roe* crystallize the crucial distinction between policy-making and policy-discovery. Policy-making is an act of *judicial assertion*—specifically, the imposition of norms on a community before it is ready to receive them. Policy-discovery is an act of *judicial self-effacement*—specifically, the discovery of unarticulated norms the community has already accepted. Policy-discovery by nature is less activist than policy-making. Both forms of policy-formulation can involve law-making, the creation of new law to enforce public policy. The new law can, of course, be a precedent borrowed from another jurisdiction.[80]

---

78. Morton J. Horwitz, *The Warren Court and the Pursuit of Justice* (New York: Hill and Wang, 1998), pp. 106–7.

79. 381 U.S. at 485. Similarly, the Court in *Grutter v. Bollinger*, 539 U.S. 306 (2003), discovered the unarticulated value of diversity in higher education and then constitutionalized that value in the Fourteenth Amendment.

80. See, e.g., *Reynolds v. Bank of America National Trust and Savings Association*, 53 Cal. 2d 49, 345 P. 2d 926 (1959) (court borrows a rule concerning compensation for loss of use

Policy-vindication is the third and final feature of the judicial policy-formulation function. It is less complex than policy-making or policy-discovery and, thus, can be explained more quickly. A judge engages in this form of policy-formulation when he promotes articulated policies; policies already advanced through an existing constitutional, statutory or common law rule; policies put into legal action by a community's extant law.

The Supreme Court's 1954 opinion in *Brown v. Board of Education*,[81] overturning the constitutionality of state school segregation statutes, illustrates policy-vindication (and a good deal more, as we shall see). The Court based its reasoning on the equality value articulated in the Fourteenth Amendment. This reasoning constitutes policy-vindication in the context of our national community, because the Fourteenth Amendment, a duly enacted law, applies nationwide. *Brown's* reasoning also reflects policy-vindication with respect to those regional communities, mainly northern states, that enacted state school desegregation statutes or general anti-discrimination laws similar to the Fourteenth Amendment. But as to regional communities that rejected racial equality by law or practice, mainly southern communities, *Brown* must be seen as an act of judicial policy-making. Because ours is a bifurcated system of government, judicial opinions can sometimes contain multiple policy-formulations.

Given the existence of an accompanying legal rule or doctrine, policy-vindication is, necessarily, an interpretive exercise. If the governing law changes, it does so by extension or contraction.[82] In contrast, policy-making and policy-discovery, because of the absence of an implementing rule of law, usually entail law-making. The judge must often create legal doctrine, or "new law," as in *Griswold*, *Roe*, and the policy-making feature of *Brown*. The conditions for rule-interpretation are simply not present.

The illustrations of policy-making discussed thus far are not intended to suggest that such policy-oriented decision making is necessarily illegitimate. As we shall see next, there are, to be sure, circumstances in which policy-making should be viewed as a legitimate exercise of judicial power.

We can perhaps better understand the "legitimacy question" regarding policy-making by beginning with a few of the reasons that establish the institutional legitimacy of other exercises of judicial policy-formulation, policy-vindication and policy-discovery. Traditionally viewed, judicial decision making in a liberal, dem-

---

of destroyed property from other jurisdictions to effectuate a policy of full compensation).
    81. 347 U.S. 483 (1954).
    82. See, e.g., Roy L. Brooks, *Rule 10b-5 in the Balance: An Analysis of the Supreme Court's Policy Perspective*, Hastings Law Journal 32 (1980):403, 413 n.45, n. 46, n. 47 (discussing judicial vindication of policies behind federal securities statutes).

ocratic society is institutionally suspect when it is untethered to authoritative text.[83] Based on this premise, the institutional legitimacy of policy-vindication can be readily established. Although not a direct, logical application of text, policy-vindication is based on the governing black-letter law. It is an interpretative exercise, the judge's reasonable elaboration of existing authoritative text based on the text's underlying policies.[84] So in a loose way, policy-vindication is tethered to text.

On the other hand, neither policy-discovery nor policy-making is directly tethered to authoritative text.[85] Nevertheless, policy-discovery is legitimate for at least two reasons. First, discovered policies, or norms, require substantial community support.[86] This requirement supplies democratic pedigree to the judge's decision making,[87] doing so in a way that is not very different from policy-vindication. That is, both forms of policy-formulation produce rules that are extrapolated from existing policies—some unarticulated (policy-discovery), others articulated (policy-vindication).

That both sets of policies predate the judge's decision in a case brings us to the second reason policy-discovery is legitimate, and also provides an additional ground for establishing the legitimacy of policy-vindication. Judicial decision making based on pre-existing norms, to quote Carl Auerbach, "ensure[s] that decisions reflect standards that the disputants either knew or had reason to know at the time of their transaction, even if the standards previously had not been officially recognized as legal rules."[88] As Theodore Eisenberg states, pre-existing norms explain how it can be "fair to resolve a dispute concerning a past transaction by applying a legal rule that is articulated after the transaction occurred."[89]

In contrast, policy-making has none of these legitimizing features. It is completely untethered to authoritative text applicable to the case, it produces *ex post facto* rules, and it embraces policies that not only lack substantial community support, but are actually adverse to the community's values. Yet, policy-making can still be a legitimate exercise of the judicial function. Let us consider how.

---

83. See Part 1, Section A (Logical Method), infra.

84. See relevant discussion appearing earlier in this Section C2.

85. Ibid.

86. Ibid.

87. Cf. Eisenberg, *The Nature of the Common Law* supra note 65, at pp. 4, 9–10 (arguing that judge-made rules supported by the general standards of a society establish judicial accountability and responsiveness to the people).

88. Auerbach, *A Rival of Some Ancient Learning*, supra note 65, at p. 541 (Eisenberg, *The Nature of the Common Law* supra note 65, at p. 10).

89. Eisenberg, *The Nature of the Common Law* supra note 65, at p 10.

Judge Richard Posner provides a conceptualization of judicial illegitimacy that seems to suggest that policy-making is a legitimate judicial function in common law cases. He argues that most of the time a judge should set "as an important goal of his decision making the cutting back of the power of his court system in relation to—as a check on—other government institutions."[90] Thus, in "areas where considerations of judicial restraint...[are] irrelevant, as they usually are when a judge is expounding private judge-made law as distinct from public law," judicial policy-making is legitimate.[91]

Judge Posner's conceptualization is problematic because he defines self-restraint primarily in terms of "separation of powers," or "structural restraint."[92] Missing from his formulation is the most important restraint of all: restraint in deference to the people—what can be called "democratic restraint." Unelected and, hence, unaccountable to the people, judges in common law cases should defer to the will of the people. Judges should respect our democratic ideal, which is to say, they should not impose alien values on a community against its will. Judges have no mandate to do so, whether dealing with common law, statutory or constitutional cases. Without a sense of democratic restraint, judges would operate outside our system of checks and balances in common law cases. No other organ of government operates with such complete power, and to allow judges to do so would constitute an undemocratic assumption of power by judges.

There are, however, two counter-arguments (of varying quality) to the democratic-restraint argument. The stronger argument asserts that policy-making respects the democratic ideal, and thereby legitimizes itself, when it makes our government more democratic than it otherwise would be. Here, the term "democracy" can be taken in its *procedural sense* (its weak sense) or its *substantive sense* (its strong sense). Procedurally, democracy simply means the right to vote. Thus, the procedural argument is that where there has been a failure of democratic process in other organs of government, judges should (indeed, they must) act out of the ordinary in deference to the democratic ideal. But "democracy [also] has its own internal morality, based on the dignity and equality of all human beings. . . . These are reflected in the supremacy of such underlying democratic values and principles as human dignity, equality, and tolerance. There is no real democracy without recognition of basic

---

90. Posner, "The Meaning of Judicial Restraint," supra note 54, at p. 11.
91. Ibid., at p. 18.
92. Ibid., at p. 11.

values and principles such as morality and justice." Thus, substantively one could argue that where an identifiable group has been subordinated and stigmatized by other organs of government—denied human dignity and equality—judges should (indeed, they must) take extraordinary measures in deference to the democratic ideal. *Brown* earned its legitimacy most directly by according substantive democracy to African Americans.[93] In short, given the fact that the judge's pursuit of the democratic ideal implicates the nation's foundational norm, it is reasonable to conclude that this judicial endeavor provides firm institutional footing for policy-making.[94]

The judicial quest for justice, the second counter-argument, offers weaker support for policy-making. Judges who routinely attempt to follow the rules (as in the case of Scalian textualism) or community norms (as in the case of sociological jurisprudence) are no less in search of justice than judges who routinely ignore them.[95] However, the quest-for-justice argument can support policy-making as a once-in-a-great-while judicial necessity, mainly as a way of avoiding harsh results. For example, Richard Weisberg notes that in *Hynes v. New York Central Railroad Company*,[96] Justice Cardozo, at the time a judge on New York's highest court, found for the sympathetic plaintiff only by "overlooking precedents and challenging accepted norms on no more authority than that afforded by his formidable value system alone."[97] *Hynes*, then, is "an example of Cardozo's bending the rules to do justice in an individual case."[98] But, as Andrew Kaufman notes, *Hynes* was "not a typical Cardozo opinion."[99] Cardozo, an adherent of the policy method,[100] typically applied "what he regarded as governing legal doctrine" or community norms.[101] He "did not usu-

---

93. Aharon Barak, "A Judge on Judging: The Role of the Supreme Court in a Democracy," *Harvard Law Review* 116 (2002): 16, 39 (Justice Barak sits on the Supreme Court of Israel). See Ely, *Democracy and Distrust*, supra note 56.

94. See Chapter 10, Section D, infra.

95. See Part I, infra, for a more detailed discussion of Scalian textualism and sociological jurisprudence.

96. 231 N.Y. 229 (1921).

97. Richard H. Weisberg, "Judicial Discretion, or the Self on the Shelf," *Cardozo Law Review* 10 (1988): 105, 108.

98. Andrew L. Kaufman, *Cardozo* (Cambridge: Harvard University Press, 1998), p. 281.

99. Ibid. Kaufman does not necessarily agree with Weisberg's reading of *Hynes*, but he offers no formal challenge either. This merely points to the difficulty of determining when the judge's policy preferences are out of sync with community norms. See relevant discussion appearing earlier in this Section C2.

100. See Part 1, Section B (Policy Method), infra.

101. Kaufman, *Cardozo*, supra note 98, at p. 281.

ally bend a rule for one case," sometimes resulting in what Cardozo "characterized as a harsh result."[102] What this suggest, of course, is that judges, especially the great ones, can be seduced by policy-making.[103]

Judge Posner's attempt to legitimize broad policy-making in common law cases does not rest on either counter-argument—the pursuit of the democratic ideal or the quest for justice in individual cases.[104] Instead, it is grounded on the argument that judicial decision making in common law cases poses no threat to other organs of government. However, this argument ignores a very real threat to the democratic ideal itself—an unelected official is having license to disregard the will of the people.[105]

Yet, Judge Posner seems to have an implicit sense of the democratic deficiency of his argument. He states that: "Within that area [i.e., the common law] the judge must draw on his own values and preferences to arrive at a decision. But he must do so in a principled fashion, 'principled' implying not merely consistent but also enjoying sufficient public approbation that the judge is not afraid to state the 'principle' in his opinions."[106] Were Judge Posner to make "public approbation" within the community affected by the decision the centerpiece or litmus test of policy-formulation in common law cases, as he has done in the written law,[107] he would be ar-

---

102. Ibid.

103. Kaufman notes that Cardozo did succumbed policy-making on a regular basis in equity cases. "Only in one class of situations did he generally decide cases on the individual equities. That was...the class of cases governed by equitable principles." Ibid. Such decision-making was not unusual because it took place in the context of equity before the merger of law and equity. But even corrective equity was deemed by some to be illegitimate judicial decision-making. See Section B, supra.

104. Another argument in favor of policy-making in common law cases can be quickly dismissed. It is as follows: policy-making is permissible because the legislature can always step in with corrective legislation. This argument concedes the wrongness of policy-making, but relies on the legislature to make laws changing the common law rules it dislikes. Putting aside problems of special interest groups and legislative inertia, this argument "embrace[s] the general proposition that a wrong may be done if it can be undone"—a proposition we, like the Supreme Court, should refuse to accept. *Stanley v. Illinois*, 405 U.S. 645, 647 (1971).

105. See discussion appearing earlier in this Section C2 concerning how courts determine the will of the people.

106. Posner, "The Meaning of Judicial Restraint," supra note 54, at p. 10.

107. Judge Posner rejects policy-making in statutory or constitutional cases not only because it usurps the authority of other organs of government (separation of powers), but because it displaces the will of the people (democratic restraint). Accordingly, Judge Posner would not create a constitutional right of same-sex marriage because that would entail the imposition of "a social policy that is deeply offensive to the vast majority of...[American] citizens." Posner, *The Problematics of Moral and Legal Theory*, supra note 73, at p. 249.

guing policy-discovery rather than policy-making, thereby avoiding the problem of illegitimacy. But in order to reach this point, Judge Posner would have to recognize the distinction between policy-discovery and policy-making suggested herein.

With this understanding of the judicial policy-formulation function—including its roots in equity and its conceptualization of the term policy—we are now able to delve deeply into a discussion of judicial methods—the logical method and policy method. As we move through Part 1 (Traditional Process), we shall encounter the following recurring question: What mix of law and policy is necessary to achieve justice in a given case? As we move through Part 2 (Critical Process), we shall face the question of justice framed in an entirely different way.

PART 1
TRADITIONAL PROCESS

This part of the book presents several traditional judicial theories, or models, advanced mainly during the twentieth century: legal formalism; Scalian textualism; legal realism; sociological jurisprudence; and legal process. Each model is a specific application of a more general judicial method. One such method can be called the "logical method" (Section A) and the other the "policy method" (Section B). We shall also attempt to understand the traditional judicial models in a more sophisticated way (Section C). Through this deeper discussion, we shall be able to synthesize the five models into three levels of judicial analysis: "Level 1" (or "judicial positivism"); "Level 2" (or "judicial pragmatism"); and "Level 3" or ("judicial nominalism").

Logical Method

For many jurists and legal scholars, the logical method represents the traditional and only legitimate approach to judicial decision making in Anglo-American law. No one has defined the contours of the logical method more accurately than Max Weber (1864–1920). A German sociologist and political economist whose understanding of America, some believe, rivals that of another famous foreign observer, Alexis de Tocqueville,[1] Weber was a scholar of tremendous range. One of his main interests was the principle of rationality—"the tendency of things to get organized and subjected to rules and orderly processes."[2] Weber believed that highly evolved legal systems are in this sense "rational" rather than "irrational." They are, in other words, legal systems with value-free judicial processes. Value judgments (whether "ethical, emotional, or political") have no objective basis, Weber argued, and, thus, do not contribute to the "orderly processes" of law.[3]

Weber identified five postulates of legal systems that have "achieved the highest measure of methodological and logical rationality."[4] Taken together, these postulates represent the logical method's basic structure:

First, that every concrete legal decision be the 'application' of an abstract legal proposition to a concrete 'fact situation'; second, that it must be possible in every concrete case to derive the decision from abstract legal propositions by means of legal logic; third, that the

---

1. See Alexis de Tocqueville, *Democracy in America*, George Lawrence, trans., J.P. Mayer, ed. (New York: Doubleday, Anchor Books, 1969). Weber came to America in 1904, three-quarters of a century after de Tocqueville. The views of America's two famous visitors are analyzed in John Patrick Diggins, *Max Weber: Politics and the Spirit of Tragedy* (New York: Basic Books, 1996), pp. 1–16.

2. Roland H. Stromberg, *European Intellectual History Since 1789* (New York: Appleton-Century-Crofts, 1968), p. 185.

3. *Max Weber on Law in Economy and Society*, Edward Shils and Max Rheinstein, trans., Max Rheinstein, ed. (Cambridge: Harvard University Press, 1954), p. 63.

4. Ibid., p. 64.

law must actually or virtually constitute a 'gapless' system of legal propositions, or must, at least, be treated as if it were such a gap-less system; fourth, that whatever cannot be 'construed' legally in rational terms is also legally irrelevant; and fifth, that every social action of human beings must always be visualized as either an 'application' or 'execution' of legal propositions, or as an 'infringement' thereof.[5]

Weber has essentially described a system of deductive reasoning; a process of logical (preferably syllogistic) legal analysis:

All P are M [Major Premise]
No S are M [Minor Premise]
Ergo, No S are P [Conclusion][6]

The major premise is the controlling rule of law; the minor premise consists of the crucial facts of the case; and the conclusion is the law of the case, or "holding." The judge moves from the major premise to the conclusion by *stare decisis* ("legal logic"). Such judicial reasoning necessarily entails rule interpretation (the expansion or contraction of doctrine) aided by the parsing of words, close factual analysis, and established legal reasoning devices — reasoning by analogy, negative *stare decisis* (accentuating the differences between the case at bar and prior cases) and affirmative *stare decisis* (accentuating the similarities between the case *sub judice* and prior cases). Policy considerations are extra-legal and, hence, beyond the bounds of legitimate judicial decision making. They are not to be read into the controlling law or otherwise factored into the decision-making process, lest the judicial process promote casuistry.

The logical method has been described as the "phonograph" theory of judicial analysis. This judicial theory portrays the judge as "merely an oral medium through which the preexisting legal principles are given expression."[7] This is as good a description as one can find.

---

5. Ibid. See also David Trubek, "Max Weber on Law and the Rise of Capitalism," *Wisconsin Law Review* 1972 (1972): 720.

6. See John T. Kearns, *Deductive Logic: A Programmed Introduction* (New York: New Century, 1969), pp. 165–93. See also Ruggero J. Aldisert, *Logic for Lawyers: A Guide to Clear Legal Thinking* (New York: C. Boardman Company, 1989), pp. 53–58.

7. Lawrence Lessig, "Understanding Changed Readings: Fidelity and Theory," *Stanford Law Review* 47 (1995): 395, 462 (quoting Robert Eugene Cushman, "The Social and Economic Interpretation of the Fourteenth Ammendment," *Michigan Law Review* 20 (1922): 737, 744.

An illustration of the logical method is presented in the court of appeals opinion in *Caterpillar, Inc. v. Lewis*.[8] This case involved application of the removal statute,[9] which permits a state-court defendant to remove her case to federal district court under certain conditions. One of these conditions, the most important, is that the district court must have valid subject matter jurisdiction at the time of removal.[10] In *Lewis*, subject matter jurisdiction was based on diversity jurisdiction,[11] yet it was clear complete diversity was lacking at the time of removal.[12] The district court, nevertheless, erroneously denied plaintiff's motion, timely made, to remand the case to state court for want of federal subject matter jurisdiction.[13] Before the trial commenced in federal court, the nondiverse defendant settled, thereby giving the court complete diversity.[14] The case proceeded to trial, which resulted in a jury verdict for the remaining defendant. Plaintiff appealed, citing as error the district court's lack of subject matter jurisdiction at the time of removal.

The Sixth Circuit reversed, reasoning as follows: "When an action is based on diversity, we must determine whether complete diversity exists at the time of removal" (major premise);[15] "complete diversity did not exist at the time the case was removed to federal court [because] at the time [defendant] Caterpillar removed the case to federal court, plaintiff, a resident of Kentucky, remained a party to the case…[as did defendant] Whayne Supply Co., a Kentucky corporation…" (minor premise);[16] ergo, "[w]e hold that the district court erred in denying plaintiff's motion to remand" (conclusion).[17] The court would have preferred not to remand the case, because of policy considerations of efficiency, but felt duty-bound to abide by the letter of the law.[18] It was left

---

8. 68 F.3d 474 (6th Cir. 1995), *rev'd* 519 U.S. 61 (1996). The circuit court's opinion is referenced in a "Table of Decisions Without Reported Opinions" appearing in the federal reporter. Because of the absence of pagination, the Westlaw citation, 1995 WL 600590, is referred to hereafter.

9. 28 U.S.C. §§ 1441–1452 (1994) (Supp. 1996).

10. See 28 U.S.C. § 1441(a); 519 U.S. at 70–71; 1995 WL 600590 *2 (cases cited therein).

11. 28 U.S.C. § 1332(a) (1994) (Supp. 1996).

12. 1995 WL 600590, *2; 519 U.S. at 70 ("[T]he Sixth Circuit correctly determined that the complete diversity requirement was not satisfied at the time of removal.").

13. 519 U.S. at 74; 1995 WL 600590, *3.

14. 519 U.S. at 73; 1995 WL 600590, *3.

15. 1995 WL 600590, *3.

16. Ibid.

17. Ibid.

18. "Unfortunately, we must remand a case that has proceeded through judgment in the district court." Ibid.

to the Supreme Court to let the verdict stand, which, reversing the court of appeals, it could only do by using an entirely different judicial method—the policy method—as we shall see later on.[19]

The Sixth Circuit's reasoning illustrates the chief characteristics of the logical method—to wit, value-free and logical judicial reasoning, ultimately creating a gapless system of rules of law. The judge "impersonally discovers and applies antecedently existing law."[20]

Two expressions of the logical method are examined in this section of Part 1. Both claim allegiance to a value-free, tightly reasoned, "rational" process of judicial decision making. The first, "legal formalism" or "formalism" (Chapter 1), purportedly gives evidence of its fidelity to the logical method through a process of selecting "clear" rules of law, followed by deduction. Legal formalism dominated judicial analysis at the Supreme Court from 1886 to 1937, but may have made something of a comeback in the mid-1990s.[21] The second judicial technique centers on Supreme Court Justice Antonin Scalia's brand of judicial decision making, which in this book is called "Scalian textualism" (Chapter 2). Scalian textualism purports to demonstrate devotion to policy-free and logical decision making through a commitment to text followed by deduction. Unlike legal formalism, Scalian textualism harbors no "exaggerated belief" in the transparency of text. Rules of law must be carefully construed before they are applied.

The structure of legal formalism and Scalian textualism can be outlined as follows:

Legal Formalism
> Point A: Dispositive Issue
> Point B: Reasoning
>> (1) Minimalist Rule
>> (2) Followed by Deduction
> Point C: Judgment

Scalian Textualism
> Point A: Dispositive Issue
> Point B: Reasoning
>> (1) Plain Meaning of Text
>>> (a) Statutory: Text Trumps Intent

---

19. See discussion of the *Lewis* case in Chapter 2, Section E, infra.

20. John Hasnas, "Back to the Future: From Critical Legal Studies Forward to Legal Realism, or How Not to Miss the Point of the Indeterminacy Argument," *Duke Law Journal* 45 (1995): 84, 89.

21. See Chapter 1, Section E, infra.

    (b) Constitutional: Intent Trumps Text
  (2) Followed by Logical Discourse
Point C: Judgment

A more detailed discussion of the structure of legal formalism and Scalian textualism follows in Chapters 1 and 2, respectively.

Chapter 1
Legal Formalism

Legal formalism prescribes a judicial process in which the judge moves from Point A to Point C by an exaggerated belief in the transparency of text followed by deduction. The syllogism is not value-free; it is infused with legal doctrines that favor a minimalist government (a government of limited powers and importance, typically supportive of private interests),[1] and sometimes with a sensitivity to special facts.

A. Overview

Legal formalism (sometimes referred to as "formalism" or "classical legal thought") refers to the judicial technique the Supreme Court employed during what is called the "Lochner Era" (circa 1886–1937). The Lochner era takes its name from the infamous case *Lochner v. New York* (1905).[2] In *Lochner*, the Supreme Court struck down a New York statute that limited to sixty the number of hours bakers could work in a week. The Court ruled that the statute was an unconstitutional infringement on an employee's freedom to contract. Lochnerian jurisprudence is almost universally regarded as a judicial embarrassment, arguably topped by few other cases in the Court's history.[3] "Lochnerizing" is a term that is often used to describe a critical error in judi-

---

1. See Preface, Section B, supra, for a discussion of minimalism.
2. *Lochner v. New York,* 198 U.S. 45 (1905).
3. Two cases with worse reputations than *Lochner* are *Dred Scott v. Sandford,* 60 U.S. 393 (1856), which gave constitutional support to the institution of slavery, and *Plessy v. Ferguson,* 163 U.S. 537 (1896) (decided during the Lochner Era), which constitutionalized racial segregation. See also Dan Simon, "A Psychological Model of Judicial Decision Making," *Rutgers Law Journal* 30 (1998): 1, 10 (noting the view of legal scholars that *Lochner's* judicial method has been "officially discredited, even scorned"). One case seems to be in strong contention with these cases: *Bush v. Gore,* 531 U.S. 98 (2000), which stopped the recount in the controversial 2000 Presidential Election. The view among many legal scholars is that this case is "quite demonstrably the worst Supreme Court decision in history.... *Dred Scott* was, by comparison, a brilliantly reasoned and logically coherent decision." Max Boot, "Rule of Law: Law Professors v. the Supreme Court," Wall Street Journal, 8/13/01, p. A13. For a more detailed discussion of *Bush v. Gore,* see Introduction, note 39, supra & Chapter 7, Section B3, infra.

37

cial judgment.[4] Exactly how to define that error is a point of contention among scholars.[5]

Lochner did not begin nor did it end the era that bears its name. One of the earliest harbingers of the era came in a dissenting opinion written by Justice Bradley in the *Slaughterhouse Cases* (1873).[6] As we shall see, this influential dissent laid the foundation for the liberty of contract doctrine, one of the legal doctrines that anchored legal formalism.[7] By 1886, most justices had become committed to legal formalism. This is evident in *Santa Clara County v. Southern Pacific Railroad* (1886),[8] a case in which the Supreme Court granted Fourteenth Amendment protection to corporations. The Lochner Era ended with the 1937 Court-packing crisis, which was brought on by the persistent efforts of "the nine old men" on the Court to block New Deal legislation. Chief Justice Rehnquist provides an efficient summary of this crisis in a law review article.[9]

Some scholars would not associate legal formalism with the Lochner Era. Fred Schauer, for example, argues that Lochnerian jurisprudence is a poor example of legal formalism, and negatively colors legal formalism's potentially beneficial use in the modern age. James Q. Wilson also sees a need to distin-

---

4. See, e.g., Laurence H. Tribe, *American Constitutional Law* 2d ed.(Mineola, N.Y.: Foundation Press,1988), p. 567. For a detailed discussion of the Lochner Court, see, e.g., Cass R. Sunstein, "Lochner's Legacy," *Columbia Law Review* 87 (1987): 873.

5. See discussion of several critical views of Lochnerian jurisprudence in Section B, infra. In this book, the Lochner-era error is define as judicial policy-making and failure to faithfully adhere to the logical method. See Sections B & E, supra.

6. In the *Slaughterhouse Cases*, 83 U.S. 36 (1873), the Court upheld the constitutionality of Louisiana's slaughterhouse monopoly on the ground that the command of the recently enacted Fourteenth Amendment that "[n]o state shall make or enforce any law which shall abridge the privileges and immunities of citizens of the United States," was not a source of substantive federal protection for natural rights and, thus, could not shield citizens from infringements by their own states; the privileges and immunities clause simply prevented states from discriminating against citizens of another state. Since on its face the clause clearly protects "rights," some scholars, including Clarence Thomas before his appointment to the Supreme Court, have argued for its resurrection. See Clarence Thomas, "The Higher Law Background of the Privileges or Immunities Clause," *Harvard Journal of Law & Public Policy* 12 (1989): 63, 68. See also Philip B. Kurland, "The Privileges or Immunities Clause: 'Its Hour Come Round at Last?'" *Washington University Law Quarterly* 1972 (1972): 405, 418–20.

7. See Section C, infra.

8. 118 U.S. 394 (1886).

9. William H. Rehnquist, "The American Constitutional Experience: Remarks of the Chief Justices," *Louisiana Law Review* 54 (1994): 1161, 1169–71.

guish legal formalism from a "hostile intellectual history" to appreciate its benefits.[10]

In viewing legal formalism as an expression of a more fundamental judicial method—the logical method discussed earlier[11]—this book thus distinguishes between purely logical or syllogistic legal analysis and a particular, discredited use of such analysis. Ideology is separated from methodology. Thus, as used in this book, legal formalism is defined as an exaggerated belief in the transparency of text followed by deduction. More specifically, the formalist, or Lochnerian, judge infuses the syllogism with legal doctrines that favor a minimalist government.[12] This is a government of limited powers; a government that seeks to minimize or shrink itself so as not to suppress individual liberty or inhibit private enterprise.[13] A minimalist government champions private interests and, at the same time, rejects the idea of government solicitude for the needs of the powerless and downtrodden. Liberty, property, free markets, and individual pluck are minimalist paths not only for individual advancement but also for collective progress.

Minimalism is not entirely noninterventionist, however. The government, including the judiciary, does intervene in markets, but not to rescue the individual from poverty, illness, or his own ignorance, or inequality.[14] The government only intervenes for the limited purpose of protecting liberty or laying the foundation for private enterprise. Minimalism is "progressive," but not "liberal."[15]

Legal formalism, in short, is a process of judicial decision making in which the use of the syllogism creates the false impression that the judicial process is value-free and, hence, unquestionably correct. Lochnerian judicial decision making is neither policy-free nor unquestionably correct.

---

10. See Frederick Schauer, "Formalism," *Yale Law Journal* 97 (1988): 509, 511–14; James Q. Wilson, "The Morality of Formalism," *UCLA Law Review* 33 (1985): 431–34.

11. See Part 1, Section A, supra.

12. See Section C, infra.

13. See Preface, Section B, supra.

14. The unstated assumption is that these conditions are of the individual's own making. In contrast to this classical liberal assumption, welfare liberalism largely assumes that these realities are socially constructed. See Preface, Section B, supra.

15. "Progressive" is defined here as the government's desire to move society forward on a number of fronts, such as socially and economically. "Liberal" is defined here to mean welfare liberalism, which is the belief that government should take steps to rescue people from socially constructed disadvantages, such as poverty and inequality. For a more detailed discussion of these and similar terms, see Preface, Section B, supra.

B. The Rise of Legal Formalism

Legal formalism arose as judicial resistance to liberal social and political reforms that began to appear in the closing decades of the nineteenth century. These reforms were designed to ameliorate socioeconomic dislocations caused not only by the nation's industrialization, but also by the diminishing supply of good free land resulting from the rapid increase in immigration. As America's economic base shifted from agriculture to manufacturing, and as free land became less abundant, traditional sources of sustenance for millions of Americans began to disappear. Moving from the countryside to the city, many Americans were unable to find work or could only find it at exploitative wages or under extreme hardship. Poverty and social discontent followed.[16] The paucity of productive land exacerbated these unsettling conditions. As Arthur Schlesinger elaborates:

> ...For three centuries the national social, economic and political life had been dominated by one outstanding influence: an abundance of unoccupied and fertile land. The free land to the west had afforded opportunities for the energetic and an outlet for the discontented. It had absorbed millions of immigrants from Europe and had, by its plentiful eastward shipment of agricultural products, kept the cost of living low....
>
> * * *
>
> With the end of the era of free land, also, the opportunities for the less fortunate to escape from intolerable conditions became more limited; there were evidences of the development of class consciousness and a tightening of the lines of battle in the conflict between capital and labor.[17]

Many thoughtful Americans in fact blamed organized money. The oft-stated charge was, "America in making her fortune was in peril of losing her soul."[18] America was becoming a nation controlled by corporations and trusts. The Standard Oil Trust, the American Tobacco Trust, and other forms of big

---

16. See, e.g., William M. Wiecek, *Liberty Under Law—The Supreme Court in American Life* (Baltimore: John Hopkins University Press, 1988), pp. 111–13; Calvin Woodard, "Reality and Social Reform: The Transition from Laissez-Faire to the Welfare State," *Yale Law Journal* 72 (1962): 286, 293.

17. *A History of American Life: The Quest for Social Justice, 1898–1914*, vol. xi, Arthur M. Schlesinger, Dixon Ryan Fox, eds. (New York: The MacMillan Company, 1931)) pp. 2–3.

18. Ibid. at p. 81.

business simply overpowered individual autonomy and well-being. Farmers and laborers targeted big business as an evil that must be met with equal force. Cooperatives and labor unions were formed to provide the desired counter-vailing pressure.[19] Congress and state legislatures, urged on by such public fig-ures like Woodrow Wilson, then president of Princeton University, responded in similar fashion by passing a plethora of new laws designed to regulate large and powerful concentrations of money in such markets as agriculture, man-ufacturing, textiles, and transportation.[20] Attempts were even made to na-tionalize railroads, install a graduated income tax, and institute direct democ-racy by initiative, referendum, or recall of elected officials.[21]

Although the welfare liberalism of these reforms was certainly new, there was also something old and very familiar about them. They were in fact expressive of a deeply held American impulse: *a preference for a government, including a judiciary, that does not indulge privilege or special interests.* This notion of civic republicanism—the idea that government must pursue social progress by championing the public good over private interests—"culminates in the open-ended obligation of government to pursue the people's welfare above all else."[22] This belief, captured in the *salus populi* maxim,[23] was perhaps at its highest pitch in pre-Lochnerian America during the "Age of Jackson" (1820–1850).

Taking its name from President Andrew Jackson, the Age of Jackson was marked by what Alexis de Tocqueville called the "feverish" pursuit of wealth.[24] Jacksonian America was also and, indeed, even more so character-ized by a general sense that trade and commerce should be democratized, so that the common man could compete across the board. As Jackson said:

> It is to be regretted that the rich and powerful too often bend the acts of government to their selfish purposes. Distinctions in society will always exist under every just government. Equality of talents, of ed-ucation, or of wealth can not be reproduced by human institutions... but when the laws undertake to add to these natural and just advan-

---

19. Ibid. at pp. 27–80.

20. See ibid. at pp. 130–203. See also Paul Johnson, *A History of the American People* (New York: HarperCollins, 1997), pp. 560–67.

21. Wiecek, *Liberty Under Law*, supra note 16, at p. 111.

22. William J. Novak, *The People's Welfare* (Chapel Hill: University of North Carolina Press, 1996), p. 46.

23. Ibid.

24. Alexis de Tocqueville, *Democracy in America*, vol. II, Francis Bowen, ed. (Cam-bridge, Mass.: Sever and Francis, 1863), p. 187, reprinted in *Ideology and Power in the Age of Jackson*, Edwin C. Rozwenc, ed. (New York: Anchor Books, 1964), p. 18.

tages artificial distinctions…to make the rich richer and the potent more powerful, the humble members of society…the farmers, mechanics and laborers…have a right to complain of the injustice of their Government.[25]

The judiciary's role in supporting progress through civic republicanism is well-illustrated in *Charles River Bridge v. Warren Bridge*.[26] This famous case is considered by many scholars to be the flagship case of the Jacksonian Era. It has a rather interesting set of facts.

In 1826, Massachusetts incorporated a company to erect a bridge across the Charles River, linking Charleston and Boston. The proprietors of this bridge, the Warren Bridge, were authorized by the enabling legislation to collect tolls until they had recovered their construction costs plus 5% profit. Tolls could be collected up to six years. The bridge was then to revert to the state and become accessible to the public free of charge, thereby facilitating commerce between the cities. Still in force, however, was another charter the legislature had granted years earlier to the Charles River Bridge Company to build and operate another toll bridge not far from the new bridge. Although the old bridge, the Charles River Bridge, would have eventually reverted to the state, it still held plenty of economic value for its proprietors. To protect their economic interests, the proprietors of the Charles River Bridge sued the proprietors of the Warren Bridge. Plaintiffs argued that the Warren Bridge charter impaired their rights as guaranteed by Article I, Section 10 of the United States Constitution ("No state shall…pass any…law impairing the obligation of contracts") as well as the Fifth Amendment ("…Nor shall private property be taken for public use without just compensation").

In an opinion written by Chief Justice Taney, the Court upheld the Warren Bridge charter. Although the case turned on a strict construction of the Charles River Bridge charter, the majority and dissenting opinions were so pregnant with contrasting conceptions of political economy that it is hard to believe these extra-legal considerations did not influence how these contracts were read. For example, Justice Story's dissenting opinion argued vigorously for the protection of vested property rights. Such protection was needed, Justice Story believed, as a necessary condition for the development of infant in-

---

25. Philip B. Kunhardt, Jr., Philip B. Kunhardt III, and Peter W. Kunhardt, *The American President* (New York: Riverhead Books, 1999), p. 354. Jackson's fight with the giant and increasingly corrupt Bank of the United States, which had controlled the national economy since the early days of the republic, illustrates the *salus populi* maxim. Jackson wanted a banking system in which small banks could compete in every state. Ibid., p. 352.

26. 11 Pet. 420 (U.S. 1934).

dustries. Equally concerned with economic development, Justice Taney, writing for the majority, refused to recognize the doctrine of vested property rights in this case. To do so, he thought, would interfere with "the happiness and prosperity of the community." Furthermore, the whole notion of vested property rights ran counter to the felt necessities of the time—the feeling that the pursuit of the public's welfare should not be held hostage to the drive for private profits. As Stanley Kutler has remarked: "the Charles River Bridge proprietors never could refute the charges that their claims to exclusive privilege constituted an intolerable stranglehold over the community.... The Charles River Bridge proprietors were victims of the popular outburst against privilege that was part of the fashionable political rhetoric of the times."[27] Consistent with the tenor of the times, the Court discovered a policy of "creative destruction" that destroyed vested rights asserted in the case.[28]

Civic republicanism continued through the Civil War, perhaps the ultimate expression of *salus populi*, and into the Reconstruction years. Not only the right to use one's property free from government interference, but also the right to contract freely was viewed as "a social, relative, and hence regulatable right.... Even religious freedom was subject to the strictures of *salus populi* and *sic utere tuo*."[29]

Many state courts played an active role in supporting *salus populi* legislation in the years following the Civil War.[30] For example, New York's highest court ruled in 1873 that the judiciary must not stand in the way of the people's needs: the construction of factories, machinery, dams, canals, and railroads.[31] The Chief Justice of the New Hampshire Supreme Court exhibited a similar attitude in rejecting a legal doctrine he considered to be antithetical to the public good. To quote Virginia Nolan and Edmund Ursin: "No friend of barbarism, [Chief Justice] Doe concluded that it 'is impossible that legal principle can throw' so serious an obstacle in the way of progress and improvement.'"[32] In short, civic republicanism—progress through indulging the "people's welfare"

---

27. Stanley I. Kutler, *Privilege and Creative Destruction: The Charles River Bridge Case* (Baltimore: The Johns Hopkins University Press, 1971), p. 155.

28. See ibid.

29. Novak, *The People's Welfare*, supra note 22, at p. 47.

30. In common law cases, some state courts did indulge special interests in the name of progress contrary to the public's preference for civic republicanism. The most notable is Chief Justice Lemuel Shaw of the Massachusetts Supreme Judicial Court. See Chapter 3, Section C1, infra, and Chapter 5, Section C1, infra.

31. *Losee v. Buchanan*, 51 N.Y. 476 (1873).

32. Virginia E. Nolan and Edmund Ursin, "The Revitalization of Hazardous Activity Strict Liability," *North Carolina Law Review* 65 (1984): 257, 261.

rather than privilege or special interests—was "a coherent, distinctive, and dominant legal-political discourse that permeated even the most unlikely texts and practices in nineteenth century American life, private as well as public."[33]

Lochner-Era judges certainly rejected many of the people's reforms.[34] Does this mean they also rejected civic republicanism? Did they believe social progress is best achieved through the indulgence of privilege or special interests? The traditional view is that they did. That is, Lochnerian judges made a conscious effort to taint the logical method with pro-business legal doctrines. The syllogisms these judges used were "designed to do little more than meet the needs of the Carnegies and Morgans at the expense of the people."[35] Morton Horwitz at one time suggested that the seeds of a pro-business judiciary were sown as early as the antebellum period with the rise of an elite legal profession. These mostly corporate lawyers subsequently joined forces with the entrenched business interests they served to "freeze" legal doctrine and, thereby, maintain the status quo in the closing decades of the nineteenth century:

> ...[T]he rise of legal formalism can be understood as resulting from the convergence and synthesis of three major factors in antebellum America. First, it is a rough measure of the rise in the power of the postrevolutionary legal profession and is a culmination of the Bar's own separate and autonomous professional interest...in representing law as an objective, neutral, and apolitical system. Second, it mirrors a convergence of interest between the elite of the legal profession and the newly powerful commercial and entrepreneurial interests, an alliance which, beginning after the Revolution, enabled the Bar to achieve real prestige and power for the first time. Finally, it represents the successful culmination of efforts by mercantile and entrepreneurial interests during the preceding half century to transform the laws to serve their interests, leaving them to wish for the first time to 'freeze' legal doctrine and to conceive of law not as a malleable instrument of their own desires and interests but as a fixed and inexorable system of logically deductible rules.[36]

---

33. Novak, *The People's Welfare*, supra note 22, at p. 49.

34. See, e.g., Sections C & D, infra; Wiecek, *Liberty Under Law*, supra note 16, at pp. 110–39; Gary D. Rowe, "Lochner Revisionism Revisited," *Law and Social Inquiry* 24 (1999): 221.

35. Rowe, "Lochner Revisionism," supra note 34, at p. 222.

36. Morton J. Horwitz, *The Transformation of American Law, 1780–1860* (Cambridge: Harvard University Press, 1977), pp. 258–59.

Also:

> ...If a flexible, instrumental conception of law was necessary to promote the transformation of the postrevolutionary American legal system, it was no longer needed since the major beneficiaries of that transformation had obtained the bulk of their objectives. Indeed, once successful, those groups could only benefit if both the recent origins and the foundations in policy and group self-interest of all newly established legal doctrines could be disguised. There were, in short, major advantages in creating an intellectual system which gave common law rules the appearance of being self-contained, apolitical, and inexorable, and which, by making 'legal reasoning seem like mathematics,' conveyed 'an air...of...inevitability' about legal decisions.[37]

Another strand of the traditional view—the view that formalist judges indulged privilege or special interests, that they jettisoned civic republicanism—defines the favored special interest in Darwinian terms. Lochnerian judges sought to achieve progress by promoting competition rather than by merely pushing business interests. These judges, it is argued, were influenced by Herbert Spencer's Social Darwinism. Indeed, Spencer's theory of natural selection took root in America at the beginning of the Lochner Era.[38] Darwinians believed, as Neil Duxbury explains, that "[g]overnmental interference with the market frustrates natural competitiveness by enabling the economically weak to survive in the market longer than they would naturally do, thereby bolstering their bargaining position to the cost of the economically fittest."[39] Dissenting in *Lochner*, Justice Holmes himself identifies the Darwinian mindset as the great error in legal formalism.[40]

More recently, revisionist scholars have argued that legal formalism's rejection of civic republicanism has merit that should not be so easily dismissed. Social progress through the protection of liberty, property, and free markets is a venerable, quintessentially American view. Lochnerian jurisprudence "should be understood not as an exercise of class justice but as an attempt to

---

37. Ibid. at p. 254.
38. See Herbert Spencer, *Social Statics: or, The Conditions Essential to Human Happiness Specified, and the First of Them Developed* (London: Chapman, 1851). Between 1860 and 1900, nearly 370,000 copies of Spencer's writings were sold in America. See Neil Duxbury, *Patterns of American Jurisprudence* (Oxford: Oxford University Press, 1995), p. 28 n.76 (citing sources).
39. Duxbury, *Patterns of American Jurisprudence*, supra note 38, at p. 28.
40. See Chapter 3, Section B1, infra.

explicate and protect the constitutional ideal of liberty."[41] The judges' reasoning, especially that of the Fuller Court, exhibited "a coherence and an inner logic" that went far beyond any provincial concern for private profits. It demonstrated "a serious, principled effort to maintain one of the central distinctions in nineteenth-century constitutional law...during a period of unprecedented class conflict."[42] Legal formalism, then, offered a competing "substantive vision of the good society."[43]

Implicit in this revisionism is the argument that legal formalism was not out of step with the judicial history that preceded it. The judges' embrace of minimalism was not new nor judicial heresy. Indeed, it harkens back to Justice Story's stance in *Charles River Bridge*. Like Justice Story, legal formalists believed that the best path to social progress was through the protection rather than the subordination of private interests (liberty and property). There is also an important institutional value at stake—to wit, judicial restraint. Lochnerian jurisprudence teaches Americans to look askance at judicial activism of the order one sees in Chief Justice Taney's opinion in *Charles River Bridge*. Such activism can erode or altogether eradicate fundamental rights. Asking judges to participate in the suppression of fundamental rights runs counter to the judicial role in a free society.

The revisionist view is problematic because it misses the timing issue. Lochnerian America was not the time to indulge private interests. Minimalism was not the correct path to social progress at that particular hour of American history. The Supreme Court's indulging of private interests destroyed the hope for personal happiness and worldly success for millions of Americans who fell through the cracks of a changing economy and population explosion. Although there is little doubt that the Supreme Court and other Lochnerian jurists thought their decision making was progressive or, at the very least, in the best interest of the country, it is also clear that it was neither. What the country needed most at the time was a government that protected child laborers and persons without property. What it needed was civic republicanism, in this instance welfare liberalism to protect the powerless from the powerful. Laissez-faire was the wrong prescription for the country's ills. Americans perceived the threat to their well-being coming not from the government, but from organized money. On this new threat, famed conservative commentator William F. Buckley, quoting Professor J. Salwyn Schapiro, notes:

---

41. Owen M. Fiss, *History of the Supreme Court of the United States, 1888–1910,* vol. 8 (New York: Macmillan, 1993), p. 19.

42. Ibid.; Howard Gillman, *The Constitution Besieged: The Rise and Demise of Lochner Era Police Powers Jurisprudence* (Durham: Duke University Press, 1993), p. 10.

43. Morton J. Horwitz, "History and Theory," *Yale Law Journal* 96 (1987): 1825, 1830.

...'Laissez faire, a revolutionary doctrine in the eighteenth century, a liberal one in the nineteenth, was repudiated [by liberals] as a reactionary one in the twentieth'; and in each case, the 'liberal' was dead on target.

Mr. Schapiro goes on: 'The old liberalism had concerned itself mainly with the protection of the individual against arbitrary acts of government. The new liberalism [of the twentieth century] sought to protect him against arbitrary acts of private organizations as well....[44]

In this book, then, the Lochner-Era judges are viewed as having committed two serious judicial errors. First, Lochnerian judges did not employ the value-free process of judicial reasoning the logical method envisions. Instead, the judges played with loaded syllogisms—syllogisms that favored a minimalist government.[45] This error has nothing to do per se with the acceptance or rejection of either civic republicanism or minimalism, and it is not contradicted by other Lochnerian theories, including the revisionist one. It is based entirely on the dictates of the logical method.[46] A second error, one not normally associated with legal formalism, is judicial policy making, which arises from the fact that the Lochner-Era judges did not change with the times. This problem is explored in greater detail later in this chapter.[47] To understand both errors, we must take a look at some of the Lochnerian opinions, focusing on the loaded syllogisms.

C. Loaded Syllogisms

Legal formalists saw their function as "chiefly to restrain the coercive power of the government in order to protect the liberty of the individual."[48] Yet, as we have seen, many Americans saw the threat to individual autonomy and well-being coming not from government, as they had once believed, but from a new phenomenon—organized money, such as corporations and trusts.[49]

---

44. William F. Buckley, Jr., *Up From Liberalism* (New York: Arlington House, 1959), p. 175.

45. The fact that the values read into the syllogism were out of step with the tenor of the times leads to another error—judicial policy-making—which, of course, the logical method seeks to prevent. For further discussion of this point, see Section E, infra.

46. Which is to say, this error might be forgivable or not even considered to be an error under a different judicial regime. See Part 1, Section B (Policy Method), infra.

47. See Section E, infra.

48. Wiecek, *Liberty Under Law*, supra note 16, at pp. 132–33.

49. See discussion at the end of Section B, supra.

Organized money became even more ominous after the Supreme Court, in *Santa Clara County v. Southern Pacific Railroad*[50] and other cases,[51] gave constitutional protection to the corporate entity. Without relying on any clear precedent, the Court ruled that corporations are "persons" within the meaning of the Fourteenth Amendment. The Court reasoned that:

> Private corporations are, it is true, artificial persons, but...they consist of aggregations of individuals united for some legitimate business....It would be a most singular result if a constitutional provision intended for the protection of every person against partial and discriminating legislation by the state, should cease to exert such protection the moment the person becomes a member of a corporation....On the contrary, we think that it is well established by numerous adjudications of the Supreme Court of the United States... that whenever a provision of the constitution, or of a law, guarantees to persons the enjoyment of property...the benefits of the provision extend to corporations, and that the courts will always look beyond the name of the artificial being to the individuals whom it represents.[52]

There is no attempt on the part of the Court to more fully explain the logic of how corporations can be "persons" within the meaning of the Fourteenth Amendment. The framers of the amendment (the 39th Congress) clearly had natural persons in mind. Linking the Fourteenth Amendment to the Thirteenth Amendment, the framers sought to protect individuals from slavery and similar forms of racial oppression, such as racial discrimination. These inequalities simply do not befall corporations, which strongly suggests the framers did not have corporations in mind when they fashioned the Reconstruction Amendments.[53]

With the legal personification of the corporate entity, corporate lawyers now had a constitutional basis for challenging legislation that sought to effectuate civic republicanism, the *salus populi* maxim.[54] Their legal argument

---

50. 118 U.S. 394 (1886).

51. See, e.g., *San Mateo County v. Southern Pacific Railroad Co.*, 116 U.S. 138 (1885).

52. Horwitz, *The Transformation of American Law*, supra note 36, at p. 70 (quoting *San Mateo County v. Southern Pacific Railroad Co.*, 116 U.S. 138 (1885)).

53. Howard J. Graham, "The 'Conspiracy Theory' of the Fourteenth Amendment," *Yale Law Journal* 47 (1938): 371(arguing that the Court's ruling can not proceed on grounds of the framers' intent because that assumes the framers saw corporations as persons).

54. See Section B, supra.

proceeded along the following three prongs:(1) the legislature had no power to regulate corporations because the Fourteenth Amendment prohibited deprivation of property; (2) even if such power existed it could only be exercised reasonably; and (3) the reasonableness test lay with the judiciary.[55] The Supreme Court found this argument compelling, not merely persuasive.

After *Santa Clara*, the Supreme Court typically injected its ideology of protecting individual (business) liberty into the judicial process through the syllogism's major premise. The Court usually did so by reading several loaded legal doctrines into the Fourteenth Amendment. Among the most important were "vested property rights," "substantive due process," and "liberty of contract." Legal formalism, in a word, took the concepts of property and contract out of the well-regulated society and, thereby, removed the threat of redistribution.

Vested property rights is a legal doctrine that arose out of the distinction between "public law" and "private law." Public law is created by political acts. Constitutional law, administrative law, and criminal law are examples of public law.[56] Private law, in contrast, is created through the voluntary acts of individuals; it comes about through the exercise of free will. Contracts, torts, property, commerce, and agency are examples of private law.[57] Unless consensual, wealth redistribution cannot take place through the private law. Only the public law, which is subject to the will of the people, can be redistributive. But redistributive laws are dangerous—they can cause wrongful takings—and, hence, must be closely scrutinized. Legal formalism took as a central legal tenet the idea that taking property from A and giving it to B violated vested property rights protected by the Fourteenth Amendment.[58]

The doctrine of vested property rights is hardly neutral. It favors entrenched interests and privilege. Property owners have superior bargaining power, which enables them to redistribute wealth *against* weaker economic groups. Many believed that this is not justice, that there is something intrin-

---

55. Arnold M. Paul, *Conservative Crisis and the Rule of Law* (New York: Harper & Row, 1969), p. 6.

56. See, e.g., Wiecek, *Liberty Under Law*, supra note 16, at p. 113; Daniel A. Farber and Philip P. Frickey, "In the Shadow of the Legislature: The Common Law in the Age of the New Public Law," *Michigan Law Review* 89 (1991): 875, 885.

57. See, e.g., P. John Kozyris, "The Conflicts Provisions of the ALI's Complex Litigation Project: A Glass Half Full?," *Louisiana Law Review* 54 (1994): 953, 963; Jean C. Love, "Legal Formalism from the Perspective of a Reasonable Law Professor," *Harvard Journal of Law & Public Policy* 16 (1993): 627, 628–29.

58. Wiecek, *Liberty Under Law*, supra note 16, at p. 114.

sically wrong with a legal system that permits private *or* public redistributions to take place regardless of the resulting inequities.[59]

Horwitz brings to light yet another problem with the public/private distinction. He uses Justice Story to illustrate his point. Horwitz observes that Justice Story, who dissented in the *Charles River Bridge* case, arguing for vested property rights,[60] employed contradictory judicial processes in the two spheres—the policy method (as we call it) in the private sphere and the logical method (as called here) in the public sphere. As Horwitz states: "[Story's] private law opinions are, by and large, highly utilitarian and self-consciously attuned to the goals of promoting pro-commercial and developmental legal doctrines. By contrast, his public law opinions are usually starkly formalistic, often antiquated."[61] Such methodological inconsistency calls into question Justice Story's commitment to *both* methods.

Substantive due process—protection from arbitrary or unreasonable government action—is another important formalistic legal doctrine read into the Fourteenth Amendment. Due process had traditionally been construed only in the procedural sense. Procedural due process, as guaranteed by the Fifth Amendment and Fourteenth Amendment, gave parties a right to be notified and heard in judicial proceedings affecting their rights. In other words, procedural due process assured the right to a day in court.[62] Thus, with dubious textual support and logic, substantive due process, in short, expanded the concept of due process.[63] The concept could now be used to overturn laws that, in the interest of civic republicanism, interfered with an individual's use of his property. Substantive due process, in short, created a federal sphere of protection around a citizen's property that no state could easily invade.[64] Like the doctrine of vested property rights, substantive due process was a nonregulatory, nonredistributive legal doctrine.

Liberty of contract is derivative of substantive due process. If individuals have a fundamental right to be free from arbitrary interference by the government, then they also have the right to contract as to the disposition of their property without interference from the state. Property thus included intangi-

---

59. See Horwitz, *The Transformation of American Law*, supra note 36, at p. 254.

60. See Section B of this chapter, supra.

61. Ibid. at p. 255.

62. Wiecek, *Liberty Under Law*, supra note 16, at p. 116.

63. See Cass R. Sunstein, *Designing Democracy: What Constitutions Do* (New York: Oxford University Press, 2001), p. 80.

64. Tribe, *American Constitutional Law*, supra note 4, at p.554 (citing *Allgeyer v. Louisiana*, 165 U.S. 578 (1897)).

ble rights, such as the right to contract to work for how ever long one desired. Juxtaposing the Fourteenth Amendment with the Declaration of Independence, Justice Bradley laid the legal foundation for the liberty of contract doctrine in his famous dissent in the *Slaughterhouse Cases*:[65]

> Rights to life, liberty, and the pursuit of happiness are equivalent to the rights of life, liberty, and property. These are the fundamental rights which can only be taken away by due process of law, and which can only be interfered with, or the enjoyment of which can only be modified, by lawful regulations necessary or proper for the mutual good of all.... This right to choose one's calling, when chosen, is a man's property and right. Liberty and property are not protected when these rights are arbitrarily assailed.[66]

Limiting such rights to "necessary or proper" regulations, Justice Bradley presaged the impending battle over state police powers, the constitutional source of *salus populi* state regulation in the nineteenth century and liberal reforms in the twentieth century.[67]

Once "discovered" in the Constitution, vested property rights, substantive due process, and liberty of contract—supposedly timeless and neutral legal doctrines designed to protect individual liberty—were applied in syllogistic fashion to the facts before the Court. This judicial method, what Edward White calls the "oracular theory of judging," purported to be apolitical and guided solely by reason. But, of course, the process was tainted *ab initio* by the major premise's slant toward minimalism. The cases in the next section clearly illustrate this process.

D. Case Illustrations

Allgeyer v. Louisiana[68] is an important case decided under legal formalism. In this case, the Supreme Court was asked to decide whether it was unconstitutional for a Louisiana statute to prohibit its citizens ("persons, corporations or firms") from dealing with out-of-state marine insurance companies that

---

65. 83 U.S. 36, 111 (1873) (Bradley, J., dissenting).
66. Ibid. at 116.
67. See, e.g., Gillman, *The Constitution Besieged*, supra note 42.
68. 165 U.S. 578 (1897).

were not registered to do business within the state. The Court answered this question syllogistically. As its major premise, the Court invoked the liberty of contract doctrine at least twice: "The liberty mentioned in [the Fourteenth Amendment is] deemed to embrace the right of a citizen to be free in the enjoyment of all his faculties, to be free to use them in all ways; to pursue any livelihood or avocation, and for that purpose to enter into all contracts which may be proper, necessary, and essential to his carrying out to a successful completion the purposes above mentioned";[69] and "pursuing an ordinary calling or trade, and...acquiring, holding, and selling property, is an essential part of...[one's] rights of liberty and property, as guaranteed by the Fourteenth Amendment."[70] As its minor premise, the Court found that the statute interfered "with the liberty of defendants in restricting their rights to place insurance on property of their own whenever and in what company they desired."[71] Ergo, the Court concluded, the statute violated the Constitution.[72] Policy considerations were supposedly not part of the process. "In such a case as the facts here present," the Court stated, "the policy of the state" in enacting the statute is of no consequence.[73]

Formalism was applied in 1895 to a case involving the constitutionality of the federal income tax. None of the loaded doctrines—vested property rights, substantive due process and liberty of contract—were expressly used in *Pollock v. Farmers Loan and Trust Co.*[74] Liberty and property themes clearly underpin the Court's reasoning, however. Chief Justice Fuller's majority opinion admitted that the Court had an objective, which was "to prevent an attack upon accumulated property."[75] Putting aside this obvious appeal to policy, the majority opinion constructs the following syllogism: the Constitution requires apportionment of direct taxes; the federal income tax was a nonapportioned direct tax; ergo, the federal income tax is unconstitutional.[76] The Court had little trouble constructing the major premise, but could only frame the minor

---

69. Ibid. at 589.
70. Ibid. at 590 (quoting *Powell v. Pennsylvania*, 127 U.S. 678, 684 (1888)).
71. Ibid. at 588–89.
72. Ibid. at 593.
73. Ibid.
74. 157 U.S. 429 (1895).
75. Ibid. at 583.
76. Ibid. at 588, 591, 607–8. Ratified in 1913, the Sixteenth Amendment to the Constitution ("The Congress shall have power to lay and collect taxes on incomes, from whatever source derived, without apportionment among the several states, and without regard to any census or enumeration") overturned *Pollock*.

premise by "disingenuously explain[ing] away contrary precedent and artfully invent[ing] legal distinctions."[77]

In *Lochner v. New York*,[78] the flagship case of the Era, the issue before the Supreme Court involved the constitutionality of a New York law that limited to sixty hours the maximum hours bakers could work per week. Citing *Allgeyer*, the Court derived the doctrine of liberty of contract from the Due Process Clause of the Fourteenth Amendment, declaring: "The general right to make a contract in relation to his business is part of the liberty of the individual protected by the Fourteenth Amendment....The right to purchase or sell labor is part of the liberty protected by this amendment."[79]

Unlike *Allgeyer*, however, the Court incorporated two additional rules of law into its major premise. The first stated that: "Both property and liberty are held on such reasonable conditions as may be imposed by the governing power of the State in the exercise of...powers relat[ing] to the safety, health, morals, and general welfare of the public."[80] Thus, under the "police powers exception," the state could interfere with freedom of contract in exercise of its police powers; i.e., to protect public safety, health, and morals. The second rule is the "reasonableness test," which the Court stated as follows: "It is impossible for us to shut our eyes to the fact that many laws of this character, while passed under what is claimed to be the police power for the purpose of protecting the public health or welfare, are, in reality, passed for other motives."[81] The "reasonableness test" gives evidence of the Court's minimalism. The Court is suspicious of interventionist legislatures which, under the guise of the "police powers exception," might attempt to create redistributive laws.

Do these additional rules add anything to the major premise? On the one hand, it could be argued that the "police powers exception" is no exception at all, and the "reasonableness test" is a non-test. Language in *Lochner* strongly suggests that the public's interest can never justify an interference with liberty of contract, and to allow such would be unreasonable; otherwise "the hours of employers could be regulated, and doctors, lawyers, scientists, all professional men, as well as artisans and athletes, could be forbidden to fatigue their brains and bodies by prolonged hours of exercise."[82] On the other hand, in

---

77. Wiecek, *Liberty Under Law*, supra note 16, at p. 123. See 157 U.S. at 608–717 (White J., dissenting).

78. 198 U.S. 45 (1905).

79. Ibid. at 53.

80. Ibid. at 56.

81. Ibid. at 64.

82. Ibid. at 60.

light of subsequent cases in which the Court upholds the constitutionality of regulatory statutes, purportedly under formalist reasoning,[83] individual liberty does not appear to be an absolute right. This does not, however, make the Court a believer in the era's welfare liberalism.

For the minor premise, the Court found that the New York maximum-hour law interfered with the individual liberty of the bakery owners and bakers alike, and did not serve a valid and genuine police purpose. Bakers "are in no sense wards of the State,"[84] and "[c]lean and wholesome bread does not depend upon whether the baker works but ten hours per day or only sixty hours a week."[85] Also, given the fact that the bakers' union promoted the maximum-hour law, the Court saw the law as promoting unions and not public welfare.[86] Thus, the maximum-hour law was read as a protective, redistributive law promoting union interests of bakers. Ergo, the Court concluded, the New York maximum-hour law was unconstitutional.

A few years after *Lochner*, the Supreme Court upheld the constitutionality of an Oregon maximum-hour law in *Muller v. Oregon*.[87] The difference between this case and *Lochner* was in the minor premise; the major premise was the same in both cases.[88] Oregon's statute dealt solely with women workers. To be sure, the statute interfered with the freedom of workers and employers alike to contract for as many hours of work as they desired, but, unlike New York's law, Oregon's law was a reasonable regulation, a valid use of the police powers, because women needed government protection. "Women's physical structure, and the functions she performs in consequence thereof, justify special legislation restricting or qualifying the conditions under which she should be permitted to toil."[89] This paternalistic view of the physical abilities of women was not manufactured by the Court. Rather, it was brought to the

---

83. See, e.g., *Block v. Hirsh*, 256 U.S. 135 (1921) (regulating the cost of rental housing); *German Alliance Ins. Co. v. Lewis*, 233 U.S. 389 (1914) (regulating the cost of fire insurance); *Muller v. Oregon*, 208 U.S. 412 (1908) (regulating maximum hours women can work). Perhaps, then, *Lochner's* major premise should be stated as follows: constitutional due process permits government interference with individual liberty only to the extent that such action is a valid and genuine (i.e., reasonable) effort to promote the health and welfare of the people.

84. 198 U.S. at 60.

85. Ibid. at 57.

86. Nancy Woloch, *Muller v. Oregon: A Brief History with Documents* (Boston: Bedford Books, 1996), pp. 14, 18.

87. 208 U.S. 412 (1908).

88. Ibid. at 418–19.

89. Ibid. at 420.

Court's attention through counsel's brief (Louis Brandeis, the famous "Brandeis brief") and presented as a "widespread belief."[90] Having satisfied the terms and conditions of the major premise, the Oregon statute passed constitutional muster.

The policy determinations in *Muller v. Oregon* were so obvious that the case cannot easily be classified under the logical method. There are, likewise, cases commonly labeled policy-oriented that can be restructured under the logical method. An example may be *Brown v. Board of Education*,[91] which overturned state school segregation statutes. *Brown* receives extensive discussion in later chapters dealing with the policy method. Here, we shall consider its potential as a logical-method case.

Judge Ruggero Aldisert restructures *Brown*'s reasoning syllogistically. Specifically: "Separate but equal educational facilities are permitted under the Constitution, but unequal facilities are not; separate educational facilities for black children are inherently unequal; [ergo,] separate educational facilities for black children are not permitted under the Constitution."[92] Although Judge Aldisert's analysis of *Brown* runs counter to conventional scholarly opinion, which sees *Brown* as a policy method case,[93] it suggests that there is often more than one way to reach the same decision (or judgment) in a case. *Muller* sends the same message.

E. Criticisms

Before considering criticisms levied against legal formalism, let us first consider an important argument that is intended to deflect many of these criticisms. Writing in 1913, Charles Warren argued that if there was a slant in the Supreme Court's deployment of the syllogism under legal formalism, it was in favor of maximalist state laws.[94] Warren's attempt to show that the Court was being falsely accused of hindering such state legislation was based upon

---

90. Ibid.

91. 347 U.S. 483 (1954).

92. Ruggero J. Aldisert, *Logic for Lawyers: A Guide to Clear Legal Thinking* (New York: C. Boardman, Co., 1989), p. 243.

93. See, e.g., Roy L. Brooks, Gilbert P. Carrasco, and Gordon A. Martin, *Civil Rights Litigation: Cases and Perspectives* (Durham: Carolina Academic Press, 1995), p. 66 ("*Brown* is famous, among other things, for introducing social science evidence to support the notion that separate education brands African American children with a badge of inferiority.")

94. See Preface, Section B, supra, for a discussion of the maximalism concept.

an exhaustive study of Supreme Court cases handed down from 1887 to 1911. His study concluded that 95% of state laws challenged on Fourteenth Amendment due process and equal protection grounds were upheld.[95] A more recent law review article evaluating Warren's study supports his "general message if not his specific numbers."[96] Covering the period of 1902–1932, the article finds "in many relevant areas the ratio of rejected challenges [of state legislation] to successful challenges approaches or exceeds five to one."[97]

To be sure, there were many Supreme Court cases decided during the Lochner Era that rejected challenges to state regulatory laws. Among these were: *Block v. Hirsh*,[98] which upheld a law regulating the cost of rental housing; *German Alliance Ins. Co. v. Lewis*,[99] which upheld the regulation of rental housing; *Bunting v. Oregon*[100] and *Muller v. Oregon*,[101] both of which upheld maximum-working-hour laws. But, as the last section of the chapter clearly indicates, there were also no dearth of cases in which the Supreme Court upheld challenges to state regulatory laws, including *Lochner* itself. So where does this leave us?

One can draw two conclusions from this case alignment. First, one can demur on the ground that the authors have missed the central charge against legal formalism made in this book.[102] Regardless of the specific judgment(Point C) in these cases, the Supreme Court moved from Point A to Point C with little devotion to the logical method. Legal formalism was not a value-free process, whether the Court ended up overturning or upholding civic republican state laws. Policy or attention to special facts was inserted into the Supreme Court's formulation of the syllogism. How else could one explain the different holdings in cases with such similar legal settings as *Lochner* and *Muller v. Oregon*?[103]

---

95. Charles Warren, "The Progressiveness *of the Supreme Court*," *Columbia Law Review* 13 (1913): 294 (article breaks down state legislation into categories—labor legislation, anti-trust legislation, and so on—and methodically lists cases which upheld a state statute).

96. Michael J. Phillips, "The Progressiveness of the Lochner Court," *Denver Law Review* 75 (1998): 453, 454.

97. Ibid., p. 500. Professor Phillips' study does not analyze Warren's other article on the *Lochner* Court, "A Bulwark to the State Police Power—The United States Supreme Court." *Columbia Law Review* 13 (1913): 667.

98. 256 U.S. 135 (1921).

99. 233 U.S. 389 (1914).

100. 243 U.S. 426 (1917).

101. 208 U.S. 412 (1908).

102. See Section B, supra.

103. See Section D, supra.

Second, legal formalism's problem extends beyond state law. It also involves federal law and the quality of regulatory federal laws the Supreme Court has overturned. Indeed, it was the Supreme Court's persistent rejection of New Deal legislation that led to the Court-packing crisis of 1937.[104]

A foundational criticism of legal formalism, one that applies to the logical method itself, is that it confounds the validity of a syllogism with its truth. If the premises of a syllogism imply its conclusion, the syllogism is valid (internally consistent) but the conclusion and its premises are not necessarily empirically true. "All Spartans are wise; Socrates is a Spartan; therefore Socrates is wise" is a syllogism that is "at once valid and unsound."[105] All Spartans are not wise, and Socrates was an Athenian.

In treating judicial decision making like mathematics, legal formalism creates the appearance that it is an apolitical process. We are thus led to believe that any disagreement we might have with the results of the process is solely a function of our inability to do the math correctly. The problem lies with us and not with the judge or her judicial method. As Lawrence Lessig has said, "to the extent that the Court succeeded in establishing...a [conceptualist] language, it succeeded in increasing its own power—in particular, its power to resist progressive legislation."[106]

Yet, it just may be that a judge's selection of legal doctrine necessarily signals a policy preference. As Judge Aldisert has observed:

> ....[I]n the formulation of major and minor premises in the law, there is more at work than rules of logic. The selection of a major premise, as we have emphasized before, is a *value judgment*. The advocate or the judge makes this value judgment. A choice is made. No unerring rules of logic dictate this important decision, which is the critical threshold, the prelude to the operation of the rules of logic.[107]

Perhaps the most serious charge made against the Lochner-Era judges is that they did not exercise judicial restraint. It was very much an activist court—a conservative activist Court. Lochnerian jurisprudence informed its major premises with doctrines like "vested property rights," "substantive due process,"

---

104. See relevant discussion in Section A, supra.

105. Richard A. Posner, *The Problems of Jurisprudence* (Cambridge, Mass.: Harvard University Press, 1990), p. 43, n.7. See John T. Kearns, *Deductive Logic: A Programmed Instruction* (Albany: State University of New York Press, 1969), p. 166.

106. Lawrence Lessig, "Understanding Changed Readings: Fidelity and Theory," *Stanford Law Review* 47 (1995): 395, 462.

107. Aldisert, *Logic for Lawyers*, supra note 92, at p. 66.

and "liberty of contract." These legal doctrines indicate judicial fidelity to minimalism. But this value system was very much out of sync with the anti-privilege, maximalist, and especially liberal mood of the era. As Roscoe Pound noted at the time, the justices' views about the state, economics, and politics differed from the dominant "social conceptions of the present."[108] As time went on, legal formalism became a drag on democratic government. "[J]udges laboring in its grip," to quote William Wiecek, "seemed at first out of touch, then antiquated, then reactionary, and finally obstructive."[109] That is judicial activism — to wit, policy-making — of the highest order.[110]

Legal formalism raises yet another question, the answer to which may be planted in Justices Taney and Story's historic debate on political economy in the *Charles River Bridge* case.[111] It is this: Do the values that inhere in legal formalism — particularly the protection of private property and contract — serve the nation's best interests? This question directly bears on the decision by Thomas Penfield Jackson, federal district court judge, in June of 2000 to order the computer giant Microsoft to split into two separate corporations, one selling Microsoft's Windows operating system and the other selling Microsoft's application programs.[112] Richard Epstein, a libertarian law professor,

---

108. Roscoe Pound, "Liberty of Contract," *Yale Law Journal* 18 (1908): 454, 455. See Novak, *The People's Welfare*, supra note 22, p. 47 (making a similar point).

109. Wiecek, *Liberty Under Law*, supra note 16, at p. 132.

110. See Introduction, Section C, supra.

111. See Section B, supra.

112. The action against Microsoft arose pursuant to a complaint filed by the United States and separate complaints filed by individual states. The district court judge determined that Microsoft maintained a monopoly in the market for Intel-compatible PC operating systems, attempted to gain a monopoly in the market for internet browsers, and illegally tied two purportedly separate products, Windows and Internet Explorer. *United States v. Microsoft Corp.*, 87 F. Supp. 2d 30 (D.D.C. 2000) ("Conclusions of Law"). The district court judge then made additional findings of antitrust violations, and to remedy these violations issued a final Judgment requiring Microsoft to submit a proposed plan of divestiture, with the company to be split into an operating systems business and an applications business. *United States v. Microsoft Corp.*, 97 F. Supp. 2d 59, 64–65 (D.D.C. 2000) ("Final Judgment"). The District Court's remedial order also contained a number of interim restrictions on Microsoft's conduct. Ibid. at 66–69. On appeal, the circuit court judges reversed the ruling to break up the software giant, and ordered the case re-assigned to a different trial judge because of ethical lapses on the part of the presiding judge. *United States v. Microsoft Corp.*, 253 F.3d 34 (D.C. Cir. 2001) (en banc) (per curiam). The Supreme Court denied a writ of certiorari, *Microsoft Corp. v. United States*, 534 U.S. 952 (2001), setting the stage for a settlement. For an analysis of the settlement agreement, see, e.g., Robert Slater, *Microsoft Rebooted: How Bill Gates and Steve Ballmer Reinvented Their Company* (New York: Penguin Books, 2004); Kara Swisher, "Behind the Blustering Over the Microsoft Settlement," Wall Street Journal, 12/3/01, p. B1; Mark Wigfield, "A Primer on the Microsoft Antitrust Case Settlement," WSJ.com (11/15/01);

and others argued that Judge Thomas Penfield Jackson's order will generate dislocations for little benefit, which will result in the consumer paying higher prices for computers and software.[113] The Justice Department's chief antitrust lawyer at the time, Joel Klein, and others argue just the opposite. They believe the break-up will spur innovations and price reductions.[114]

Beyond the *Microsoft* case, there is evidence that legal formalism, though scorned historically, may be making something of a comeback. This is particularly so in cases involving the cyberspace economy. Some judges are resurrecting this old judicial method to create a new legal regime based on private-law conceptions of property and contract to protect digital works in the new economy.[115]

The return of legal formalism may extend beyond cyberspace cases. Some members of Congress as well as a number of legal scholars have argued that the Supreme Court has embarked upon a campaign of legal formalism. Between 1995 and 2000, the Court struck down all or part of 25 socially regulatory federal statutes. For example, in *United States v. Morrison*[116] a sharply divided Court overturned a provision of the Violence Against Women Act that authorized a private right of action for any victim of a gender-motivated violent crime. Congress, the Court ruled, exceeded its powers under the Commerce Clause and Section 5 of the Fourteenth Amendment. Cases like *Morrison* might well give the "nine old men" reason to smile in their graves.[117]

Rob Pegoraro, "U.S. Settlement Leaves Microsoft More Entrenched," washingtonpost.com (11/9/01).

113. See Richard A. Epstein, "The Price of a Judge's Hubris," Wall Street Journal, 6/9/00, at p. A18.

114. See Richard B. Schmitt, "A Breakup Primer for Microsoft?," Wall Street Journal, 6/6/00, at p. B1. For further discussion of these opposing viewpoints, see the following pages of the Wall Street Journal: 6/3/2000, at pp. A1 (2 articles), B1; 6/7/2000, at pp. A28, C1; 6/5/2000, at p. A32.

115. See Julia E. Cohen, "Lochner in Cyberspace: The New Economic Orthodoxy of 'Rights Management,'" *Michigan Law Review* 97 (1998): 462.

116. 120 S.Ct. 1740 (2000).

117. *See, e.g.,* Joseph Biden, "On Judicial Imperialism," *Congressional Record*, vol. 146, no. 99 (106th Congress, July 26, 2000); Harry F. Tepker, Jr., "Writing the Law of Work on Nero's Pillars: The 1998–99 Term of the U.S. Supreme Court," *The Labor Lawyer* 15 (1999): 181 (cases and articles collected therein); Jeffrey Rosen, "The Next Court," *The New York Times Magazine*, 10/22/00, at p. 76. See also, *Alden v. Maine*, 527 U.S. 706 (1999) (private suit for damages under the Fair Labor Standards Act against nonconsenting states in their own courts violates state sovereign immunity), where Justice Souter argued in dissent that "[t]he resemblance of today's state sovereign immunity to the Lochner era's industrial due process is striking." *United States v. Lopez*, 514 U.S. 549 (1995) (federal statute prohibiting knowing possession of firearms in or near schools held unconstitutional), was one of the first cases to give some hint of a return to legal formalism.

Chapter 2
Scalian Textualism

Scalian textualism prescribes a judicial process in which the judge at Point B reads text closely to find plain-meaning rules, followed by deduction (logical discourse). In statutory interpretation, text trumps intent; in constitutional interpretation, intent trumps text. Any holding not tethered to text (including the whole of the common law) lacks democratic pedigree.

A. Overview

Textualism is the belief that authoritative text should control judicial decision making. The meaning of a statutory or constitutional provision is to be determined by giving it a plain, or ordinary, reading. Blackstone sounded a similar chord: "Words are generally to be understood in their usual and most known signification;…as their general and popular use."[1] As a general guide to legal interpretation, textualism has broad appeal. Even Justice Oliver Wendell Holmes, the most important proponent of the policy method,[2] could accept a characterization of the interpretive enterprise at this level of generality. He remarked that "we ask, not what [the Framer] meant, but what those words would mean in the mouth of a normal speaker of English, using them in the circumstances in which they were used…."[3]

Differences among jurisprudents develop when interpretive difficulties arise, such as when the text is ambiguous or when following the plain meaning of an unambiguous text will lead to an unreasonable outcome. Under these circumstances, some legal theorists are more textualist than others. Frederick Schauer, for example, would not stick to the text if that would lead to absurd results.[4] Justice Antonin Scalia, however, would disagree with Schauer's "presumptive formalism." He would remain faithful to the text, as we shall see.

---

1. William Blackstone, *Commentaries on the Laws of England*, vol. I (Oxford: The Clarendon Press, 1765, Special Edition for the Legal Classic Library, Birmingham, Ala.: 1983).

2. See Part 1, Section B, infra.

3. Oliver Wendell Holmes, "The Theory of Legal Interpretation," *Harvard Law Review* 12 (1899): 417–18.

4. See Frederick Schauer, "Is the Common Law Law?," *California Law Review* 77 (1989): 455, 470. See also Frederick Schauer, "Formalism," *Yale Law Journal* 97 (1988): 509.

This chapter focuses on Justice Scalia's brand of textualism.[5] In a series of cases, law review articles, and most formally in the Tanner Lectures given at Princeton University,[6] Justice Scalia has elaborated on what some have called "the new textualism" and others "democratic formalism."[7] Scalian textualism, as it is called here, has had an impact on the judicial process, especially at the Supreme Court. As Philip Frickey points out:

> The Court is less likely to cite legislative history today, and when it does, the citations seem less important to the outcome. The Court pays careful attention to statutory text and is much more likely than in earlier eras to use dictionaries to assist in constructing statutory meaning.... [In cases where the voting is close] a Justice who is happy to consult legislative history might decide against using it to keep Justice Scalia and Justice Thomas, who shares Scalia's approach, on board with the majority result.[8]

We shall focus on the major features of Justice Scalia's brand of textualism—his statutory textualism and his constitutional textualism. Scholarly crit-

---

5. Although Fred Schauer and other scholars have advanced interesting textualist theories, see, e.g., Robert H. Bork, *The Tempting of America* (New York: Free Press, 1990), pp. 133 160; William H. Rehnquist, "Observation: The Notion of a Living Constitution," *Texas Law Review* 54 (1976): 693, Justice Scalia's brand of textualism seems to have drawn the most attention. See, e.g., Philip P. Frickey, "Revisiting the Revival of Theory in Statutory Interpretation: A Lecture in Honor of Irving Younger," *Minnesota Law Review* 84 (1999): 199; William N. Eskridge, Jr., "Textualism, The Unknown Ideal?," *Michigan Law Review* 96 (1998): 1509; John Manning, "Textualism as a Nondelegation Doctrine," *Columbia Law Review* 97 (1997): 673; Jerry L. Mashaw, "Textualism, Constitutionalism, and the Interpretation of Federal Statutes," *William & Mary Law Review* 32 (1991): 827; Frederick Schauer, "Statutory Construction and the Coordinating Function of Plain Meaning," *Supreme Court Review* 1990 (1990): 231. See generally, Symposium, "Formalism and Statutory Interpretation," *Chicago Law Review* 66 (1999): 636, 671, 685, 698.

6. See Antonin Scalia, *A Matter of Interpretation: Federal Courts and the Law* (Princeton: Princeton University Press,1997). See e.g., *Printz v. United States*, 521 U.S. 898 (1997) (writing for the Court); *Chisom v. Roemer*, 501 U.S. 380, 404 (1991) (Scalia, J., dissenting); *Green v. Bock Laundry Mach. Co.*, 900 U.S. 504, 527 (1989) (Scalia, J., concurring in the judgment). See also, Antonin Scalia, "The Rule of Law as a Law of Rules," *University of Chicago Law Review* 56 (1989): 1175; Antonin Scalia, "Originalism: The Lesser Evil," *University of Cincinnati Law Review* 57 (1989): 849.

7. See Eskridge, "Textualism," supra note 5, at p. 1509; Cass R. Sunstein, "Justice Scalia's Democratic Formalism," *Yale Law Journal* 107 (1997): 529; William N. Eskridge, Jr., "The New Textualism," *UCLA Law Review* 37 (1991): 621.

8. Frickey, "Revisiting the Revival of Theory in Statutory Interpretation," supra note 5, at p. 205.

icism of both sides of Scalian textualism will also be considered. We begin, however, with the basic thinking behind Scalian textualism.

B. Basic Approach

Scalian textualism is based on a unique view of judicial decision making in three contexts—common law, statutory law, and constitutional law. In actuality, it is a denigration of the common-law tradition. Decisional law, Justice Scalia argues, is ill-suited for democratic government. It is democratically challenged; it has inferior "democratic pedigree," to borrow from Cass Sunstein.[9] Justice Scalia contends:

> [T]he common-law tradition...would be an unqualified good, were it not for a trend in government that has developed in recent centuries, called democracy. In most countries, judges are no longer agents of the king, for there are no kings.[10]

In addition to his belief that the common law is institutionally suspect in a democratic society, Justice Scalia asserts that judge-made law is too particularized and, hence, unpredictable or indeterminate.[11] Doctrines designed to constrain judicial discretion, most notably the doctrine of *stare decisis*, are easily circumvented by "the art, or the game," of distinguishing earlier cases. The holding of a case, which stands as precedent for future cases, can be read broadly—i.e., as the "analytical principle that produced the judgment"—or narrowly—i.e., as limited to the "facts that were before the court." Judges "will squint narrowly," Justice Scalia argues, "when they wish to avoid an earlier decision." Thus, Justice Scalia concludes, it is "[b]y reason of the doctrine of *stare decisis*, as limited by the principle...[of distinguishing earlier cases], that the common law grew in a particular fashion—rather like a Scrabble board. No rule of decision previously announced could be *erased*, but qual-

---

9. See Sunstein, "Justice Scalia's Democratic Formalism," supra note 7, at p. 530.

10. Scalia, *A Matter of Interpretation*, supra note 6, at p. 9.

11. This view can be contrasted with Aristotle's view, discussed in the Introduction, Section B, supra, that law's inherent defect lies in its universality. See Introduction, Section B, supra. It can also be contrasted with the postmodernist view, discussed in Chapter 9, that law is not particularized enough, hence the ironic need to resort to *general* rules of law. See Chapter 9, Section C3, infra.

ifications could be *added* to it. The first case lays on the board.... And the game continues."[12]

Justice Scalia's criticism of the common law is not intended to "scrape[] [it] away as a barnacle on the hull of democracy."[13] Rather, it is designed to set up his theory of textualism in the other contexts, statutory and constitutional. Justice Scalia wishes to keep the common-law mind-set out of statutory and constitutional interpretation:

> I... question whether the *attitude* of the common-law judge — the mind-set that asks, 'What is the most desirable resolution of his case, and how can any impediments to the achievement of that result be evaded?' — is appropriate for most of the work that I do, and much of the work that state judges do. We live in an age of legislation, and most new law is statutory law.[14]

Justice Scalia also contends that removing common-law proclivities from judicial interpretation of the written law would enable the written law to retain much of its democratic fiber as it works its way through the judicial process, and would bring greater internal consistency to its development. Judicial interpretation would be more logical, less policy-oriented. Judges would efface themselves, thereby allowing rules of law produced through the democratic process to reign supreme, as should be the case in a socio-legal order like ours. Quoting the historian Lawrence Friedman, Justice Scalia notes, again, that "in modern times, 'the main business of government, and therefore of law [is] legislative and executive.... Even private law, so-called [has been] turning statutory.' "[15]

Justice Scalia insists that his analytical technique is "formalistic":

> Of all the criticisms leveled against textualism, the most mindless is that it is 'formalistic.' The answer to that is, *of course it's formalistic!* The rule of law is *about* form. If, for example, a citizen performs an act — let us say the sale of certain technology to a foreign country — which is prohibited by a widely publicized bill proposed by the administration and passed by both houses of Congress *but not yet signed by the President*, that sale is lawful. It is of no consequence that every-

---

12. Scalia, *A Matter of Interpretation*, supra note 6, at pp. 8–9.
13. Ibid. at p. 12.
14. Ibid. at p. 13.
15. Ibid. (quoting Lawrence M. Friedman, *A History of American Law* (New York: Simon and Schuster, 1973), p. 590).

one knows both houses of Congress and the President wish to prevent the sale.... [The bill must be signed into law by the President before it takes effect.] Long live formalism. It is what makes a government a government of laws and not of men.[16]

This quotation certainly suggests that it is the logical method, and not legal formalism itself, that Justice Scalia admires and seeks to incorporate in his judicial technique. He desires a judicial process that places constraints on judicial discretion by requiring the judge to apply established rules of law logically. Following this judicial method, Justice Scalia believes, produces consistent, reliable, and democratic outcomes. Justice Scalia is very much against a judicial process that "load[s] the dice for or against a particular result."[17] As we saw in the last chapter, legal formalism's syllogism was "loaded."[18] Scalian textualism, as Judge Richard Posner has suggested, entails "mainly the careful reading of texts to find rules in them, followed by deduction from the rules to the outcome of the particular case."[19] Unlike legal formalism, it does not harbor an "exaggerated belief in the transparency of statutory or constitutional language and hence in the possibility of definitely correct answers to difficult interpretive questions."[20] The distinctiveness of Scalian textualism, what Judge Posner might call the "nonpejorative" use of the logical method, is more than apparent when discussed in its primary mode—statutory and constitutional interpretation.

Scalian textualism is manifested one way in statutory cases—called "contextualist" textualism, or "semantic intentionalist" textualism—and quite another way in constitutional cases—called "originalist" textualism, or "expectations originalist" textualism. The terms "semantic intentionalist" and "expectations originalist" arise from a criticism of Scalian textualism by Ronald Dworkin. Justice Scalia agrees with Dworkin's characterization of his statutory textualism, but not with Dworkin's description of his constitutional textualism.[21] We shall look at Justice Scalia's statutory textualism first.

---

16. Ibid. at p. 25.

17. Ibid. at p. 27.

18. See Chapter 1, Section C.

19. Richard A. Posner, *The Problems of Jurisprudence* (Cambridge, Mass.: Harvard University Press, 1990), p. 40.

20. Ibid.

21. See Scalia, *A Matter of Interpretation*, supra note 6, at pp. 117–26, 144–49.

C. Statutory Textualism

Contextualist textualism holds that when faced with a problem of statutory construction, the judge should remain faithful to the interpretive foundation in textualism discussed at the beginning of this chapter. The judge, in other words, should follow the ordinary meaning of the statute even if that would lead to an absurd or unreasonable outcome.[22] This is quite different from Frederick Schauer's "presumptive textualism," also mentioned at the beginning of this chapter.

Justice Scalia's brand of statutory textualism, contextualist textualism, carries at least two important textualist implications. Permitting unreasonable outcomes means, most prominently, that Scalian textualism rejects intentionalist textualism. This form of textualism relies on the intent of the framers, the legislative history, to determine statutory meaning. Justice Scalia argues, "if what the legislature *intended*, rather than what it *said*, is the object of our inquiry," judges would always give effect to legislative intent, even when the letter of the law is clear. Intent is not altogether irrelevant, however. "We look for a sort of 'objectified intent,'" Justice Scalia says, "intent that a reasonable person would gather from the text of the law, placed alongside the remainder of the *corpus juris*."[23] Scalian textualism also rejects strict constructionist, or literalist, textualism, which construes a statute narrowly. "I am not a strict constructionist, and no one ought to be ...," Scalia says. "A text should not be construed strictly...[or] leniently; it should be construed reasonably, giving the words their ordinary meaning."[24] To illustrate the difference between his brand of textualism, contextualist textualism, and literalist textualism, Justice Scalia refers to the Supreme Court's opinion in *Smith v. United States*:[25]

> ...The statute at issue [in the case] provided for an increased jail term if, during and in relation to...[a] drug trafficking crime, the defendant uses...a firearm. The defendant in this case had sought to purchase a quantity of cocaine, and what he had offered to give in exchange for the cocaine was an unloaded firearm, which he showed to the drug-seller. The Court held, I regret to say, that the defendant was subject to the increased penalty, because he had used a firearm dur-

22. Eskridge, "Textualism," supra note 5, at p. 1512. See Section A, supra.
23. Scalia, *A Matter of Interpretation*, supra note 6, at pp. 16–17, 29–37.
24. Ibid. at p. 23.
25. 508 U.S. 223 (1993).

ing and in relation to a drug trafficking crime. The vote was not even close (6–3). I dissented. Now I cannot say whether my colleagues in the majority voted the way they did because they are strict-construction textualists, or because they are not textualists at all. But a proper textualist, which is to say my kind of textualist, would surely have voted to acquit. The phrase 'uses a gun' fairly connoted use of a gun for what guns are normally used for, that is, as a weapon. As I put the point in my dissent, when you ask someone, 'Do you use a cane?,' you are not inquiring whether he has hung his grandfather's antique cane as a decoration in the hallway.[26]

Ronald Dworkin argues that Justice Scalia's interpretation of the statute in the firearm case reveals incoherence in his theory because it "allows respect for intention to trump literal text."[27] While Justice Scalia's interpretation of the statute may be consistent with legislative intent, it could also be argued that his interpretation represents the ordinary meaning or usage of the phrase "uses a gun," and that he did not resort to legislative intent to determine such meaning. The fact that Justice Scalia's interpretation of the statute may be in agreement with its legislative intent is simply fortuitous.

To help determine ordinary meaning, the judge can resort to certain canons of statutory construction. Some canons work better than others, Justice Scalia believes, in elucidating the plain meaning of the text. The helpful ones are the traditional Latin-derived canons, such as *expressio unius est exclusio alterius*, meaning: "Expression of the one is exclusion of the other." Elaborating, Justice Scalia states: "What this means is this: If you see a sign that says children under twelve may enter free, you should have no need to ask whether your thirteen-year-old must pay. The inclusion of the one class is an implicit exclusion of the other." Other acceptable canons include "the rule that when the text of a statute is clear, that is the end of the matter"; and the canon "that ambiguities in a newly enacted statute are to be resolved in such fashion as to make the statute, not only internally consistent, but also compatible with previously enacted laws." Such canons are "commonsensical," Justice Scalia maintains.[28]

Other canons of statutory construction are, on the other hand, unacceptable because they "load the dice for or against a particular result," as do certain statutory presumptions. These slanted or nonneutral presumptions and

---

26. Scalia, *A Matter of Interpretation*, supra note 6, at pp. 23–24.
27. Ibid. at p. 116.
28. Ibid. at pp. 16, 25, 26.

rules of construction include the "rule of lenity" (ambiguities in criminal statutes must be resolved in defendant's favor) and the "rule of Indian preference" (ambiguities in Indian treaties or statutes dealing with Indians are to be resolved in favor of Indians). They are disfavored, Justice Scalia maintains, because it is unclear what gives courts authority to use them or how much judicial weight is to be given to them. As a consequence, they fuel arbitrariness and unpredictability in judicial decision making.[29]

Justice Scalia does, however, favor some loaded presumptions and canons of construction; namely, those that are "validated by sheer antiquity" or that are designed to lead us to the ordinary meaning of a statute. These additional considerations change the status of some disfavored rules of construction. For example, the rule of lenity is acceptable because of its antiquity. Likewise, the rule that Congress' abrogation of Eleventh Amendment immunity must be expressed rather than implied is acceptable because it moves us closer to ordinary meaning, or, as Justice Scalia says, it is "merely a normal interpretation" of what we would expect from such an extraordinary congressional act.[30]

In his Tanner Lectures, Justice Scalia primarily relies on an 1892 case, *Holy Trinity Church v. United States*,[31] to illustrate his brand of statutory textualism. The Supreme Court in this case disregarded the plain meaning of a federal statute that banned the importation of "any" foreign labor under contracts for the performance of "labor or service of any kind." The Court unanimously held that the Church of the Holy Trinity, an Episcopal church located in New York City, could pay the way for a British pastor, The Reverend E. Walpole Warren, to travel to the United States as the congregation's new rector. Speaking for the Court, Justice David Brewer cited "the familiar rule that a thing may be within the letter of the statute and yet not within the statute, because not within its spirit, nor within the intention of its makers."[32] Congress intended to prevent the importation of cheap, unskilled labor, not "brain toilers."[33] Substituting clear legislative intent for the plain meaning of the text was injudicious, Justice Scalia charges. A Scalian textualist would have ruled that the church violated "the letter of the statute, and was therefore within the

---

29. Ibid. at pp. 27–29(citing *United States v. Bass*, 404 U.S. 336, 347–49 (1971) (the rule of lenity); *Montana v. Blackfeet Tribe of Indians*, 471 U.S. 759, 766–68 (1985) (Indian treaties or statutes).

30. Ibid. at p. 29.

31. 143 U.S. 457 (1892).

32. Ibid. at p. 459.

33. Ibid. at pp. 462–65.

statute: end of case."[34] One legal historian, Carol Chomsky, argues that the Court's reasoning is sound when viewed in the context of the entire historical record.[35]

William Eskridge provides a more contemporary illustration of Scalian statutory textualism. It concerns a famous yet controversial incident involving two professional basketball teams:

> In May 1997, the New York Knickerbockers basketball team was poised to reach the finals of its division in the National Basketball Association (NBA). The Knicks led the rival Miami Heat by three games to two and needed one more victory to win the best-of-seven semifinal playoff series. Game six would be in New York; with their star center, Patrick Ewing, playing well, victory seemed assured for the Knicks. A fracas during game five changed the odds. During a fight under the basket between Knicks and Heat players, Ewing left the bench and paced in the middle of the court, away from the fight. Rule 12A, Section IX(c), of the NBA Rules provided: 'During an altercation, all players not participating in the game must remain in the immediate vicinity of their bench. Violators will be suspended, without pay, for a minimum of one game,' commencing 'prior to the start of their next game.' Applying the rule, NBA Commissioner David Stern suspended Ewing and another player for game six in New York, which the Knicks lost; two other players were suspended for game seven in Miami, which the Knicks also lost. Having lost the series, four games to three, the Knicks cried foul: the rule should not have been applied to Ewing because he did not leave the bench to join the altercation. The rule was not intended to apply to Ewing; it was not fair to apply the rule to someone who was not contributing to the fight: 'we wuz robbed.'
>
> The foregoing argument, made not only by the Knicks but also in print by philosopher Ronald Dworkin and proceduralist Linda Silberman, both law professors at New York University, reflects good old-fashioned common law reasoning from a rule to a new and perhaps unanticipated fact situation. Justice Antonin Scalia...says humbug to all that. Apply the rule according to its plain meaning. Do not consider the 'intent' of its drafters. Unfairness is irrelevant when the

---

34. Scalia, *A Matter of Interpretation*, supra note 6, at p. 20.

35. Carol Chomsky, "Unlocking the Mysteries of *Holy Trinity*: Spint, Letter, and History in Statutory Interpretation," *Columbia Law Review* 100 (2000): 901.

rule applies as a matter of plain textual meaning. Stern did the right thing and for the right reasons. Ewing must be suspended. He and his colleagues will know better than to leave the bench during the next melee.[36]

Thus, for Justice Scalia, reading statutes is a very simple matter: text trumps intent. "It is the law that governs, not the intent of the lawgiver."[37]

Justice Scalia supports his view of statutory construction with three primary arguments. The first is essentially an economic argument: researching legislative history is time-consuming and costly and "more likely to produce a false or contrived legislative intent than a genuine one."[38] Even Eskridge, a harsh critic of Scalian textualism, finds "support" for this argument in his own reading of statutes.[39] Eliminating intent from the judicial inquiry is therefore likely to save time and money not only for judges and their law clerks, but also for practicing lawyers.

A second argument in favor of excluding legislative intent is ideological. Relying solely on statutory text brings the interpretive enterprise in line with the logical method's goal of judicial restraint. The murkiness of searching for legislative intent gives cover to judges who wish to slip policy into the judicial process. Eliminating legislative intent reduces judicial discretion and, consequently, inconsistency and uncertainty in statutory cases. This, in turn, promotes the rule of law and democratic government.[40] Eskridge argues that this benefit is offset by the cost of "new errors" that would be introduced by eliminating legislative intent, "including greater need for the legislative process to sacrifice parts of its limited agenda to monitor and respond to textualist decisions."[41] When a judge considers only the statutory text in the face of unambiguous, contradictory legislative intent she forces the legislature to redeploy its limited resources to rewrite the statute, when she could have reached the correct result by simply consulting the statute's legislative history.

Justice Scalia's final argument in support of ignoring legislative intent is essentially institutional. Excluding legislative history from the judicial process will improve legislative drafting or, in other words, force law-makers to perform in a constitutionally responsible fashion. "If, for example, legislative his-

---

36. Eskridge, "Textualism," supra note 5, at pp. 1509–10.

37. Scalia, *A Matter of Interpretation*, supra note 6, at p. 17.

38. Ibid. at p. 32.

39. Eskridge, "Textualism," supra note 5, at p. 1540.

40. See Scalia, *A Matter of Interpretation*, supra note 6, at p. 30; Sunstein, "Justice Scalia's Democratic Formalism," supra note 7, at pp. 531–32, 538.

41. Eskridge, "Textualism," supra note 5, at p. 1541.

tory will not be used, legislators will be under considerable pressure to increase statutory clarity."[42] Again, Eskridge sees this benefit as "virtually nil" when compared to its cost—namely,the "increased willingness of judges to overrule [administrative] agency interpretations of statutes because the agency is influenced by legislative expectations that judges think contrary to statutory text."[43] This criticism of Scalian textualism relates to a larger matter discussed near the end of this chapter; namely, Justice Scalia's failure to factor administrative agencies into his view of the judicial process.[44] We shall turn to this and other criticisms of Scalian textualism after we consider its constitutional side.

D. Constitutional Textualism

Scalian textualism in constitutional cases is discerningly different from its profile in the statutory context. Interpretation is less semantical and more historical in the constitutional setting—what might be called "originalist textualism." But Justice Scalia's basic concern—the lack of democratic pedigree and the absence of the rule of law in untethered judicial decision making—remains constant in both milieus. Common-law constitutionalism is no less detrimental to democratic government and the rule of law than common-law legislation, in Justice Scalia's opinion.

Accordingly, Justice Scalia rejects the idea of "the Living Constitution, a body of law (unlike normal statutes) [that] grows and changes from age to age, in order to meet the needs of a changing society."[45] This does not mean Justice Scalia is against change in the law. To the contrary, he favors change created democratically. He believes change should come through legislation rather than through text-free constitutional interpretation inherent in the Living Constitution. The latter "is preeminently a common-law way of making law, and not the way of construing a democratically adopted text."[46] Furthermore, policy-formulation and law-making the Living Constitution inevitably invites "actually reduces the capacity for democratic experimentation, by allowing judges to prevent elected officials from engaging in new experiments."[47]

---

42. Sunstein, "Justice Scalia's Democratic Formalism," supra note 7, at pp. 538–39. See ibid. at pp. 531–32.
43. Eskridge, "Textualism," supra note 5, at p. 1541.
44. See Section E, infra.
45. Scalia, *A Matter of Interpretation*, supra note 6, at p. 38.
46. Ibid. at p. 40.
47. Sunstein, "Justice Scalia's Democratic Formalism," supra note 7, at p. 537.

The evolutionary approach, Justice Scalia argues, has prevented the admissibility of evidence of guilt unlawfully seized by the police, has prohibited the termination of welfare payments prior to a due process hearing even when evidence of fraud is received, and has placed other new restrictions on democratic government.[48]

We assume "that evolution will always be in the direction of greater personal liberty," Justice Scalia says. But "the record of history refutes the proposition that the evolving Constitution will invariably enlarge individual rights."[49] Propelled by this assumption, the Living Constitution threatens the Bill of Rights, an anti-majoritarian prescription, by permitting a judge to interpret the Constitution any way "the majority wants."[50] What Justice Scalia fears most is that a "moral reading" of the Constitution will lead to "a reduction of the rights of individuals," because the moral precepts of future societies may not be as "moral" as those that underpin the Constitution as originally conceived.[51]

Rather than viewing the Constitution as a "morphing" document, Scalian textualism treats it as a text frozen in time and place—1791 America.[52] The judge should stay within the original meaning of the Constitution. Thus, Justice Scalia's constitutional textualism begins exactly where his statutory textualism begins—namely, with the ordinary meaning of individual words at the time they were written. It is quite obvious that in some cases, such meaning can be easily discerned.[53] But in most cases it cannot be so effortlessly determined. The judge will have to go back in time to ascertain plain meaning. This is done mostly by consulting the writings of informed people of the time, especially the Framers and the authors of *The Federalist Papers*. Again, the objective is to learn "how the text of the Constitution was originally understood."[54] The Constitution is timeless because it is changeless.

Of course, any reliance on *The Federalist Papers* is problematic. These papers are "a series of propaganda documents penned by supporters of the Con-

---

48. Scalia, *A Matter of Interpretation*, supra note 6, at pp. 41–42.

49. Ibid. at pp. 42, 43.

50. Ibid. at p. 47.

51. Ibid. at p. 149. Here is where Scalia earns his conservative stripes. See discussion of his conservatism in Preface, Section B, supra.

52. This is the date the Bill of Rights was ratified and thus became part of the Constitution.

53. For example, in *Maryland v. Craig*, 497 U.S. 836, 862 (1992), Justice Scalia wrote a dissenting opinion in which he argued that the plain meaning of the word "confrontation" in the Sixth Amendment's Confrontation Clause includes a "face-to-face" meeting.

54. Scalia, *A Matter of Interpretation*, supra note 6, at p. 38. See ibid. at pp. 133–38 (response to Professor Tribe).

stitution to persuade New York to ratify it."[55] Although, as Eskridge points out, "they were written by smarter and more far-sighted people, . . . they are on the whole less reliable sources for figuring out 'the objective indication of the words, rather than the intent of the [Framers].'"[56]

In addition to the Framers' intent and other writings of the period, a Scalian textualist uses certain other interpretive aids in construing the Constitution. These devices include eighteenth or nineteenth century dictionaries,[57] supported by literature.[58] Several additional devices are delineated in a highly controversial case, *Printz v. United States*.[59] In this case, the Supreme Court struck down the Brady Act's requirement that local law enforcement officers perform background checks on prospective gun buyers. Justice Scalia, writing for the Court, held that the Constitution prohibits Congress from passing laws that require state executives to enforce federal statutes. Such federal "commandeering" of the state legislature was not expressly prohibited by the constitutional text, Justice Scalia conceded: "There is no constitutional text speaking to this precise question."[60] However, looking to "historical understanding and practice,...the structure of the Constitution, and...the jurisprudence of this Court," Justice Scalia derived the prohibition from the constitutional powers of the states.[61] Given the fact that the Constitution grants powers to the states, it is logical to infer a constitutional prohibition against Congress' interfering with the exercise of such powers.[62]

The inability to identify a particular constitutional provision as the source for the governing rule of law (the prohibition against commandeering) would have been a nonstarter for judges proceeding under legal formalism. They would have looked for textual support—perhaps the Tenth Amendment. The transparency of the meaning or application may be exaggerated, but at least

---

55. Eskridge, "Textualism," supra note 5, at p. 1520 (citing sources).

56. Ibid.

57. For example, in *National Endowment for the Arts v. Finley*, 524 U.S. 569, 595 (1998), Justice Scalia wrote a concurring opinion in which he used a 1796 dictionary to define the word "abridging" in determining whether a statute "abridged" First Amendment rights.

58. For example, in *Coy v. Iowa*, 487 U.S. 1012, 1016–1017 (1988), Justice Scalia cites William Shakespeare's *Richard II* to support the dictionary meaning of the word "confrontation" in the Sixth Amendment's Confrontation Clause. This type of support seems to be off target as it is not set within the time of the Constitution.

59. 521 U.S. 898 (1997).

60. Ibid. at 905.

61. Ibid.

62. For an interesting criticism of this case, see Vicki C. Jackson, "Federalism and the Uses and Limits of Law: Printz and Principle?," *Harvard Law Review* 111 (1998): 2180.

there is an attempt to be textual in the analysis. In this particular instance, legal formalism is not only more textual than Scalian textualism, but is also closer to their common foundation—the logical method. This observation speaks to the first of many criticisms that can be made of Scalian textualism.

E. Criticisms

At times, Justice Scalia's reading of the Constitution hardly satisfies the most important requirement of the logical method—textual support. In *Printz*, for example, Justice Scalia has no constitutional text to pull down. Yet, in spite of that, he relies on extra-textual material—in that case, the structure of the Constitution and the Supreme Court's jurisprudence of federalism, and in other cases, *The Federalist Papers*—to render a decision *based on the Constitution*. Given the absence of authoritative text, the holding's textualist pedigree is quite dubious.

Perhaps Scalian textualism should be viewed as aspirational in its adherence to the logical method. Certainly Justice Scalia has no taste for the policy method in statutory or constitutional interpretation, and certainly his goal is to "address[] the text of the [statutory or] constitutional provision that is at issue."[63] But, clearly, Justice Scalia commits the very sin he accuses constitutional law classes and casebooks of making—starting constitutional analysis with Supreme Court cases rather than the text.

Another problem with Scalian constitutional textualism concerns its preference for the Dead Constitution. It is difficult to understand how Justice Scalia can disparage the Living Constitution and adopt an expansive reading of the constitutional text simultaneously.[64] Justice Scalia would apply the First Amendment's protection of speech and press to handwritten letters, even though the latter is technically neither speech nor press. Hasn't he just updated the Constitution? Justice Scalia justifies his modernization of text as a "reasonable construction" of the Constitution.[65] But reasonable on what basis? Certainly not on the basis of the original meaning of the text.

At this point, one might wonder what precisely is the source of the tension between Scalian constitutional textualism and the Living Constitution, which

---

63. Scalia, *A Matter of Interpretation*, supra note 6, at p. 39.

64. "[W]ords and phrases [are to be given] an expansive rather than [a] narrow interpretation though not an interpretation that the language will not bear." Ibid. at p. 37.

65. Ibid. at p. 38.

represents the modern theory of constitutional interpretation. Some scholars would argue that it is the originalism element in Scalian constitutional textualism that clashes with the expansion of rights under the Constitution. These scholars, such as Robert Bork[66] and Leonard Levy,[67] seek to defend originalism against attacks by "liberal" constitutional theorists, such as Alexander Bickel,[68] John Hart Ely,[69] Laurence Tribe,[70] and Justice William Brennan. Indeed, Justice Brennan gave a speech in 1985 that captures the essence of the Living Constitution. Referring to the Bill of Rights and the Reconstruction Amendments (Thirteenth, Fourteenth, and Fifteenth Amendments), Justice Brennan stated: "The precise rules by which we have protected fundamental human dignity have been transformed over time in response to both transformations of social condition and evolution of our concepts of human dignity."[71]

In contrast to what Bork and Levy suggest in their writings, Michael Perry argues that minimalism and not originalism is the part of Scalian constitutional textualism that is in conflict with the Living Constitution.[72] Like minimalism in the context of legal formalism, discussed in the last chapter, minimalism here signifies a weak government.[73] It seeks to reduce the discretion (and hence power and importance) of the judiciary. In contrast, originalism, Perry argues, is constitutional interpretation that seeks to find the firmest textual support possible for rights—e.g., the "antidiscrimination directive" rather than the "reasonableness directive" for abortion rights,[74] the Ninth Amendment rather than the Due Process Component of the Fifth Amendment for the prohibition against racial discrimination by the federal government.[75]

---

66. See, e.g., Bork, *The Tempting of America*, supra note 5.

67. Leonard Levy, *Original Intent and the Framers' Constitution* (New York: MacMillan, 1988).

68. Alexander M. Bickel, *The Least Dangerous Branch: The Supreme Court at the Bar of Politics* (Indianapolis: Bobbs-Merrill, 1962).

69. John H. Ely, *Democracy and Distrust: A Theory of Judicial Review* (Cambridge: Harvard University Press, 1980).

70. Laurence Tribe, *American Constitutional Law* 2d ed. (Mineloa, N.Y.: Foundation Press, 1988), p. iii.

71. William J. Brennan, Jr., Speech at the *Text and Teaching Symposium*, Georgetown University, Washington, D.C., 10/12/85.

72. See Michael Perry, *The Constitution in the Courts: Law or Politics?* (New York: Oxford University Press, 1994).

73. See Chapter 1, Section B, supra.

74. See Perry, *The Constitution in the Courts*, supra note 72, at pp. 180–89.

75. See ibid. at pp. 145–48.

Perry believes that originalism does not require minimalism, that both theo-ries are in fact distinct. Originalism, but not minimalism, provides the basis for constitutionalizing a wide range of rights. Thus, Perry would disagree with many "liberal" grounds for constitutionalizing rights, and, at the same time, disagree with "conservative" theorists who would deny the expansion of rights on originalist grounds. Perry's theory of originalism makes a significant con-tribution to legal theory.

The difference between Perry's originalism and Justice Scalia's originalism is quite apparent when applied to the most important civil rights case in his-tory, *Brown v. Board of Education*.[76] Perry would actively search for and find firm textual support in the Fourteenth Amendment for the Supreme Court's invalidation of the state school segregation statutes.[77] Justice Scalia's original-ism (text frozen in time), his constitutional conservatism,[78] could not ration-ally sustain the Court's reasoning in *Brown*. His originalism would reject read-ing the Fourteenth Amendment as a prohibition against segregation in public education, because such a reading does not demonstrate the degree of fealty to the Amendment's original meaning that Justice Scalia's originalism seems to require. Surely the Amendment's framers, the Thirty-ninth Congress, in-tended the Amendment to be read in harmony with the then-common mean-ing of segregation—that is, "separate but equal." Indeed, Congress made no attempt to desegregate the public schools of Washington, D.C. These schools as well as the public schools in the home districts of virtually every congress-man who voted for the Amendment were segregated both before and after the Amendment's passage.[79] It is not enough to argue, as some have, that the Framers' understanding of racial segregation "was completely inconsistent with

---

76. 347 U.S. 483 (1954).

77. See Perry, *The Constitution in the Courts*, supra note 72, at pp. 42–46.

78. See Preface, Section B, supra.

79. Compare Roy L. Brooks, *Integration or Separation? A Strategy for Racial Equality* (Cambridge: Harvard University Press, 1996), pp. 206–13 (arguing that the Fourteenth Amendment could be read as a prohibition against racial subordination as opposed to racial separation). The view that *Brown* cannot be squared with originalism is overwhelmingly supported by legal scholars. For further discussion of the question, see, e.g. Michael W. McConnell, "Originalism and The Desegregation Decisions," *Virginia Law Review* 81 (1995) 947 (arguing compatibility); Michael J. Klarman, "Brown, Originalism, and Constitutional Theory: A Response to Professor McConnell," *Virginia Law Review* 81 (1995): 1881 (argu-ing non-compatibility, the majority position); Michael W. McConnell, "The Originalist Case For Brown v. Board of Education," *Harvard Journal of Law and Public Policy*, 19 (1996): 457 (replying to Klarman's response); Boris I. Bittker, "Interpreting the Constitu-tion: Is the Intent of the Framers Controlling? If Not, What Is?" *Harvard Journal of Law and Public Policy*, 19 (1995): 9 (taking the majority position).

the equal protection of the laws they mandated."[80] Quite obviously, neither they nor the average American at the time saw any such inconsistency. Though "separate but equal" has not been part of the common meaning of the Equal Protection Clause since at least the time of *Brown*, it was part of the Clause's common understanding during the years following the Civil War. Otherwise, the Amendment would never have been proposed let alone ratified,[81] and, equally telling, Justice Harlan's dissenting opinion would have been the majority opinion in *Plessy v. Ferguson*.[82] Given all we know about the aftermath of the Civil War, it is ludicrous to suppose that the lawmakers of the era intended, hoped, or expected that racial mixing (the *sine qua non* of *Brown's* reasoning) would be a "consequence" of the Equal Protection Clause.

An integral part of Justice Scalia's originalism, minimalism (specifically, the notion of an impotent judiciary) is also incompatible with *Brown's* reasoning. The Court in *Brown* enlarged itself by overturning every state school segregation statute in the nation, as well as reversing 75 years of its own precedents. A Scalian textualist, in short, would be hard pressed to find textual support for the Supreme Court's construction and application of the Fourteenth Amendment in *Brown* not only on originalist grounds, but also on minimalist grounds. School segregation, as evil as it is, must be eradicated through the democratic process. This is the conclusion one logically draws from a fair reading of Scalian textualism.

The relationship between Scalian statutory textualism and Scalian constitutional textualism is also grounds for criticism. This relationship, at a minimum, seems incoherent. Justice Scalia completely ignores legislative history in the statutory context, but freely consults it in the constitutional context. While in statutory cases he disregards the spirit of the law in favor of the letter of the law, as his discussion of the *Holy Trinity* case illustrates,[83] in constitutional cases, he allows nontextual matters to trump text, as demonstrated in *Printz* and other cases discussed earlier.[84]

Such inconsistency in Scalian textualism raises questions concerning Justice Scalia's commitment to the Dead Constitution. As Professor Eskridge has observed:

---

80. Bork, *The Tempting of America*, supra note 5, at p. 169.

81. Segregation was widely practiced in the North as well as in the South during Reconstruction (1865–1877). See, e.g., John Hope Franklin, *Reconstruction: After the Civil War* (Chicago: University of Chicago Press, 1961); W.E.B. DuBois, *Black Reconstruction in America* (New York: Atheneum, 1992, reprint of 1935 edition).

82. 163 U.S. 537 (1896).

83. See Section C, supra.

84. See Section D, supra.

The dead Constitution that Scalia described in the Tanner Lectures came alive in *Printz* because Scalia cobbled together a constitutional limit from several sources: historical practice, including early congressional assertions of authority and the debates surrounding the Constitution's ratification; the Constitution's overall commitment to the principle of Federalism, which would be undermined by national commandeering of state and local officials; and the Court's own decision in *New York v. United States*,[85] which struck down national commandeering of state legislatures and which Scalia extended to commandeering of local law enforcement officers.[86]

Perhaps it is possible at some level to reconcile the theoretical inconsistency between Scalian statutory and constitutional textualism by distinguishing between "*kinds* of intention," as suggested earlier.[87] But if it is acceptable to Scalian textualists to give effect to what the lawmakers intended, hoped, or expected would be the "consequences" of their words in the constitutional text, why is it not equally acceptable to do so in the statutory text? The answer seems to be that Scalian textualists cannot reconcile or otherwise explain away this inconsistency.

Of course, one could argue that there is no inconsistency here, because in both instances Justice Scalia is looking for ordinary, or original, meaning. It is just that in order to arrive at such meaning in constitutional cases, one has to go back in time to 1791. In this search for original meaning, one must necessarily resort to legislative history and other institutional conventions to get a sense of the way in which society saw things at the time. Legislative intent is not, however, so important in determining the ordinary meaning of a document enacted in our lifetime. The problem with this argument is that Justice Scalia rejects legislative intent even when construing statutes as old as the Constitution. Also, for someone who is so concerned about democratic process, Justice Scalia is quite willing to ignore an essential ingredient of that process—to wit, legislative intent—when construing statutes.

Beyond mere disagreement with Justice Scalia's reasons for excluding legislative intent from statutory interpretation, one finds a host of other problems. Eskridge, perhaps Scalia's most persistent critic, delineates several, including the problem of coherence ("Is Scalia a 'true' textualist?"); the problem

---

85. 505 U.S. 144 (1992).
86. Eskridge, "Textualism," supra note 5, at pp. 1516–17.
87. See Section C, supra.

of context ("Are text-based or linguistic sources, such as dictionaries, less manipulable than legislative history?"); the problem of loose canons ("What role do the variegated canons of statutory construction play in a new textualist methodology?"); the problem of normativity ("Can normative considerations be excluded from statutory cases, even for an honest textualist such as Scalia?"); and the problem of omission (the failure to take account of administrative agencies).[88] Let us consider a few of these problems.

The problem of coherence is manifested in several ways. First, it is fairly obvious that Justice Scalia is not a true textualist, because he relies on canons as well as the text. This makes him, as Phil Frickey would say, a "text-plus-canons" textualist. Worse, some of the canons Justice Scalia favors "are based on judicially identified policies." Thus, illicit judicial reasoning is brought into statutory interpretation by Trojan Horses pregnant with the common-law mindset. The canon governing statutory waivers of sovereign immunity is an example. "One thinks that Justice Scalia would find such canons anti-democratic," Frickey observes, "for they are judicially created requirements that may dislodge an interpretation consistent with ordinary meaning."[89]

Second, Justice Scalia is at best a selective adherent of the logical method. He slips into the policy method from time to time, even joining opinions that are openly policy-oriented. For example, Justice Scalia neither dissented from nor concurred in the Supreme Court's reasoning or decision in *Caterpillar Inc. v. Lewis*.[90] Without protest, he went along with the other justices as they completely disregarded the unambiguous text of the removal statute, which required the establishment of original jurisdiction at the time of removal.[91] The justices were guided instead by "a main theme of the removal scheme Congress devised."[92] They found policy "considerations of finality, efficiency, and economy…[to be] overwhelming."[93]

This leads to what some scholars see as a third and certainly more serious problem of coherence in Scalian textualism. It is argued that Justice Scalia has, at times, abandoned his judicial method for the sake of political expediency.

---

88. See ibid. at pp. 1515–56.

89. Frickey, "Revisiting the Revival of Theory in Statutory Interpretation," supra note 5, at pp. 206–7.

90. 519 U.S. 61 (1996).

91. For a more detailed discussion of the facts of the case, see Part 1, Section A, supra, which correctly applies the logical method to the case.

92. 519 U.S. at 76. This sounds like legislative intent or spirit, which is an unacceptable source of interpretation in Scalian textualism.

93. Ibid. at 75. Supposedly, Scalian textualism rejects common-law legislation.

An oft-cited example is *Montana v. Egelhoff*.[94] Writing for the majority, Justice Scalia held that a Montana statute that disallowed the introduction of evidence of intoxication in determining the existence of the mental-state element of a criminal offense did not violate constitutional due process. To reach this holding, Justice Scalia had to construe the original meaning of the Due Process Clause in a manner that was different from the Montana Supreme Court's reading of the Clause, which was that "the Due Process Clause guarantees a defendant the right to present and have considered by the jury 'all relevant evidence to rebut the State's evidence on all elements of the offense charged.' "[95] Justice Scalia could not, however, find historical writings probative of the Due Process Clause's original meaning as regards the presentation of evidence in a case like the one *sub judice*. But rather than conceding the issue for lack of textual support, he primarily relied on relatively recent Supreme Court cases for the proposition that the Due Process Clause permits restrictions on the introduction of evidence that do not offend our fundamental notions of justice.[96] Justice Scalia, it is argued, was not going to permit a defendant to use a lawless act (intoxication) to escape liability for an even greater lawless act (double murder) just because textual support for throwing him in jail was unavailable. The thought of a person literally getting away with murder was just too much for Justice Scalia's law-and-order conservatism to accept. Cases like *Egelhoff* have given some scholars cause to believe that Justice Scalia is quite prepared to jettison textualism when it conflicts with his ideological or political values.[97]

Greater stability and certainty in the law is one of the stated benefits of Scalian textualism. These qualities, of course, go to the heart of the logical method. Many scholars have found, however, that Scalian textualism has brought greater instability to various areas of the law.[98] This condition pri-

---

94. 518 U.S. 37 (1996).

95. Ibid. at 41–42 (quoting *Montana v. Egelhoff*, 272 Mont. 114, 125, 900 P. 2d 260, 266 (1995)).

96. See ibid. at 42 (citing *Taylor v. Illinois*, 484 U.S. 400, 410 (1988); *Michigan v. Lucas*, 500 U.S. 145, 151 (1991)). Justice Scalia also relied on another nontextual source, Federal and Montana Rule of Evidence 403, which provides: "Although relevant, evidence may be excluded if its probative value is substantially outweighed by the danger of unfair prejudice, confusion of the issues, or misleading the jury, or by needless presentation of cumulative evidence."

97. See, e.g., David M. Zlotnick, "Justice Scalia and His Critics: An Exploration of Scalia's Fidelity to His Constitutional Methodology," *Emory Law Review* 48 (1999): 1377, 1379.

98. See, e.g., Richard J. Lazarus & Claudia M. Newman, "City of Chicago v. Environmental Defense Fund: Searching for Plain Meaning in Unambiguous Ambiguity," *New York*

marily arises from mixed signals being sent to the courts of appeal by a Supreme Court (including Justice Scalia himself) that is textualist one moment and policy-oriented the next. *Caterpillar, Inc. v. Lewis*, discussed a moment ago, is one such example. Frickey gives another example, which, because of its importance, is quoted here at length.

> …Title VII of the Civil Rights Act of 1964 outlaws discrimination in employment on the basis of such factors as race or gender. Suppose an employee is fired and, believing that the discharge was racially motivated, files a complaint with the federal Equal Employment Opportunity Commission, the first step in bringing a Title VII action. Suppose further that, while the charge is pending, the former employee seeks another job. If the former employer gives the former employee a negative job reference in retaliation for his or her filing of the complaint with the EEOC, is that actionable under Title VII?
>
> * * *
>
> A case of this kind, *Robinson v. Shell Oil Co.* divided the United States Court of Appeals for the Fourth Circuit sitting en banc. Seven judges followed the plain meaning [of the statute] and denied relief; four dissented. The majority concluded that the statute unambiguously failed to protect former employees from retaliation. Indeed, the statute defines 'employee' as 'an individual employed by an employer,' and there was no doubt that, at the time of the alleged retaliation, this person was not employed by that employer. The majority said that they were 'simply prohibited from reading into the clear language of the definition of 'employee' that which Congress did not include.' The majority acknowledged that most of the courts of appeals had gone the other way on this question, avoiding a literal interpretation because that produced a result defeating the underlying purposes of Title VII. This purposive approach…came under heavy fire from the Fourth Circuit majority, which called it an abandonment of 'the es-

---

University Environmental Law Journal 4 (1995): 1 (environmental law); Jack M. Beermann, "The Supreme Court's Narrow View on Civil Rights," *Supreme Court Review* 1993 (1993): 199 (civil rights law); William N. Eskridge, Jr., "Reneging on History? The Court/Congress/President Civil Rights Game," *California Law Review* 79 (1991): 613 (civil rights); Philip P. Frickey, "Congressional Intent, Practical Reasoning, and the Dynamic Nature of Federal Indian Law," *California Law Review* 78 (1990): 1137 (Indian law).

tablished analytical framework for statutory construction' in pursuit of a reliance 'on broad considerations of policy.' The majority stated that 'these decisions fail to heed the Supreme Court's repeated mandate' to follow ordinary statutory textual meaning, citing a Supreme Court opinion written by Justice Thomas that is very Scalia-like in its analysis. The majority concluded that, 'although extending Title VII to cover former employees is tantalizing fruit, our judicial inquiry must cease when the language of a statute is plain and unambiguous. Such is the rule of law.'

* * *

I was quite surprised when the Supreme Court reversed unanimously—in an opinion by Justice Thomas! You have to wonder if the judges in the majority of the Fourth Circuit felt that they had been victimized by a bait and switch. Justice Thomas concluded that 'employee' was ambiguous in Title VII—it could mean former employees as well as current ones. After all, the definition of an employee is someone 'employed by an employer,' which could be 'is employed' or 'was employed,' Justice Thomas wrote, and without a verb derived from the infinitive 'to be' preceding the verb 'employed,' the statute is ambiguous. Some provisions of Title VII seem to assume that 'employee' means former employees, while others do not. This broader statutory context, along with 'a primary purpose of [the] antiretaliation provisions: maintaining unfettered access to statutory remedial mechanisms,' supported an interpretation protecting former employees as well as current employees and applicants for employment.

* * *

…Again, the limiting device proposed by Justice Scalia—courts must stick to 'ordinary meaning' even when there is no plain meaning— failed to work itself into a Supreme Court opinion that Justice Scalia himself joined. In this light, even if the majority of the Fourth Circuit was wrong to conclude that the definition of 'employee' was completely unambiguous, were they not right that the definition had an ordinary meaning excluding former employees? Justice Thomas worked hard to create enough doubt on the question of ambiguity to allow him to peek outside the provision at broader considerations. At that point, the case became an exercise in pragmatism, and an easy one at that.

Robinson suggests that, like beauty, ambiguity is in the eye of the beholder. In *Robinson* ambiguity becomes a magically liberating factor, a beautiful thing for judges—even if, or one might say, especially if, it is selectively employed.[99]

Thus, the promise of consistency under Scalian textualism is often more illusionary than real.

The failure to take into account the role administrative agencies play in our scheme of government is a serious flaw in Scalian statutory textualism. Administrative agencies, not courts, perform most of the important work of statutory interpretation and application.[100] This is perhaps how it should be, because, unlike judges, agency officials are experts and focused on single industries. No judge knows as much as the Surgeon General about public health matters, or as much as the Federal Aviation Administration (FAA) staff about technical aviation issues.

In addition to greater technical knowledge, federal agencies have greater accountability than federal courts. As the Supreme Court has said in *Chevron U.S.A., Inc. v. Natural Resources Defense Council*:[101] "While agencies are not directly accountable to the people, the Chief Executive is."[102] With an umbilical cord to the presidency, federal agency officials have "a kind of democratic pedigree" federal judges do not have.[103] Thus, "it is entirely appropriate," the Supreme Court ruled in *Chevron*, "for [administrative agencies]... to make...policy choices—resolving the competing interests which Congress itself did not resolve, or intentionally left to be resolved by the agency charged with the administration of the statute in light of everyday realities."[104]

All this would seem to undercut Justice Scalia's legitimacy argument, his concern for judicial law-making and policy-formulation in statutory cases. When a court defers to an agency's interpretation of a statute, as the Supreme Court has said it should do when the statute is ambiguous,[105] the judicial enterprise acquires a degree of democratic pedigree. Also, the judge is likely to produce a technically correct decision. After all, legitimate and correct statutory interpretation is what Scalian textualism is supposedly all about.

For all its flaws, Scalian textualism presents a set of ideas that has intrinsic appeal. Adhering to the plainest meaning of text promotes democratic gov-

---

99. Frickey, "Revisiting the Revival of Theory in Statutory Interpretation," supra note 5, at pp. 212–15 (citations omitted).

100. See Sunstein, "Justice Scalia's Democratic Formalism," supra note 7, at p. 550.

101. 467 U.S. 837 (1984).

102. Ibid. at 865.

103. Sunstein, "Justice Scalia's Democratic Formalism," supra note 7, at p. 551.

104. 467 U.S. at 865.

105. Ibid. at 842, 845.

ernment in at least two related ways. First, it protects against an overreaching judiciary (whether liberal or conservative) which would otherwise be able to take advantage of the fact that words are easily susceptible to multiple meanings. Second, it reminds judges of their institutional obligations to the rule of law and democratic ideals. As we move to the policy method, the reader should ask whether Justice Scalia's important message has fallen on deaf ears or whether it is merely being expressed in a different way.

Section B

Policy Method

"The life of the law has not been logic: it has been experience."[1] This, perhaps the most famous aphorism in Anglo-American law, comes from Justice Oliver Wendell Holmes. It is intended to debunk the logical method, and, at the same time, convey the essence of an alternative judicial technique that can be called "the policy method."

It is a fallacy, Holmes asserted, to believe that "the development of the law is logic,...that there is a fixed quantitative relation between every phenomenon and its antecedents and consequents."[2] Holmes argued that "the logical method...flatter[s] that longing for certainty and for repose which is in every human mind. But certainty generally is illusion, and repose is not the destiny of man."[3] When one looks at what judges actually do, rather than what they say they do, it becomes quite apparent that, although judges couched their opinions in "the language of logic" and purport to reason deductively, "[b]ehind the logical form lies a judgment as to the relative worth and importance of competing legislative grounds, often an inarticulate and unconscious judgment, it is true, and yet the very root and nerve of the whole proceeding."[4]

Justice Benjamin Cardozo made a similar rhetorical attack on the logical method. Quoting Roscoe Pound, who, like Holmes, was an early opponent of the logical method, Cardozo wrote of "the dangers of a 'jurisprudence of conceptions'..., the extension of a maxim or definition with relentless disregard of consequences to 'a dryly logical extreme.' The approximate and relative become the definite and absolute."[5]

---

1. Oliver Wendell Holmes, *The Common Law*, Mark DeWolfe Howe, ed. (Cambridge: Belkamp Press of Harvard University Press, 1963), p. 5.

2. Oliver Wendell Holmes, "The Path of the Law," *Harvard Law Review* 10 (1897): 457, 465.

3. Ibid. at p. 466.

4. Ibid.

5. *Hynes v. New York Central Railroad Co.*, 231 N.Y. 229, 235 (1921) (citing Roscoe Pound, "Mechanical Jurisprudence," *Columbia Law Review* 8 (1908): 605, 608, 610).

The logical method's formalism sits in stark contrast to the policy method's consequentialism.[6] Whereas the logical method insists that judges should not displace logical discourse with public policy considerations, the policy method makes no pretense of being value-free. Whereas the logical method is committed to a normativity of consistency—the internal order of the law—the policy method is self-consciously attuned to the consequences judicial decisions have on society. And whereas the logical method entails the parsing of words and the use of legal reasoning devices,[7] the policy method involves all that, but mostly (and decisively) the weighing of competing policy considerations in an attempt to arrive at justice, the social end of Western legal systems.[8]

Although judicial analysis under the policy method, like that under the logical method, typically begins with a generalized rule of law, rules alone do not determine the outcome of cases. Rules may guide judicial decision making, but policies decide cases. Hence, policy-formulation is much more conspicuous under the policy method than under the logical method. Readers of judicial opinions fashioned under the policy method are left to deal with the resulting twists and turns in judicial reasoning as best they can. "If our opinions seem on occasion to be internally inconsistent, to contain a logical fallacy, or to insufficiently distinguish a prior case," Chief Justice Rehnquist has said in paraphrasing a former Chief Justice, "let the law reviews figure out what [they mean]."[9]

Three expressions of the policy method are examined in this section of Part 1. Each regards policy-formulation as a legitimate judicial function in the process of moving from Point A to Point C. They differ, however, in the degree to which they are committed to the use of policy in the judicial context. The first judicial model is legal realism (Chapter 3), whose heyday was the 1920s and 30s, but returned to Yale Law School in the 1970s. With its unabashed incorporation of judicial policy-making, legal realism is the most judicially assertive of the traditional judicial models studied in Part 1 of this book.

Sociological jurisprudence (Chapter 4) is the next policy-method model. Developed by Roscoe Pound, a prolific scholar and at one time a dean at Harvard Law School, as a criticism of both legal formalism and legal realism, so-

---

6. See, e.g., Roberto Unger, "The Critical Legal Studies Movement," *Harvard Law Review* 96 (1983): 565. See also, Ernest J. Weinrib, "Legal Formalism: On the Imminent Rationality of Law," *Yale Law Journal* 97 (1988): 949.

7. See Part 1, Section A, supra.

8. See Introduction, Section B, supra.

9. Linda Greenhouse, *"Rehnquist Asks Limit to Automatic Appeals,"* New York Times, Sept. 16, 1984, at 15.

ciological jurisprudence limits the judicial policy-formulation function primarily to policy-vindication. Policy-discovery is, however, permitted in certain cases. But policy-making is never allowed.

The final judicial model is legal process (Chapter 5). Perhaps the most sophisticated of the policy-method models, legal process was developed in part as a criticism of preceding judicial models (particularly sociological jurisprudence), but mostly in reaction to the administrative state created in the 1930s. Legal process permits policy-discovery in most cases, but never policy-making. James Landis, a Harvard Law School dean, and Henry Hart and Albert Sacks, two very influential Harvard Law professors, gave important shape to legal process. Its heyday was the 1950s and 60s, but it continues to influence judicial decision making.

The structure of the traditional policy-method models can be outlined as follows:

Legal Realism
  Point A: Dispositive Issue
  Point B: Reasoning
    (1) Progressive (Liberal) Policy
      (a) Unrestrained by Prior Rules or Community Values
      (Policy-making)
    (2) Followed by Ex Post Facto Application of Rules
  Point C: Judgment

Sociological Jurisprudence
  Point A: Dispositive Issue
  Point B: Reasoning
    (1) Progressive and Ethical Rule
    (2) Shaped by:
      (a) Policy-vindication in Statutory and Constitutional Cases
      (b) Rule-application in "Spurious Interpretation" Cases
      (c) Policy-discovery in Common Law Cases
  Point C: Judgment

Legal Process
  Point A: Dispositive Issue
  Point B: Reasoning
    (1) Defer to Duly Enacted Rules
    (2) Policy-discovery in Other Cases, Except "Genuine Interpretation"
      Cases, which Requires Policy-vindication
    (3) Follow (1) and (2) with "Reasoned Elaboration"
  Point C: Judgment

A more detailed discussion of the structure of legal realism, sociological jurisprudence, and legal process follows in Chapters 3, 4, and 5, respectively.

Chapter 3
Legal Realism

Legal realism prescribes a judicial process in which progressive, largely liberal ends justify judicial means.[1] *In moving from Point A to Point C, the judge (rule-and fact-skeptic) reacts to the underlying policies in the case, which can entail policy-making, and uses the rules to provide ex post facto "legal" rationales for her policy choices. "'Judgment for the plaintiff,' runs the old anecdote of Marshall; 'Mr. Justice Story will furnish the authorities.'"*[2]

A. Background

Legal realism arose as a challenge to the orthodoxy of legal formalism and in response to several forces unrelated to law that converged in America during the late nineteenth and early twentieth centuries. Lon Fuller writes that legal realism "may have reached its flower" between 1929 and 1934.[3] Yet, the imprint of legal realism can certainly be seen beyond the 1920s and 1930s in landmark Supreme Court cases like *Shelley v. Kraemer* (1948)[4] and *Brown v. Board of Education* (1954),[5] both discussed in this chapter.[6] It can also be seen in legal education. Such well-known legal realists as Myres McDougal, Thomas Emmerson, and Charles Black were teaching at Yale Law School well into the 1970s.[7] Certainly the legal realism of Justices Thurgood Marshall and William Brennan has left large footprints on the American socio-legal landscape.

---

1. Again, "progressive" is not synonymous with welfare liberalism. The former means to move society forward on a number of fronts, such as social, economic, and cultural. The latter is the belief that the government should intervene in social or economic arrangements to rescue the individual from poverty, illness, ignorance, or inequality. Progressive outcomes can be attempted through classical liberal or conservative principles. See Preface, Section B, supra.

2. Karl N. Llewellyn, *The Bramble Bush: Some Lectures on Law and Its Study* (Birmingham: The Legal Classics Library, Special Edition, 1986), p. 29.

3. Lon L. Fuller, "American Legal Realism," *University of Pennsylvania Law Review* 82 (1934): 429, 429.

4. 334 U.S. 1 (1948).

5. 347 U.S. 483 (1954).

6. See Sections B1, B2, and C2, infra.

7. For an illuminating look at legal realism at Yale Law School, see Laura Kalman, *Legal Realism at Yale, 1927–1960* (Chapel Hill: University of North Carolina Press, 1986).

The impact of legal realism can also be seen in the lower federal courts. Some trial judges have attempted to effectuate nothing less than the wholesale restructuring of social institutions from public schools to prisons. In these cases, called "public law litigation" or "institutional reform litigation," the trial judge micro-manages the daily operations of an institution found to be in violation of constitutional or statutory law. "The trial judge," as Abraham Chayes put it, "has passed beyond even the role of legislator and has become a policy planner and manager."[8]

For all of its influence, legal realism is something of a mystery. Karl Llewellyn, one of legal realism's central figures, insisted in 1931 that there is no realist "school," only a congeries of perspectives that have left and right wings.[9] Some contemporary scholars define legal realism as a reform movement that attacks "traditional abstractions and nonempirical concepts of justice," while others define it more modestly as a pragmatic critique of formalist modes of reasoning that functioned to maintain the status quo. Then there are those who see legal realism as more of a historical phenomenon associated with the rise of American legal education in the twentieth century than as an actual method of judicial decision making. Finally, a few scholars believe there is no jurisprudence of legal realism, that legal realism does not exist apart from the personal views of its principal exponents—Karl Llewelyn, Jerome Frank, Underhill Moore, Leon Green, Herman Oliphant, Walter Wheeler Cook, and perhaps one or two others.[10]

Despite this array of views, this chapter finds in legal realism a core set of beliefs that distinguishes it from other theories of judicial decision making. All legal realists are rule-skeptic and fact-skeptic. As discussed in greater de-

---

8. Abraham Chayes, "The Role of the Judge in Public Law Litigation," *Harvard Law Review* 89 (1976): 1281, 1302. See, e.g., Malcolm M. Feeley and Edward L. Rubin, *Judicial Policy Making and the Modern State: How the Courts Reformed America's Prisons* (Cambridge: Cambridge University Press, 1998); Stephen Garvey, Book Review: "Did Making Over the Prisons Require Making Up the Law?," *Cornell Law Review* 84 (1999): 1476.

9. See Karl Llewellyn, "Some Realism about Realism," *Harvard Law Review* 44 (1931): 1222, 1254.

10. For a general discussion of these views, see, e.g., Michael Martin, *Legal Realism: American and Scandinavian* (New York: Peter Lang Publishing, Inc., 1997), pp. 2, 23; John Henry Schlegel, *American Legal Realism and Empirical Social Science* (Durham: The University of North Carolina Press, 1995), pp. 2–11; John Brigham, *The Constitution of Interests: Beyond the Politics of Rights* (New York: New York University Press, 1996), pp. 52–54; Virginia E. Nolan & Edmund Ursin, "Dean Leon Green and Enterprise (No-Fault) Liability: Origins, Strategies, and Prospects," *Wayne Law Review* 47 (2001): 91; Brian Leiter, "Rethinking Legal Realism: Toward a Naturalized Jurisprudence," *Texas Law Review* 76 (1997): 267.

tail later in this chapter, rule-skepticism is the belief that law is not a body of rules but a set of facts that give rise to competing policy choices. When judges move from Point A to Point C, they react primarily to the underlying policies in the case and use the rules to provide *ex post facto* "*legal*" rationales for their policy choices. Thus, rules are inherently inconsistent, and law is infinitely indeterminate. The life of the law has not been the syllogism, but rather the policy choices judges have made, consciously or unconsciously, throughout the years.[11] Fact-skepticism is the belief that the "facts" upon which both judge and jury rely in rendering their decisions are "subjective" facts. They are facts "found" by the judge and jury and are not necessarily the "actual objective" facts that took place prior to the trial.[12]

To gain a deeper understanding of legal realism, one must delve into its past, paying particular attention to the legal, philosophical, economic, political and social science forces that have given shape to its development. These forces converged on the American scene between the 1880s and 1930s. They enrich our knowledge of the theory and structure of judicial decision making under legal realism.

B. Shaping Forces

1. Major Legal Force

The legal force that had the greatest impact on legal formalism is easy to discern—Oliver Wendell Holmes. It would not be incorrect to regard Holmes as the "father" of legal realism; for his pre-judicial writings (i.e., his writings before he became a judge and ultimately a Supreme Court justice) have given legal realism its central organizing theme. In these and in later writings, Holmes attacked the logical method's syllogistic approach to deciding cases.[13] Having spent nearly ten years studying the English common law system, Holmes felt comfortable coming to the conclusion that judges render decisions based not on deductive reasoning but on consequentialist reasoning. He believed that cases are decided based on "[s]ome belief as to the practice of the community or of a class, or…some attitude of yours upon a matter not

---

11. For a similar understanding of legal realism, see Brian Leiter, Review Essay: "Positivism, Formalism, Realism," *Columbia Law Review* 99 (1998): 1138, 1148.

12. Julius Paul, *The Legal Realism of Jerome N. Frank: A Study of Fact-Skepticism and the Judicial Process* (The Hague: Martinus Nijhoff, 1959), p. 73.

13. See Part 1, Section A, supra.

capable of exact quantitative measurement, and therefore not capable of founding exact logical conclusions."[14] Holmes elaborated on this idea in his most famous and impressive scholarly work, *The Common Law* (1881): "The felt necessities of the time, the prevalent moral and political theories, intuitions of public policy, avowed or unconscious, even the prejudices which judges share with their fellow-men, have had a good deal more to do than the syllogism in determining the rules by which men should be governed."[15] Holmes, in short, liberated judicial reasoning from the syllogism's straitjacket and made it more instrumental.

Although it appears, as we shall see in Section C, infra, that Holmesian consequentialism incorporated policy-making in the unwritten law, there is little doubt that it did not embrace policy-making in the context of the written law. Holmes dissented in *Lochner*, a case involving the written law. This case is considered by many to be the poster child of legal formalism.[16] Suggesting at most policy-discovery, Holmes wrote:

> This case is decided upon an economic theory which *a large part of the country does not entertain.* If it were a question whether I agreed with that theory I should desire to study it further and long before making up my mind. But I do not conceive that to be my duty, because I strongly believe that my agreement or disagreement has nothing to do with the right of a *majority* to embody their opinions in law.... The Fourteenth Amendment does not enact Mr. Herbert Spencer's Social Statics.... Some... laws embody convictions or prejudices which judges are likely to share. Some may not. But a constitution is not intended to embody a particular economic theory, whether of paternalism and the organic relation of the citizen to the State or of laissez faire. It is made for people of fundamentally differing views, and the accident of our finding certain opinions natural and familiar or novel and even shocking ought not to conclude our judgment upon the question whether statutes embodying them conflict with the Constitution of the United States.
>
> I think that the word liberty in the Fourteenth Amendment is perverted when it is held to prevent the natural outcome of a *dominant*

---

14. Oliver W. Holmes, "The Path of the Law," *Harvard Law Review* 10 (1897): 457, 466.

15. Oliver W. Holmes, *The Common Law*, Mark DeWolfe Howe, ed. (Cambridge, Mass.: Harvard University Press, 1963), p. 5.

16. For a discussion of the case, see Chapter 1, supra.

opinion, unless it can be said that a rational and fair man necessarily would admit that the statute proposed would infringe fundamental principles as they have been understood by the traditions of our people and our law....[17]

Some might argue that Holmes was being hypocritical in *Lochner* because he seemed to read "his personal views" (which we may take to mean "non-dominant" views[18]) into the Constitution when he wrote the majority opinion in *Buck v. Bell.*[19] This case, which may exceed *Lochner* in its infamy,[20] rejected a Fourteenth Amendment challenge to a Virginia statute that authorized the forced sterilization of the daughter of a supposedly mentally disabled woman on grounds that "[t]hree generations of imbeciles are enough."[21] In rejecting the challenge, Holmes, writing for the Court, sought to vindicate "the general declarations of the Legislature," among which was the desire to prevent the state from being "swamped with incompetence" by "those who had already sapped the strength of the State."[22] Holmes seemed to suggest that eugenics was an established social norm in his day, and that the legislature had embraced this norm.[23] Thus, in both *Lochner* and *Buck v. Bell,* it could be argued that Holmes's policy-formulation does not go as far as policy-making. Indeed, in *Lochner,* Holmes rejected the majority's reading of the Fourteenth Amendment because, as he says in his dissent quoted above, "This case is decided upon an economic theory which *a large part of the country does not entertain.*"

As we shall see in the next section, later generations of legal realists envision a more assertive judiciary whether in the common-law or the constitutional context. But first, a look at the nonlegal influences on legal realism.

---

17. 198 U.S. 45, 75–76 (1905) (emphasis supplied).

18. My conception of policy-making is discussed in the Introduction. See Section C2 therein.

19. 274 U.S. 200 (1927).

20. See discussion in Chapter 1, Section A, supra.

21. 274 U.S. at 207. Neither Carrie Buck, her mother, nor her daughter was mentally retarded. They were simply poor and without effective legal representation. For an interesting account of the background of the case, see Roy L. Brooks, Gilbert P. Carrasco, Michael Selmi, *Civil Rights Litigation: Cases and Perspectives* 2nd edition (Durham: Carolina Academic Press, 2000), pp. 1055–56.

22. 274 U.S. at 207.

23. Ibid. See also Brooks, *Civil Rights Litigation,* supra note 21, at p. 1055. Yet, in his *Lochner* dissent Holmes seems to suggest that, at least in the employment context of 1905, Social Darwinism was not a dominant community norm.

2. Major Nonlegal Forces

Forces outside the law also gave shape to legal realism. In his classic work, *Social Thought in America: The Revolt Against Formalism* (1957), Morton White called attention "to a very strong cultural and intellectual tie between our most distinctive philosophy and our most distinctive philosophy of law."[24] White was referring to the relationship between pragmatism and legal realism. Pragmatism, "the search for fact, for concreteness, for truth behind appearances," was in the air everywhere in America from the closing decades of the 1800s to the 1930s. It was in education, literature, the arts, and social criticism.[25] Many of the legal realists named earlier in this chapter, particularly Llewellyn, Frank, Oliphant, Cook and Moore, had direct contact with Charles Sanders Peirce (1839–1914), William James (1842–1910), and John Dewey (1859–1952), the three most important American pragmatists.[26] Some legal realists taught at Columbia University during Dewey's long tenure there and, hence, were colleagues of his. All read and cited works authored by pragmatists. Holmes himself was a friend of both Peirce and James.[27]

While there is little doubt that legal realists were influenced by the pragmatists, there is a difference of opinion among legal scholars as to whether legal realism puts forth a conceptual and normative jurisprudence commensurate with pragmatism. Some, such as Michael Moore, argue that legal realism does not.[28] Others, such as Brian Leiter, argue that legal realism can be seen in the context of not only pragmatism, but also naturalism, which is the idea that the causal explanations we give (a descriptive task) shape the justifications we make (a normative task).[29] Still others, such as Robert Summers,

---

24. Morton White, *Social Thought in America: The Revolt Against Formalism* (Boston: Beacon Press, 1957), p. 62.

25. Yosal Rogat, "Legal Realism," *The Encyclopedia of Philosophy*, vol. 4, Paul Edwards, ed. (New York: The Macmillan Publishing Company and The Free Press, 1967), p. 421. See ibid. at p. 217.

26. See generally Louis Menand, *The Metaphysical Club: A Story of Ideas in America* (New York: Farrar, Straus and Giroux, 2001).

27. See generally, Martin, *Legal Realism*, supra note 10, at pp. 11–12; Morton J. Horwitz, *The Transformation of American Law: 1870–1960: The Crisis of Legal Orthodoxy* (New York: Oxford University Press, 1992), pp. 194–95; John Brigham, *The Constitution of Interests: Beyond the Politics of Rights* (New York: New York University Press, 1996), p. 59.

28. See Michael S. Moore, *Educating Oneself in Public: Critical Essays in Jurisprudence* (New York: Oxford University Press, 2000), pp. 30–37, 193–97.

29. See Leiter, "Rethinking Legal Realism," supra note 10; Leiter, "Positivism, Formalism, Realism," supra note 11.

argue that legal realism offers a sophisticated legal theory that can stand on its own.[30]

Legal realists were also influenced by economic changes taking place in America at the time. Three related developments took shape between the 1860s and 1920. First, the size of business organizations increased dramatically. In 1904, for example, "approximately 1 percent of the total number of businesses in the United States produced annually 40 percent of the nation's industrial goods." Some national markets, such as oil and tobacco, were controlled by a few businesses, sometimes just one.[31] Second, almost all the businesses in 1860 performed a single task, e.g., manufacturing, marketing, or financing. By 1920, almost all the dominant businesses were multi-unit enterprises, operating multiple smaller businesses.[32] Third, and perhaps most important, "the complexity and interconnectedness" of individual firms as well as the entire economic system increased dramatically. "The expansion of national and then international markets and the maturation of the financial system made the fates of many economic actors turn upon forces they neither controlled nor understood."[33]

Legal realists believed legal rules should keep pace with these important economic changes. As early as 1896, Holmes and other legal realists expressed the view that the law of torts should be consciously shaped to give greater attention to this economic transformation. Many argued that some form of enterprise liability—vicarious liability or even strict liability in some cases—should be imposed on firms to provide legal redress for the many torts committed in the normal operation of these new businesses. The underlying assumption of this view was that judges should not favor business interests, that indulging such interests was not the democratic way to achieve social and economic progress. This view of progress contrasts sharply with an earlier view

---

30. Robert Summers, *Institutionalism and American Legal Theory* (Ithaca, NY: Cornell University Press, 1982); Robert Summers, "On Identifying and Reconstructing a General Theory—Some Thoughts Prompted by Professor Moore's Critique," *Cornell Law Review* 69 (1984): 1014. The disagreement between Professors Summers and Moore about legal realism is ultimately a disagreement about what constitutes good legal theory. Professor Moore, as well as Professor Leiter, subscribe to H.L.A. Hart's notion about legal theory. See discussion in Preface. This book argues that legal realism is nominalistic in form. See discussion of judicial nominalism in Chapter 7, Section B1, infra.

31. *American Legal Realism*, William W. Fischer, III, Morton J. Horwitz, Thomas A. Reed, eds. (New York: Oxford University Press, 1993), pp. 130–32. This is part of the organized money phenomenon discussed in Chapter 1, Section B, supra.

32. *American Legal Realism*, supra note 31, at pp. 130–32.

33. Ibid.

expressed by such judges as Lemuel Shaw whose activism helped to lay the foundation for legal realism. Chief Justice Shaw and other judges of his era believed social and economic progress was best achieved by favoring business interests.[34] As we shall see in a moment, legal realists were considerably more liberal than Chief Justice Shaw, though no less activist.[35]

In 1885, the American Economic Association was founded on the basis of anti-laissez-faire, welfare statist principles. The association spoke out against business combinations, which were thought to be the inevitable result of free competition, and developed arguments for public ownership of monopolies, or at least their regulation. They also argued that government should intervene in the market to improve working conditions, prohibit child labor and protect unions. These arguments reflected the emerging twentieth-century movement in welfare liberalism.[36]

Legal realists aligned themselves politically with this movement.[37] They did so most prominently by targeting legal doctrines that stood in the way of liberal reforms. These doctrines were primarily the ones formalist judges read into the Fourteenth Amendment to protect private property and contracts—vested property rights, substantive due process, and liberty of contract—including the private/public distinction in law that underpinned these doctrines.[38] The gravamen of their argument was that these formalist legal doctrines as well as the line between the private domain (in which property and contracts are beyond the law's redistributive reach) and the public domain (which gives the government limited redistributive powers under its police powers) were artificial and not in the public's best interest. As Walter Volkomer explains:

> [T]he ability of some parties (e.g., employers) to force others (e.g., unskilled laborers) to enter into and abide by certain agreements depends to a large extent on the existence and enforcement of the law of contracts and property; . . . the content of the body of ostensibly

---

34. See discussion in Section C1, infra.

35. For a more detailed discussion of the tort reforms discussed in this paragraph, see, *American Legal Realism,* supra note 31, at pp. 132–33. See generally Edmund Ursin, "Judicial Creativity and Tort Law," *George Washington Law Review* 49 (1981): 229.

36. See Chapter 1, Section B, supra. See also Horwitz, *The Transformation of American Law,* supra note 27, at p. 166. For a discussion of the term "welfare liberalism," see Preface, Section B, supra.

37. See, e.g., Walter E. Volkomer, *The Passionate Liberal: The Political and Legal Ideas of Jerome Frank* (The Hague: Martinus Nijhoff, 1970).

38. See Chapter 1, Section C, supra.

'private' law is largely determined by 'public' policies (like fostering commerce, encouraging the transmission of property between generations in a nuclear family, or discouraging unionization); . . . that the state consequently is responsible to a substantial degree for the distribution of wealth and power.[39]

Legal realism's relentless attack on the private/public distinction obtained dramatic success in 1948 when the Supreme Court issued its opinion in *Shelley v. Kraemer.*[40] In that case, the justices held that judicial enforcement of private, racially discriminatory contracts (racially restrictive covenants) constituted "state action" within the meaning of the Fourteenth Amendment's Equal Protection Clause. The Court said: "in granting judicial enforcement of the restrictive agreements in these cases, the States have denied petitioners the equal protection of the laws."[41] While *Shelley v. Kraemer* can be viewed as a victory for legal realism, it has not torn down the wall separating the private and public spheres. The Supreme Court has not adopted the realist position that "if enforcement of private contracts is state action, then all private activity is public activity, and all private law is public."[42]

Social science advances in the academy had a profound impact on the methodological as well as the ideological development of legal realism. Following the social scientists, the legal realists asserted that the world "must be known through science if it is to be 'really' known."[43] Law, therefore, must be an empirical study of events. More than a body of rules, law is a set of facts that can and should be observed in the official acts of judges and other public officials. The legal skeptics, as legal realists were sometimes called, argued that they were not denying the existence of rules of law (engaging in what Morris Cohen called "nominalism"), but were simply insisting, in the words of Jerome Frank, that "legal rules exist and must be studied.... [K]nowledge of the rules is but a small part of what lawyers and judges use in their work and...a definition of law as rules does an injury to clear thinking about law."[44] Studying rules scientifically, legal realists came to what was certainly a radical opinion at the time—rule-

---

39. *American Legal Realism,* supra note 31, at p. 99. See also Horwitz, *The Transformation of American Law,* supra note 27, at pp. 165–67, 169–70.

40. 334 U.S. 1 (1948).

41. Ibid. at 19.

42. Horwitz, *The Transformation of American Law,* supra note 27, at p. 207.

43. Brigham, *The Constitution of Interests,* supra note 10, at p. 59.

44. Jerome Frank, "Are Judges Human?" *University of Pennsylvania Law Review* 80 (1931): 17, 44–45. See Paul, *The Legal Realism of Jerome N. Frank,* supra note 12, at pp. 24, 34.

skepticism. "Rules, whether stated by judges or others, whether in statutes, opinions or text-books by learned authors, are not the law, but are only some among many of the sources to which judges go in making the law of the cases tried before them."[45] Karl Llewellyn in *The Bramble Bush* embellished the notion of rule skepticism with this famous observation: "Within the law, I say,…rules guide, but they do not control decision. There is no precedent the judge may not at his need either file down to razor thinness or expand into a bludgeon."[46]

Frank's attack on the "myth" of rule-certainty, his insistence that law is not a body of rules, but a set of facts, found wide support among legal realists. It was, in fact, a binding belief among them. No doubt, Frank lost followers as he attempted to explain why judges, lawyers, and the public at large believed in rule-certainty. Borrowing from child psychologists, such as Jean Piaget, Frank argued that we hold onto rules as a substitute for our fathers. But even Frank did not accept this as a complete explanation. He viewed the notion of rule-certainty as a father-substitute to be only a "partial explanation."[47]

Frank was not only a rule-skeptic but also a fact-skeptic. Facts, Frank argued, are "subjective," because they are "those facts that are *found* by the judge and the jury, not the *actual* objective facts that took place in a particular place at a particular time *prior* to trial."[48] Furthermore, he asserted that "no one can prophesy which lawsuits will be 'contested' or what conflicting testimony will be introduced in a lawsuit."[49] By "contested" lawsuit, Frank meant "a case in which a question of fact is raised and in which conflicting testimony is introduced with respect to the facts in question."[50]

Using the following formula, Julius Paul summarizes how Frank conceptualizes the difference between the myth and the reality of judicial decision making:

> [T]he conventional formula is R (legal rules) x F (the facts of a case) gives D (the decision in the case). The actual process of adjudication, according to Frank, is S (all of the stimuli surrounding the judge and the case) x P (the personality of the judge) gives D (the decision). But the latter formula has no predictive value, so Frank uses this formula instead: R (legal rules) x SF (the subjective facts) gives D (the decision).[51]

---

45. Jerome Frank, *Law and the Modern Mind* (New York: Tudor Publishing, Co., 1936), p. 127.

46. Llewellyn, *The Bramble Bush*, supra note 2, at p. 180.

47. See, e.g., Paul, *The Legal Realism of Jerome N. Frank*, supra note 12, at pp. 24, 35, 73.

48. Ibid. at p. 73 (emphasis in original).

49. Frank, "Are Judges Human?," supra note 44, at p. 48.

50. Jerome Frank, "What Courts Do In Fact," *Illinois Law Review* 26 (1932): 645, 650 n.10.

51. Paul, *The Legal Realism of Jerome N. Frank*, supra note 12, at p. 73.

Frank's fact-skepticism caused a rift among the ranks of the legal realists. Some realists took it to its logical extension to mean unfettered judicial discretion. In other words, the judge's view of the facts was colored by his idiosyncracy, which made predicting future judicial outcomes impossible. Another group of legal realists took a different view. They argued that judicial decisions "fall into discernible patterns (making prediction possible), though the patterns are not those one would expect from examining the existing rules. Rather, the decisions fall into patterns correlated with the underlying factual scenarios of the disputes at issue." Hence, it is "the judicial response to...the distinctive factual pattern that determines the outcome of the case."[52]

C. Structure and Illustrations

With this understanding of the ideological underpinnings of legal realism, we can better understand how it operates as an expression of the policy method. Rule- and fact-skeptic, the judge moves from Point A to Point C by reacting to the underlying policies in the case. The judge exercises the judicial policy-formulation function in a manner that moves society forward. Usually, this entails no more than policy-discovery; however, policy-making, in the pursuit of progressive, typically welfare-liberal social ends, is a distinct possibility. Finally, rules are used almost as an afterthought to add legal cogency to the judge's reasoning. This process is well illustrated in the following cases.

1. Unwritten Law

An oft-cited illustration of legal realism in the common law context is a case that was decided nearly a century before the heyday of legal realism, and a half-century before the country and its political leaders would turn to welfare liberalism as the primary means of pursuing social progress.[53] Thus, the case, *Farwell v. Boston & Worcester R.R. Corp.*,[54] can only illustrate legal realism's judicial activism. Missing is the legal realist's "passionate liberalism."[55]

---

52. Leiter, "Positivism, Formalism, Realism," supra note 11, at p. 1148. See also Leiter, "Rethinking Legal Realism," supra note 10, at pp. 268–69.

53. For a discussion of welfare liberalism, see Preface, Section B, supra; Chapter 1, Section B, supra.

54. 45 Mass. 49 (1842).

55. See, e.g., Volkomer, *The Passionate Liberal: The Political and Legal Ideas of Jerome Frank*, supra note 37.

The author of *Farwell* was the Chief Justice of the Massachusetts Supreme Judicial Court, Lemuel Shaw. As Edmund Ursin points out, "Holmes was a great admirer of Shaw." Indeed:

> In *The Common Law*, Holmes wrote of Shaw that 'the strength of that great judge lay in an accurate appreciation of the requirements of the community whose officer he was.' Although Holmes conceded that '[s]ome, indeed many, English judges could be named who have surpassed him in accurate technical knowledge,' he argued that 'few have lived who were his equals in their understanding of the grounds of public policy to which all laws must ultimately be referred.'...Shaw's [judicial] process perspective is the premise of *The Common Law* as well as of Holmes's later work.[56]

The facts of the case were as follows. Two persons were employed by a railroad company. One was injured through the careless and negligent acts of the other while on the job. The injured party sued the railroad company for damages. The controlling law was an English precedent called the doctrine of *respondeat superior*. As stated by Chief Justice Shaw, "It is laid down by Blackstone, that if a servant [employee], by his negligence, does any damage to a stranger, the master [employer] shall be answerable for his neglect. But the damage must be done while he is actually employed in the master's service; otherwise, the servant shall answer for his own misbehavior."[57] Thus, an employer was vicariously liable for the wrongful acts committed by its employees against strangers, persons other than fellow employees. Justice Shaw was unwilling to extend the doctrine of *respondeat superior* to injuries committed by fellow employees. Instead, he adopted the "fellow-servant" rule, which barred an injured employee from recovering from his employer for on-the-job injuries committed by a fellow employee. Chief Justice Shaw then went beyond the facts of the case to adopt another doctrine that further limited the ability of employees to recover from their employers for on-the-job injuries. He adopted the doctrine of assumption of risk, which required employees to assume ordinary risks associated with their jobs.[58]

It is difficult to overstate the devastation Chief Justice Shaw's rulings caused to worker welfare. As Edmund Ursin explains:

---

56. Ursin, "Judicial Creativity," supra note 35, at pp. 271–72.
57. 45 Mass. at 55.
58. Ibid. at 56, 57, 59.

... [T]he fellow-servant rule and the doctrine of assumption of the risk, when coupled with the defense of contributory negligence (of which Shaw was a 'leading exponent'), left injured employees virtually without recourse when an injury occurred during their employment. Indeed, in the bulk of industrial accidents, injured workers were likely to be left with only a lawsuit against an equally poor fellow employee, and thus with no practical means of recovering for medical bills, lost wages, and the like. This outcome is representative of the general pattern of Shaw's holdings. The historian Leonard Levy in his study of Shaw concludes: '[T]he evidence drawn from case law...indicates that the Shaw court was biased in favor of railroads.'[59]

Although Chief Justice Shaw's reasoning lacked the liberalism of legal realists, it captured their judicial activism. The fellow-servant rule and the doctrine of assumption of risk were adopted by Chief Justice Shaw to effectuate and to add legal cogency to a policy preference—namely, the protection of the infant railroad industry—the judge felt needed to be imposed on the community. Chief Justice Shaw was willing to override the community's preference for civic republicanism—the belief that the government should pursue progress without indulging privilege or special interests[60]—for the sake of his own estimate of what it took to achieve social and economic progress.[61] As Ursin said earlier, Holmes admired Shaw's "accurate appreciation of the requirements of the community."[62]

---

59. Ursin, "Judicial Creativity," supra note 35, at p. 260 (citations omitted).

60. See Chapter 1, Section B, supra. *Charles River Bridge*, decided only 7 years before *Farwell*, captured the tenor of the times. There, the Supreme Court refused to indulge privilege as a means of achieving social progress. See ibid.

61. "The Chief Justice, like so many of his time, linked that which was beneficial to railroads with industrial expansion, which in turn was linked with the grand march of the Commonwealth toward a more prosperous life....Scholars are generally in agreement that the tort law of this era was responsive to the perceived need to protect infant industry from excessive liability." Ursin, "Judicial Creativity," supra note 35, at p. 260. Chief Justice Shaw's attitude toward railroads was consistent with special interest legislation enacted by some of the states. Then, as now, special interests were a constant threat to civic republicanism.

62. See Section C1, supra. Holmes permitted policy-making in common law cases. Judges in these cases where not limited to policy-discovery; there was no substantial-community-support requirement. See Introduction, Section C2, supra. As Auerbach, notes: "Nothing in Holmes' writings on the common law indicates that he would require common law judges to ascertain whether...policies have substantial popular support before using them to reach their decisions." Carl A. Auerbach, "A Rival of Some Ancient Learn-

2. Written Law

While Holmes would encourage judicial policy-making in the context of the unwritten law (but not in the context of the written law, as his reasoning in cases like *Lochner* and *Buck v. Bell* makes clear[63]), later generations of legal realists would permit policy-making in both areas of the law. True, legal realism's welfare liberalism was in sync with the policy aspirations of most Americans during its heyday (between 1929 and 1934[64]), and, to that extent, it did not counsel policy-making. However, the potential was there, and clearly manifested in cases like *Brown v. Board of Education.*[65] Indeed, *Brown* is often cited as a classic example of legal realism.

In *Brown*, the Supreme Court overturned state school segregation laws on the ground that such statutes violated constitutional equal protection. Although known among legal scholars and judges as the quintessential policy-method case, *Brown* can also be explained as a logical-method case. As discussed earlier,[66] Judge Aldisert demonstrates how the Supreme Court could have reached the same decision (or judgment) in the case by deductive reasoning. Even though legal realists would agree with the judgment the syllogism reaches, as it went in favor of the plaintiffs, they would jettison the syllogism in favor of a consequentialist approach to judicial decision making. Specifically, they would opt for an approach that is fact-skeptic, rule-skeptic, and produces progressive welfare liberal outcomes. This ultimately entails policy-making, as the following analysis illustrates.

A judge proceeding under the legal realist judicial model would give primary attention to the facts of the case. Policies, all important in legal realism, are derived from the facts; not the "actual objective" facts but the court's "subjective" facts. Accordingly, the Court in *Brown* begins by developing an understanding of the essential facts of the case—namely, gross inequality in facilities and per pupil spending on African American and white students attending racially segregated public schools in the South. These facts, which tell but a portion of the story about the African American educational experience at the time,[67] were well-documented in school desegregation litigation leading up to *Brown*. Using

---

ing: A Critique of Eisenberg's The Nature of the Common Law," *Minnesota Law Review* 75 (1991): 539, 551.

63. See Section B1, supra.
64. See Section A, supra.
65. 347 U.S. 483 (1954).
66. See discussion at end of Chapter 1, Section D, supra.
67. For a more complete telling of this story, see Section D, infra.

sociological research conducted by such eminent scholars as W.E.B. DuBois,[68] Horace Mann Bond,[69] and Gunnar Myrdal,[70] NAACP lawyers were able to document substantial racial inequality in school buildings, per pupil expenditures for textbooks and equipment, and teacher salaries throughout the South, even among African American and white schools in the same school district. "[T]he typical black teacher labored in a poorly equipped classroom, taught larger classes for fewer days per year, and earned less doing it than did her white counterpart."[71] Southern states frequently allocated 2 to 5 times more money per pupil to white students than to African American students.[72] Testifying during the trial phase of *Briggs v. Elliot*[73] as to the condition of the African American schools in Clarendon County, South Carolina, Matthew Whitehead stated:

> The total value of the buildings, grounds, and furnishings of the two white schools that accommodated 276 children was four times as high as the total for the three Negro schools that accommodated a total of 808 students. The white schools were constructed of brick and stucco; there was one teacher for each 28 children; at the colored schools, there was one teacher for each 47 children. At the white high school, there was only one class with an enrollment as high as 24; at the Scott's Branch high school for Negroes, classes ranged from 33 to 47. Besides the courses offered at both schools, the curriculum at the white high school included biology, typing, and bookkeeping; at the black high school, only agriculture and home economics were offered.

---

68. See W.E.B. DuBois and Augustus Dill, *The Common School and the Negro American* (New York: Russell and Russell, 1969, originally published in 1911).

69. See Horace Mann Bond, *The Education of the Negro in the American Social Order* (New York: Octagon Books, 1966, originally published in 1934); Horace Mann Bond, *Negro Education in Alabama: A Study in Cotton and Steel* (New York: Octagon Books, 1969, originally published in 1939).

70. See Gunnar Myrdal, *An American Dilemma: The Negro Problem and Modern Democracy* (New York: Harper and Brothers, 1944).

71. Robert A. Margo, *Race and Schooling in the South, 1880–1950: An Economic History* (Chicago: University of Chicago Press, 1990), p. 56. "In the Deep South States of Louisiana and Mississippi, black teachers earned about 80 percent of what white teachers earned [in 1980]." Ibid. at p. 54. See also, Thurgood Marshall, "Teacher Salary Cases" in *The Negro Handbook 1946–1947*, Florence Murray, ed. (New York: A. A. Wynn, 1947), pp. 40–50.

72. Walter G. Stephan, *Blacks and Brown: The Effects of School Desegregation on Black Students* (prepared for the United States Department of Education, National Institute of Education, 1983), p. 3 (sources cited therein).

73. 98 F. Supp. 529 (1951).

There was no running water at one of the two outlying colored grade schools and no electricity at the other one. There were indoor flush toilets at both white schools but no flush toilets, indoors or outdoors, at any of the Negro schools—only outhouses, and not nearly enough of them.[74]

With this understanding of the essential facts, the Court begins its legal analysis. Rule-skeptic, the Court does not feel constrained to begin its reasoning with *Plessy v. Ferguson*'s holding, as legal formalists would do. In other words, the Court does not feel bound by *Plessy*'s interpretation of the Fourteenth Amendment's Equal Protection Clause—namely, separate and equal facilities are permitted under the Constitution, but separate and unequal facilities are not. Using *Plessy* as precedent does not afford the Court the flexibility needed to rest its reasoning on a liberal value—equal educational opportunity, or racial equality—inherent in the facts of the case. This value goes to the heart of the case. It, therefore, needs to go into the heart of the Court's reasoning. Starting its reasoning with the Fourteenth Amendment's Equal Protection Clause itself—"No State shall...deny to any person within its jurisdiction the equal protection of the laws"—gives the Court enough space in which to incorporate the racial equality value into its reasoning.

To be sure, there are competing policy considerations in the factual pattern before the Court, comity and freedom of association primarily. But from the Court's perspective, these countervailing policies are outweighed by the more progressive racial-equality policy. Thus, the Supreme Court gives the Equal Protection Clause a progressive and liberal interpretation, one that has the potential of moving society forward socially and educationally, and one that attempts to rescue African Americans from a life of racial inequality.[75]

To reach this construction of the Equal Protection Clause, the Court had to frame the issue of the case as a *frontal attack* on rather than as an embrace of *Plessy*:

Does segregation of children in public schools solely on the basis of race, even though the physical facilities and other 'tangible' factors may be equal, deprive the children of the minority group equal educational opportunities? We believe that it does....To separate negro children from others of a similar age and qualifications solely because of their race generates a feeling of inferiority as to their status in the

---

74. Richard Kluger, *Simple Justice* (New York: Alfred A. Knopf, 1976), p. 332.
75. See Preface, Section B, supra, for a discussion of these terms.

community that may affect their hearts and minds in a way unlikely ever to be undone.... 'Segregation of white and colored children in public schools has a detrimental effect upon the colored children. The impact is greater when it has the sanction of the law; for the policy of separating the races is usually interpreted as denoting the inferiority of the negro group. A sense of inferiority affects the motivation of a child to learn'.... We conclude that in the field of public education the doctrine of 'separate but equal' has no place. Separate educational facilities are inherently unequal.[76]

This frontal attack on *Plessy* is about as thorough or complete as it can be. Not only does the Court reject *Plessy's* interpretation of the Constitution, it also rejects *Plessy's* findings as to the socio-psychological effect segregation has on African Americans. Chief Justice Warren finds the "psychological knowledge at the time of *Plessy v. Ferguson*" to be unsupported by "modern authority." Furthermore, he rejects "any language in *Plessy v. Ferguson* contrary to" the finding that segregation in public schools is detrimental to the hearts and minds of African American children.[77]

The imposition of the racial equality value—defined in *Brown* as equal educational opportunity and refined in subsequent Supreme Court cases to include racial integration[78]—on the southern states was an act of policy-making. Southerners were not ready to accept this value. They made their views on the matter abundantly clear not only by the arguments they advanced in *Brown*, but also by their open racial hostility, including the passage of numerous segregation statutes such as the ones before the Court. Such judicial assertiveness was warranted, legal realists argued, because the federal government should not permit "a massive intentional disadvantaging of the Negro race, as such, by state law."[79] "When the directive of equality cannot be followed without displeasing white[s], then something that can be called a 'freedom' of the white[s] must be impaired."[80]

There is a sense in which *Brown* can also be viewed as a policy-vindication opinion. Effectuating the racial equality value in the context of the national

---

76. 347 U.S. at 494.

77. Ibid. at 493–94.

78. See, e.g., *United States v. Hall*, 472 F.2d 261, 265 (5th Cir. 1972) (cases cited). See generally Roy L. Brooks, *Rethinking the American Race Problem* (Berkeley: University of California Press, 1990), pp. 25–33.

79. Charles Black, "The Lawfulness of the Segregation Decisions," *Yale Law Journal* 69 (1960): 421, 421.

80. Ibid. at p. 429. See also Michael Heyman, "The Chief Justice, Racial Segregation, and the Friendly Critics," *California Law Review* 49 (1961): 104; Louis Pollack, "Racial Dis-

community—a community that is coextensive with the federal judiciary's jurisdiction—or in the context of northern states that had passed school desegregation statutes or anti-discrimination laws similar to the Constitution's Equal Protection Clause is policy-vindication, not policy-making. Racial equality, in these contexts, is an articulated value; it has already been put into play by extant laws.[81] Policy-vindication under such progressive and liberal circumstances would be an acceptable form of judicial decision making for legal realists.[82]

D. Criticisms

Brown illustrates legal realism's flaws as well as its virtues. While it places the judge in a position to "do the right thing," legal realism also places her on a pedestal. The judge is positioned as a kind of philosopher-king, capable of wisely resolving any problem over which he can exercise jurisdiction. This notion of the judge often founders on the shoals of reality. In *Brown*, for example, none of the federal judges, including the Supreme Court justices, fully understood the social science data on which they made factual findings. The famous "dolls test" that was used to establish as a legal fact the proposition that "segregation produced confusion in African American children and proved debilitating to their development of a healthy sense of self-worth," on closer examination "actually revealed a *lesser* percentage of out-group preference among southern children who attended segregated schools than among northern children who attended racially mixed schools."[83] Also, "racial anguish…was more prevalent among integrated than segregated children."[84] In the end, "[t]hese findings tend to contradict the [social scientists] and the Supreme Court's conclusion that segregation (certainly more than integration) debilitated the African American child's sense of self-worth."[85]

Brown's central legal ruling—"separate educational facilities are inherently unequal"—has been criticized by African American scholars on the political right as well as the political left. Conservative Supreme Court Justice Clarence

---

crimination and Judicial Integrity: A Reply to Professor Wechsler," *University of Pennsylvania Law Review* 108 (1959): 1.

81. See Introduction, Section C2, supra.

82. For a more detailed discussion of this aspect of *Brown*, see Chapter 4, Section D3, infra.

83. Brooks, *Rethinking the American Race Problem*, supra note 78, at p. 14.

84. Ibid.

85. Ibid.

Thomas, for example, faults *Brown* for creating "a jurisprudence based upon a theory of black inferiority."[86] Liberal Alex Johnson flat out states that *"Brown* was a mistake."[87] *Brown* was not only factually wrong, but it has helped to spread a negative image of African Americans that continues to dog them to this day. This image suggests that a black child must capture a white child to obtain a quality education. Perhaps most deleterious to African Americans today, *Brown's* central legal ruling has prevented the Court from drawing a crucial distinction between racial segregation (involuntary racial isolation meant to stigmatize a race) and racial separation (voluntary racial isolation that promotes self-help).[88] Both forms of racial isolation have been held to be unconstitutional. As the Court said in *Brown*, " 'separate but equal' has no place [in our Constitution]."[89] (Compare the critical theorists' approach to *Brown* in Part 2.)

If there is one thing that jurists from Justices Thomas and Scalia at the federal level to Judge Robert Satter at the state level, and that scholars from Fred Schauer, a proponent of the logical method, to Ronald Dworkin, an adherent to a moralist policy method, have in common it is their criticisms of legal realism. All believe legal realism's policy-making feature is, to quote Dworkin, "lawless." Although each defines policy-making as the judge's assertion of "personal" values,[90] their collective criticism applies with equal force to the clarifying definition of policy-making used in this book.[91] When a judge imposes values on a community before the community is ready to accept them, she acts in an imperialist fashion. She undermines the traditional relationship between the judiciary and the legislature—the notion that judges apply law and legislators and the people make policy through the legislative and constitutional processes, respectively.[92]

The claim of institutional illegitimacy is often met with an argument most forcibly made by Charles Black in 1960. In his book, *The People and the Court: Judicial Review in a Democracy*,[93] meant to be a defense of Warren Court ac-

---

86. Ibid. at p. 17.
87. Ibid.
88. Ibid. at pp. 204–5.
89. 347 U.S. at 494. See Roy L. Brooks, *Integration or Separation? A Strategy for Racial Equality* (Cambridge: Harvard University Press, 1996), pp. 204–5.
90. See Introduction, Section C2, supra.
91. See ibid.
92. For further discussion of the legitimacy question, see, e.g., Ronald Dworkin, *Law's Empire* (Cambridge, Mass.: Belknap Press, 1986); Leiter, "Rethinking Legal Realism," supra note 10, at pp. 267–68.
93. Charles L. Black, *The People and the Court: Judicial Review in a Democracy* (New York: The Macmillan Co., 1960).

tivism, Black argues that policy-making performed in the execution of the Supreme Court's institutional obligation to determine the constitutionality of acts of Congress and state legislation (i.e., the doctrine of judicial review),[94] is a necessary feature of a democratic society. Judicial policy-making makes democratic government possible; for, it enables the Supreme Court to stand in the path of unjust majorities, both local and national. If the Supreme Court did not speak out against state segregation statutes in *Brown v. Board of Education* or against the federal school segregation law in *Bolling v. Sharpe*,[95] *Brown*'s companion case, who would have?

There is typically a two-fold rejoinder to this argument. First, policy-making is quite acceptable so long as the preferred policies are of the sacred, high-minded type imposed on the South in *Brown*. But what happens if the Court, as in the *Lochner* Era, imposes less lofty policies on the community?[96] What does one do in that case? Unelected, the justices cannot be kicked out of office at the next election. That, indeed, is why President Roosevelt resorted to his controversial Court-packing plan in 1937. This strategy nearly caused a constitutional crisis, however, which was narrowly averted when the "old nine men" lost their majority through retirement.[97] The door swings both ways.

The second rejoinder goes to the appearance of judicial impartiality. Judges who engage in policy-making soil their robes by entering the hurly-burly world of politics. They create at least the appearance, if not the reality, of taking sides. When judges lose their appearance of impartiality, they also lose any justification for the deference they are normally accorded.

Lon Fuller raised yet another problem as far back as 1934. Rule-skepticism—the belief that legal rules are questionable because reality is too amorphous and complex to be tamed by rules[98]—can be carried too far. Legal realism seems to be saying that because all legal concepts inevitably distort reality ("Rules are made up of concepts, and concepts are but the shadowy figments of our own minds, wholly unworthy of the simple faith the conceptualist places in them"[99]), we should not trust universals and abstractions. This tends toward "nominalism," "the belief that universals exist only in the mind of the

94. See *Marbury v. Madison*, 1 Cranch 137, 2 L.Ed. 60 (1803).

95. 347 U.S. 497 (1954).

96. See Chapter 1, Section E, supra.

97. See William H. Rehnquist, "The American Constitutional Experience: Remarks of the Chief Justices," *Louisiana Law Review* 54 (1994): 1161, 1171. See Chapter 1, Section A, supra.

98. See Section B2, supra.

99. Fuller, "American Legal Realism," supra note 3, at pp. 443–44.

individual."[100] Fuller's charge of anti-conceptualism is somewhat of a harbinger of the charge made against postmodernism in critical theory.[101]

A final criticism of legal realism has to do with its stance on the coextensiveness of law and morality. Michael Martin sees a contradiction in the legal realist position that legal issues and moral issues should be separate in the actual execution of the policy-formulation function:

> …American legal realists, like the legal positivists, advocated separating what law is from what it should be morally, thus rejecting the view of natural-law theory that law and morality were conceptually connected. But, despite what critics say, this separation did nothing to prevent moral evaluation of the law; in fact, it is compatible with allowing for the influence of morality on the law. Indeed, American legal realists argued that extralegal factors such as moral beliefs influenced judicial decisions. Moreover, nothing in the position of American legal realism would prevent it from acknowledging that empirical knowledge is relevant but not determinative in making policy. The American legal realists would have thought it obvious that ethical and value considerations are crucial in making social and legal policy. However, like legal positivists, they would have insisted that policy questions about what the law is be separated from questions of what it should be.[102]

Roscoe Pound, the creator of sociological jurisprudence, our next judicial model, took a different stance. For him, there was no separating law from morality.

---

100. Ibid.
101. See Chapter 9, Section C3, infra.
102. Martin, *Legal Realism*, supra note 10, at p. 81.

Chapter 4
Sociological Jurisprudence

Sociological jurisprudence prescribes a judicial method that enforces progressive and ethical rules certified by social science,[1] limited by policy-discovery in the context of the unwritten law and policy-vindication in the context of the written law. The goal in moving from Point A to Point C is to close the gap between law-in-theory and law-in-action by using the "is" of sociology to produce the "ought" of law.

A. Background

Sociological jurisprudence emerged as part of the late-nineteenth-century attack on legal formalism.[2] To this extent, it aligns itself with progressive legal scholars.[3] During the late 1920s, however, sociological jurisprudents took issue with what they perceived to be extreme pronouncements of judicial policy-formulation coming from the legal realists, scholars with whom they had had an agreeable relationship in the early struggle against legal formalism. It is as much the fight with legal realism as the struggle against legal formalism that defines sociological jurisprudence. Hence, both conflicts are discussed in this chapter.[4]

The persons most associated with sociological jurisprudence are Eugen Ehrlich (1862–1922) and Roscoe Pound (1870–1964). For Ehrlich, "[t]he quest for the 'living law'—the law that actually governs human conduct—was an absolute necessity."[5] Thus, Ehrlich distinguished between what he called the "positive law" (formal law, specifically statutory law) and the "living law" (social customs, or the law society actually followed). He argued that positive

---

1. Roscoe Pound, the creator of sociological jurisprudence, believed in social engineering, not unlike legal realists. But, unlike legal realists, he believed such welfare liberalism should come through the legislature and not through the courts. See Sections B, C, & D2, infra. For a more general discussion of the politico-economic aspirations of sociological jurisprudence, see Preface, Section B, supra.

2. See Chapter 1, Section B, supra.

3. See Chapter 3, Section A, supra.

4. See, e.g., Morton J. Horwitz, *The Transformation of American Law, 1870–1960: The Crisis of Legal Orthodoxy* (New York: Oxford University Press, 1992), pp. 7, 193.

5. Carl A. Auerbach, "The Relation of Legal Systems to Social Change," *Wisconsin Law Review* 1980 (1980): 1227, 1257.

law is ineffective when incongruent with living law. For example, the 55 m.p.h. speed limit imposed by the federal government to save gas during the oil shortage of the 1970s was largely ignored by motorists who were accustomed to traveling at 65 m.p.h. Thus, Ehrlich's great contribution to a sociological understanding of law was to focus attention on the distinction between "what the lawmakers felt people should do and what people felt was right."[6]

Perhaps no scholar is more closely identified with the introduction and development of sociological jurisprudence than Roscoe Pound, a prolific scholar and one of the great deans of Harvard Law School.[7] As early as 1905, Pound articulated the need for a jurisprudence founded on a knowledge of the social and political sciences.[8] But it was not until 1911 and 1912 that he was able to announce the emergence of sociological jurisprudence as a complete theory of law, outlining its purpose and scope.

B. Basic Approach

Pound's approach to law began with a criticism of two opposing theories of judicial decision making: legal formalism and legal realism.

1. Criticism of Legal Formalism

As much a rejection of the logical method as a criticism of legal formalism, Pound's judicial theory maintained that syllogistic or deductive judicial reasoning produced law that was "backward[]...in meeting social ends."[9] Pound offered two explanations as to why this was so. First, law teaching and legal scholarship during legal formalism's heyday were greatly influenced by the values of an "individualistic agricultural society," while society had become more

---

6. Sheryl J. Grana and Jane C. Ollenburger, *The Social Context of Law* (Upper Saddle River, N.J.: Prentice-Hall, Inc., 1999), p. 34.

7. For a synthesis of Pound's juristic theory and philosophy, see Roscoe Pound, *Jurisprudence* (St. Paul: West Publishing Co., 1959) written in five volumes. A bibliography of Pound's writings up to 1940 lists 15 books and 241 major articles. Edwin W. Patterson, *Jurisprudence: Men and Ideas of Law* (Brooklyn: Foundation Press, 1953), p. 511. Pound was born in 1870 and died in 1964. The best biography on Pound is David Wigdor, *Roscoe Pound: Philosopher of Law* (Westport, Conn.: Greenwood Press, 1974).

8. Roscoe Pound, "Do We Need a Philosophy of Law?" *Columbia Law Review* 5 (1905): 339, 344, 351. See also, Edward White, "From Sociological Jurisprudence to Realism: Jurisprudence and Social Change in Early Twentieth-Century America," *Virginia Law Review* 58 (1972): 999, 1004.

9. Ibid. at p. 510.

"interdependent, urbanized, [and] industrial."[10] Second, and more fundamentally, the logical method's mechanical approach to judicial decision making (what Pound called "mechanical jurisprudence") simply could not keep up with rapid social change.[11] Although he repeatedly condemned mechanical jurisprudence, Pound noted that it might be useful in the fields of property law and commercial transactions, because one fee simple is like every other, and one promissory note is like another.[12]

Overall, Pound criticized the attempt by formalist judges to decide cases syllogistically.[13] "Law, then, is not the simple thing that we sought to make it in our legal theory in the last century," Pound contended. "It is not something established definitely and absolutely by the will of the sovereign."[14] Law has a purpose, Pound wrote, and that purpose is "the administration of justice." As Pound wrote:

> Law...must be judged by the results it achieves, not by the niceties of its internal structure, it must be valued by the extent to which it meets its end, not by the beauty of its logical processes or the strictness with which its rules proceed from dogmas it takes for foundation.[15]

Pound not only criticized the methodology of legal formalism—the logical method, the tradition of Harvard's legendary dean, Christopher Columbus Langdell—but he also found fault with its ideology—minimalism.[16] He was very much a person of his times, the Progressive Era in American history.[17] It is little wonder, then, that Pound would later list progress as one of the interests law should serve.[18] We shall say a bit more about these interests later in this chapter.

---

10. Horwitz, *The Transformation of American Law*, supra note 4, at p. 188.

11. Ibid.

12. See, Roscoe Pound, "The Theory of Judicial Decision," *Harvard Law Review* 36 (1923): 940, 952.

13. See, White, "Jurisprudence and Social Change," supra note 8, at p. 1003.

14. Roscoe Pound, "The Theory of Judicial Decision," supra note 12, at pp. 641, 660.

15. Roscoe Pound, "Mechanical Jurisprudence," *Columbia Law Review* 8 (1908): 605, 605. See Roscoe Pound, "Liberty of Contract," *Yale Law Journal* 18 (1909): 454, 462.

16. See Neil Duxbury, *Patterns of American Jurisprudence* (New York: Oxford University Press, 1995), p. 54. See Preface, Section B, supra,& Chapter 1, Section B, supra, for a discussion of minimalism.

17. See Chapter 1, Section B, supra, & Chapter 3, Section B2, supra.

18. See Roscoe Pound, *Outlines of Lectures on Jurisprudence* 5th ed. (Cambridge, Mass.: Harvard University Press, 1943), pp. 104–11; Patterson, *Jurisprudence*, supra note 7, at pp. 523–24. For a definition of the word "progress," see Preface, Section B, supra.

Pound sought to create in sociological jurisprudence a jurisprudence considerably more instrumental and consequential than anything theretofore produced through the logical method. Specifically, he wanted law to be a science in the sense of what we now think of social engineering. He wanted to create the means by which social problems could be resolved through the legal order. "The sociological movement in jurisprudence," Pound said, "is a movement for pragmatism as a philosophy of law; for the adjustment of principles and doctrines to the human conditions they are to govern rather than to assume first principles; for putting the human factor in the central place...."[19]

A comparison between sociological jurisprudence and the sociology of law gives us a more precise understanding of the former. Both concepts are closely related. In fact, "the emergence of sociological jurisprudence paralleled the development of the socialization of law."[20] As Edward McLean explains, quoting Pound:

> 'The one [sociological jurisprudence] is a theoretical, the other [sociology of law] an applied science.' Sociological jurisprudence...focuses on the social control exercised by law....The means needed for the successful ordering of society, Pound feels, cannot be fashioned without expanding the scope of legal inquiry so that it incorporates data drawn from other sciences directed to the understanding of social order.[21]

In short, sociological jurisprudence, like legal realism, makes the essential claim that law should adjust relations and interests to achieve social justice. "Legal precepts are to be regarded more as guides to results which are socially just and less as inflexible molds."[22]

2. Criticism of Legal Realism

Although critical of legal formalism, Pound did not want to go as far as legal realism. He had no taste for its judicial swagger.[23] Pound argued that:

---

19. Pound, "Mechanical Jurisprudence," supra note 15, at p. 610. See Edward B. McLean, *Law and Civilization: The Legal Thought of Roscoe Pound* (Lanham, Maryland: University Press of America, 1992), p. 201.

20. McLean, *The Legal Thought of Roscoe Pound*, supra note 19, at p. 199.

21. Ibid.

22. Roscoe Pound, "The Scope and Purpose of Sociological Jurisprudence," *Harvard Law Review* 25 (1912): 489, 516.

23. See note 1, supra, in addition to this subsection. See also Section C, infra.

Radical non-realism seems to deny that there are rules or principles or conceptions of doctrines at all, because all judicial action, or at times much judicial action, can not be referred to them; because there is no definite determination whereby we may be absolutely assured that judicial action will proceed on the basis of one rather than another of two competing principles;...because much takes place within the course of adjudication which does not fit precisely into the doctrinal plan. Such a view is not without its use as a protest against the assumption that law is nothing but a simple aggregate of rules. But nothing would be more unreal...than to conceive of the administration of justice...as a mere aggregate of single determinations.[24]

Pound's criticism of legal realism raised the wrath of Karl Llewellyn, Jerome Frank, and other legal realists who branded him an apostate for having criticized a theory of law he himself helped to create.[25] Pound, however, felt justified in his criticism of legal realism. He did not want the canon—the policy method—that he had helped to articulate to be hijacked by policy-making.[26] Instead, he proposed a middle ground between legal formalism and legal realism.

C. Structure

Presaging legal process, discussed in the next chapter, Pound believed the judiciary's policy-formulation function should be constrained in light of the courts' limited fact-finding capability and nondemocratic character. To this extent, my reading of Pound is consistent with that of Edmund Ursin, who argues that "Pound stressed both competence and political accountability arguments for limiting the judicial role."[27] Ursin, however, goes on to observe in a footnote: "Pound at times envisioned what appears to be a more creative role for the judiciary."[28] As we shall see, these seemingly conflicting views of

---

24. Roscoe Pound, "The Call for a Realistic Jurisprudence," *Harvard Law Review* 44 (1931): 697, 707–8.

25. See, e.g., Karl Llewellyn, "Some Realism About Realism—Responding to Dean Pound," *Harvard Law Review* 44 (1931): 1222.

26. For other differences between Pound and the legal realists, see, e.g., N.E.H. Hull, *Roscoe Pound and Karl Llewellyn: Searching for an American Jurisprudence* (Chicago: University of Chicago Press, 1997), pp. 144–45.

27. Edmund Ursin, "Judicial Creativity and Tort Law," *George Washington Law Review* 49 (1981): 229, 279–80.

28. Ibid. at p. 280 n.328.

Pound's judicial theory are consistent if contextualized. Pound allowed for a more "active" judiciary in common law cases than in statutory or constitutional cases. For reasons of competency and accountability, Pound argued that judges must defer to the written law. Hence, through sociological jurisprudence, Pound constructed a system of judicial decision making that consisted of policy-discovery in common law cases and policy-vindication in statutory and constitutional cases. Policy-making was not permitted in any context.

These features of sociological jurisdiction can be seen in several of Pound's works, beginning with an important article titled, "The Scope and Purpose of Sociological Jurisprudence," in which Pound writes: "The main problem to which sociological jurists are addressing themselves today is to enable and compel law-making, and also interpretation and application of legal rules, to take more account...of the social facts upon which law must proceed and to which it is to be applied."[29] To illustrate his views, Pound points approvingly to Judge Winslow's judicial philosophy expressed in *Borgnis v. Falk Co.*:[30]

> Public policy on a given subject is determined either by the Constitution itself or by statutes passed within constitutional limitations. In the absence of such constitutional or statutory determination only may the decisions of the courts determine it.... [W]here the Legislature has not spoken on a subject, and the courts in the course of their duty have declared the principle of common law applicable thereto, public policy may be truly said to be thus created.[31]

This quotation suggests that Pound, by way of Judge Winslow, believes courts are limited to policy-vindication in statutory and constitutional matters but free to create public policy in the common law setting.[32] Although the word "create" at the end of the above quotation seems to suggest otherwise, I believe neither Judge Winslow nor certainly Pound subscribed to the notion that judges are free to "make" public policy (i.e., impose policy on unaccepting communities[33]) even in common law cases. Pound's view of the judiciary's policy-formulation function did not envision a judge forcing policy down the throat of an unwilling community. His strong criticism of policy-making,

---

29. Pound, "The Scope and Purpose of Sociological Jurisprudence," supra note 22, at pp. 512–13.

30. 133 N. W. 209 (1911).

31. Ibid. at 216. See Pound, "The Scope and Purpose of Sociological Jurisprudence," supra note 22, at p. 513 n.94.

32. See Section D, infra.

33. See Introduction, Section C2, supra, for the book's definition of "policy-making."

whether in pursuit of welfare-statist outcomes under legal realism or mini-malist ends under legal formalism, makes it prudent to read the word "create" in Judge Winslow's opinion to mean "discover." Furthermore, Pound did not believe in social ordering through private dispute resolutions: "It is a sound instinct of the community that objects to the settlement of questions of the highest social impact in private litigations between John Doe and Richard Roe."[34] Hence, common law judges are free to discover public policy, not cre-ate public policy. They are free, in other words, to find unarticulated norms a community is ready to accept or has already accepted, but they are not free to impose unwanted norms on a community.[35]

Pound understood that a judge is often called upon to choose from conflict-ing community interests or values. It is therefore important for a judge to have a clear picture of the judiciary's institutional role in our government. For this reason Pound sought to articulate the social ends of policy-discovery and pol-icy-vindication or, more generally, the judicial function. He asserted that the judiciary, and the whole of law as well, must promote "social interests."[36] Pound articulated six classes of social interests, general progress and morality being the most important.[37] Judges, then, are to discover and vindicate public policies that will lead to social progress and, at the same time, add to the moral life of the community. This is very much a value-laden process. Interests must be weighed and balanced not solely in the pursuit of progress,[38] as legal realists would have it, but also in the pursuit of morally acceptable outcomes.[39]

---

34. Roscoe Pound, "Common Law and Legislation," *Harvard Law Review* 21 (1908): 382, 404.

35. Support for this reading of Pound can be found in the works of other scholars as well. Edward McLean, for example, suggests that Pound's concept of social engineering en-visioned the judge as an engineer of man's behavior. The judge is neither a creator nor de-stroyer of social interests. Instead, she merely facilitates social change by protecting emerg-ing social interests. See McLean, *The Legal Thought of Roscoe Pound*, supra note 19, at pp. 200–5.

36. Pound, *Outlines of Lectures On Jurisprudence*, supra note 18, at pp. 104–11; Pat-terson, *Jurisprudence*, supra note 7, at p. 524. Professor Patterson, a distinguished legal scholar in his own right, was a fellow traveler, an intellectual friend of Pound.

37. "Social interest in general security"; "social interest in security of social institutions"; "social interest in general morals"; "social interest in conservation of social resources"; "so-cial interest in general progress"; "social interest in the individual life." Pound, *Outlines of Lectures on Jurisprudence*, supra note 18, at pp. 104–11; Patterson, *Jurisprudence*, supra note 7, at pp. 523–24.

38. See Preface, Section B, supra, for a definition of the word "progressive."

39. For further discussion of the balancing test, see McLean, *The Legal Thought of Roscoe Pound*, supra note 19, at pp. xv–xvi.

Moral decision making is, indeed, an important component of sociological jurisprudence. Pound argued for a close relationship between law and morality. He believed the judge should frame in his mind's eye an ideal picture of the social and legal order, infused with utilitarian moral principles, and render decisions that bring this image to life. The effectiveness of law depends upon this union of law and morality:

> In general law cannot depart far from ethical custom nor lag far behind it. For law does not enforce itself. Its machinery must be set in motion and kept in motion and guided in its motion by individual human beings; and there must be something more than the abstract content of the legal precept to move these human beings to act and to direct their action.[40]

Pound, in short, believed law that was both socially progressive and morally acceptable to the community was the best way to close the gap between, in the words of Ehrlich, "what the lawmakers felt people should do and what people felt was right."[41]

D. Illustrations

Having clarified the structure of sociological jurisprudence, let us consider some examples of its basic application in common law, statutory, and constitutional settings. This exercise should help crystallize our understanding of Pound's approach to judicial decision making.

1. Common Law Setting

Unfortunately, Pound gives no clear illustrations of the application of his theory in common law cases. The following hypothetical, however, illustrates Pound's view. It is an extension of Lon Fuller's catcher's mitt story presented in the Introduction.[42] Assume Jack Jones sues the baseball team of which he is a member for taking away his baseball mitt and giving it to Sue Smith, a teammate, who is a better player at Jones's position. If Jones is going to sit on the bench and not play, he wants his mitt to sit with him. He also wants to retain his position on the team. Jones's legal theory is the common law tort of trespass, which lies

---

40. Roscoe Pound, *Law and Morals* (Chapel Hill: University of North Carolina Press, 1924), p. 122.
41. Grana and Ollenburger, *The Social Context of Law*, supra note 6, at p. 34.
42. See Introduction, Section C2, supra.

against those charged with direct and immediate aggression to the person, chattels or land of the plaintiff.[43] Alternatively, Jones charges breach of contract in which he alleges that players have an implied agreement with management that permits players to exercise control over the equipment they bring to the team.[44] How might a judge proceeding under sociological jurisprudence rule?

The issue is whether the team is liable to Jones in tort or contract. A judge might rule that once a player voluntarily joins a team, he or she waives all claims against the team, in tort or contract, arising from the allocation of equipment among players, that such player cedes control of any equipment brought to the team while remaining a member of the team. If other cases higher in rank suggest a different ruling, the judge will simply distinguish them on their facts or narrowly interpret the ruling for which they stand.

Note, however, that the actual basis of the judge's waiver ruling is a progressive and ethical public policy discovered by the judge from extant community values. Such a policy might be one that favors apportioning equipment in accordance with player ability. A competing policy, also taken from community expectations, is one that favors apportionment based on ownership. The latter public policy, which certainly helps plaintiff's case, is weaker because it is arguably less progressive and utilitarian than the former public policy. In other words, the player-ability policy is progressive because the team, which is the relevant community here, is likely to win more games with it. Likewise, the policy is utilitarian because it is likely to bring the greatest happiness to the team as a whole. This conclusion is, of course, only a projection based on social science data, perhaps a survey of the players' views. No one actually goes out and assesses the rule's effect in the case *sub judice*. This is not sociology of law; it is sociological jurisprudence.[45]

One might wonder how progressive or ethical the player-ability policy would be under a different set of facts. Suppose, for example, the baseball team was by design less competitive. Suppose it was a little league team rather than a professional team. Perhaps other public policies, not necessarily the equipment-ownership policy, might prove to be more progressive or more ethical.

It is important to be able to see the structure of sociological jurisprudence analysis in the resolution of the above hypothetical.[46] Analysis begins at Point

---

43. See, e.g., *Waco Cotton Oil Mill of Waco v. Walker*, 103 S.W.2d 1071, 1072 (1937).

44. This assumes, of course, that Jones is able to allege the conditions of an implied contract. See, e.g., *Bowen v. Income Producing Mgmt., Inc.*, 202 F.3d 1282, 1284 (10th Cir. 2000) (discussing several conditions).

45. For a discussion of the distinction, see Section B1, supra.

46. See Section C, supra, for a general discussion of this structure.

A with the statement of the dispositive issue: Is the team liable in tort or contract to Jones for tendering his mitt to Smith? Moving from Point A to Point C, the judge finds a socially progressive policy that promises to bring the greatest success and happiness to the team. This policy—the player-ability policy—has not been articulated through an extant rule of law, but it inheres as a long-standing custom in the relevant community (the team). The policy taps into the community's competitive spirit; it is a familiar and acceptable norm. Next, the judge searches for a rule of law to implement the discovered policy. The waiver rule fits this bill. Finally, the judgment of the case, which is implicit in the discussion under Point B, orders the dismissal of Jones's action.

It should also be noted that the waiver ruling is a new rule of law. This is perfectly permissible under sociological jurisprudence. "[J]udicial law-making," Pound argued, is "a necessary element in the determination of all but the simplest controversies."[47] Justice Benjamin Cardozo, also an adherent of the policy method, expressed a similar view:

> A rule which in its origin was the creation of the *courts themselves,* and was supposed in the making to express the mores of the day, may be abrogated by the courts when the mores have so changed that perpetuation of the rule would do violence to the social conscience.... This is not usurpation. It is not even innovation. It is the reservation for ourselves of the same power of creation that built up the common law through its exercise by the judges of the past.[48]

2. Statutory Setting

While policy-discovery and law-making are permitted in common law cases under sociological jurisprudence, the judge is far more restricted when interpreting statutes and construing constitutions. Here, the judicial function of policy-formulation consists of no more than policy-vindication, the promotion of "the social purposes which law subserves."[49] Through the "interpretation and application of legal rules,"[50] the judge gives effect to articulated social interests or norms that underpin the written law. This process enables legislatures and courts to largely remain "in their respective spheres of law-

---

47. Wigdor, *Philosopher of Law,* supra note 7, at pp. 189–90 (sources cited therein).
48. Benjamin N. Cardozo, *The Growth of the Law* (New Haven: Yale University Press, 1924), pp. 136–37.
49. Pound, "The Scope and Purpose of Sociological Jurisprudence," supra note 22 at p. 516.
50. Ibid. at p. 513.

making and interpretation."[51] Thus, while Pound recognized the necessity of judicial law-making in the common law context, he believed "legislative law-making must be the chief reliance of modern society."[52]

Pound gave several reasons to support this position. Most importantly, he believed "legislation is the more truly democratic form of law-making."[53] Also, the legislature, having superior fact-finding resources, is better equipped to fashion laws that can scientifically respond to social needs and, hence, adequately promote social interests, or public policies.[54] Frequent conflicts between courts and legislatures on labor matters during the Lochner Era fueled Pound's belief in the superiority of legislative law-making.[55]

Given this view of legislation, it was easy for Pound to advocate judicial deference to the legislature's will. The Poundian judicial attitude toward statutory construction was expressed in *Borgnis v. Falk Co.*,[56] a case briefly mentioned earlier in this chapter.[57] In this case, the Wisconsin Supreme Court upheld the legality of the state's recently enacted workmen's compensation law. Responding to the plaintiffs' contention that the legislature, in passing the law, unlawfully abolished well-established common-law defenses available to the employee, the court stated:

> The precedent once made was generally followed, until it became buttressed by a multitude of decisions in practically all of the jurisdictions whose jurisprudence is founded upon the English common law. But…the conditions surrounding employer and employed have vastly changed during the last half century, and now the Legislature, having become convinced that new conditions call for a change in rules of liability, have declared that such a change shall be made. They have changed the rule established by the courts, because they deem another rule better fitted to deal with the problems of the time, or, in

---

51. Patterson, *Jurisprudence*, supra note 7, at p. 518.

52. Roscoe Pound, "Common Law and Legislation," *Harvard Law Review* 21 (1908): 382, 404.

53. Ibid. at p. 406.

54. Ibid. at p. 405 (noting that the courts, unlike legislative committees, are unable "to investigate conditions of manufacture, to visit factories and workshop and see them in operation and to take the testimony of employers, employees, physicians, social workers, and economists as to the needs of workmen and of the public….").

55. See ibid. at p. 404.

56. 133 N.W.209 (1911). See Pound, "The Scope and Purpose of Sociological Jurisprudence," supra note 22, at p. 513 n.94.

57. See Section C, supra.

other words, because they deem it best to establish a changed public policy.[58]

Courts must yield to elected lawmakers; they must not stand in the way of progress and democratic process.[59]

Pound's deference to progressive legislation led him to criticize a state court's invalidation of a workmen's compensation law in *Ives v. South Buffalo Ry. Co.*[60] Pound took note of the care with which the legislature had arrived at its decision to enact the new law, a feature of legislation that made it difficult for courts to second guess such laws. Prior to enacting this law, the New York legislature created a bipartisan commission to study the problem of industrial accidents.[61] The commission determined that the current system of dealing with industrial accidents was economically, morally, and legally unsound.[62] These findings were based on an abundance of information, including statistical tables, works of philosophical writers, and laws regulating industry in other states and countries.[63] But, unlike the *Borgnis* court, the *Ives* court disregarded this evidence and its supporting social policies, stating that "[u]nder our form of government, however, courts must regard all economic, philosophical, and moral theories, attractive and desirable though they may be, as subordinate to the primary question of whether they can be molded into statutes without infringing upon the letter or spirit of our written constitutions."[64]

Similarly, Pound criticized the Supreme Court's opinion in *Atkins v. Children's Hospital.*[65] A majority of the justices struck down a minimum wage law, which was enacted for the purpose of protecting "women and minors...from conditions detrimental to their health and morals, resulting from wages which are inadequate to maintain decent standards of living...."[66] The formalist Court took little notice of the relevant social factors articulated through statistics. It simply held that the statute interfered with freedom of contract and,

---

58. 133 N.W. at 216–17.

59. See, e.g., Roscoe Pound, "The New Deal in the Courts: A Changing Ideal of Justice," New York Times 9/9/34, p. 8–3; Hull, *Roscoe Pound and Karl Llewellyn*, supra note 26, at p. 256 (discussing Pound's support for a child labor amendment).

60. 94 N.E. 431 (1911). See Pound, "The Theory of Judicial Decision," supra note 12, at p. 653 n.3.

61. 94 N.E. at 435.

62. Ibid. at 437.

63. Ibid. at 436.

64. Ibid. at 437.

65. 261 U.S. 525 (1923).

66. Ibid. at 542.

hence, was in violation of the Fifth and Fourteenth Amendments to the Constitution.[67] Pound saw this case as an example of well-made legislation completely derailed by judges who were not in touch with the needs of an industrial society.[68]

Under sociological jurisprudence, there appears to be little for judges to do when reviewing statutes. Indeed, Pound limited "genuine" statutory interpretation to just two areas:

> The difficulty calling for interpretation may be, (a) which of two or more co-ordinate rules to apply, or (b) to determine what the lawmaker intended to prescribe by a given rule, or (c) to meet deficiencies or excesses in rules imperfectly conceived or enacted. The first two are cases for genuine interpretation. The third case, when treated as a matter of interpretation, calls for spurious interpretation.... [The latter's objective] is to make, unmake, or remake, and not merely to discover. It puts meaning into the text as a juggler puts coins, or what not, into a dummy's hair, to be pulled forth presently with an air of discovery. It is essentially a legislative, not a judicial process, made necessary in formative periods by the paucity of principles, feebleness of legislation, and rigidity of rules characteristic of archaic law. So long as a law is regarded as sacred, or for any reason as incapable of alteration, such a process is necessary to growth, but surviving into periods of legislation, it becomes a source of confusion.[69]

Arguably, the Supreme Court's interpretation of the removal statute in *Lewis*[70] falls into the spurious interpretation category. Although the statute was clear on its face, the Court sought to remedy a perceived deficiency in its application. The Court did not like the outcome of the statute in that particular case and, consequently, simply amended the statute by judicial fiat. This sort of thing would not bother legal realists nor, as we shall see, legal process jurisprudents.[71]

---

67. Compare ibid. at 562 (Taft, J., dissenting) (rejecting the courts disregard for the "evils of the sweating system and of the long hours and low wages...").

68. See, Roscoe Pound, "A Survey of Social Interests," *Harvard Law Review* 57 (1944): 1, 29 n.136. (approving the legislation that was at issue in *Adkins*). See also Patterson, *Jurisprudence*, supra note 7, at p. 525.

69. Roscoe Pound, "Spurious Interpretation," *Columbia Law Review* 7 (1907): 379, 381–82.

70. See Chapter 2, Section E, supra.

71. See Chapter 5, infra.

It is instructive to compare and contrast sociological jurisprudence with Scalian textualism, discussed in Chapter 2. Like the latter, the former could theoretically give effect to a statute whose consequences were absurd or outrageous. Justice Scalia would do so if the "ordinary meaning" of the statute so dictated. Pound would do so in the course of avoiding a "spurious interpretation," presumably even if the statute is nonprogressive or immoral. Unambiguous statutes are to be enforced as written, unless they conflict with other statutes. Of course, Pound assumed, perhaps naively given the many state statutes mandating racial segregation during his day, that legislation is likely to be progressive and moral more times than not.

Sociological jurisprudence, unlike Scalian textualism, is respectful of legislative intent. For Pound, intent trumps text. For Justice Scalia, text trumps intent. Hence, Pound most likely would have sided with the majority in the *Holy Trinity Church,* which read the statute barring foreign laborers in light of the legislative desire to exclude only manual laborers.[72]

3. Constitutional Setting

The judicial process under sociological jurisprudence becomes slightly more activist when the Constitution comes into play. Because statutes must be "passed within constitutional limitations,"[73] constitutional policies are vindicated over statutory policies. Whether progressive or not, a statute must fall if it fails to comport with the Constitution. This makes the judge a bit more active in constitutional cases. Policy-discovery is still not permitted, however. Policy-vindication, with constitutional policies ranked higher than statutory policies, is the most the judge can do.

An illustration of policy-vindication in the constitutional setting, resulting in the overturning of a statute, is the Supreme Court's 1954 decision in *Brown v. Board of Education,*[74] which banned segregation in public schools. We have already analyzed *Brown* from the perspectives of legal formalism,[75] Scalian tex-

---

72. See Chapter 2, Section C, supra.

73. *Borgnis v. Falk,* 133 N. W. 209, 216 (1911). As stated earlier, Pound approved of the reasoning in this case.

74. 347 U.S. 483 (1954). This decision is commonly known as *"Brown I"* in contradistinction to *"Brown II,"* Brown v. Board of Education, 349 U.S. 294 (1955), which ruled that *Brown's* school desegregation mandate must be executed "with all deliberate speed."

75. See Chapter 1, Section D, supra.

tualism,[76] and legal realism.[77] Now we shall look at the case through the eyes of a sociological jurisprudent. This tells us, once again, that cases can be decided on different grounds.

In *Brown*, the Court begins by developing an understanding of the essential facts of the case—namely, gross inequality in facilities and per pupil spending on African American and white students attending racially segregated public schools in the South. As discussed in Chapter 3, these facts were well-documented in school desegregation litigation leading up to *Brown* in a nontraditional way.[78] Moving to its legal analysis, the Court starts with a generalized rule of law applicable to the facts, the Fourteenth Amendment Equal Protection Clause which states: "No State shall…deny to any person within its jurisdiction the equal protection of the laws." The Court decides not to go with its then-current interpretation of the clause (*Plessy v. Ferguson*'s "separate but equal doctrine," which would permit school segregation to continue if the white and African American schools were "equal"[79]) because of the overwhelming policy consideration of equal educational opportunity. Derived from the Equal Protection Clause, this policy is not only progressive—educationally enlightening in post-World War II America—but also morally correct—it promotes human dignity and the greatest good for all Americans.

The sociological jurisprudence perspective on *Brown* can be summarized as follows: *Brown* extends existing constitutional law, the Equal Protection Clause, to a new factual pattern through the effectuation of articulated constitutional policies. The Court's technique is classic policy-vindication. But does policy-vindication provide a full account of *Brown*'s reasoning? This is merely one of several questions discussed next.

E. Criticisms

As we saw in the last chapter,[80] there is an unmistakable element of policy-making in the Supreme Court's reasoning in *Brown*. The Court imposes the racial equality norm, albeit technically limited to public education in grades K-12, upon a community (the South) before the latter is willing to accept it. This goes far beyond policy-vindication. Pound would probably attempt to

---

76. See Chapter 2, Section D, supra.
77. See Chapter 3, Section C2, supra.
78. See ibid.
79. 163 U.S. 537 (1896).
80. See Chapter 3, Section C2, supra.

explain away the policy-making problem by suggesting that the concept of "community" must at times be extended nationwide. According to Pound, "many things which were of purely local concern even a generation ago have nation-wide effects, and can be dealt with only through the power of the general government."[81] The argument, then, is that *Brown* can be understood solely as a policy-vindication case in that the equality norm is a national norm derived from the extant law of the land, the Fourteenth Amendment.

This sense of community, it is interesting to note, is coextensive with Justice Story's concept of "general law" expressed in the famous case of *Swift v. Tyson.*[82] Representing a way of conceptualizing law that was still prevalent during the first third of the twentieth century, the heyday of Pound's most important writings, the "general law" was described by Justice Holmes as a "transcendental body of law outside of any particular State but obligatory within it."[83] Federal courts are empowered to say what the "general law" is, as to which the state courts must follow. But as to "local law," the law that exists within each state and varies from state to state, the tables are turned: state courts lead and federal courts follow. Pound would likely view the issue in *Brown* as one that falls within the "general law." Ergo, the national community must be viewed as the only relevant community for purposes of deciding the segregation question.

One does not, however, find this argument persuasive. Our system of government is bifurcated. There is a central government, and there are regional governments defined along state, county, and city lines. Our concept of federalism—which raises the difficult yet enduring question concerning the proper allocation of power between the central and regional governments—presupposes this bifurcation. Thus, one could certainly argue that *Brown* must be read from a policy perspective that entails policy-vindication at one level (the national level) and policy-making at another level (the regional level consisting of those states that rejected racial equality under the law). This is not to say that *Brown* was wrongly decided. The point is simply that the Court's reasoning in the case cannot be explained or justified on policy-vindication grounds alone.

---

81. Hull, *Roscoe Pound and Karl Llewellyn*, supra note 26, at p. 256 (quoting statement made by Pound).

82. 16 Pet. (U.S.) 1, 10 L.Ed. 865 (1842), *rev'd, Erie Railroad Co. v. Thompkins*, 304 U.S. 64 (1938).

83. *Black & White Taxicab & Transfer Co. v. Brown & Yellow Taxicab & Transfer Co.*, 276 U.S. 518, 532 (1928) (Holmes, J., dissenting). Later, the Supreme Court rejects Justice Story's concept of federal general law. See *Erie Railroad Co. v. Tompkins*, 304 U.S. 64 (1938).

Pound's view concerning the relationship between law and morality is also problematic. We have seen from Prohibition and attempts to wipe out prostitution how difficult it is to legislate morality or to define "common" moral values even on utilitarian grounds. It is easy to understand why some judicial theorists prefer to draw a line between that which is illegal and that which is immoral, the latter covering more ground than the former. Cursing in church may be immoral but it is not illegal. Adultery is immoral but is no longer illegal in most states. Legal realists, who do not deny that moral precepts *influence* the law, do not believe in the coextensiveness of law and morality.[84] They believe, instead, that legal sanctions and the felicity calculus will ensure law's effectiveness. On this point, the legal realists are closer to Holmes, the "father" of the policy method, than are sociological jurisprudents. Holmes said in "The Path of the Law":

> If you want to know the law and nothing else, you must look at it as a bad man, who cares only for the material consequences which such knowledge enables him to predict, not as a good one, who finds his reasons for conduct, whether inside the law or outside of it, in the vaguer sanctions of conscience.[85]

Judge Richard Posner, who is often thought of as our most scholarly jurist since Holmes, flatly states that "moral theory has nothing *for law*,"[86] and "moral arguments are weak arguments in court."[87]

On the other hand, even if severe sanctions will ensure the effectiveness of the law, we may still want law to *teach* morality, as it often does. *Brown* is as much a case about public morality—the nation as a whole operates on a higher moral plane without racial apartheid—as it is a case about public law. But what type of morality should law teach? If law does not teach moral absolutes, does it not then teach moral relativism? If we are to believe that every culture and every era has its own standards of right and wrong, how do we universally condemn the Nazis for the Holocaust or Americans who traded in human bondage?[88]

---

84. See Chapter 3, Section D, supra.

85. Oliver Wendell Holmes, "The Path of the Law," *Harvard Law Review* 10 (1897): 457, 459.

86. Richard A. Posner, *The Problematics of Moral and Legal Theory* (Cambridge, Mass.: Harvard University Press, 1999), p. 141.

87. Richard Posner, "1997 Oliver Wendell Holmes Lectures: The Problematics of Moral Theory," *Harvard Law Review* 111 (1997): 1637, 1705.

88. Consider the story of "The Lottery," Shirley Jackson's short story of a small town in which a woman is stoned to death by her family (husband, daughter, and 4-year-old son).

Sociological jurisprudence's fidelity to statutory law seems a bit obsessive. Statutory rules that lead to absurd or outrageous results receive greater judicial deference than statutory rules that conflict or are ambiguous. The latter are subject to judicial interpretation while the former are not; they are simply applied as read. This unwise and unnecessary act of judicial deference can lead to situations in which the court unwittingly gives its imprimatur to the very evils Pound sought to condemn—nonprogressive or immoral legislation. Segregation statutes, which were prevalent during Pound's entire life, are a prime example. There is nothing in Pound's system of statutory interpretation that authorizes a judge to set aside these undemocratic and morally outrageous statutes.[89]

Are judges competent to handle social science data? Pound's vision was to close the gap between law-in-theory and law-in-action by using the "is" of sociology to produce the "ought" of law, "with the social scientist in the role of midwife," as Duncan Kennedy tells us. Kennedy further explains:

> Expertise, data, training, and scientific method were crucial not just to provide a context for value judgments about desirable law reform, but to suggest and validate them. In practice, the social interests of sociological jurisprudence are very similar to the principles of classical legal thought, or similar at least in that the trick is to find a governing interest for a domain and then implement it.[90]

Lawyers are crucial to the judicial process. They are responsible for bringing relevant social science data to the judge's attention through briefs modeled after the famous Brandeis Brief submitted in *Muller v. Oregon*. As discussed in Chapter 1,[91] a unanimous Supreme Court in *Muller* upheld a state maximum hour statute for women. The decision in that case was reached on the strength of Brandeis' brief supporting the statute. The Brief contained "two pages of legal argument and ninety-five pages of sociological and economic data about the conditions of working women's lives in factories."[92]

The stoning is part of an annual ritual of human sacrifice to make the crops grow. Should we defend the killing on the ground that it is part of the town's culture?

89. In its constitutional mode, sociological jurisprudence does, however, provide for the overturning of segregation statutes. But, as mentioned earlier in this Section E, policy-vindication only sustains a partial invalidation of these statutes.

90. Duncan Kennedy, "From the Will Theory to the Principle of Private Autonomy: Lon Fuller's 'Consideration and Form,'" *Columbia Law Review* 100 (2000): 94, 120.

91. See Chapter 1, Section D, supra.

92. Horwitz, *The Transformation of American Law*, supra note 4, at p. 209.

In spite of the Brandeis Brief (and in many respects because of it), judges have at best a spotty record of handling social science data in a competent manner. Judges have been misled by "junk science," empirical findings that do not follow truth-seeking norms. For example, judges have relied upon the pseudo-science justifications of eugenics to uphold state sterilization statutes[93] and state "antimiscegenation laws 'to keep the white race pure' and African Americans 'in their place.'"[94] The judge's reasoning in *Scott v. Georgia* provides a good illustration:

> The amalgamation of the races is not only unnatural, but is always productive of deplorable results. Our daily observation shows us that the offspring of these unnatural connections are generally sickly and *effeminate*, and that they are inferior in physical development and strength to the full-blood of either race. It is sometimes urged that such marriages should be encouraged for the purpose of elevating the inferior race. The reply is that such connections never elevate the inferior race to the position of the superior, but they bring down the superior to that of the inferior. They are productive of evil, and evil only, without any corresponding good.[95]

The problem of "junk science" speaks to a larger problem in sociological jurisprudence. Judges who rely upon sociological studies in their decision making may be unaware of the interplay between social science inquiry and values, and, hence, may mistakenly believe they are working within a value-free system. Social science, however, is not a value-free discipline; it slants one way or another both in terms of the problems selected for study ("for example, whether…[the researcher] selects a problem with great relevance for public policy or one of wholly academic interests") and in terms of the analysis of the problem selected (for example, "every social science study necessarily implicates the investigator in the perspective of an actual hierarchical position, seeing social life from either the social top or the bottom, and is therefore inherently biased"[96]).

Was it the inherent bias of social science inquiry or the inherent incompetency of the judiciary in handling social science data that gave rise to the

---

93. See, e.g., *Buck v. Bell*, 274 U.S. 200 (1927) (opinion written by Holmes).

94. Lisa J. McIntyre, *Law in the Sociological Enterprise: A Reconstruction* (Boulder: Westview Press, Inc., 1994), p. 158.

95. Ibid. at pp. 158–59 (quoting *Scott v. Georgia*, 39 Ga. 321 (1869)).

96. Donald J. Black, "The Boundaries of Legal Sociology," in *Sociological Theories of Law*, Kahei Rokumoto, ed. (New York: New York University Press, 1994), pp. 38–39.

Supreme Court's misreading of the social science evidence in *Brown*? The famous dolls test tended to contradict rather than support the Supreme Court's conclusion that segregation more than integration debilitated the African American child's sense of self-worth.[97] Kenneth Clark, the most famous of the social scientists who conducted the dolls test, suggests that he and other social scientists certainly had good reason to put a certain spin on their findings if in fact they had set out to do so:

> The underlying problem was that the Negro was regarded as semi-human or in some subtle way as sub-human; and not only as different, but as different and inferior. The common denominator of *Dred Scott, Plessy v. Ferguson*, and almost all court decisions up to *Brown* was that the Negro in some way was special and inherently unworthy of the rights which white American citizens would be expected to have without question and without litigation. Indeed, the fact that the Negro was required to persist in seeking judicial determination of his rights was, in itself, indicative of the basic racist realities of the society of which he was a part.[98]

The problem of "junk science" is not limited to high-profile cases like *Brown*. Michael Rustad and Thomas Koenig have studied the way partisan organizations distort social science research in amicus briefs, arguing that "although the amicus briefs contain no outright fabrications,...[one finds] a pattern of over-generalizations from limited social science data, selective distortions of findings, normative statements that appear to be empirical information, and citations to questionable research specifically produced for litigation."[99]

A final criticism of sociological jurisprudence is the charge that it is more "activist" than it claims to be. Far from being a mere reaction to extant social phenomena, sociological jurisprudence decision making can effectuate change. *Brown*, for example, had a profound effect on race relations in our society. The Court's decision in that case affected the course of society as much as (if not more than) the course of society affected it. This is not necessarily a good or a bad thing; it is simply an acknowledgment of the fact that sociological ju-

---

97. See Chapter 3, Section C2, supra, for a more detailed discussion.

98. Kenneth B. Clark, "The Social Scientists, the Brown Decision, and Contemporary Confusion," in *Argument: The Complete Oral Argument Before the Supreme Court in Brown v. Board of Education of Topeka, 1952–55*, Leon Friedman, ed. (New York: Chelsea House Publishers, 1969), p. xxxi.

99. Michael Rustad and Thomas Koenig, "The Supreme Court and Junk Social Science: Selective Distortions in Amicus Briefs," *North Carolina Law Review* 72 (1993): 91, 91.

risprudence can on occasion deliver more judicial assertiveness than it perhaps intends to deliver.

Despite these criticisms, sociological jurisprudence is here to stay. Judges
will no doubt continue to use sociological findings in their reasoning. In the
wake of *Brown*, the "United States Supreme Court has received empirical social science data on many occasions," including cases involving obscenity, jury
size, death penalty discrimination, and employment discrimination.[100] Also,
as Judges Peggy Fulton Hora and William Schma have remarked, sociological
jurisprudence greatly informs the concept of "therapeutic jurisprudence,"
which is "the use of social science to study the extent to which a legal rule or
practice promotes the psychological and physical well-being of the people it
affects."[101] Therapeutic considerations do not necessarily trump other considerations. For example, a judge would likely uphold a printed story that says
negative things about a public figure on grounds of freedom of the press, even
though the public figure may be adversely affected emotionally and psychologically by the judge's ruling. Therapeutic jurisprudence's only purpose is to
bring therapeutic considerations to the attention of the judge so that they can
be balanced against other relevant considerations, all in an effort to maximize
the success of a law in achieving its goal.[102] If therapeutic jurisprudence is half-
way successful, that would be a lasting tribute to sociological jurisprudence.

---

100. Ibid. at p. 111.
101. Peggy Fulton Hora, William G. Schma, and John T.A. Rosenthal, "Therapeutic
Jurisprudence and the Drug Treatment Court Movement: Revolutionizing the Criminal
Justice System's Response to Drug Abuse and Crime in America," *Notre Dame Law Review*
74 (1999): 439, 443.
102. See ibid. at p. 445.

Chapter 5
Legal Process

Legal Process prescribes a judicial process in which the means justify the ends. Moving from Point A to Point C, the judge defers to the substantive results of duly established institutional procedures, exercising all the while "reasoned elaboration from existing arrangements." This process incorporates policy-vindication in statutory cases involving "genuine interpretation" problems and policy-discovery in all other cases, but never policy-making. The judicial process thus exemplifies the principle of "reasonable persons pursuing reasonable purposes reasonably."[1]

A. Background

Legal process attempts to make the art of judging more than just the will of the judge. The judge proceeding under the legal process model is constrained by institutional rules of decision, the search for "right" answers, limited fact-finding capability, and, most importantly, the ideal of democratic government. Although the process jurist is decidedly not a legal realist,[2] neither is she a devotee of the logical method.[3] Fundamentally, legal process "emphatically accept[s] the social welfare implications of realist work in assuming the range of questions across the substantive field [of law] were rooted in issues of social policy."[4]

---

1. Henry M. Hart, Jr. and Albert M. Sacks, *The Legal Process: Basic Problems in the Making and Application of Law*, William N. Eskridge, Jr. and Philip P. Frickey, eds. (New York: Foundation Press, 1994), p. 1378. "[D]ecisions which are the duly arrived at result of duly established procedures [for making decisions] of this kind ought be accepted as binding upon the whole of society unless and until they are changed." Ibid. at p. 4. See Daniel B. Rodriguez, Review Essay, "The Substance of the New Legal Process," *California Law Review* 77 (1989): 919, 942.

2. See Chapter 3, supra.

3. See Part 1, Section A, supra.

4. Gary Minda, *Postmodern Legal Movements: Law and Jurisprudence at Century's End* (New York: New York University Press, 1995), pp. 34, 35. See Laura Kelman, Review Essay, "Eating Spaghetti with a Spoon," *Stanford Law Review* 49 (1997): 1547, 1563. For a discussion of process-oriented thoughts in legal realism and the logical method, see Neil Duxbury, *Patterns of American Jurisprudence* (Oxford: Clarendon Press, 1995), pp. 149, 210–12, 298.

Similarities and differences between legal process and sociological jurisprudence are also apparent.[5] Both maintain that the judicial policy-formulation function must of necessity be limited because of limited judicial competency and accountability. Judicial policy-making is, therefore, not allowed under either judicial theory. But although judicial self-effacement is a feature of both judicial models, legal process certainly gives less deference to the legislative branch than does sociological jurisprudence. As we shall see, legal process's fidelity is conditional—it is conditioned on "purposive action" and "reasoned elaboration."

Another difference between legal process and sociological jurisprudence concerns their treatment of the social sciences. Unlike sociological jurisprudence, legal process displays "a decidedly casual attitude towards the social sciences."[6] Perhaps this is because by the time legal process came along in the 1930s, reaching its heyday in the 1950s and 1960s, the sociological perspective in law "no longer caused any great shakes."[7] As Duxbury observes: "A consequence of this sentiment is that, in process literature, social science perspectives rarely if ever take center-stage and an interdisciplinary ethos features in only a very informal and unobstrusive manner."[8]

Some scholars assert that legal process is less a school of thought than an attitude toward law. This attitude is deeply embedded in American legal culture, they argue, and is "premised in every instance on the belief that those who respect and exercise the faculty of reason will be rewarded with the discovery of *a priori* criteria which gives sense and legitimacy to their legal activities."[9] Perhaps it is true that the pioneers of legal process were not interested in developing a distinct jurisprudence. It is, however, also true that these jurisprudents—particularly James Landis, Henry Hart, and Albert Sacks—have, in fact, influenced the way in which judges approach their craft.

1. Landis

James Landis, the dean of Harvard Law School in the 1930s, shaped the early development of legal process. As early as 1915 and more so in the 1930s, he advanced the idea that theories about the judicial process must be cognizant of the regulatory system created by New Deal legislation. Administrative agen-

---

5. See Chapter 4, supra, for a discussion of sociological jurisprudence.
6. Duxbury, *Patterns of American Jurisprudence*, supra note 4, at p. 209.
7. Ibid.
8. Ibid.
9. Ibid. at p. 208.

cies play an important role in our legal system. They are the day-to-day enforcers of legislation designed to regulate industry.

Institutionally, administrative agencies are more knowledgeable about the industries they regulate than either the judiciary or Congress. The personnel of the Department of Agriculture, for example, know more about agricultural matters than most judges or congresspersons. They are experts (scientists, academics, and businesspersons) hired for the specific task of continuous regulation of a single industry.[10]

Landis believed judges should give deference to administrative agencies not just because of their superior knowledge but for other reasons as well. He argued, for example, that judicial deference made for competent and efficient regulatory law. Because of the way in which they are arranged, courts have limited factfinding capability and, in addition, can only take an ad hoc approach to regulatory issues—issues that require systemic rulemaking. Overall, administrative agencies are more flexible than courts. Indeed, Landis argued that the sprawling administrative structure that took final shape in the 1930s "sprung from a distrust of the ability of the judicial process to make the necessary adjustments in the development of both law and regulatory methods as they related to particular industrial problems."[11] Landis, of course, was referring to legal formalism, which had been the dominant form of judicial decision making since the beginning of the century.[12]

By the mid-1930s, Landis was giving voice to a process of judicial decision making that was to become the organizing principle for legal process. He argued for a type of adjudication that "does not embrace policy-making; and [he believed] if the integrity of adjudication is to be preserved, judicial restraint must dominate the courts."[13] Here, of course, Landis was referring to legal realism, which was in its "flower" as legal formalism was in its decline during this time.[14]

2. Hart and Sacks

In the years following World War II, two Harvard legal scholars, Henry Hart and Albert Sacks, brought legal process to its full articulation. These men were

---

10. See, e.g., James M. Landis, *The Administrative Process* (New Haven: Yale University Press, 1938), pp. 6–46; Felix Frankfurter, "The Task of Administrative Law," *University of Pennsylvania Law Review* 75 (1927): 614, 617–19. See generally, Duxbury, *Patterns of American Jurisprudence*, supra note 4, at pp. 151–53.

11. Landis, *The Administrative Process*, supra note 10, at p. 30. See also ibid, at pp. 31–36.

12. See Chapter 1, supra.

13. Duxbury, *Patterns in American Jurisprudence*, supra note 4, at pp. 234–35.

14. See Chapter 3, supra.

part of a generation of legal scholars (which included the likes of Herbert Wechsler, Alexander Bickel, Harry Wellington, and Gerald Gunther) and judges (most prominently Felix Frankfurter, John Harlan, and Learned Hand) who had seen the rise of Hitler and Fascism, felt the shock of Pearl Harbor and the horror of Dachau, witnessed the potential for nuclear annihilation in pictures and news footage from Hiroshima, and feared the spread of Communism beyond eastern Europe. America's mid-twentieth century culture instilled in these scholars and judges a longing for order, stability, consensus, institutional comity, democratic process, and an apolitical, rational process of judicial decision making. The politico-economic implications of this type of judicial process were quite clear: society should move forward but only cautiously and orderly; in other words, only through Burkean conservative means.[15] Edmund Ursin correctly suggests that in the absence of the post-World War II politically conservative climate, legal process may not have developed in quite the way it did.[16]

Hart and Sacks recorded their legal theory in an unpublished manuscript titled, *The Legal Process: Basic Problems in the Making and Application of Law.* Although never published during Hart and Sacks' lifetimes, even after several revisions, this manuscript influenced generations of public law scholarship.[17] The publication of Hart and Sacks' teaching materials on legal process was eventually brought about through the efforts of two legal scholars, William Eskridge and Philip Frickey, some forty years after the final draft.[18] The story of legal process is for all practical purposes the story of Hart and Sacks.

---

15. See Preface, Section B, supra.

16. See Edmund Ursin, "Judicial Creativity and Tort Law," *The George Washington Law Review* 49 (1981): 229, 286. On the political, economic, and social environment of legal process, see, e.g., Morton J. Horwitz, *The Transformation of American Law, 1870–1960* (Cambridge, Mass.: Harvard University Press, 1977), p. 523; Duxbury, *Patterns of American Jurisprudence,* supra note 4, at pp. 242–43, 250, 298; Gerald B. Wetlaufer, "Systems of Belief in Modern American Law: A View from Century's End," *American University Law Review* 49 (1999): 1, 20–24; William N. Eskridge, Jr. and Philip P. Frickey, "The Making of the Legal Process," *Harvard Law Review* 107 (1994): 2031, 2033.

17. See, e.g., William N. Eskridge, Jr. and Gary Peller, "The New Public Law Movement: Moderation as a Postmodern Cultural Form," *Michigan Law Review* 89 (1991): 707; William N. Eskridge, Jr. and Philip P. Frickey, "Legislation Scholarship And Pedagogy in the Post-Legal Process Era," *University of Pittsburgh Law Review* 48 (1987): 691, 698. See generally, Duxbury, *Patterns of American Jurisprudence,* supra note 4, at pp. 251–52.

18. See Hart and Sacks, *The Legal Process,* supra note 1.

B. Components of Legal Process

1. Purposive Action

Legal process under Hart and Sacks takes as a basic assumption the belief that all legal institutions—courts, legislatures, and administrative agencies—act legitimately if they act with a "purpose." By "purpose," or "purposive action," legal process means that these institutions must direct their actions toward a public good:

> The social problem has been broadly described as that of 'establishing, maintaining and perfecting the conditions necessary for community life to perform its role in the complete development of man.' If this be right, it would follow that the ultimate test of the goodness or badness of every institutional procedure and of every arrangement which grows out of such a procedure is whether or not it helps to further this purpose.[19]

Legislators, for example, act legitimately if they do so for the public good, not just out of political will or whim.

Although a condition for legitimate governance, purposive action does not give the judge the unbridled right to second guess legislative or administrative rules. Nor does it give the judge power to make policy, even in common law cases. Unelected and unaccountable to the people, the judge has a more limited function in our democratic form of government. The role of the judge is, in the main, to observe two principles: "institutional settlement" and "reasoned elaboration."

2. Institutional Settlement and Reasoned Elaboration

Institutional settlement and reasoned elaboration give legal process its distinctive features. They carry forth the policy method's basic assumption that law is policy, which is to say, law is the elaboration and enforcement of public policy. These principles establish a permissible level of judicial policy-formulation. In so doing, institutional settlement and reasoned elaboration help the judge to achieve the core aspiration of the legal process method, which is to resolve legal problems "as coherent[ly] and as rational[ly] as possible through procedural justifications consistent with political pluralism."[20] Before linking these principles to an appropriate level of policy-formulation, let us clarify their meaning.

---

19. Ibid. at p. 102.
20. Eskridge and Frickey, "Legislation Scholarship," supra note 17, at p. 698.

The principle of institutional settlement is an attempt to make a proper allocation of decision-making authority within our system of government in accordance with the design of decision-making structures.[21] This principle works as a principle of comity among legal institutions. It recognizes and respects the institutional competency of legislators, administrators, and judges. Each is competent in his own sphere of expertise: the legislator in making policy; the regulator in making regulatory rules; and the judge in making process-oriented decisions. Institutional settlement, in short, insists that "decisions which are the duly arrived at result of duly established procedures...ought to be accepted as binding upon the whole society unless and until they are duly changed."[22]

Focusing on process rather than the results of process yields certain benefits, according to Hart and Sacks. For example, process that "is soundly adapted to the type of power to be exercised is conducive to well-informed and wise decisions."[23] Also, by emphasizing procedure over substance, the judge is able to avoid the illegitimacy problem—the problem of mixing law and politics—that legal realists inevitably encounter. "Legitimate legal decision making turns on process values, not substantive theory."[24] When judges make policy, they lose sight of their limited institutional role in our democratic system of government. What Hart and Sacks could have also said is that when judges take on the appearance of politicians, they lose the appearance and perhaps the reality of judicial objectivity. Finally, process-based decision making, according to Hart and Sacks, produces ethical results. Procedure, they argued, "provides the objective process through which the law...achieve[s] ethically desirable outcomes."[25] Thus, while legal realism and sociological jurisprudence argued over the coextensiveness of law and morality, legal process sought to mediate the tension between law and morality through procedure.[26]

The principle of reasoned elaboration—"*reasoned elaboration from existing arrangements*"—comes into play when judges attempt to explain the rationale behind the judgment in a case, particularly the applicability (or non-

---

21. See Richard H. Fallon, Jr., "Reflections on the Hart and Wechsler Paradigm," *Vanderbilt Law Review* 47 (1994): 953, 971–72.

22. Eskridge and Frickey, "The Making of the Legal Process," supra note 16, at p. 2045 (quoting Hart and Sacks, *Legal Process*, supra note 1, p. 4).

23. Ibid. at p. 2044 (quoting Hart and Sacks, *Legal Process*, supra note 1, p. 173).

24. Minda, *Postmodern Legal Movements*, supra note 4, at p. 35. See Hart and Sacks, *Legal Process*, supra note 1, at p. iv; Neil Duxbury, "Faith in Reason: The Process Tradition in American Jurisprudence," *Cardozo Law Review* 15 (1993): 601, 661–62.

25. Minda, *Postmodern Legal Movements*, supra note 4, at p. 35.

26. Eskridge and Frickey, "The Making of the Legal Process," supra note 16, at p. 2040.

applicability) of general rules. Reasoned elaboration penetrates the formal rules that give support to the holding. It connects the judge's reasoning to the stuff of which decisions are duly made. Rules "do not transparently tell officials and citizens what to do in specific situations, but that does not mean that officials simply interpret ambiguous language to reflect their own political values."[27] Instead, the judge or other official applying a general rule ("a general directive arrangement") must "elaborate the arrangement in a way which is consistent with other established applications of it."[28] Furthermore, she "must do so in the way which best serves the principles and policies it expresses."[29] As Eskridge and Frickey point out, in extending the principle of reasoned elaboration to legal interpretations, Hart and Sacks *"presumed that 'every statute and every doctrine of unwritten law developed by the decisional process has some kind of purpose or objective,' and that each should be applied in ways that subserve both their purposes and the general purposes of the law."*[30]

In short, "reasoned elaboration from existing arrangements" primarily means judges must fully articulate the grounds upon which they rely, including the public policies underlying the rules of law they make or interpret. Hart and Sacks, as Ursin notes, "do not argue that courts may only deduce rules from pre-existing precedent. Indeed, they envision courts overruling precedent."[31] Courts may overturn precedent on the basis of "existing arrangements," meaning "existing community values"—*reasoned elaboration from existing community values.* This suggests, at most, policy-discovery.

Thus, taken together, the principles of institutional settlement and reasoned elaboration legitimize a degree of judicial activism. Judges ought to formulate policy and make law on matters that fall within their institutional competency. "[B]asic principles and policies form the basis for extending a rule or statute to a novel context, reformulating old rules or provisions, and even for replacing prior rules or practices with new ones."[32] "Process jurisprudence is not antithetical to judicial activism."[33]

---

27. Ibid. at p. 2043.

28. Ibid.

29. Ibid. (citing Hart and Sacks, *Legal Process*, supra note 1, at pp. 162–68).

30. Ibid. (quoting and citing Hart and Sacks, *Legal Process*, supra note 1, at pp. 421–27 (regarding the unwritten law) and pp. 166–67, 1179–203 (regarding the written law)) (emphasis supplied).

31. Ursin, "Judicial Creativity and Tort Law," supra note 16, at p. 238 n.42.

32. Eskridge and Frickey, "The Making of Legal Process," supra note 16, at p. 2044 (citing Hart and Sacks, *Legal Process*, supra note 1, at pp. 386–406, 1407–26, 565–89).

33. Duxbury, *Patterns of American Jurisprudence*, supra note 1, at p. 264.

At the same time, the principles of institutional settlement and reasoned elaboration also inject a measure of judicial restraint into the decision-making process. Judges ought not to make policy. Judicial policy-making is an illegitimate exercise of the judicial policy-formulation function. As Justice Frankfurter, a major contributor to the development of legal process, said in a school flag-salute case: "As judge we are neither Jew nor Gentile, neither Catholic nor agnostic.... As a member of this Court I am not justified in writing my private notions of policy into the Constitution, no matter how deeply I may cherish them or how mischievous I may deem their disregard."[34] Let us take a closer look at the structure of legal process, along with a few illustrations.

C. Structure and Illustrations

Legal process envisions different levels of judicial policy-formulation, depending on the type of case. Policy-making is never permitted, however. This extreme form of judicial activism moves the judiciary into areas of governance that only our elected officials should and can perform legitimately and competently. Legislatures create policy, courts create law.[35] But courts can effectuate discovered policies and vindicate extant policies depending on the legal setting.

1. Common Law Setting

Moragne v. States Marine Lines[36] illustrates the legal process model applied in the common law setting. The issue in this case, the opinion of which was written by Justice Harlan, was whether an action lies under general maritime law for death caused by violation of a maritime duty.[37] In answering this question, Justice Harlan "surveyed case law, statutory law, and ancient English legal history to determine the source and reason for the continuing vitality of the ancient rule against non-statutory wrongful death actions in admiralty." The old common

---

34. *West Virginia Bd. of Educ. v. Barnette*, 319 U.S. 624, 646–47 (1943). See *Sweeney v. New Hampshire*, 354 U.S. 234, 255, 266–67 (1957) (Frankfurter, J.). See generally Alexander Bickel, *Least Dangerous Branch: The Supreme Court at the Bar of Politics* (Indianapolis: Bobbs-Merrill, 1962).

35. See Hart and Sacks, *Legal Process*, supra note 1, at p. iv; Duxbury, "Faith in Reason," supra note 24, at p. 661.

36. 398 U.S. 375 (1970).

37. Ibid. at 377.

law rule, if the Court had upheld it, would have precluded the decedent's widow (Moragne) from recovering. Harlan noted that numerous state and federal wrongful death statutes, "taken as a whole, make it clear that there is no present public policy against allowing recovery for wrongful death," that such statutes "evidence a wide rejection by the legislators" of the common law precedent, and that "[t]he policy thus established has become itself part of our law" to be applied in statutory and common law cases.[38] The Court, then, discovered a public policy from the current structure of statutory law and used it to update the common law, creating new law.[39] Adding more richness to the Court's reasoning, Justice Harlan went on to contend that "a judicious reconsideration of precedent cannot be as threatening to public faith in the judiciary as continued adherence to a rule unjustified in reason, which produces different results for breaches of duty in situations that cannot be differentiated in policy."[40]

It is important to see here that legal process is less concerned with judicial law-making in common law cases than with the exercise (or lack thereof) of reasoned elaboration. Justice Harlan's law-making was acceptable because he offered reasoned justification in support of it. Most significantly, he relied on a policy that had "become itself part of our laws." "If a decision is to be rational," Hart and Sacks insisted, "it must be based upon some rule...or [policy]. If the rule...or [policy] is to make any appeal to the parties it must be something that *pre-existed* the decision. An explanation in terms of a...[policy] created *ad hoc* to explain the decision it purports to govern lacks the persuasive power necessary to make adjudication effective."[41] Reasoning based on

---

38. Ibid. at 390–91.

39. Ibid. at 397–98. Had the issue of the case been one of statutory construction, the court's decision would have involved the extension of a pre-articulated statutory policies; i.e, policy vindication. Had the court followed the existing common law rule, it would have vindicated a common law policy in admiralty law.

40. Ibid. at 405. "Respect for the process of adjudication should be enhanced, not diminished, by our ruling today." Ibid. See, e.g., *Boys Markets, Inc. v. Retail Clerks Union, Local 770*, 398 U.S. 235 (1970) (Justice Brennan, on behalf of the Court, announced that *stare decisis* does not bar the Court's reconsideration of prior decisions); *Helvering v. Hallock*, 309 U.S. 106 (1940) (Justice Frankfurter's argument that *stare decisis* "is a principle of policy and not a mechanical formula of adherence to the latest decision"). Judge Guido Calabresi proposed that if judges engaged in common law legislation, the legislature would be induced to respond by changing obsolete statutes. Robert Weisberg, "The Calabresian Judicial Artist: Statutes and the New Legal Process," *Stanford Law Review* 35 (1983): 213, 256.

41. Hart and Sacks, *Legal Process*, supra note 1, at p. 398 (quoting Lon Fuller, "The Forms and Limits of Adjudication," the unpublished version presented at Harvard Law School, November 19, 1957, subsequently published at *Harvard Law Review* 92 (1978): 353 (first emphasis supplied).

discovered policies is within the court's institutional competency, but reasoning based on new policies—alien policies—is not.[42] Read in tandem with *Moragne*, the next case helps to crystallize this important point.

Hart and Sacks criticized the type of judicial law-making that took place in *Norway Plains Co. v. Boston & Me. R.R.*[43] Written by Lemuel Shaw, the legendary Chief Justice of the Supreme Judicial Court of Massachusetts from 1830 to 1860, whom Justice Holmes, the legal realist, greatly admired,[44] *Norway Plains* involved the question of whether railroads are subject to the same standards of liability as common carriers. At the time the case arose, railroads were an infant industry.[45] Chief Justice Shaw held that railroads are common carriers of merchandise and, hence, assume the "extraordinary responsibility" of such carriers for the safe carriage of their merchandise. But as to the question of when such liability ceases, Chief Justice Shaw went on to hold that the traditional rule terminating common-carrier liability upon delivery or due tender of the goods does not apply to railroads. Instead, railroad liability terminates when the goods are deposited at the platform of the destination station whether or not the consignee has notice of the goods delivery or an opportunity to cart them away. This new law was created to implement a new policy the court made up *ad hoc*: "We need to encourage this infant industry of carriage by railroad," Chief Justice Shaw declared. "In my judgment, a special liability as insurer of the safe carriage of goods will operate as a deterrent to the growth of the industry."[46]

Hart and Sacks saw such reasoning as illicit judicial activism, a judicial usurpation of the legislative function. The court's law-making was institutionally suspect because it was based upon policy-making. Unlike Justice Harlan, whose law-making in *Moragne* was predicated upon a policy that "pre-existed the decision," Chief Justice Shaw, Hart and Sacks believed, used law-making as a vehicle for imposing a policy—the protection of an infant industry—on a community before it was ready to accept it. Chief Justice Shaw, thereby, engaged in an act of governance more suited for democratically selected law-makers. Hart and Sacks cited a New Hampshire opinion on a similar issue, handed down just two years after *Norway Plains*, in which the

---

42. See Introduction, Section C2, supra, for a discussion of the judicial policy-formulation function.

43. 67 Mass. (1 Gray) 263 (1854).

44. Ursin, "Judicial Creativity," supra note 16, at p. 271. See Chapter 3, Section C1, supra.

45. See discussion of a similar case decided by Chief Justice Shaw in Chapter 3, Section C3, supra.

46. Hart and Sacks, *Legal Process*, supra note 1, at p. 374.

court, "with all…respect for the eminent" Chief Justice Shaw, refused to engage in such activism.[47] Chief Justice Shaw, in short, was guilty of "treating the judicial power as a discretionary power rather than as a power of reasoned elaboration."[48]

It might be useful to point out at this juncture a similarity between legal process and the judicial theory of Ronald Dworkin.[49] Like Hart and Sacks, Dworkin takes strong exception to the claim that judges may legitimately exercise "discretion" when cases fall between the cracks of extant rules of law. Dworkin, however, seemingly disagrees with Hart and Sacks as to the specific source on which judges can legitimately rely for such interstitial decision making. For Dworkin it is "principles"; for Hart and Sacks it is "policy." There is not much difference in this distinction when one considers the unsustainable dichotomy between "principles" and "policies," Dworkin and others urge.[50] Also, Hart and Sacks even concede that "principles and policies are closely related, and for many purposes need not be distinguished from each other."[51] The influence of legal process in Dworkin's work is quite apparent.[52]

2. Statutory Setting

Reasoned elaboration dictates even more judicial restraint in statutory matters. While policy-making is no more permitted in the written law than it is in the unwritten law, policy-vindication is the primary mode of policy-formulation in statutory cases. Policy-discovery is the exception. Referring to the three classes of interpretive problems Roscoe Pound identified in the last chapter,[53] Hart and Sacks require policy-vindication in what Pound called "genuine interpretation" cases. These are cases where the judge is called upon to determine which of multiple coordinate statutory rules to apply or what the legislature meant a statute to prescribe.[54] But as to "spurious interpretation" cases — cases in which the statutory language is unam-

---

47. Ibid. at p. 377.

48. Ibid. at p. 374. Unfortunately, Hart and Sacks do not locate the dividing line between discretion and reasoned elaboration. See Ursin, *Judicial Creativity*, supra note 16, at p. 239.

49. See Introduction, Section C1, supra, for a discussion of Dworkin.

50. See ibid.

51. Hart and Sacks, *Legal Process*, supra note 1, at p. 141.

52. See Ursin, "Judicial Creativity," supra note 16, at p. 235, for further discussion.

53. See Chapter 4, Section D2, supra.

54. See ibid. See also Hart and Sacks, *Legal Process*, supra note 1, at pp. 1111–380, especially pp. 1374–80.

biguous but leads to absurd or outrageous results[55]—the judge is free to discover policy. Indeed, the judge may even have an institutional duty to do so; for, as Hart and Sacks argued, "courts are to be criticized when they 'pass the buck to the legislature and avoid taking an open and honest responsibility of their own for the growth of the law.' "[56] We shall return to this point shortly.

It is interesting to note that Hart and Sacks are more activist than Justice Scalia and Pound in "spurious interpretation" cases. Justice Scalia and Pound feel constrained to do very little, if anything, in such cases. Both would simply apply the unambiguous rule.[57] In contrast, Hart and Sacks would proceed to policy-discovery. Indeed, they severely criticized Pound, their former dean, for not permitting greater judicial discretion in these cases.[58]

Let us look more closely at the application of legal process in the statutory context, starting with "genuine interpretation" cases.

Justice Harlan's dissenting opinion in *National Labor Relations Board v. Fruit and Vegetable Packers and Warehousemen, Local 760*,[59] illustrates the proper application of legal process to "genuine interpretive" problems. Policy-vindication is permitted, policy-discovery is not. In *National Labor Relations Board*, the majority construed a statute creatively so as to uphold a union's secondary picketing of retail stores, the purpose of such picketing being to persuade customers not to buy the product of the primary employer. Justice Harlan argued that the majority's decision was not based on the statutory language, legislative history, or any other legislative evidence—in other words, there was no attempt at policy-vindication.[60] The Court created a tenuous distinction between general and limited product picketing, Justice Harlan contended, that went beyond and *against* legislative policy.[61] In short, the Court, to borrow from Hart and Sacks, did not "[r]espect the position of the legislature as the chief policy-determining agency of the society."[62]

The role of the judge under the legal process model is quite different, more activist, in "spurious interpretation" cases, however. Policy-discovery is permitted and even required in such cases. Hart and Sacks drafted a prob-

---

55. See Chapter 4, Section D2, supra.
56. See Duxbury, "Faith in Reason," supra note 24, at p. 661 (sources cited therein).
57. See Chapter 2, Section C, supra; Chapter 4, Section D2, supra.
58. See Hart and Sacks, *Legal Process*, supra note 1, at p. 89.
59. 377 U.S. 58 (1964).
60. Ibid. at pp. 80–84 (Harlan, J., dissenting).
61. Ibid. at pp. 82–83 (Harlan, J., dissenting).
62. Hart and Sacks, *Legal Process*, supra note 1, at p. 1174.

lem for use in their casebook, called "The Case of the Spoiled Heir,"[63] that illustrates policy-discovery. This problem was based on a controversy decided in *Riggs v. Palmer*.[64] Hart and Sacks approved of the state court's analysis in *Riggs*.

The court in *Riggs* ignored the express language of a statute that would have allowed a murderer to receive a devise as the named beneficiary of the estate of a person whom he had murdered. Despite the unambiguous language of the New York statute, which commanded the enforcement of decedent's duly executed will, the court canceled the devise based on what it believed to be the public good—namely, a wrongdoer should not be permitted to benefit from his or her own wrongdoing, lest the law encourage the intentional or reckless taking of life. Basing the decision on this widely held community value was the rational thing to do, Hart and Sacks observed. It was reasoned elaboration.[65]

How does legal process attempt to square judicial policy-discovery in "spurious interpretation" cases with the principle of institutional settlement? The reasons judges are permitted to discover policy in "spurious interpretation" cases has to do as much with the institutional competency of legislatures as it does with the institutional competency of courts. Although each organ of government has a special expertise, they share a common purpose, which is to advance the public good (purposive action).[66] If a statute produces outrageous outcomes, the judge is obligated to act on the public's behalf because it is likely that democratic process and reasoned elaboration were not fully adhered to in the enactment of the statute. There was a failure of legislative process. Bad ends suggest bad means, thereby nullifying institutional settlement.

One picks up this line of thought from Justice Felix Frankfurter's views on statutory interpretation. Justice Frankfurter drew a sharp distinction between legislative intent and the public good. Judges are to avoid legislative intent when interpreting statutes, Frankfurter argued, because legislative intent is "subjective." "We do not delve into the minds of legislators or draftsmen, or committee members," Frankfurter said.[67] Instead, judges must interpret statutes just like they decide cases—in the public's interest and with reasoned elaboration. Hart and Sacks did not go as far as Frankfurter—legislative intent remains part of the judicial inquiry, as Harlan's dissent in *National Labor*

---

63. Ibid. at p. 68.

64. 115 N.Y. 506, 22 N.E. 188 (1889), reproduced in *Legal Process*, supra note 1, at p. 80.

65. Hart and Sacks, *Legal Process*, supra note 1, at pp. 84–85.

66. See Section B1, supra.

67. Felix Frankfurter, "Some Reflections on the Reading of Statutes," *Columbia Law Review* 47 (1947): 527, 539.

Relations Board well illustrates—but legislative intent was subject to close scrutiny under the purposive action directive.

It is worth noting that Justice Frankfurter's distinction between "subjective" legislative intent and "objective" legislative purpose has drawn criticism from Kent Greenawalt on several grounds. For example, Greenawalt argues that objective legislative purpose involves some element of a judge's subjective attitudes.[68] However, the distinction is still quite useful in helping us understand why legal process permits policy-discovery in "spurious interpretation" cases. Judges ought not to be required to vindicate legislative mean-spiritedness, such as the personal views of a powerful United States Senator comparing homosexuals to "kleptomaniacs and alcoholics with impunity."[69] Judges are institutionally competent to step into the legislative sphere and proceed with good purpose when legislative promulgations or procedures shock the conscience.[70]

3. Constitutional Setting

The directive that cases be decided in the public's interest applies with equal force to constitutional interpretation. In this context, the source of institutional competency comes largely from the doctrine of judicial review announced in *Marbury v. Madison*.[71] Again, policy-discovery, but not policy-making, is within the judiciary's institutional competency. Speaking to the Court's interpretive duty in reading the Due Process Clause, Justice Frankfurter said in *Rochin v. California*:[72]

> ....The faculties of the Due Process Clause may be indefinite and vague, but the mode of their ascertainment is not self-willed. In each case 'due process of law' requires an evaluation based on a disinterested inquiry pursued in the spirit of science, on a balanced order of facts exactly and fairly stated, on the detached consideration of conflicting claims, on a judgment not ad hoc and episodic but duly

68. Kent Greenawalt, "Variation on Some Themes of A 'Disporting Gazelle' and His Friends: Statutory Interpretation as Seen by Jerome Frank and Felix Frankfurter," *Columbia Law Review* 100 (2000): 176, 202–3.

69. Ronald J. Krotoszynski, Jr., "The New Legal Process: Games People Play and the Quest for Legitimate Judicial Decision Making," *Washington University Law Quarterly* 77 (1999): 993, 1043 (sources cited).

70. Cf. *Rochin v. California*, 342 U.S. 165, 172 (1952) (Frankfurter, J.) overruled on other grounds by *Mapp v. Ohio*, 367 U.S. 643 (1961).

71. 1 Cr. 137, 2 L.Ed. 60 (1803).

72. 342 U.S. 165 (1952) reversed on other grounds by *Mapp v. Ohio*, 367 U.S. 643 (1961).

mindful of reconciling the needs both of *continuity* and of change in a *progressive* society.

Applying these general considerations to the circumstances of the present case, we are compelled to conclude that the proceedings by which this conviction was obtained do more than offend some fastidious squeamishness or private sentimentalism about combatting crime too energetically. This is conduct that *shocks the conscience....* This course of proceeding by agents of government to obtain evidence is bound to offend even hardened sensibilities. They are methods too close to the rack and the screw to permit constitutional differentiation.[73]

"The judge is a legislature with a difference," Hart and Sacks wrote in *Legal Process.* "[H]is training, the procedures he follows, and the traditions of legal reasoning entitle us to repose greater confidence in his probity and competence."[74]

The legal process model is thought to have an indisposition to constitutional cases like *Brown v. Board of Education*.[75] This conventional characterization of legal process is based primarily upon a single article written by Herbert Wechsler, an influential legal process scholar.[76] Wechsler was critical not only of *Brown*, but of the Warren Court generally. He felt that the Court's opinions were morally sound but jurisprudentially weak, because they lacked reasoned elaboration. Of *Brown*, in particular, he said, "[t]he problem inheres strictly in the reasoning of the opinion."[77] Wechsler at times seemed to be saying that the Warren Court opinions lacked *any* legal basis. "[T]he Court has been decreeing value choices in a way that makes it quite impossible to speak of principled determinations or the statement and evaluation of judicial reasons, since the Court has not disclosed the grounds on which its judgments rest."[78]

Hart and Sacks, in fact, disagreed with Wechsler's criticism of *Brown* and strongly defended the opinion, while assiduously criticizing most other War-

---

73. Ibid. at p. 172 (emphasis added).

74. Hart and Sacks, *Legal Process,* supra note 1, at pp. 84–85.

75. See, e.g., Minda, *Postmodern Legal Movements,* supra note 4, at pp. 38–43; Duxbury, *Patterns in American Jurisprudence,* supra note 4, at pp. 274–75, 278–89; Horwitz, *The Transformation of American Law,* supra note 16, at pp. 266–68, 342 n.37; Gary Peller, "Neutral Principles" in 1950s, *University of Michigan Journal of Law Reform* 21 (1988): 561.

76. Herbert Wechsler, "Toward Neutral Principles of Constitutional Law," *Harvard Law Review* 73 (1959): 1.

77. Ibid. at p. 32.

78. Ibid. at p. 20. See Minda, *Postmodern Legal Movements,* supra note 4, at pp. 38–43 (discussing Wechsler and Alexander Bickel's attack on the Warren Court).

ren Court opinions on legal process grounds.[79] Eskridge and Frickey point out in their introduction to *Legal Process* that "[w]hen Louis Pollak published a critical response to Wechsler in 1959, Sacks praised it and rejected Wechsler's analysis. In the classroom, Hart endorsed *Brown* and explicitly disagreed with Wechsler's analysis."[80] Eskridge and Frickey also make the point that Hart and Sacks, the latter five years before Wechsler's article,[81] as well as the vast majority of legal process scholars,[82] saw *Brown* "as consistent with the purposes of the fourteenth amendment, within the Court's rather than the legislature's institutional competence, and as appropriate for the Court to do, notwithstanding the fierce opposition in the South, because the Court is 'a politically sheltered institution whose function it is to seek to reflect the sober second thought of the community.'"[83]

This analysis suggests that Hart and Sacks viewed *Brown* as a policy-discovery case. Had the South been thinking soberly, it would have embraced the equality value mandated by the Constitution, especially where education is concerned. An educated citizenry serves the community's best interest. This thinking assumes a regional (southern) community. But it is possible that Hart and Sacks had in mind a national community as well. The latter suggests an additional legal process defense of *Brown*.

When federal law is at stake, Hart and Sacks may have believed that the term "community" should be given a broad, nationwide definition. From this perspective it can be argued that the Court in *Brown* merely vindicated a norm (racial equality) which had already been effectuated through a "community"-wide rule—the Fourteenth Amendment's Equal Protection Clause. The argument is problematic, however, because, as we noted in the last chapter,[84] one could just as easily discern two applicable "communities," one national and the other regional or local. States do, in fact, count under our bifurcated

---

79. See Albert Sacks, "The Supreme Court, 1953 Term Foreward," *Harvard Law Review* 68 (1954): 96, 99–103 (criticized the Warren Court for its overapproval of the summary judgment); Henry Hart, Jr., "The Supreme Court, 1958 Term-Foreward: The Time Chart of the Justices," *Harvard Law Review* 73 (1959): 84, 100 ("too many of the Court's opinions are about what one would expect could be written in twenty-four hours.... [F]ew of the Court's opinions, far too few, genuinely illumine the area of law with which they deal"). See also *Legal Process*, supra note 1, at p. cix (Hart and Sacks joining Wechsler's criticism of the Warren Court).

80. Hart and Sacks, *Legal Process*, supra note 1, at p. cix (sources cited therein).

81. Ibid., at p. cviii (sources cited therein).

82. Ibid.(sources cited therein).

83. Ibid. at cix (sources cited therein).

84. See Chapter 4, Section E, supra.

government; hence the notion of federalism. While it could be argued that the Court in *Brown* merely engaged in policy-vindication at the national level, it must be acknowledged that the Court clearly engaged in policy-making at the regional level in the South. It was no secret that the South was not ready to accept the racial equality norm. The Court, to its good credit, found the moral strength to impose this noble value on the South, even though only "with all deliberate speed."[85]

Is *Brown* more defensible on legal process grounds if viewed in light of the state school segregation statutes it overruled? Clearly, these statutes were enacted under the most undemocratic and repressive regime on American soil since the institution of slavery. With millions of African Americans denied the right to vote, the institutional procedures that produced these statutes were hardly "duly established." Institutional comity is not required when there has been so blatant a failure of democratic process. Indeed, institutional settlement is no more required here than in statutory cases involving mean-spirited legislative intent.[86] But, of course, *Brown* was not a statutory case and, even if it were, this argument does not explain the policy-making. "Spurious interpretation" cases warrant only policy-discovery. Hart and Sacks may have agreed with the reasoning in *Brown*, but they could not have done so on legal process grounds.

D. Criticism

Legal process has been criticized on several other grounds as well. One misplaced criticism can be raised and discarded quickly. It is the commonly made argument that "the abstract concepts upon which Legal Process arguments depend are as indeterminate as substantive concepts were shown to be by Legal Realism and that, at bottom, decisions allocating responsibility to one or another institution or court are nothing but thinly disguised substantive decisions."[87] But as Richard Fallon points out, legal process does not deny that judgments allocating decision-making authority reflect substantive commitments as to what constitutes good outcomes. "The best Legal Process scholarship continues to consider issues of how to get the 'best' performances from various institutions of government, including courts."[88]

---

85. Brown v. Board of Education, 349 U.S. 294 (1955) (Brown II).
86. See Section C2, supra.
87. Fallon, "Reflections on the Hart and Wechsler Paradigm," supra note 21, at pp. 972 (summarizing and responding to criticism).
88. Ibid.

Some argue that the degree of judicial deference to administrative agencies that legal process seems to demand is wrongheaded if not outright dangerous. Administrative agencies may seem more expert than courts in the matters they regulate diurnally, but they do not always proceed with purposive action. For example, Congress authorizes the Immigration and Naturalization Service (INS) to detain "removable aliens" (i.e., those who have entered the United States) for only a reasonable time beyond the expiration of a ninety-day period after entry of a final order of removal.[89] Yet, the INS has repeatedly abused this grant of authority by indefinitely detaining hundreds if not thousands of removable aliens whose homeland does not have a repatriation agreement with the United States. Such detention amounts to a life sentence in some cases.[90] Legal process is not, however, without an answer to this type of problem. Hart and Sacks were worldly enough to know that administrative agencies can run amok and, therefore, are in need of judicial scrutiny. They not only required institutions, including administrative agencies, to act purposively, but also with reasoned elaboration. Both are prerequisites for institutional comity.

A related criticism of legal process is that the principle of institutional settlement naively assumes the procedures themselves are fair and those executing them are honest and competent; otherwise, routine institutional deference makes no sense.[91] Given the existence of racial segregation statutes and public laws authorizing discrimination based on gender and a host of other invidious bases, it is difficult to find optimistic pluralism in the 1950s legislative process.[92] Today, legal process assumptions of legislative rationality, proceduralism, and openness are woefully unrealistic. These assumptions have been undercut by findings in public choice scholarship to the effect that "the primary motivation of the legislator is to be re-elected."[93] As Eskridge and Frickey further explain:

> Public choice scholarship applies principles of market economics to explain institutional and political behavior and decisionmaking. The public choice approach assumes that people are 'egoistic, rational utility maximizers' in political as well as economic arenas. Under the public choice vision of legislation, many, if not most, important pub-

---

89. See 8 U.S.C. §1231(a)(6); *Ma v. Reno*, 208 F.3d 815, 830 (9th Cir. 2000).

90. See *Ma v. Reno*, 208 F.3d at 818.

91. Eskridge and Peller, "The New Public Law Movement," supra note 17, at p. 724.

92. See, e.g., Roy L. Brooks, Gilbert P. Carrasco, and Michael Selmi, *Civil Rights Litigation: Cases and Perspectives* 2d ed. (Durham: Carolina Academic Press, 2000), pp. 5–9, 21–26, 257–61, 343–45, 507–11, 605–7, 869–71, 989–92.

93. Eskridge and Frickey, "Legislation Scholarship," supra note 17, at p. 705.

lic problems are not resolved by the legislature. Even when the legislature does act on an important issue, the resulting statute 'tends to represent compromise because the process of accommodating conflicts of group interest is one of deliberation and consent.... What may be called public policy is the equilibrium reached in [the political] struggle at any given moment.' The legislature is a political battlefield; most of its activity is no more purposive than the expedient accommodation of special interest pressures. 'It is hard to imagine a more effective way of saying that Congress has no mind or force of its own' than the prognosis of public choice theory.[94]

Other scholars have also argued that politicians and special interests often conspire to pass legislation to the detriment of the national interests.[95]

Another chief concern regarding legal process is its failure to specify the mechanism by which a judge determines when an unambiguous statutory command leads to an absurd or otherwise irrational result that would justify policy-discovery. The prescribed outcome in *Riggs* was obviously not only absurd but outrageous. But what about less obvious cases, such as a case like *Lewis*,[96] in which following the statute's unambiguous language would have wiped out the federal adjudication post-judgment and returned the case to state court for want of federal subject matter jurisdiction. Is this a case that calls for policy-discovery or policy-vindication under the legal process method? Is there a consensus, based on the common values and aspirations of the American people, that returning the case to state court is irrational or otherwise unacceptable?

Understanding precisely how judges make choices—how they draw lines—is a problem that is not unique to legal process. It is endemic to judicial decision making in general. Many legal scholars and judges attempt to explain line-drawing by reference to "principles." Roscoe Pound defined "principles" as "authoritative starting points for legal reasoning."[97] Once formulated, Ben-

---

94. Ibid. at p. 703 (citations omitted).

95. See, e.g., Kevin Phillips, *Arrogant Capital: Washington, Wall Street, and the Frustration of American Politics* (Boston: Little, Brown and Company, 1994); Elizabeth Garrett, "Who Directs Direct Democracy?" *The University of Chicago Law School Round Table* 4 (1997): 17; Donald L. Barlett and James B. Steele, "Big Money Politics: Who Gets Hurt," *Time* 2/7/00, p. 38.

96. See Chapter 2, Section E, supra, for a discussion of the case.

97. Roscoe Pound, "Roscoe Pound," in Julius Rosenthal Foundation, *My Philosophy of Law: Credos of Sixteen American Scholars* (Boston: Boston Law Book Co., 1941), p. 249, at p. 257.

jamin Cardozo said, a principle "becomes a datum, a point of departure, from which new lines will be run, from which new courses will be measured."[98] Yet it is difficult to believe the judge's subjective attitude does not ultimately determine her choice of "principles," "consecrated principles" or "policies." The line-drawing question is still in search of a good answer.

Eskridge and Frickey make a similar point. They argue that legal process offers "no rigorous methodology for making significant policy judgments."[99] Whether policy-discovery or policy-vindication (as in a case when two statutes collide), Hart and Sacks do not articulate the process by which judges may prefer one public policy over another. Policies are essential to sound judicial reasoning—reasoned elaboration—but what makes the selection of one public policy over a contraposed one sound if they both promote the public's interest?

It is possible that Hart and Sacks did not think deeply about this question. Such a question would not figure prominently in Hart and Sacks's vision of a relatively homogeneous, nondiverse society. This raises doubts about legal process's suitability for our modern, culturally diverse society. Legal process seems resistant to dramatic social change necessary to accommodate the interests of new social groups. It primarily relies upon traditional institutions to resolve conflicts through established procedures.[100] In the context of a changing, culturally diverse society, these procedures can operate in a most undemocratic way.

Finally, while legal process disparages formalism, it creates its own type of formalism. By insisting that judges must rely on only established institutional structures, legal process manufactures a kind of "institutional formalism." The judiciary, it is argued, would in fact be stifled if it always adheres to duly established institutional boundaries or existing community arrangements. Sometimes judicial creativity is needed to resolve pressing social, economic or political problems.[101] Exhibit A: *Brown v. Board of Education.*

For all its flaws, the legal process model has had a profound impact on American law. Erwin Griswold, the dean of Harvard Law School during legal process's heyday in the 1950s, gave evidence of this influence when he com-

98. Benjamin N. Cardozo, *The Nature of the Judicial Process* (New Haven: Yale University Press, 1921), p. 48.

99. Eskridge and Peller, "The New Public Law Movement," supra note 17, at p. 725 (referring to comments by Judge Posner).

100. See, e.g., Edward Purcell, *The Crisis of Democratic Theory: Scientific Naturalism and the Problem of Value* (Lexington: University Press of Kentucky, 1973), pp. 254–55.

101. See Horwitz, *The Transformation of American Law,* supra note 16, at p. 254.

mented on his law school's handling of Hart and Sacks' legal process teaching material: "By word of mouth the materials became known elsewhere, and a considerable number of teachers in other schools sought to make use of them. I suddenly found myself a publisher, dealing with requests that forty copies be sent here, and sixty copies be sent there, and this process continued."[102] Indeed, many members of the Supreme Court were educated under the legal process method.

But it is not simply familiarity that accounts for the enduring appeal of legal process. The notion of process-values seems basic to fair governance. This is especially so if the critics are correct, as I think they are, in their charge that government officials are not all the things Hart and Sacks wanted them to be: rational, honest, public-interested. In a Hobbsian state of nature, we may want procedure to prevail over the whims of humans. This may be the only way to ensure fairness.

Hart and Sacks believed that if all the proper procedures were followed during the course of institutional decision making—courts, legislatures, administrative agencies, and so on—and if institutional comity was practiced, institutional outcomes were less likely to be questioned or overruled. Procedure, in short, serves to legitimize institutional outcomes.[103] The end results reached are the "right" or best results and "ought to be accepted as binding on the whole society unless and until they are duly changed."[104]

Legal process has a particular appeal for legal scholars. The basic thinking behind legal process, planted by Landis in the 1930s, that decision-making authority within our system of government should be allocated in accordance with decision-making structure, provides a rational paradigm for the study of federal jurisdiction and other federal court issues. Reasoned elaboration is, in a sense, the unspoken standard by which rigorous legal scholarship is measured. Perhaps this is why it is difficult to think of legal process as time-bound or antiquated. Perhaps this is why its "view of the cathedral" seems timeless.[105]

---

102. Hart and Sacks, *Legal Process*, supra note 1, at p. vii.
103. Eskridge and Frickey, "Legislation Scholarship," supra note 17, at p. 696.
104. Hart and Sacks, *Legal Process*, supra note 1, at pp. 4–5.
105. See Fallon, "Reflections on the Hart and Wechsler Paradigm," supra note 21, at pp. 971–72.

Section C

A Philosophical Synthesis

We have thus far considered several traditional theories, some more pre-scriptive than descriptive, concerning the processes or methods by which American judges decide cases. Along the way, we have attempted to present these judicial methods in three different, largely harmonious intellectual struc-tures: (1) the prism of "progressive" and "nonprogressive" judicial decision making, essentially a "nonlegal" or extra-judicial conceptualization;[1] (2) the "points" in judicial decision making (Points A, B, and C), a linear judicial con-ceptualization;[2] and (3)the diverse expressions of the logical method or pol-icy method, a more complex judicial conceptualization.[3] We now move to a more sophisticated intellectual framework, largely compatible with the oth-ers, that not only reconceptualizes our current understanding of traditional process, but also synthesizes the five traditional judicial models into three dis-tinct levels of judicial analysis.

Section C has two chapters. Chapter 6 unearths philosophical presupposi-tions that give conceptual structure to traditional judicial analysis. Philo-sophical methods help to clarify the intellectual foundations that shape the ju-dicial outlook. Chapter 7 uses these philosophical traditions as a foundation for synthesizing traditional process into alternative levels of judicial decision making. These levels of judicial analysis take increasingly assertive judicial stances.

---

1. See Preface, Section B, supra, & Part1 passim.
2. See Introduction, Section A, supra, & Part1 passim.
3. See Introduction, Sections A & B, supra, & Part1 passim.

Chapter 6
Philosophical Foundations

A. Introduction

Philosophy plays an important role in judicial reasoning. It provides the analytical structure for much of what we call traditional judicial decision making. Three philosophical methods have had the greatest impact on judicial reasoning: *pragmatism*; *nominalism*; and *positivism*.

These terms are sometimes difficult to pin down. One reason, as we shall see, is that philosophers themselves do not always use the terms consistently.[1] But even when consistent definitions are employed, the distinction between pragmatism and nominalism can at times be quite elusive.[2] This gives rise to the argument that there are really only two philosophical methods (nominalism and positivism) structuring judicial analysis. Some would even go so far as to argue that there is but one underlying philosophical method (nominalism). In other words, unless a judge proceeds in a positivist manner, following the governing law closely, how are we to know she has not slipped into nominalism, visceral judicial decision making? Is it possible that all judges in reality proceed in a nominalist fashion, and merely attempt to create the appearance of fidelity to text and precedent?

We shall not attempt to answer these important questions until the end of the next chapter.[3] Our initial challenge is to try to understand enough of the underlying philosophical approaches to enable us to proceed to the next chapter with a measure of confidence.

B. Human Temperaments

1. Pragmatism and Nominalism

"The history of philosophy is to a great extent that of a certain clash of human temperaments."[4] William James, a great American philosopher, made

---

1. See Sections B1 & B2, infra.
2. See Section B1, infra.
3. See Chapter 7, Section C, infra.
4. William James: Pragmatism and Other Writings, Giles Gunn, ed. (New York: Penguin Books, 2000), p. 8.

this observation in 1907, a time in which one of the most important intellectual clashes in America was well under way. Some argued that it is not only possible but also desirable to make assessments about beliefs based upon an objective, transcendental frame of reference. Our conceptual tools (words and beliefs) and resulting conduct could and should be derived from a theoretically "clear" or "pure" position. This method of investigation is "rationalistic (going by 'principles')." James called it "the tender-minded."[5]

A contrasting intellectual temperament that subsequently developed took the world as it is, warts and all. Believers in this perspective argued that "ideas should never become ideologies," they should not be used to justify the status quo or to dictate or renounce transcendental imperatives. As Louis Menand explains:

> [These philosophers] believed that ideas are not 'out there' waiting to be discovered, but are tools—like forks and knives and microchips—that people devise to cope with the world in which they find themselves. They believed that ideas are produced not by individuals, but by groups of individuals—that ideas are social. They believed that ideas do not develop according to some inner logic of their own, but are entirely dependent, like germs, on their human carriers and the environment. And they believed that since ideas are provisional responses to particular and unreproducible circumstances, their survival depends not on their immutability but on their adaptability.[6]

This method of inquiry is "empiricist (going by 'fact')." James called it the "tough-minded."[7]

The tough-minded intellectual temperament describes pragmatism, a philosophy created in the late nineteenth century by Charles Peirce[8] and subsequently developed by William James[9] and John Dewey,[10] especially James. At its core, the pragmatic method attempts "to interpret each notion by tracing its respective practical consequences."[11] The pragmatist "turns away from ab-

---

5. Ibid. at pp. 10–11.

6. Louis Menand, The Metaphysical Club: A Story of Ideas in America (New York: Farrar, Straus and Giroux, 2001), pp. xi–xii.

7. William James, supra note 4, at pp. 10–11.

8. See, e.g., Collected Papers of Charles Sanders Peirce, Charles Hartshorne, Paul Weiss, and Arthur Burks, eds. (Cambridge: Harvard University Press, 1931–1966).

9. See, e.g., William James, supra note 4.

10. See, e.g., John Dewey, Reconstruction in Philosophy (Boston: Beacon Press, 1948).

11. William James, supra note 4, at p. 25.

straction and insufficiency, from verbal solutions, from bad *a priori* reasons, from fixed principles, closed systems, and pretended absolutes and origins."[12]

Although commonly viewed as a distinctly American philosophy (Peirce, James, and Dewey being Americans), James himself traced pragmatism to the beginning of Western philosophy, and, hence, saw nothing new in it. As he stated, "There is absolutely nothing new in the pragmatic method. Socrates was…adept at it. Aristotle used it methodologically. Locke, Berkeley, and Hume made momentous contributions to the truth by its means."[13] Yet, the American brand of pragmatism has a more modern articulation. It draws heavily from the modern scientific method, which came into wide acceptance in the second half of the nineteenth century. Indeed, both Peirce and James were scientists. Pragmatism, then, cannot be fully understood without some understanding of the scientific method.

Two features of modern science have infused the pragmatic method: induction and Darwinism. Induction proceeds from the belief that "a physical fact is as sacred as a moral principle."[14] Hence, rather than proceeding from a set of abstractions about things, the modern scientist "observe[s] first and constructs generalizations later."[15] Induction is the life blood of Darwinian thought.

Charles Darwin profoundly changed the way we understand ourselves, nature, and, indeed, the cosmos. His contributions to human understanding arguably equal those of Isaac Newton (the principle of gravity and laws of motion) and Albert Einstein (special and general theories of relativity). Darwin argued that all forms of life (from the ant to the Queen of England) evolved from the same organism. New species develop on this "tree of life" in response to environmental changes—drastic climatic shifts, a new predator arrives on the scene, and so on. They do not appear in preordained ways at God's will. Indeed, God is made a remote figure in Darwin's universe. Nature takes center stage. Species that adapt to changing environments survive; those that do not become extinct. Hence, forces of nature "select" which species survive and which do not. New species develop by mutation, and mu-

---

12. Ibid. at p. 27.

13. Ibid.

14. Louis Agassiz, "Evolution and Permanence of Type," Atlantic Monthly, 33 (1874): 95.

15. Menand, The Metaphysical Club, supra note 6, at p. 100. "The notion that the scientist is working with actual things, rather than with prior abstract conceptions about things, suggests that the world is being taken on its own terms. The scientist is not speculating about unseen or unverifiable agencies; he or she is simply assembling reliable data and generating testable hypotheses. A personal preference for one outcome over another is not being permitted to override the evidence of the senses." Ibid., at p. 101.

tations occur by chance. In taking this view, Darwin, some argue, moved science from a conviction that there is mathematical certainty in the universe—a universe under God's firm control—to the realization that the world is governed by unpredictability or chance. Specifically, Darwin's theory of natural selection by chance variation teaches us "that the phenomenal world—the world we can see and touch—is characterized, through and through, by change, and that our knowledge of it is characterized, through and through, by uncertainty."[16]

Induction and Darwin's notion of chance and change were not lost on the pragmatist. As a method of inquiry, pragmatism implies empiricism, with its rejection of truth as a static proposition. Truth is a moving target. There are no final philosophical conclusions, just as there are none in science. We operate on the basis of hypotheses, not absolutes.

Such thinking opens the door to pure chance, and in walks nominalism—the philosophy of particulars. "Nominalism is the doctrine that reality is just one unique thing after another, and that general truths about those things are simply conventions of language, simply names."[17] The nominalist view is nicely captured in the life-as-weather metaphor advanced in a famous article written in 1858 by the scientist Chauncey Wright.[18] With some help from Menand, the metaphor unfolds as follows:

> '[U]nlike planetary perturbations, the weather makes the most reckless excursions from its averages, and obscures them by a most inconsequent and incalculable fickleness.'... We accept this state of affairs about the weather—that it is a perfectly lawful, rather mundane phenomenon whose complexity nevertheless vastly exceeds our ability to understand it—and yet we freely pontificate about the causes of human unhappiness and the future progress of society, things determined by factors presumably many times more complex than the weather.[19]

Thus, Wright believed that life, like the weather, is too complex for us to comprehend with certainty. Life's events are not themselves uncertain; it is only our *knowledge* of these events that is uncertain or imperfect.

---

16. Ibid. at p. 207.

17. Ibid. at p. 228.

18. See Chauncey Wright, "The Winds and the Weather," Atlantic Monthly, 1 (1858): 273.

19. Menand, The Metaphysical Club, supra note 6, at pp. 207–8 (quoting "The Winds and the Weather," at p. 273).

Wright sought to maintain an absolute distinction between science and metaphysics, the philosophy of universals (e.g., the meaning and origin of life). Science deals with facts and their accompanying instability, while metaphysics with values and their presumption of order, Wright argued. But even scientists, including Darwin, had a difficult time adhering to this distinction. Most followed in the direction of Herbert Spencer, the Social Darwinist, whom Wright declared "is not a positivist."[20] Spencer saw continuity in science, the theory of natural selection in particular, prompting Wright to respond:

Everything out of the mind is a product, the result of some process. Nothing is exempt from change. Worlds are formed and dissipated. Races of organic beings grow up like their constituent individual members, and disappear like these. Nothing shows a trace of an original, immutable nature, except the unchangeable laws of change. These point to no beginning and to no end in time, nor to any bounds in space. All indications to the contrary in the results of physical research are clearly traceable to imperfections in our present knowledge of all the laws of change, and to that disposition to cosmological speculations which still prevails even in science.[21]

Again, "the universe is only weather." In its totality, it has no intelligible order—no beginning, no end, no development from lower to higher—and, hence, no meaning that we can divine.[22]

Justice Holmes, the "father" of the policy method,[23] greatly admired Wright's philosophy. Like Wright, Justice Holmes believed that change is constant, that metaphysical theories do not affect people's choices, and that there should be a separation between science and metaphysics. Justice Holmes, in fact, had more admiration for Wright than he did for his pragmatist friends.[24] Justice Holmes's last recorded embrace of Wright came in 1929, the end of his long judicial career, and, thus, raises several important questions about Justice Holmes's judicial method. For example, even though Justice Holmes is

---

20. Chauncey Wright, "The Philosophy of Herbert Spencer," North American Review 100 (1865): 436.

21. Ibid. at pp. 454–55.

22. See Menand, The Metaphysics Club, supra note 6, at pp. 210–11.

23. See Part 1, Section B, supra.

24. Menand, The Metaphysics Club, supra note 6, at p. 217. Recall Holmes's dissent in Lochner, discussed in Chapter 3, Section B1, supra, in which he states, "The Fourteenth Amendment does not enact Mr. Herbert Spencer's Social Statics."

commonly thought to be a pragmatist,[25] he may in fact have been a nominalist masquerading as a pragmatist. Was he? More broadly, can a reasonable distinction be drawn between nominalism and pragmatism, at least in the context of law if not in the context of philosophy? Does nominalism necessarily lead to emotivism (the belief in noncognitive processes; i.e., the notion that a statement's meaning is the emotion—such as, love, pleasure, fear, anger, or pain—it communicates without conveying the truth) or even to nihilism?

What is clear is that Wright's nominalism did not get very far in pragmatist circles. Justice Holmes, for one, did not carry nominalism into the mainstream of his judicial philosophy (or so it would appear[26]) even though he thought Peirce "overrated" and "lost sympathy with the views of his friend William James, which he thought too hopeful and anthropocentric."[27] Peirce and James expressly rejected Wright's philosophy,[28] and, in the process, sought to clarify the distinction between pragmatism and nominalism.

James argued that science (facts) and metaphysics (values) cannot be separated. Indeed, the belief that they should (or should not) be separated is itself a metaphysical choice. Everything we do serves some interest, or value—so we had better know what these values are. Our beliefs reflect our way of coping with the world.[29]

We cannot, however, be absolutely certain about the truth of this or any other proposition, James asserted. Agreeing with Wright (and, of course, with Darwin), James accepted the fact that the human condition is such that certainty is beyond our reach. But we are saved from nominalism, emotivism or nihilism, James believed, if we recognize the existence of free will. James defined free will as "the sustaining of a thought *because I chose to* when I might have other thoughts."[30] Freedom exists because there is no other way to explain why one person believes in one thing (say, necessity or determinism) while another person believes in the opposite (free will). We prove the existence of free will (and, hence, reason and moral agency) when that which

---

25. See, e.g., Richard A. Posner, The Problematics of Moral and Legal Theory (Cambridge: The Belknap Press of Harvard University Press, 1999), p. 240.

26. In addition to the discussion of some of the opinions written by Justice Holmes in Chapter 3, Section B1, supra, see, e.g., Richard A. Posner, "Pragmatic Adjudication," in The Revival of Pragmatism: New Essays on Social Thought, Law, and Culture, Morris Dickstein, ed. (Durham: Duke University Press, 1998), pp. 235–36 (suggesting that Holmes had standards, that he did not decide constitutional cases from the gut).

27. Menand, The Metaphysics Club, supra note 6, at p. 217.

28. See, e.g., ibid. at p. 228.

29. See ibid. at pp. 101, 219.

30. Ibid. at p. 219 (emphasis in original).

we do makes a practical difference to someone. Thus, Wright was right in his insistence that one cannot predict the effect belief has in individual cases, but he was wrong to deduce from that the conclusion that "we must affirm nothing."[31]

Pragmatism, then, attempts to distinguish itself from nominalism and other philosophical methods by making the following claims collectively.[32] First, philosophy is simply a method of coping with everyday life; it is not a path to certainty about the world in which we live. Second, results, not (deductive) logic, are what make beliefs true. Third, concepts (whether scientific or metaphysical) are not immutable or determinate; they do not name actual entities, but are, instead, only tools of analysis; they "do not exist independent of our interests."[33] Finally, pragmatism is more than a theory about knowledge and truth—more than an epistemology. It is also a theory about "social character." Pragmatism acknowledges the reality of the social, just as nominalism acknowledges the reality of the individual. "James and Dewey," Richard Rorty notes, "took for granted...the ideal of universal human fraternity."[34] The community trumps the individual in pragmatism. As Peirce suggested in 1871:

> The question whether the *genus homo* has any existence except as individuals is the question whether there is anything of any more dignity, worth, and importance than individual happiness, individual aspiration, individual life. Whether men really have anything in common, so that the *community* is to be considered as an end to itself...is the most fundamental practical question in regard to every public institution the constitution of which we have it in our power to influence.[35]

---

31. Ibid. at p. 213.

32. See William James, supra note 4, at pp. 24–41, 74–104; Menand, The Metaphysical Club, supra note 6, at pp. 219–30.

33. Menand, The Metaphysical Club, note 6, at p. 225. For example, the legal concept of "proximate cause" is only a metaphor. "[Since] every event has a multiplicity of independent causes,...'proximate cause' is just the antecedent event people choose to pick out in order to serve whatever interest they happen to have in the case at hand." Ibid. at p. 223.

34. Richard Rorty, "Pragmatism as Romantic Polytheism," in The Review of Pragmatism: New Essays on Social Thought, Law, and Culture, Morris Dickstein, ed. (Durham: Duke University Press, 1998), p. 25.

35. Menand, The Metaphysical Club, supra note 6, at p. 229 (quoting Charles Sanders Peirce, "Fraser's The Works of George Berkeley," in Writing of Charles S. Peirce: A Chronological Edition, Peirce Edition Project, vol. 2 (Bloomington: Indiana University Press, 1982), p. 487).

Pragmatism's political side—community welfare and solidarity trumps individual independence—is very much reflected in Justice Holmes's jurisprudence.[36] Perhaps it arises in reaction to his participation in America's greatest sectional strife, the Civil War (an event which also supports the pragmatist claim that beliefs do matter). Justice Holmes's strong support of community interest would seem to place him squarely within the pragmatist camp.

2. Positivism

Another important clash of intellectual temperaments that helps explain traditional judicial decision-making centers on the meaning of law itself. The most important figure on this subject is not an American but an Englishman—H.L.A. Hart. Hart practiced law in England in the 1930s, but turned his attention to philosophy and eventually to legal philosophy after World War II. Hart had in common with a school of thought called "logical positivism" the desire to ask the right philosophical questions—namely, questions regarding the appropriate *use* of words or concepts rather than "senseless" metaphysical questions (questions dealing with the essence of things) that can only lead to "senseless" metaphysical answers.[37]

Applying his analytical method to the meaning-of-law question, Hart began with a criticism of a position advanced in the nineteenth century by Jeremy Bentham and John Austin. Bentham defined law as the sovereign's prerogative: "whatever is given for law by the person or persons recognised as possessing the power of making laws, is *law*."[38] "Every *law* or *rule...is a command,*" Austin wrote, and a command "*issued by a sovereign legislature...would probably be called a law.*"[39] Thus, for Bentham and Austin, law is whatever the sovereign commands. More specifically, law has two elements—coercion and the citizens' habits of obedience.[40] Hart found this concept of law deficient because it did not explain what some philosophers call the "normativity" of law.

---

36. See, e.g., *Buck v. Bell* discussed in Chapter 3, Section B1, supra. See also, Posner, "Pragmatic Adjudication," supra note 26, at p. 236 (noting Holmes's frequent use of communitarian phrases such as "the traditions of our people").

37. This aspect of Hart's philosophy is often called "ordinary language philosophy." For a more detailed discussion of this philosophy and its relation to logical positivism, see, e.g., Richard Rorty, The Linguistic Turn (Chicago: University of Chicago Press, 1967).

38. Jeremy Bentham, An Introduction to The Principles of Morals and Legislation (New York: Hafner Publishing Company, 1948), p. 330 (emphasis in original).

39. John Austin, The Province of Jurisprudence Determined (London: John Murray, 1832), pp. 5, 14 (emphasis in original).

40. See H.L.A. Hart, Essays on Bentham (Oxford: Clarendon Press, 1982), p. 78.

This is the idea, as Hart stated, that "where there is law, there human conduct is made in some sense non-optional or obligatory."[41] Defining law as citizens' habits of obedience backed by the coercive power of the state fails to differentiate legal obligations from "obligations" that arise from wrongful force, such as the "obligation" to obey a gunman who commands, "Your money or your life."[42]

Hart's concept of law centers on what he called the "rule of recognition." A legal system exists only when officials within the society (the elites) adopt a certain "internal attitude" towards a rule; namely, that the rule should be enforced.[43] Thus, traffic rules are "laws" because the police and judges enforcing them believe in their legitimacy (but not necessarily in their justness, as we shall see momentarily). The "your-money-or-your-life" rule is not "law" because no one involved in the transaction believes it is legitimate.

Hart's central concept—law is a system of legitimate, state-enacted rules—has been attacked by several philosophers. The best known is Ronald Dworkin,[44] who argued that, in a country with a rich institutional history such as the United States and England, law cannot properly be conceived of as a static system of rules. Instead, law is a living phenomenon that consists of not only state-enacted rules but also long-established custom (or policy).[45] Another critic, Lon Fuller, argued that law is not just a system of rules. Rather, it is a system of a particular species of rules. These are rules that have an "inner morality," which is to say rules that are applied publicly, prospectively, and consistently.[46] And, finally, Joseph Raz criticized Hart's failure to stipulate the

---

41. Ibid. at p. 80.
42. Ibid.
43. Ibid. at p. 55.
44. See discussion of Dworkin in Introduction, Section C1, supra.
45. See Ronald Dworkin, Taking Rights Seriously (Cambridge: Harvard University Press, 1977), pp. 14–80); Ronald Dworkin, "The Model of Rules," University of Chicago Law Review 35 (1967): 14. See also relevant discussion in Introduction, Section C1, supra. Hart responded that he was addressing a different question than Dworkin. Hart was looking at the question of law externally—that is, from the perspective of the social scientist, asking what does she think law is?—whereas Dworkin was asking an internal question—what does a judge think law is? See, e.g., Hart, Essays on Bentham, supra note 40, at pp. 144–53; H.L.A. Hart, "Law in the Perspective of Philosophy: 1776–1976," New York University Law Review 51 (1976): 538.
46. See, e.g., Lon Fuller, "Positivism and Fidelity to Law—A reply to Professor Hart," Harvard Law Review 71 (1958): 630, replying to H.L.A. Hart, "Positivism and the Separation of Law and Morals," Harvard Law Review 71 (1958): 593. Hart responded to this argument at various times, including in 1958 in his Harvard article, each time arguing that procedural fairness strictly administered "is unfortunately compatible with very great in-

necessity for just laws. In other words, Hart did not think that our use of the word "law" necessarily implied that law must be moral:

> Not only may vast numbers be coerced by laws which they do not regard as morally binding, but it is not even true that those who do accept the system voluntarily, must conceive of themselves as morally bound to do so, though the system will be most stable when they do so. In fact, their allegiance to the system may be based on many different considerations: calculations of long-term interest; disinterested interest in others; an unreflecting inherited or traditional attitude; or the mere wish to do as others do.[47]

How, Raz asked, could Hart assert coherently that a judge is obligated to follow the law yet she does not have to *believe* in the law's justness?[48] Should Hart acknowledge that judges and other state officials must at the very least claim (even if they do not believe) that the system of rules they are called upon to

---

iquity." H.L.A. Hart, The Concept of Law (Oxford: Oxford University Press, 1961), p. 202. See also, Grant Gilmore, The Ages of American Law (New Haven: Yale University Press, 1977), p. 111 ("In Hell there will be nothing but law, and due process will be meticulously observed.").

47. H.L.A. Hart, The Concept of Law, supra note 46, at p. 198.

48. Is Raz suggesting that a judge who does not believe in the justness of the law he is called upon to enforce is not obligated to enforce it? Raz argues that the law (qua law) obligates judges no more than it obligates citizens: "Both courts and ordinary citizens are legally bound to so act. Neither are necessarily morally so bound." Joseph Raz, "Symposium: The Works of Joseph Raz: Facing Up: A Reply," Southern California Law Review 62 (1989): 1153, 1170 n. 28. On the other hand, Michael Moore ascribes to Raz the belief that law does obligate judicial obedience, not just as a conceptual matter (i.e., if judges do not feel obligated by a legal system's rules, there can be no legal system from a positivist point of view), but also as a moral matter. Moore quotes Raz as saying, "the courts are bound to apply laws regardless of their view of their merit.... [L]egal systems consist of laws which the courts are bound to apply and are not at liberty to disregard whenever they find their application undesirable, all things considered." Michael S. Moore, Educating Oneself in Public: Critical Essays in Jurisprudence (New York: Oxford University Press, 2000), p. 133 (quoting Raz; emphasis supplied). Moore also notes that even Raz concedes the point that judicial oaths or vows "may impose a moral obligation to obey." Ibid. at p. 135. But Raz seems to suggest that these reasons may not bind judges morally in all cases. See Raz, "A Reply," at p. 1170 n. 28 ("Moore is right to say that I subscribe to the common view that there are additional reasons for obeying the law which apply to judges, at least in reasonably just societies. But I am not convinced that those amount to a binding moral obligation in all cases."). My thanks to my colleague Michael Moore for helping me think through this issue.

enforce is just? Isn't that a necessary and sufficient condition for any concept of law?[49]

None of these critics, with the exception of Dworkin, really question the validity of Hart's central message that law is a system of rules with a certain pedigree; to wit, state-enacted rules held to be legitimate by their enforcers. This, of course, is essentially the Bentham/Austin model, the main difference being Hart's emphasis on the normativity of law. Dworkin calls the Bentham/Austin/Hart stance "legal positivism," or "positivism."[50] As we shall see next, positivism has had a significant impact on the manner in which judges structure their reasoning.

---

49. See, e.g., Joseph Raz, The Concept of a Legal System 2d ed. (Oxford: Oxford University Press, 1980), pp. 234–38. Michael Moore observes that Hart could concede that officials must believe in the system's justness before it can be called "law," without Hart himself asserting that the system must be just in order for it to be law. See Moore, Educating Oneself in Public, supra note 48, at p. 3. Hart's response as to why he refused to accept the weaker form of positivism is instructive: "I myself wonder at times why I do not take the easier line; what prevents me is the simple empirical doubt as to whether all officials do believe this (Oliver Wendell Holmes did not!) and if they do not whether a system with all the other features of law cannot exist as a legal system." Ibid. (quoting personal correspondence with Hart).

50. See, e.g., Dworkin, Taking Rights Seriously, supra note 45, at pp. 16–17. Dworkin admits, however, that "not every philosopher who is called a positivist would subscribe" to his definition. Ibid. at p. 17.

Chapter 7
Levels of Judicial Analysis

A. Introduction

Positivism, pragmatism, and nominalism roughly translate into three basic levels of judicial decision making, what can be called: "Level 1," or "judicial positivism"; "Level 2," or "judicial pragmatism"; and "Level 3," or "judicial nominalism." The five traditional judicial models discussed in Chapters 1–5 (Part 1, Section A and Section B) can now be sorted and synthesized within this new framework. Like other structures discussed in this book—"progressive"/"nonprogressive" dichotomy, linear judicial decision making (Points A, B, and C), and the logical/policy method distinction[1]—the levels of judicial analysis render fascinating juxtapositions that shed new light on familiar judicial theories.[2]

B. Judicial Temperaments

1. Level 1: Judicial Positivism

Judicial positivism can be defined as judicial decision making that attempts to adhere to consistency with past judicial, legislative, regulatory, and constitutional rules. The judicial positivist not only believes that the positivist account of law—to wit, law is a system of state rules and these rules are exhaustive of the law[3]—is descriptively accurate, but also that it is prescriptively sound. Judges should not enforce rights or impose correlative duties that do not arise directly or logically from the positive law:[4]

---

1. See Section C, supra.

2. Not surprisingly, some of the traditional judicial models seem more aspirational than fully operational in their representation of a particular level of judicial analysis.

3. See, e.g.,Ronald Dworkin, *Taking Rights Seriously* (Cambridge: Harvard University Press, 1977), p. 16 ("The set of these valid legal rules is exhaustive of 'the law'; so that if someone's case is not clearly covered by such a rule..., then that case cannot be decided by 'applying the law.'").

4. Ibid. ("To say that someone has a 'legal obligation' is to say that this case falls under a valid legal rule that requires him to do or to forbear from doing something.").

The judicial positivist would begin and usually end with a consideration of cases, statutes, administrative regulations, and constitutional provisions—the 'authorities' to which the judge must defer in accordance with the principle that judges are duty-bound to secure consistency in principle with what other officials have done in the past. If the authorities all line up in one direction, the decision of the present case is likely to be foreordained, because to go against the authorities would, unless there are compelling reasons to do so, violate the duty to the past. The most compelling reason would be that some other line of cases had adopted a principle inconsistent with the authorities directly relevant to the present case. It would be the judges' duty, by comparing the two lines and bringing to bear other principles manifest or latent in case law, statute, or constitutional provision, to find the result in the present case that would promote or cohere with the best interpretation of the legal background as a whole.[5]

There is little mystery which traditional judicial models exhibit positivist tendencies. Legal formalism (Chapter 1) and Scalian textualism (Chapter 2) are models of judicial consistency, or so they attempt to be. The judge proceeding thereunder will not be influenced by policy considerations, other than the policy of consistency.[6]

Judicial positivism's normativity—its idea that judicial decision making should be consistent not only with prior judicial rulings, but also with other governmental rulings—yields distinct advantages, especially in a heterogeneous society. Perhaps the most important is that it creates conditions necessary for the ordering of civic and personal affairs. "People repeatedly subjected, like Pavlov's dogs, to two or more inconsistent sets of directions, without means of resolving the inconsistencies, could not fail in the end to react as the dogs did. The society, collectively, would suffer a nervous breakdown."[7]

Separation of powers is another stated benefit of judicial positivism. Power concentrated in the hands of legislators or judges cannot and should not be

---

5. Richard Posner, *The Problematics of Moral and Legal Theory* (Cambridge: The Belknap Press of Harvard University Press, 1999), pp. 241–42. See Richard A. Posner, "Pragmatic Adjudication," in *The Revival of Pragmatism: New Essays on Social Thought, Law, and Culture*, Morris Dickstein, ed. (Durham: Duke University Press, 1998), pp. 237–38.

6. For a discussion of the nondistinction between "policies" and "principles," see relevant discussion in Introduction, Section C1, supra.

7. Henry Hart, "The Relations Between State and Federal Law," *Columbia Law Review* 54 (1954): 489, 489.

tolerated under our democratic form of government. Judicial positivism limits the judicial power of democratic government to the application of extant rules. Law-making and, most importantly, policy-formulation are government functions given to the legislative branch of government, which is more accountable to the people.

It can also be argued that judicial positivism cloaks the powerless with inviolable rights—rules that the powerful can neither modify nor eliminate arbitrarily. In this sense, judicial positivism is similar to what Rodney Blackman calls "procedural natural law." Here, "law" is seen as containing certain "fixed elements" all of which guard against arbitrary or irrational government acts, and thereby give "law" its moral dimension.[8]

Perhaps the most serious charge against judicial positivism is that it is difficult for human beings wearing black robes to follow without failure. It takes some doing for a judge to remain faithful to a style of judging that is too slow to change with the changing times. Congress is too slow to act, and when it does, it is often handcuffed by special interest groups. The injustice that can result from the application of "dead" law can be too much for warm-blooded judges to ignore. Parties to a lawsuit care little about the internal consistency of legal propositions when justice is denied.[9]

In spite of these considerations, judicial positivism has a powerful hold on judicial behavior. Perhaps it is the psychology of consistency, as Dan Farber suggests, that explains its strong appeal.[10] Or perhaps judicial positivism gives judges a way to achieve peace of mind; in other words, to disengage emotionally from the imponderable human elements that often come together in a single case. Whatever the reason, judicial positivism's imprint on the judicial process cannot be gainsaid. "The judicial opinion continues to be based largely on syllogistic forms of argumentation; judges maintain remarkably high levels of confidence in their decisions; and opinions portray the chosen decision as singularly correct."[11]

---

8. See Rodney J. Blackman, *Procedural Natural Law* (Durham: Carolina Academic Press, 1999).

9. Justice is the primary objective of Western legal systems. See Introduction, Section B, supra.

10. See Daniel Farber, Symposium contribution, "The Ages of American Formalism," *Northwestern University Law Review* 90 (1995): 89, 105.

11. Dan Simon, "A Psychological Model of Judicial Decision Making," *Rutgers Law Journal* 30 (1995): 1, 10–11.

2. Level 2: Judicial Pragmatism

If it is true that most judges, especially at the lower court level, tend to be judicial positivists, it is equally true that most of our great judges have been judicial pragmatists. Richard Posner, Chief Judge of the Seventh Circuit, lists the following among the Supreme Court justices with significant pragmatist leanings: Holmes, Brandeis, Cardozo, Frankfurter, Jackson, Douglas, Brennan, Powell, Stevens, White, and Breyer.[12] Although not a Supreme Court justice, Posner, arguably the greatest intellectual and scholarly judge on or off the Supreme Court since Holmes, places himself in the pragmatist camp as well.[13]

Judicial pragmatism does not have a universally agreed upon definition. Dworkin, for example, defines it as follows: "The pragmatist thinks judges should always do the best they can for the future, in the circumstances, unchecked by any need to respect or secure consistency in principle with what other officials have done or will do."[14] Posner, who also calls Dworkin a pragmatist,[15] restates Dworkin's definition to read as follows: "Pragmatist judges always try to do the best they can do for the present and future, unchecked by any *felt* duty to secure consistency in principle with what other officials have done in the past."[16] Posner's "pragmatist" judge seems less predisposed to dismiss past rules than Dworkin's. However, Dworkin's use of the word "unchecked" could mean that the judge will absolutely not respect past rules just as much as it could mean that he is free to choose not to do so. The latter meaning removes any real distinction between Dworkin's and Posner's definitions. The former meaning more properly describes nominalism, although, as we noted earlier, the line between pragmatism and nominalism can be thin at times.[17]

By definition, then, pragmatic adjudication seeks to produce the best results for society that a legal system can produce "unchecked by any *felt* duty to secure consistency in principle." This conceptualization of judicial pragmatism does not, of course, mean that precedent is totally irrelevant. Following precedent in a given case—that is, simply applying the extant rules—may lead to the best results for society, such as maintaining a consistent set of rules. Level 2, to this limited extent, is consistent with Level 1, and even in-

---

12. Posner, *The Problematics of Moral and Legal Theory*, supra note 5, at p. 240.
13. Ibid.
14. Ronald Dworkin, *Law's Empire* (Cambridge, Mass.: Belknap Press, 1986), p. 161.
15. See Posner, *The Problematics of Moral and Legal Theory*, supra note 5, at pp. 240, 252–55 (also distinguishing his approach from Dworkin's).
16. Ibid. at p. 241 (emphasis in original).
17. See Section A & Section A1, supra.

corporates Level 1. A pragmatist judge could come out the same way as a positivist judge (but on pragmatic grounds) just as he might come out the same
way as a nominalist judge (but for pragmatic reasons). This internal flexibility is quite in line with the philosophical side of pragmatism: As Rorty observes, "The frequent complaint that a philosopher who holds the pragmatic
theory of truth cannot give you a reason to be a fascist is perfectly justified.
But neither can that person give you a reason not to be a fascist."[18] In short,
"[a] pragmatic judge...need not be recognizable by a distinctive style of judging....[H]e is open to any pragmatic argument in favor of rules [or against
rules, including the argument that] judges cannot be trusted to make intelligent decisions unless they are guided by rules...."[19]

What this means, of course, is that the criteria for the "best results" for
which the pragmatic judge is striving must remain open. The "best results" are
not necessarily utilitarian. They can, for example, be egalitarian in the sense of
Dworkin's "forward-looking" notion of the judicial process's purpose—"it aims
at a structure of law and community that is egalitarian."[20] Basically, the "best
results" depend on the circumstances surrounding the case, mostly *the relevant
values*. What this means is that the "best results," as Posner asserts, "are not simply what is best for the particular case without regard for the implications for
other cases....[Thus,] [p]ragmatism will not tell us what is best; but, provided
there is a fair degree of value consensus among the judges, as I think there is,
it can help judges seek the best results unhampered by philosophical doubts."[21]

Judicial pragmatism presupposes a concept of law that is very different from
the one embraced by judicial positivism. In fact, it is very Dworkian: law is a
living organism that consists of not only state-enacted rules but also long-established custom or community norms, including its moral precepts. Judicial
pragmatists believe this account of law is both descriptively accurate and prescriptively sound.[22]

---

18. Richard Rorty, "Pragmatism as Romantic Polytheism," in *The Review of Pragmatism: New Essays on Social Thought, Law, and Culture*, Morris Dickstein, ed. (Durham:
Duke University Press, 1998), p. 25.

19. Posner, "Pragmatic Adjudication," supra note 5, at p. 247. See also, Posner, *The
Problematics of Moral and Legal Theory*, supra note 5, at pp. 261–62.

20. Ronald Dworkin, "In Praise of Theory," *Arizona State Law Journal* 29 (1997): 353, 364.

21. Posner, *The Problematics of Moral and Legal Theory*, supra note 5, at p. 262. See
also ibid. at p. 253.

22. See, e.g., Dworkin, *Taking Rights Seriously*, supra note 3, at pp. 14–80; Posner, *The
Problematics of Moral and Legal Theory*, supra note 5, at pp. 240–62. See especially, ibid.,
at pp. 257, 262 (suggesting that law can arise from "a fair degree of value consensus among
the judges" who are community-connected).

Again, it is important to note that consistency does matter under judicial pragmatism. It is just that it does not possess the special power it commands under judicial positivism. Judicial pragmatism reduces consistency to a value, one of several to be considered in a given case.

Mostly, though, judicial pragmatism implicates policy-formulation. It suggests that the judge, operating within the corporateness of the judicial process, will effectuate articulated norms (policy-vindication) as well as enforce unarticulated community norms (policy-discovery), but the judge will not impose norms on a community before the community is ready to accept them (policy-making). The pragmatist "ideal of universal human fraternity"[23] would seem to preclude what might be viewed as a judge's hostile takeover of the community. Sociological jurisprudence (Chapter 4) and legal process (Chapter 5) contain the predominant features of judicial pragmatism.

Judicial pragmatism's basic stance (its normativity) is that a judge should have the freedom and flexibility to be as consistent or as inconsistent in principle as is necessary to get the best results out of our legal system. The crucial question, of course, is how much inconsistency and at what price? Do we really want to take the chance that some day some court might decide to chip away at a fundamental right simply because, on balance, it is in the community's best interest to do so? What is there, save the judge's confirmation promise, to stop a judge from disregarding all law, from morphing judicial pragmatism into judicial nominalism?

3. Level 3: Judicial Nominalism

True to its philosophical temperament, judicial nominalism has no respect for consistency, except to the extent that it can help the judge arrive at the best results in the particular case. Judicial nominalism is case-specific decision making. The judicial nominalist is a judicial particularist. She is a judge who gives the parties to the case her undivided attention and her deepest sensibility. Justice will be done in *this* case; individual justice will not be held hostage to community justice.

Whose sense of justice is this? The answer is clear—the judge's. In an interview reflecting on some thirty years on the bench, Judge Skelly Wright,

---

23. See Chapter 6, Section B1, supra. Judge Posner seems to jettison pragmatism in common law cases on the ground that judicial decision making in such cases poses no threat to other organs of government. For a criticism of this position, see Introduction, Section C2, supra. Justice Holmes also seems to have taken a similar position in common law cases. See Chapter 3, Section C1, supra.

one of the most celebrated federal judges in the last half of the twentieth century, said:

> I guess I am an activist, but I want to do what's right. When I get a case, I look at it and the first thing I think of automatically is what's right, what should be done—and then you look at the law to see whether or not you can do it. That might invert the process of how you should arrive at a decision, of whether you should look at the law first, but [with me] it developed through making decisions, which involves resolving problems.... And I am less patient than other judges with law that won't permit what I conceive to be fair. Now, there's a legitimate criticism of that, because what's fair and just to X may not be fair and just to Y—in perfect good faith on both sides. But if you don't take it to extremes, I think that it's good to come out with a fair and just result and then look for law to support it.[24]

Thus, in attempting to define judicial nominalism, one can restate Dworkin's definition of judicial pragmatism as follows: a judicial nominalist always tries to achieve the best results in the present case "unchecked by a need to respect or secure consistency in principle with what other officials have done or will do."[25] The judge makes no pretense of respecting past rules. Cases are decided by "fundamental principles" or principles of morality deeply rooted in the judge's gut rather than in community standards. Justice is the measure of the chancellor's foot.[26]

Unlike the judicial positivist or judicial pragmatist, the judicial nominalist has no concept of law. The latter is rule-skeptic and fact-skeptic.[27] Nominalists, Dworkin writes:

> ...urge that we solve [legal] problems by ignoring them. In their view the concepts of 'legal obligation' and 'the law' are myths, invented and sustained by lawyers for a dismal mix of conscious and subconscious motives. The puzzles we find in these concepts are merely symptoms that they are myths. They are unsolvable because [they are] unreal,

---

24. Jack Bass, *Unlikely Heroes* (New York: Simon and Schuster, 1981), p. 116.

25. Dworkin, *Law's Empire*, supra note 14, at p. 161.

26. This expression is a reference to equity jurisdiction discussed in the Introduction, Section B, supra. As discussed in the Introduction, Section C2, supra, the judge's values are never inconsistent with some community; they are always in harmony with a community. The problem here is that they are not in harmony with the community affected by the case. That, indeed, is the central problem with policy-making.

27. These terms are discussed in Chapter 3, supra.

and our concern with them is just one feature of our enslavement. We would do better to flush away the puzzles and the concepts altogether, and pursue our important social objectives without this excess baggage.[28]

Judicial nominalists argue that all judges are human beings and, therefore, engage in gut-reaction, visceral decision making. Every judge has his or her own "puke" test and will use it when the occasion arises. A sympathetic party[29] or a "hard case" usually present such an occasion. "Hard cases" have so much doubt, so much uncertainty, so many imponderables as to make logical reasoning or consistent policy rulings impossible.[30]

A case that is not particularly hard, but which seems to involve a politically "sympathetic" party, is the Supreme Court's controversial opinion in *Bush v. Gore*.[31] This case dealt with the historic 2000 Presidential Election between the Republican candidate, Texas Governor George W. Bush, and the Democratic candidate, Vice President Albert Gore. Here we see judicial nominalism masquerading as judicial positivism or, some would argue, judicial pragmatism.

Under intense pressure to decide the case within a matter of days rather than months, which is its customary time frame, the Court struck down Florida's statutory scheme governing the manual recount of disputed electoral ballots. Seven of the justices reasoned that the absence of uniform standards governing manual recounts violated the Fourteenth Amendment's Equal Protection Clause. Five of the justices (Chief Justice Rehnquist and Justices Scalia, Thomas, O'Connor, and Kennedy), however, went on to rule that the recount must end. By so ruling, these justices placed the Court, America's least democratic governmental institution, in the middle of a presidential election, America's most sacred democratic practice. Although typically not policy-

---

28. Dworkin, *Taking Law Seriously*, supra note 3, at p. 15.

29. See discussion of Justice Cardozo's lapse into judicial policy-making in Introduction, Section C2, supra.

30. Responding to this situation, Chief Justice Rehnquist said in a speech: "If our opinions seem on occasion to be internally inconsistent, to contain a logical fallacy, or to insufficiently distinguish a prior case, I commend you to the view attributed to Chief Justice Hughes upon his retirement from our Court in 1941. He said that he always tried to write his opinions logically and clearly, but if a Justice whose vote was necessary to make a majority insisted that particular language be put in, in it went, and let the law reviews figure out what it meant." Linda Greenhouse, "Rehnquist Asks Limit to Automatic Appeals," New York Times, Section 1 (Main), 9/16/84, p. 27.

31. 531 U.S. 98 (2001).

makers, these justices did not hesitate in this one instance to enlarge the judicial power of the United States beyond the expectations of most Americans.[32]

Continuing along its nominalist path, the justices also ignored well-settled
precedent. For example, the Court completely disregarded the "intent test" in
equal-protection law. For more than twenty-five years prior to this case, the
Supreme Court had consistently ruled that a violation of the Equal Protection
Clause is triggered only by the establishment of a discriminatory animus on
the part of the state actor.[33] Indeed, the intent test had allowed scores of facially neutral state laws to withstand constitutional challenge even though each
had a discriminatory effect on people of color or women.[34] In *Bush v. Gore,*
no one so much as alleged that the Florida legislature acted with invidious intent in the enactment of the state election code.

---

32. Apparently, the Court's decision did not affect the outcome of the election as was
once thought. A recount of some of the disputed Florida ballots (the "undervotes," which
are ballots that registered no presidential preference, and the "overvotes," ballots that registered two votes for one candidate, or votes for multiple candidates) by the New York
Times, The Wall Street Journal, the Washington Post, and CNN several months after the
election revealed that Bush won Florida and, hence, the 2000 Presidential election. On this
basis it could be argued that the Supreme Court did not decide the election. On the other
hand, it was also revealed that a statewide recount to determine the "intent" of voters would
have given Florida and, hence, the election to Gore. See, e.g., Philip Terzian, "Media's Vote
Tally is in: President Bush is President," San Diego Union-Tribune, 12/2/01, p. G4; Martin
Plissner, "Majority of Voters Should Pick the President," San Diego Union-Tribune,
11/18/01, p. G4. See generally, Jackie Calmes and Edward P. Foldessy, "Florida Revisited:
In Election Review, Bush Wins Without Supreme Court Help—Still, Majority of State Voters Would Have Picked Gore But for Poor Ballot Design," Wall Street Journal, 11/12/01, p.
A1. The media's vote tally does not, of course, excuse or justify the fact that by stopping
the electoral process, the Supreme Court made a major inroad on a political matter that
Congress, through statutes, and the people, through the Constitution, had reserved for
themselves.

33. See, e.g., *Adarand Constructors, Inc. v. Pena,* 515 U.S. 200 (1995); *City of Richmond
v. Croson,* 488 U.S. 469 (1989); *Rogers v. Lodge,* 458 U.S. 613 (1982); *Mt. Healthy City School
Board of Education v. Doyle,* 429 U.S. 274 (1977); *Washington v. Davis,* 426 U.S. 229 (1976);
Harper v. Virginia Board of Elections, 383 U.S. 665 (1966).

34. The Court has, for example, upheld state land use laws that had an exclusionary
effect on African Americans as well as state employment laws that had an exclusionary effect on women. The Court has, in addition, required a showing of discriminatory intent
on the part of a state actor as a precondition to sustaining the constitutionality of public
affirmative action programs. For a discussion of these cases and the intent test in general,
See, e.g., Roy L. Brooks, *Rethinking the American Race Problem* (Berkeley: University of
California Press, 1990), pp. 51–54, 84–87.

In an unmistakably unpositivist act, the justices expressly ruled that their reasoning on the equal protection issue was "limited to the present circumstances."[35] This unprecedented attempt to strip the Court's reasoning of its precedential value—taking it out of the doctrine of *stare decisis* by mere incantation—was smoking-gun evidence of the Court's rejection of judicial positivism. Essentially conceding this point, Judge Posner contends, however, that the Court's opinion can best be explained and justified as an exercise in judicial pragmatism. The justices averted a looming national crisis by ending the disputed election then and there rather than allowing it to take its constitutionally scripted course—to wit, a decision in the House of Representatives—wherein partisan forces could run amok.[36] The few legal scholars who have come forth to defend the majority's opinion have done so largely on this ground.[37]

But this argument begs many questions. Did the Court merely substitute its own partisanship for that of Congress's? Were the justices intent on achieving what they believed to be justice in this one, special case? Were they so focused on the particulars of the case that prior rules and countervailing community norms carried little weight at this singular moment in American history?

For most legal scholars, *Bush v. Gore* looks, smells, and quacks like judicial nominalism. As one commentator has observed, most legal scholars see the case as "quite demonstrably the worst Supreme Court decision in history....*Dred Scott* was, by comparison, a brilliantly reasoned and logically coherent decision."[38] Akhil Amar, one of the leading constitutional law scholars in the country, concurs: "Many of us thought that courts do not act in an openly political fashion."[39] Suzanna Sherry, a persistent critic of critical theory, similarly concludes, "There is really very little way to reconcile this opinion other than that they wanted Bush

---

35. 531 U.S. at 109.

36. See Richard A. Posner, *Breaking the Deadlock: The 2000 Election, the Constitution, and the Courts* (Princeton, N.J.: Princeton University Press, 2001).

37. See, e.g., Vincent Bugliosi, *The Betrayal of America: How the Supreme Court Undermined the Constitution and Chose Our President* (New York: Nation's Books, 2001) p. 47 (discussing scholars who support the court's opinion).

38. Max Boot, "Rule of Law: Law Professors v. the Supreme Court," Wall Street Journal, 8/13/01, p. A13.

39. Ibid. Jack Balkin and Sanford Levinson have characterized the Court's opinion as "muddled reasoning [that] barely passes for legal doctrine." Jack M. Balkin and Sanford Levinson, "Understanding the Constitutional Revolution," *Virginia Law Review* 87 (2001): 1045, 1060. Moreover, they argue that the opinion represents "low politics"; that is, it "does not promote any of [the] larger ideological goals [e.g., federalism]. It simply installed a Republican president in the White House." Ibid. at p. 1062.

to win."[40] Echoing the scholarly sentiment, a federal judge, who was a Republican appointee and former Supreme Court law clerk, laments that he "had long since become accustomed to watching the justices 'making it up as they go along.' That aspect of the majority opinion, which is analytically weak and untethered to precedent, did not particularly bother him." It was the Court's blatant partisanship that he could not get over.[41] Alan Dershowitz captures the views of most legal scholars and court watchers in the following passage:

> In future election cases, don't try to hold the Court to what it said in *this* case, because it decided this case not on general principles applicable to all cases, but on a principle that has never before been recognized by this court. The purpose of the remarkable cautionary line—which is virtually an admission that this decision does not fit into a line of continuing precedents—was to cobble together a majority for Bush consisting of justices who almost never find equal-protection violations (except, perhaps, when white people are 'discriminated' against by affirmative action) and who do not want a broad equal-protection decision waiting out there to be used as a precedent in other cases in which the result would be inconsistent with the political or ideological results they generally prefer.[42]

---

40. Bugliosi, *The Betrayal of America*, supra note 37, at pp. 46–47.

41. Linda Greenhouse, *High Court Appears Diminished in Process*, San Diego Union-Tribune, 12/14/00, at p. A24.

42. Alan M. Dershowitz, *Supreme Injustice: How the High Court Hijacked Election 2000* (New York: Oxford University Press, 2001), pp. 81–82 (emphasis in original). For a collection of thoughtful views on the case, see *The Vote: Bush, Gore and the Supreme Court*, Cass R. Sunstein and Richard A. Epstein, eds. (Chicago: University of Chicago Press, 2001). It should also be noted that the positivist justices seemed to pick the moment that would ensure a political victory for the Republican litigant not only to embrace policy (an illicit consideration under positivism), but also to reject the policy of comity that they had so relentlessly advanced during the five-year period before *Bush*. Between 1995 and 2000, these justices struck down all or part of 25 socially progressive federal statutes on grounds of comity. See, e.g., Jeffrey Rosen, "The Next Court," *The New York Times Magazine*, 10/22/00, at p. 76. For example, in one of the most important cases, *United States v. Morrison*, 529 U.S. 598 (2000), these justices voted to overturn a provision of the Violence Against Women Act that authorized a private right of action for any victim of a gender-motivated violent crime. Congress, they ruled, exceeded its powers under the Commerce Clause and Section 5 of the Fourteenth Amendment. Likewise, in *Alden v. Maine*, 527 U.S. 706 (1999), the judicial conservatives ruled that a private suit for damages under the Fair Labor Standards Act against nonconsenting states in their own courts violates state sovereign immunity. And in *United States v. Lopez*, 514 U.S. 549 (1995), they overturned a federal statute prohibit-

Justice under judicial nominalism depends not on prior rules or on community expectations, but on who decides.[43]

Legal realism (Chapter 3) is the only traditional judicial model discussed herein that suggests judicial nominalism. Skeptical, particularized, and instrumental (i.e., given to the *ex post facto* use of rules), legal realism displays the predominant intellectual temperament of judicial nominalism. This is not to say, of course, that legal realism and judicial nominalism are coextensive substantively. The former has a specific agenda whereas the latter does not. Legal realism seeks to promote welfare liberalism while judicial nominalism is "empty" and thus can be used to accommodate the full range of politico-economic norms from classical conservatism to welfare liberalism.[44] It is judicial nominalism's structure that legal realism mimics—the attempt to do justice in the particular case even if that leads to policy-making.

There is, however, disagreement among legal scholars concerning legal realism's philosophical method. Michael Moore, for one, argues that legal realism has no philosophical base. Brian Leiter, on the other hand, argues that it does have philosophical pedigree—to wit, pragmatism. Here, it is argued that legal realism's philosophical method is nominalism. As previously discussed,[45] many legal theorists argue that it makes no sense to argue the point.

Judicial nominalism's normativity—its commitment to the best results in particular cases—is problematic. Certainly there is the potential for a "nervous breakdown" in a society governed by inconsistent laws. Essentially a roving moral commissioner, the judge's moral viewpoint gives license to just about any type of judicial action. Abortion-clinic bombers could be subjected

---

ing a person from knowingly possessing a firearm in or near schools. For further discussion, see, e.g., Balkin and Levinson, "Understanding the Constitutional Revolution," supra note 39; Joseph Biden, "On Judicial Imperialism," *Congressional Record*, vol. 146, no. 99 (106th Congress, July 26, 2000); Harry F. Tepker, Jr., "Writing the Law of Work on Nero's Pillars: The 1998–99 Term of the U.S. Supreme Court," 15 *The Labor Lawyer* 181 (1999); (cases and articles collected therein); Rosen, "The Next Court." It is worth noting that the dissenting judicial pragmatists (Justices Stevens, Souter, Ginsburg, and Breyer) were characteristically inconsistent. They supported the comity policy even though they had consistently rejected it in the federalism cases that preceded *Bush*. See, e.g., *Morrison, Alden,* and *Lopez,* supra.

43. Even though the judge's personal values are shared by fellow citizens, regardless of the number, somewhere in the United States, see Introduction, Section C2, supra, the nominalist judge is less concerned with (and certainly does not feel constrained by) the thought of imposing alien values on the community affected by the decision in the case.

44. See Preface, Section B, supra.

45. See Chapter 3, Section B2, supra. See also Preface, Section A, supra.

to punishment in some courts while treated with encomium in other courts. The rule of law ceases to exist.[46]

Equally troubling to many traditionalists is the cognate problem of legitimacy. They argue that "a visceral, personalized, rule-less, free-wheeling, unstructured conception of judging"[47] gives the judiciary a legislative appearance. The problem, of course, is that, unlike legislators, federal judges are unelected and, hence, unaccountable to the American people. Judges thereby operate without a democratic mandate—much like fishing without a license.

Three other problems should also be noted here. First is the problem of judicial impartiality. A nominalist judge loses the appearance of impartiality and the deference that comes with it. Judges face this hazard whenever they step away from the text. The second problem concerns institutional competency. Although judges are certainly able to formulate public policy, the question is can they do it competently? Unlike legislators, judges lack the investigatory machinery, including the power of the purse, which is necessary for developing the factual foundation for intelligent policy promulgations. Policy-formulation, so boldly featured in judicial nominalism, is intensively fact-driven. Finally, it is argued that judicial nominalism not only offers a judicial technique that is beyond the ability of judges, but it also provides "a thin and unsatisfactory epistemology."[48] Unlike other levels of judicial analysis, especially judicial positivism, judicial nominalism displays little in the way of textual analysis, the sort of reasoning judges are most likely to identify as their craft's unique epistemology.

A normativity of particulars is not entirely defenseless, however. It assures, as much as any judicial temperament can, that each litigant will receive a *full* day in court. The litigants' interests will not be sacrificed for another interest they do not themselves represent; an interest—such as, institutional comity or federalism[49]—the judge deems to be more important than the litigants' interests. Judicial nominalism empowers the individual in yet another way. It gives her a voice in a government that is too often influenced by special interests operating within the legislative and executive branches. This concern goes

---

46. See discussion of judicial positivism in Section B1, supra.

47. Posner, *The Problematics of Moral and Legal Theory*, supra note 5, at p. 240, citing Jeffrey Rosen's characterization of Posner's method of judging as nominalistic. See Jeffrey Rosen, "Overcoming Posner," *Yale Law Journal*, 105 (1995): 581, 584–96.

48. Ibid., referring to Paul Bator's characterization of Posner's judicial technique as nominalistic. See Paul M. Bator, "The Judicial Universe of Judge Richard Posner," *University of Chicago Law Review* 52 (1985): 1146, 1161. *The Problematics of Moral and Legal Theory*, supra note 5, is Posner's attempt to recast his judicial method in pragmatist terms.

49. See discussion in note 42, supra.

beyond the usual problem of legislative sluggishness in responding to pressing social issues. It involves the protection of a citizen's "participatory interest," the right to effective participation in one's own governance.[50]

Many of the perceived deficiencies of judicial nominalism go directly to its legitimization of judicial policy-formulation, especially policy-making. Yet the legitimacy of policy-formulation, as a judicial function, can be supported on a number of grounds. For example, the grant of jurisdiction over a case not only limits the matters on which the judge may expound, but also gives the judge authority to decide such matters fully, completely, and adequately. Policy-formulation on matters outside the judge's jurisdiction would be an illegitimate act, as would be the application of rules of law to such matters. Also, judges are institutionally empowered to make policy as a prelude to creating legal doctrine. Policy-formulation is a legitimate judicial function because it is a by-product of doctrinal creation, an unquestionably legitimate and necessary judicial function. Of course, the most serious criticisms of policy-formulation concern policy-making. This heightened level of judicial assertiveness has been defended as a necessity in the quest for justice in individual cases.[51] It can also be argued that broad policy-making in pursuit of the democratic ideal when other governmental institutions are experiencing democratic failure is not only a legitimate judicial function in a democratic society like ours, but also a necessary one. Exhibit A: *Brown v. Board of Education* and its progeny.[52]

Judicial nominalism may, at bottom, offer what can be called "truth in judging" in at least some cases. Gut-reaction decision making may be the only way some cases get decided. How is a judge who cares deeply about young people likely to respond to a case involving a 15-year-old boy who faces a life sentence under a three-strikes rule for stealing a bike? Although couched in legalese, the judge's response "is bound in the end to be an emotional rather than a closely reasoned one, because so many imponderables enter into that response."[53]

---

50. See Frank I. Michelman, "The Supreme Court and Litigation Access Fees," *Duke Law Journal* 1973 (1973): 1153, 1172–77.

51. For a more detailed discussion, see Introduction, Section C2, supra.

52. For a more detailed discussion, see ibid.

53. Posner, "Pragmatic Adjudication," supra note 5, at p. 246. Judge Posner uses a marijuana-selling case to illustrate this point. Also, in an attempt to cast the decision-making as pragmatic, he adds: "But emotion is not glandular secretion. It is influenced by experience, information, and imagination, and can thus be disciplined by fact." Ibid. The notion of informed emotional judgments better describes judicial nominalism than judicial pragmatism, because the latter is disciplined not only by the facts of the case, but also by what goes on before and after the case; i.e., by rules and community norms. That Judge Posner

Judicial nominalism may be descriptively correct in some cases, but is it prescriptively sound?

C. Summary

For any given legal problem there are any number of ways of finding an answer. The levels of analysis in traditional process offer three such methods, which can be summarized as follows.

Level 1/judicial positivism is the search for justice disciplined by prior rules, or the principle of *stare decisis*. It posits a policy-free process of judicial decision making. Policy (except the underlying policy of consistency) is an extrajudicial consideration. The judge proceeds logically as illustrated by legal formalism or Scalian textualism.

Level 2/judicial pragmatism is the search for justice disciplined by what comes before the case (precedent, community norms, and existing institutional arrangements) and by what comes after the case (the consequences a decision in the case will have on a particular community). This style of judging theorizes a result-oriented process of judicial decision making. It subscribes to the notion that law and culture must move in the same direction. Level 2 naturally lends itself to policy-formulation in the form of policy-vindication or policy-discovery, but not policy-making. The latter is illegitimate. Judicial decision making proceeds in a fashion similar to sociological jurisprudence or legal process.

Level 3/judicial nominalism is the search for justice disciplined only by the facts of the case, also a result-oriented process of judicial decision making. Unlike Level 1 or Level 2, judicial reasoning is not constrained by factors that reside outside of the judge. The judge's personal sense of fairness or justice, which the judge may or may not attempt to hide behind bogus Level 1 or Level 2 analysis, ultimately decides the case. Justice is "the measure of the chancellor's foot," which he will not hesitate to use to clomp down on a community. Policy-formulation in all its manifestations, including policy-making, is, therefore, a normal feature of the judicial process. The judge proceeds in a fashion similar to legal realism.

Taken together, the levels of judicial analysis paint two contrasting pictures regarding the judicial decision making process. One picture has the judge delicately balancing himself on a tightrope high above a water tank. Swimming in the water below is a shark. The tightrope represents Level 1

---

would discuss judicial pragmatism in this fashion simply underscores the thin line between judicial pragmatism and judicial nominalism.

analysis, the water tank Level 2 analysis, and the shark Level 3 analysis. Lawyers for the parties are at opposite ends of the water tank, busily shaking the poles to which the tightrope is attached in an attempt to dump the judge into the water tank. Clearly, the judge wishes to proceed at Level 1, but the lawyers are equally clear in their intent that the judge proceed at Level 2. They will argue rules, but they know that given the fact that the governing law is unclear, their best hope of winning lies in the competing policy considerations inherent in the case. Thus, the lawyers want the judge to face these issues. The danger facing the judge is that the shark, always swimming in the waters of Level 2, may devour him if he falls off the tightrope.[54] Is this picture correct? Do judges come to the bench intent on following the rules, fighting to stay out of shark-infested Level 2 waters? Does the picture portray Level 3 in an unduly negative light?

Perhaps the following is a more accurate picture. Level 3 is depicted as a large elephant. The judge struggles to push the elephant up a few steps and into a tiny cage, which represents Level 1. After all this muscling, the judge is able to get only a very small part of the elephant into the cage. Most of the elephant ends up resting on the second step, Level 2.[55] Do judges come to the bench with an innate desire to do justice in individual cases, only to be met by structural limitations of the judicial process? "If our opinions seem on occasion to be internally inconsistent, to contain a logical fallacy, or to insufficiently distinguish a prior case," Chief Justice Rehnquist once said, "I commend you to the view attributed to Chief Justice Hughes upon his retirement from our Court in 1941. He said that he always tried to write his opinions logically and clearly, but if a Justice whose vote was necessary to make a majority insisted that particular language be put in, in it went, and let the law reviews figure out what it meant."[56]

This brings us face-to-face with the central conundrum of our legal system, a problem that traces back to ancient Greece: what is the proper mix of law and policy in a given case? What ratio will deliver justice? *Too much policy kills law; too much law kills justice.*

Critical process, to which we shall now turn, poses a new set of problems for our legal system. These problems are unique to contemporary American society.

---

54. I am indebted to Kenneth M. White, USD Law, Class of 2002, for suggesting this picture. Mr. White was a student in my Fall 2001 jurisprudence class.

55. This picture was suggested by Sahyeh S. Fattahi, USD, Class of 2002, also a student in my Fall 2001 jurisprudence class.

56. Linda Greenhouse, "Rehnquist Asks Limit to Automatic Appeals," New York Times, Section 1 (Main), 9/16/84, p. 27.

PART 2
CRITICAL PROCESS

Recall for a moment Holmes's opening salvo in *The Common Law*: "The life of the law has not been logic; it has been experience." This empirical assertion raises a fundamental question: whose experience or values does the law validate? Is it those of cultural "insiders" (elite, straight white males, such as the captains of industry and most members of Congress and the Supreme Court itself) or is it those of cultural "outsiders," historically disadvantaged groups (mainly, people of color, women, and homosexuals)? Part 2 sets forth the response of critical theory (Section A) and, ultimately, "critical process" (Section B)to this query. The latter is critical theory, a theory of legal criticism, transformed into a theory of judicial decision making. It is critical-theory-in-action in the context of litigation. Structurally, critical process is a progressive judicial theory (Preface, Section B) that fits firmly within the policy method (Part 1, Section B). It does not, however, fit comfortably within the levels of analysis (Part 1, Section C). At the same time, critical process has a fundamentally unique judicial outlook and operation. Faithful to critical theory's central tenet, critical process views the socio-legal order as "racist," "sexist," and "homophobic." These ugly words do not completely comport with traditional usage. They convey a penetrating message about the realities of life many Americans experience in our socio-legal environment. Critical process invites us to stretch our thinking about law and judicial decision making beyond traditional process.

CRITICAL THEORY

The one irreducible fact we take from our study of traditional process in Part 1 is this: human temperament motivates the judicial enterprise much more so than the "mathematics" of any particular judicial method. Indeed, as we have seen, each traditional judicial technique is flawed; none is perfectly coherent; none is able to satisfy our complex notion of justice, a sensibility that seems to mutate with each new factual pattern. No judge or legal scholar can, therefore, claim to be driven to (or away from) a particular judicial theory on the basis of overwhelming powers of reason. Something other than reason helps to motivate a judge to embrace, say, Scalian textualism over legal process or legal realism over sociological jurisprudence. Something other than sheer logic brings a judge to the conclusion that Level 2 is a "better" judicial technique than Level 1, for instance. Reason helps to make the selection, but it does not decide; temperament decides. Temperament impels judges to make tradeoffs, and they are ultimately judged by these tradeoffs.

These important observations provide a springboard for considering critical theory.[1] "Criticalists," or "crits," can be understood as proceeding from the premise that no judge is driven to a particular jurisprudence by logical necessity. Every judge, particularly a Supreme Court Justice, has a choice in the matter. Call it culture, call it politics. Here it is called temperament, or "human temperament" to borrow from William James. Every judge is ultimately guided by some largely indefinable inward reaction to a set of facts. Why not, then, deploy the power and majesty of the judicial process in a way that will be most beneficial to the have-nots and have-lesses of our society? Why not begin with people of color, women, and homosexuals—the cultural "outsiders" of American society?

These questions assume that none of the traditional judicial models adequately serves outsider needs. This assumption is tested throughout Part 2.

---

1. For a collection of seminal works on critical theory, see Chapter 8 n. 3, infra.

However, a close reading of Part 1 also supports this assumption. Juridical subordination—structural limitations that disadvantage outsiders—can be found in traditional process. Let us consider legal formalism first. Syllogistic reasoning loaded with minimalist legal doctrine did not serve the needs of society's downtrodden and powerless at the beginning of the twentieth century, and will not serve the needs of outsiders in the twenty-first century either. This fact was brought to light in our discussion of the Supreme Court's recent return to formalism.[2] For example, between 1995 and 2000, the Court struck down all or part of 25 socially progressive federal statutes similar to the one in *United States v. Morrison*.[3] In that case, a sharply divided Court overturned a provision of the Violence Against Women Act that authorized a private right of action for any victim of a gender-motivated violent crime. Congress, the Court ruled, exceeded its powers under the Commerce Clause and Section 5 of the Fourteenth Amendment. Cases like *Morrison* give outsiders reason to worry about legal formalism.

Outsiders have even more reason to fear Justice Scalia's jurisprudence. Justice Scalia's strong preference for the Dead Constitution,[4] his fundamental belief that "the record of history refutes the proposition that the evolving Constitution will invariably enlarge individual rights,"[5] is dangerously wrong. Quite simply, if one is a person of color, a women or a homosexual, society *has* gotten better since 1791. Slavery is gone, women have a broad range of legal rights, and homosexuals, having garnered legal rights under many local laws, are unabashedly demanding the same rights under federal law. The new restrictions on democratic government Justice Scalia decries—such as, the

---

2. See Chapter 1, Section E, supra.

3. 529 U.S. 598 (2000). See, e.g., Jack M. Balkin and Sanford Levinson, "Understanding the Constitutional Revolution," *Virginia Law Review* 87 (2001): 1045; Joseph Biden, "On Judicial Imperialism," *Congressional Record*, vol. 146, no. 99 (106th Congress, July 26, 2000); Harry F. Tepker, Jr., "Writing the Law of Work on Nero's Pillars: The 1998–99 Term of the U.S. Supreme Court," *The Labor Lawyer* 15 (1999): 181 (cases and articles collected therein); Jeffrey Rosen, "The Next Court," *The New York Times Magazine*, 10/22/00, at p. 76. See also, *Alden v. Maine*, 527 U.S. 706 (1999) (private suit for damages under the Fair Labor Standards Act against nonconsenting states in their own courts violates state sovereign immunity), where Justice Souter argued in dissent that "[t]he resemblance of today's state sovereign immunity to the *Lochner* era's industrial due process is striking." *United States v. Lopez*, 514 U.S. 549 (1995) (federal statute prohibiting knowing possession of firearms in or near schools held unconstitutional), was one of the first cases to give some hint of a return to legal formalism.

4. See Chapter 2, Sections D & E, supra.

5. Antonin Scalia, *A Matter of Interpretation: Federal Courts and the Law* (Princeton: Princeton University Press,1997), p. 43.

Miranda warning and the expansion of due process rights[6]—could just as easily be described as hallmarks of a democratically mature society, especially for those who do not occupy positions of power.

Most tellingly, Justice Scalia's originalism (text frozen in time) with its implicit minimalism (the reduction of judicial power) can not sustain the Supreme Court's reasoning in the most important civil rights case in history, *Brown v. Board of Education.*[7] Reading the Fourteenth Amendment as a prohibition against segregation in public education does not demonstrate the degree of fealty to the Amendment's original meaning that Justice Scalia's originalism seems to require.[8] Also, overturning every state school segregation statute as well as 75 years of its own precedents enlarges the Court beyond the constraints of Justice Scalia's minimalism.[9] A Scalian textualist, in short, would be hard pressed to find textual support for the Supreme Court's construction of the Fourteenth Amendment in *Brown* on either originalist or minimalist grounds.[10] School segregation, as wrong as it is, must be eradicated through democratic process, even if there is no hope of that ever happening in the foreseeable future.[11]

Level 2 judicial models can be as culturally myopic as Level 1 models. One need only mention the absence of any discussion of the segregation laws in either sociological jurisprudence or legal process despite the fact that these laws were ubiquitous during the heyday of both models.[12] Level 2's major defect

---

6. See Chapter 2, Section D, supra.

7. 347 U.S. 483 (1954).

8. See Chapter 2, Section E, supra.

9. See ibid.

10. Compare Roy L. Brooks, *Integration or Separation? A Strategy for Racial Equality* (Cambridge: Harvard University Press, 1996), pp. 206–13 (arguing that the Fourteenth Amendment could be read as a prohibition against racial subordination as opposed to racial separation). The view that *Brown* cannot be squared with originalism is overwhelmingly supported by legal scholars. For further discussion of this point, see, e.g. Michael W. McConnell, "Originalism and The Desegregation Decisions," *Virginia Law Review* 81 (1995) 947 (arguing compatibility); Michael J. Klarman, "Brown, Originalism, and Constitutional Theory: A Response to Professor McConnell," *Virginia Law Review* 81 (1995): 1881 (arguing non-compatibility, the majority position); Michael W. McConnell, "The Originalist Case For Brown v. Board of Education," *Harvard Journal of Law and Public Policy*, 19 (1996): 457 (replying to Klarman's response); Boris I. Bittker, "Interpreting the Constitution: Is the Intent of the Framers Controlling? If Not, What Is?" *Harvard Journal of Law and Public Policy*, 19 (1995): 9 (taking the majority position).

11. This book argues that the failure of democratic process in other organs of government legitimizes judicial policy-making. See Chapter 10, Section D, infra.

12. See Chapters 4 & 5, supra.

has less to do with its methodology than its ideology. Judicial pragmatism does not permit a judge under any circumstance to impose norms on a community before the community is willing to accept them. In other words, judges cannot engage in judicial policy-making. At most, they are permitted to discover or vindicate policies.[13] This type of judicial self-restraint makes it impossible for Level 2 judges to sustain cases like *Brown*—cases on which outsiders place a great deal of value—without sacrificing intellectual integrity.[14]

Judge Posner himself makes the point that a pragmatic judge would not create a constitutional right of same-sex marriage because that would entail imposition of "a social policy that is deeply offensive to the vast majority of… [American] citizens."[15] Not unlike Justice Scalia, Judge Posner counsels patience and democratic process. But to homosexuals, such advice can seem insensitive and even cruel, especially when the democratic process has failed them. The problem with judicial pragmatism from an outsider perspective, then, is that it offers little protection from unjust majorities.

If judicial nominalism's normativity—its commitment to the best results in particular cases—is problematic to many traditionalists, it ought to be of greater concern to outsiders, but for different reasons. Visceral judicial decision making can easily facilitate outsider subordination, because it gives the judge too much discretion.[16] Unbridled judicial power can act as an easy cover for conscious or unconscious bias against outsiders. Indeed, some critical theorists have picked up this theme in their scholarship concerning rules. "Rule flexibility is disfavored because it can provide an easy pretext for subordination, allowing racial or gender prejudice and domination to go unchecked."[17]

The deficiencies in traditional process catalogued above—loaded syllogism, frozen constitutional text, and minimalism at Level 1; the prohibition against policy-making under any circumstance at Level 2; and unbridled judicial discretion at Level 3—may be epiphenomenal of a more basic defect that operates at all levels of traditional process. Whether Level 1, 2, or 3, traditional

---

13. See ibid. Justice Holmes's policy-formulation in statutory and constitutional cases is similarly restrained. For example, in *Lochner*, Holmes rejects the majority's reading of the Fourteenth Amendment because, as he says in his dissent, "This case is decided upon an economic theory which *a large part of the country does not entertain*." See Chapter 3, Section B1, supra.

14. See Chapter 4, Section D3, supra; Chapter 5, Section C3, supra.

15. Richard A. Posner, *The Problematics of Moral and Legal Theory* (Cambridge: Harvard University Press, 1999), p. 249.

16. See Chapter 3, supra.

17. Roy L. Brooks, *Critical Procedure* (Durham: Carolina Academic Press, 1998), pp. 11–12 (sources cited therein).

process makes a basic assumption that critical theorists flatly reject. Though it usually goes unstated, this assumption holds that American society and its institutions, including its legal institutions, are fundamentally neutral as to matters of race, gender, and sexual orientation. Criticalists not only reject this "objectivist" assumption as dangerously naive,[18] but, as we shall see in Chapters 8 and 9, their entire approach to law is predicated upon its rejection. Criticalists, in other words, are "anti-objectivists." The logical extension of anti-objectivism is a judicial process that permits policy-making disciplined by an awareness of anti-objectivism. Chapters 10, 11, and 12 attempt to enlarge upon this theme.

---

18. A criticalist might say just look at the law's attitude toward homosexuals revealed in Judge Posner's observation's above. For a more detailed discussion of the law's treatment of homosexuals, see Chapter 8, Section B2, infra; Chapter 9, Section B1, infra.

Chapter 8
Critical Theory: Central Element

In the context of law, critical theory operates as a theory of legal criticism.[1] It derives from a larger project developed in cultural studies.[2] Both intellectual enterprises incorporate a congeries of interdisciplinary theories. Each, however, has a distinct focus. Critical theory in cultural studies seeks to help us better understand how culture works. Critical theory in law attempts to increase our understanding of how law works, not internally (not in terms of the nuts and bolts of legal rules) but externally (in other words, in terms of the effect law has on power arrangements within the larger culture). To that extent, critical theory is resolutely critical of the existing legal order; it is, in other words, "oppositional." Furthermore, most of its constituent theories— e.g., Critical Race Theory, Critical Feminist Theory, Critical Asian Theory, LatCrit Theory and QueerCrit Theory[3]—are singularly sensitive to matters of race, gender or sexual orientation.[4] Hence, when used in the context of law

---

1. See Sections A2 & B, infra.

2. See Section A1, infra.

3. Among the literally thousands of pieces of scholarship written on some aspect of critical theory, see, in addition to sources cited in this chapter, e.g., *Crossroads, Directions, and a New Critical Race Theory*, Francisco Valdes, Jerome McCristal Culp, and Angela P. Harris, eds. (Philadelphia : Temple University Press, 2002); Richard Delgado and Jean Stefancic, *Critical Race Theory: An Introduction* (New York: New York University Press, 2001); *The Politics of Law: A Progressive Critique*, 3d ed., David Kairys, ed. (New York: Basic Books, 1998); *Feminist Legal Theory II: Positioning Feminist Theory Within the Law*, vol. 2, Frances E. Olsen, ed. (New York: New York University Press, 1995); *Critical Race Theory: The Cutting Edge*, 2d ed., Richard Delgado and Jean Stefancic, eds. (Philadelphia: Temple University Press, 2000); *Homosexuality: Opposing Viewpoints*, Mary E. Williams, ed. (San Diego: Greenhaven Press, 1999); William N. Eskridge, Jr., *Gaylaw: Challenging the Apartheid of the Closet* (Cambridge: Harvard University Press, 1999); *Critical White Studies: Looking Behind the Mirror*, Richard Delgado and Jean Stefancic, eds. (Philadelphia: Temple University Press, 1997); *The Latino/a Condition: A Critical Reader*, Richard Delgado and Jean Stefancic, eds. (New York: New York University Press, 1998); *Critical Race Feminism: A Reader*, Adrien Katherine Wing, ed. (New York: New York University Press, 1997); *Critical Race Theory: The Key Writings that Formed the Movement*, Kimberlè Williams Crenshaw, Neil Gotanda, Garry Peller, and Kendall Thomas, eds. (New York: New Press, 1995); Mari J. Matsuda, Charles R. Lawrence III, Richard Delgado, and Kimberlè Williams Crenshaw, *Words That Wound: Critical Race Theory, Assaultive Speech, and the First Amendment: New Perspectives on Law, Culture and Society* (Boulder: West View Press, 1993).

4. See Sections A2d & A3, infra.

today, the term "critical theory" mainly refers to these outsider legal theories, collectively, and less so to the Critical Legal Studies,[5] the latter of which generally ignores matters of race, sex, and sexual orientation.[6] Critical theory, then, is an amalgamation of theories that take an outsider's stance against the received tradition in law.[7]

As is true of most legal theories, our understanding of critical theory significantly increases when it is viewed through the eyes of Holmes, the most important figure in traditional process.[8] Recall again his opening salvo in *The Common Law*: "The life of the law has not been logic; it has been experience."[9] Criticalists can be understood as raising and answering the following question: whose experiences or values does Anglo-American law tend to validate? In other words, does law validate the life experiences of cultural insiders (again, white heterosexual males, especially the captains of industry, members of Congress, Supreme Court justices, and other elites) or those of cultural outsiders (again, mainly people of color, women, and homosexuals)? The criticalist answer to this question is "anti-objectivism"—law, like the larger society, is not in reality objective or neutral when it comes to matters of race, sex, and sexual orientation, but instead leans imperceptibly toward insiders. Hence, law is corrupt; it is "racist," "sexist," and "homophobic."[10]

The criticalist claim of anti-objectivism (including the terms used to describe it) is highly controversial. Some would even say it is "dangerous." Let us consider the origins of critical theory before examining the anti-objectivism claim.

---

5. See Section A2a, infra.

6. See Section A2d, infra. Sometimes the term "outcrit" is used to make a similar distinction. See Francisco Valdez, "Theorizing Outcrit Theories: Coalitional Method and Comparative Jurisprudential Experience—Racecrits, Queercrits and Latcrits," *University of Miami Law Review* 53 (1999): 1265.

7. There is also an outsider perspective in cultural studies. See, e.g., *Critical Race Theory Perspectives on the Social Studies: The Profession, Policies, and Curriculum*, Gloria Ladson-Billings, ed. (Greenwich, Conn.: Information Age Pub., 2003); *Cultural and Literary Critiques of the Concepts of "Race,"* E. Nathaniel Gates, ed. (New York: Garland Pub., 1997).

8. See Part 1, Section B (The Policy Method), supra.

9. Oliver Wendell Holmes, Jr., *The Common Law*, Mark DeWolfe Howe, ed. (Cambridge: Harvard University Press, 1963), p. 5.

10. See Section B, infra.

A. Intellectual History

Critical theory's story covers no small amount of intellectual terrain. It begins with the complex concept of "hegemony."[11] After a period of time, it makes its way into legal analysis through structuralism (with a fair amount of internal discord),[12] only to be challenged in short order by postmodernism.[13] These are the important moments in critical theory's history.

1. Hegemony

Hegemony comes from the Greek word *hegemonia*, meaning predominant influence.[14] As originally used, hegemony described the power or controlling influence one Greek city-state exerted over other Greek city-states. This feature of hegemony—power or controlling influence—has remained with the term throughout the ages. Accordingly, during the age of colonial powers, it was said that France exercised hegemony over her colonies and Prussia over Germany.[15] Similarly, during this post-Cold War Era, scholars and commentators see an "American hegemony" or "shades of American hegemony," arguing, *inter alia*, that the United States exerts unchallenged military power in the world in pursuit of democracy, plus unequaled economic power in pursuit of free markets.[16]

The concept of hegemony applies domestically as well as internationally. Indeed, it is the domestic application that is most important for purposes of

---

11. See Section A1, infra.

12. See Section A2, infra.

13. See Section A3, infra.

14. *The American Heritage College Dictionary*, 4th edition (New York: Houghton Mifflin Co., 2004), p. 642.

15. See Douglas Litowitz, "Gramsci, Hegemony, and the Law," *Brigham Young University Law School* 2000 (2000): 515, 519.

16. See, e.g., Norm Chomsky, *Hegemony or Survival: America's Quest for Global Dominance* (New York: Henry Holt and Company, 2003); Michael A. Harmony, "Harmony or Hegemony? The American Military Role in the Pursuit of Justice," *Connecticut Journal of International Law* 19 (2004): 231; Randolph B. Persaud, "Shades of American Hegemony: the Primitive, the Enlightened, and the Benevolent," *Connecticut Journal of International Law* 19 (2004): 263; John E. Noyes, "American Hegemony, U.S. Political Leadership, and General International Law," *Connecticut Journal of International Law* 19 (2004): 293. See also, Sara Dillon, "Looking for the Progressive Empire: Where is the European Union's Foreign Policy?" *Connecticut Journal of International Law* 19 (2004): 275.

understanding critical theory. In this context, hegemony has come to mean more than just the exertion of force or coercion. Also, hegemony may (or may not) operate at multiple levels in a society, as we shall see.[17]

Hegemony was first applied systematically in the domestic context by nineteenth- and twentieth-century European intellectuals who sought to explain the failure of the Marxist prediction of a proletarian revolution and the concomitant decline of capitalist societies. Marxism is a complex system of thought.[18] At its most basic level, Marxism analyzes anything and everything from a "scientific law" of "historical materialism," or "dialectic materialism." This concept incorporates two main features. The first comes not from Karl Marx directly but from Marx's predecessor, the German philosopher George Wilhelm Friedrich Hegel. Hegel posited a "theory of ideas," or consciousness: the best of opposing thoughts—the "thesis" and the "antithesis"—synthesizes into a higher level of consciousness—the "synthesis." The object of history is to create synthesis after synthesis, or new knowledge, moving toward "absolute knowledge." In this way, our ideas are constantly turning into higher forms of consciousness.[19]

Hegel described an "idealist" dialectic ("the mind contemplating itself"). Marx then sets this dialectic on top of a materialist foundation, ultimately shifting the focus to class struggle. Thus, the second feature of Marxism, sometimes referred to as "economic determinism" or "economism," posits that all societies (whether socialistic or capitalistic) have a basic structure that consists of an economic base or "infrastructure" (the means of production, e.g., slave-based, mercantile or capitalistic) that *determines* its "superstructure" (law, education, religion, politics, the arts, morality, and all other cultural or ideological phenomenon).[20] Hegel's dialectic and Marx's materialism—together,

---

17. See Section A3, infra.

18. For a collection of original works written by Karl Marx (1818-1863) and Frederick Engels (1820-1895), see the Marxists Internet Acheive, <http://www.marxists.org/archive/marx/txindex.htm>.

19. "Hegel thought that the life of reason proceeded by a continuing sequence of ideas, in which the opposition between two positions might eventually be resolved by moving the debate to a new level. First, someone develops a systematic theory—which Hegel's predecessor, Fichte, called a 'thesis.' Then it is challenged, Fichte said, by those who support the antithesis; finally, a new view develops that takes what is best of each to produce a new synthesis. Hegel's suggestion is that the new idea can be said to 'transcend' the old debate, moving it to a higher level." Kwame, Anthony Appiah, *Thinking It Through: An Introduction to Contemporary Philosophy* (New York: Oxford University Press, 2003), p. 378.

20. Litowitz, "Gramsci, Hegemony, and the Law," supra note 15, at p. 528 (Marxists had "espoused a deterministic causality from the base (relations of production) to the superstructure (law, morality, and ideology).")

dialectic materialism—yield the Marxist proposition that history is a story of economic struggle between the oppressor and the oppressed (such as, the slaveholder versus the slave, and the lord versus the serf). In capitalist societies, the class conflict is between the bourgeoisie and proletariat. Thus, capitalism, like all economic systems, is always in a state of crisis. Marx predicted that the conflict between capital and labor would result in the working class rising up and overthrowing the system of capitalist exploitation.[21]

The trouble was the subordinated classes seemed quite content to go along with this system of exploitation. Why did they not see that revolution was manifestly within their material interests as the Marxists had predicted? Why did the dominated classes in advanced capitalist societies seem so complacent? Why did socialist revolutions fail to materialize in these societies?

The answer, later Marxists would argue,[22] was because Marx presented an under-theorized, or perhaps a wrongly theorized, notion of class domination. Marx's materialism overshadowed his (or Hegel's) idealism. Economic determinism, the hidden process by which economic reality engenders idealism (culture, ideas or "what is in your head") had less explanatory power than Marx had supposed. Idealism (superstructure) was more important in explaining class domination than Marx had theorized.

These Marxists, then, rejected the crude deterministic notion of their teacher on the ground that social ideology, or message, was too powerful to downplay. Marxist economic determinism failed to understand how the ruling ideology "disguises" itself through media, religion, and other social institutions, and, hence, becomes unrecognizable as exploitation. People walk around with preconceived, unexamined notions about life shaped by the class elites. Economic determinism, then, missed the point that the very ideology that subserves the interest of the ruling class, that allows them to stay in power, was "internalized and endlessly reinforced in schools, churches, institutions, scholarly exchanges, museums, and popular culture."[23] Whereas crude determinism treated these and other institutions as merely epiphenomenal (as secondary and resultant),

---

21. See *The Communist Manifesto : New Interpretations*, Mark Cowling, ed. (New York: New York University Press, 1998)(includes, in full, *The Manifesto of the Communist Party*, written by Karl Marx and Frederick Engels, Terrell Carver, trans., first published in 1848).

22. My excellent research assistant, Timothy S. Carey, USD Law Class of '05, believes there is evidence that Marx expressed the answer (hegemony) himself in his earlier "humanistic" essays. Mr. Carey, thus, asserts that "Marx had, arguably, two phases of socialist theory and it is his 'scientific' phase that most directly lends itself to the deterministic reading." Only a fool would disagree with a research assistant of Mr. Carey's caliber.

23. Litowitz, "Gramsci, Hegemony, and the Law," supra note 15, at p. 519.

the later Marxists treated them as primary elements essential to an understanding of how class domination is accepted at many levels in a society.

In giving such primacy to idealism, these Marxists not only helped to explain why a Marxist revolution in capitalist societies had not materialized, but they also began to articulate a more nuanced conceptualization of hegemony. One of the earliest deployments of the refined term came during the Russian Revolution. "The term *gegemoniya* (hegemony) was one of the most central political slogans in the Russian Social-Democratic movement, from the late 1890's to 1917."[24] Russian writers as early as 1883 "urged the imperative necessity to wage a *political struggle* against Tsarism, not merely an *economic struggle* against its employers."[25] No one, however, has done more to position hegemony within an idealist framework, thereby giving the concept its modern meaning, than the Italian intellectual, Antonio Gramsci.[26]

Antonio Gramsci was a labor leader who eventually became the Secretary of the Italian Communist Party and a member of the Italian Parliament. Gramsci's fortune took a turn for the worse in 1926 when he was imprisoned by Mussolini. During his imprisonment from 1926–1937, Gramsci sought to clarify the concept of hegemony.[27] His efforts were published posthumously

---

24. Perry Anderson, "The Antinomies of Antonio Gramsci," *New Left Review*, 100 (1976): 5, 15.

25. Ibid. (italics added). In 1898, Axlerod took the notion of hegemony further and argued against economism and for a leading political role for the proletariat in fighting Tsarism. Ibid. In a letter to Struve written in 1901, Axlerod offered, " 'By virtue of the historical position of our proletariat, Russian Social-Democracy can acquire hegemony (gegemoniya) in the struggle against absolutism." Ibid., at pp. 15–16. Lenin was soon to follow, and in a letter to Plekhanov, as well as in a 1902 article titled, "What is to be Done?," urged the formation of a revolutionary newspaper to organize the political consciousness of the proletariat. Ibid. Finally, the term was worked into the documents of the 3rd International (Comintern) and in the 4th Congress of the Comintern. It "was- for what seems to be the first time- extended to the domination of the bourgeoisie over the proletariat, if the former succeeded in confining the latter to a corporate role by inducing it to accept a division between political and economic struggles in its class practice." Ibid., at p. 18. Through Comintern, the concept was thoroughly placed in the international socialist movement and "transmission of the notion of hegemony to Gramsci, from the Russian to the Italian theatres of the socialist movement, can with reasonable certainty be located in these successive documents...." Ibid. My thanks to Timothy S. Carey, USD Class of '05, for his help in developing these points.

26. *See, e.g., Antonio Gramsci*, James Martin, ed. (New York: Routledge, 2001); Walter L. Adamson, *Hegemony and Revolution: A Study of Antonio Gramsci's Political and Cultural Theory* (Berkeley: University of California Press, 1980).

27. According to Litowitz, Gramsci "claimed that the concept [of hegemony] was created by Lenin."Litowitz, "Gramsci, Hegemony, and the Law," supra note 15, at p. 520.

along with other essays in the *Prison Notebooks*.[28] A Marxist, Gramsci saw hegemony as the controlling ideology in a society that subserves the interest of the dominant class. Hegemony is the social narrative that emanates from the ruling class, and is exerted over the dominated classes not only by physical force or coercion,[29] but also, and more importantly, by a kind of "consensus" imbibed through interaction with schools, churches, the media, and other social institutions (superstructures). As Gwyn Williams explains:

> By 'hegemony' Gramsci seems to mean a sociopolitical situation, in his terminology a 'moment,' in which the philosophy and practice of a society fuse or are in equilibrium; an order in which a certain way of life and thought is dominant, in which one concept of reality is diffused throughout society in all its institutional and private manifestations, informing with its spirit all taste, morality, customs, religious and political principles, and all social relations, particularly in their intellectual and moral connotations. An element of direction and control, not necessarily conscious, is implied. This hegemony corresponds to a state power conceived in stock Marxist terms as the dictatorship of a class.[30]

Thus, for Gramsci, hegemony is the unconscious force in a society that creates consensual submission. Hegemony results in consensual submission. It commands subtle acceptance throughout society of "one concept of reality" as universal and rational. The prevailing social ideology (or "master narrative") is taken as natural, neutral, and "an intractable component of common sense."[31] Exploitation could not be achieved through the power of force alone. It must also rely on the power of knowledge. In this regard, language plays an important role. Language, in other words, does not provide a transparent representation of reality, but, instead, embodies a belief system that shapes a society's values and beliefs. This, then, is the real import of hegemony.

Gramsci's explication sheds light on American society in the twenty-first century. Many Americans vote against their economic interests in presidential

---

28. *See* Antonio Gramsci, *Pre-Prison Writings*, Richard Bellamy, ed. Virginia Cox, trans.(New York : Cambridge University Press, 1994); *Prison Notebooks /Antonio Gramsci*, Joseph A. Buttigieg, ed., Joseph A. Buttigieg and Antonio Callari, trans. (New York: Columbia University Press, 1996).

29. See sources cited in note 16, supra.

30. Gwyn Williams, "Gramsci's Conxept of 'Egomania,'" *Journal of History of Ideas*, 21 (1960): 586–87.

31. Litowitz, "Gramsci, Hegemony, and the Law," supra note 15, at p. 519.

elections when they feel strongly about social issues.[32] When, for example, they "no longer feel that they can transmit their culture to their young," they will "keep voting on social issues…rather than vote on their economic plight."[33] This culture (what some might call "traditional values"), Gramsci would argue, is part of the prevailing social ideology. It is "internalized and endlessly reinforced in schools, churches, institutions, scholarly exchanges, museums, and popular culture,"[34] and, hence, is regarded as natural and commonsensical to a majority of Americans. While a critical theorist can certainly expose the incongruence between voting and economic interests, her real job is to unearth the power hierarchies and agendas hidden in the dominant social ideology.[35]

2. Structuralism in the Law

a. Critical Legal Studies

During the 1970s and earlier 1980s, Critical Legal Studies (CLS) applied Gramsci's conceptualization of hegemony to the law.[36] These mostly white male legal scholars attempted to describe ("deconstruct") the entrenched nature of extant legal conventions and institutions. Law imbibes the dominant social perspective; it is a hegemonic instrument. As such, law sets the conditions for self-actualization, both individually and institutionally. Law creates "artificial structures that contained permissible legal [or authoritative] discourse."[37] Hegemonic legal structures legitimate, validate, regulate and simultaneously silence and subordinate. CLS spent a good deal of time attempting to map out their view of law's hegemony—the fundamental structure that gives shape to legal reasoning, rules, and doctrines.

Robert Gordon, for example, attempted to unearth the basic structure of the law of contracts in his innovative scholarship. As Litowitz correctly notes,

---

32. See Thomas Frank, *What's The Matter with Kansas: How Conservatives Won the Heart of America* (New York: Metropolitan Books/Henry Holt and Company, 2004).

33. John Leo, "On Society: Pain in the Heartland," *US. News and World Report*, Sept. 6, 2004, p. 86.

34. Litowitz, "Gramsci, Hegemony, and the Law," supra note 15, at p. 519.

35. See, for example, the discussion of formal equal opportunity in Section A2b, infra.

36. For a collection and discussion of this scholarship, see, e.g., Roy L. Brooks, Civil Rights Symposium—"Racial Subordination Through Formal Equal Opportunity," *San Diego Law Review* 25 (1988): 879, 984–87 (sources cited therein).

37. Litowitz, "Gramsci, Hegemony, and the Law," supra note 15, at p. 532.

"tracing the background assumptions that shape the court's reasoning about law," Gordon sought to bring "to light the hidden commitments and conflicts that haunt the deep structure of contract law."[38] Thus, CLS moved from class, which had preoccupied the Marxists, to "complex cultural codes" that drive not only law, but also religion, art, and other belief (or idealist) systems within the culture.

Many scholars posit that Marxism was superceded by "structuralism" in CLS; hence, the formulation "hegemony as class versus hegemony as structure."[39] Although it is true that no "explicit appeal to dominant and subservient classes" was made in most CLS discourse on hegemony,[40] it may be more accurate to view both CLS theorists and Marxists as structuralists in a broad sense. Keep in mind that deterministic Marxism holds that a direct and causal (epiphenominal) relationship exists between the economic *structure* and superstructures. Thus, Marxism can be viewed as a brand of "structuralism." It is thoroughly modern (as opposed to "postmodern," more about which in a moment) and it is certainly open to a post-structural critique of its "structurality," given the "center"(historical materialism) and the structure that develops around it. Hence, it may be more accurate to refer to Marxists as *class-structuralists* and to CLS theorists as *cultural-structuralists*; in other words, hegemony viewed as a class system that shapes values versus hegemony viewed as a cultural system that shapes values.

But even this formulation is a bit problematic, because not all CLS theorists in the 1970s and 1980s were non-Marxists. Some remained faithful to Gramsci's class bent, and thus saw law as an instrument of class domination. Gordon, himself, seemed conflicted. At times he seemed to be a cultural-structuralist, viewing law as a reinforcement of hegemonic cultural codes, but at other times he seemed to be a class-structuralist, seeing law as protecting and perpetuating hegemonic class domination.[41]

b. Critical Race Theory

Critical Race Theory (CRT) took the CLS analysis of structuralism in the law in a new, race-conscious direction. CRT began in the 1970s with the work

---

38. Ibid., p. 533 n.70.
39. Ibid., p. 533.
40. Ibid. *See* Robert W. Gordon, "New Developments in Legal Theory," in *The Politics of Law: A Progressive Critique*, David Kairys, ed. (New York: Pantheon Books, 1982), p. 281; Robert W. Gordon, "Unfreezing Legal Reality: Critical Approaches to Law," *Florida State University Law Review* 15 (1987): 195.
41. See Gordon, "New Developments in Legal Theory," pp. 280–87.

of American legal scholars who were dissatisfied with the slow pace of racial progress through law. Federal civil rights laws prohibiting housing and employment discrimination illustrate the problem. As enacted by Congress and interpreted by the Supreme Court, these statutory laws had (and for the most part still have) little bite. For example, they impose difficult standards of proof on plaintiffs, and, in the case of employment discrimination law, ponderous procedural requirements, all of which have decelerated the pace of racial progress after the civil rights gains of the 1960s.[42]

Professors Derrick Bell (an African American)[43] and Alan Freeman (a white American),[44] followed by others,[45] argued that in order to understand the slow pace of racial progress in this post-Civil Rights Era, one must "pierce the veil of presuppositions on which civil rights doctrine relies" — namely, "a world of autonomous and responsive law; shared values such as individualism and color-blindness;... and [the presumption of] gradual linear civil rights."[46] Attempting to close the gap between civil-rights myth and reality, these pioneers described the Anglo-American legal order as "a world where law is more responsive to power than to powerlessness; where values are contradictory, conflicting, and bound up with patterns of domination and hierarchy;... and where cyclical failure is as plausible as linear progress."[47]

Although this discussion is not very different in tone from CLS, it had and continues to have powerful racial implications, one of which is the unsteadiness or uncertainty of racial progress. Race crits argued that racial remedies, or, more broadly, the nation's dominant racial norm—formal

---

42. For a summary and analysis, see Roy L. Brooks, *Rethinking the American Race Problem* (Berkeley: University of California Press, 1990), pp. 1, 54–66, 90–94.

43. See, e.g., Derrick A. Bell, Jr., *Race, Racism and American Law* 1st ed., 2d ed., 3d ed. (Boston: Little, Brown and Company, 1973, 1980, 1992). The 4th & 5th editions were published by Aspen Law & Business in 2000 and 2004, respectively. See also discussion of Bell's ideas in Section B, infra.

44. See, e.g., Alan Freeman, "Legitimizing Racial Discrimination Through Antidiscrimination Laws: A Critical Review of Supreme Court Doctrine," *Minnesota Law Review* 62 (1978): 209; Alan Freeman, Book Review, "Race and Class: The Dilemma of Liberal Reform," *Yale Law Journal* 90 (1980): 1880.

45. See, e.g., *The Politics of Law: A Progressive Critique*, David Kairys, ed. (New York: Pantheon Books, 1982); Sidney Willhelm, Book Review, "The Supreme Court: A Citadel for White Supremacy," *Michigan Law Review* 79(1981): 847.

46. Derrick A. Bell, Jr., *Race, Racism and American Law*, 2d ed., 1984 Supplement (Boston: Little, Brown and Company, 1984), p. 3.

47. Ibid. See also infra note 80.

equal opportunity[48]—operates as "a homeostatic device." This device, as Richard Delgado and Jean Stefancic explain, "ensures that racial progress occurs at just the right pace. Too slow would make minorities impatient and risk destabilization; too fast could jeopardize important material and psychic benefits for elite groups."[49] Derrick Bell elaborated on this theme with his "interest-convergence principle," more commonly known as the "white self-interest principle." In his explication, Bell also indicated how racial progress occurs given America's anti-objectivism (its permanent racism), discussed in the next section of this chapter. Bell asserted that "the degree of progress blacks have made away from slavery and toward equality has depended on whether allowing blacks more or less opportunity best served the interests and aims of white society."[50] Similarly, Malcolm X articulated the white self-

---

48. Formal equal opportunity (FEO)calls for color-blind racial remedies. Color-consciousness is the law is prohibited. But FEO's racial omission tenet is sometimes in tension with another of its tenets—racial integration. For a critical analysis of FEO, see Brooks, *Rethinking the American Race Problem*, supra note 42, at ch. 1.

49. Delgado and Stefancic, *Critical Race Theory*, supra note 3, p. 31.

50. Derrick A. Bell, *Race, Racism and American Law* 2d ed. (Boston: Little, Brown and Company, 1980), p. 39. See also Derrick A. Bell, "Brown v. Board of Education and the Interest-Convergence Dilemma," *Harvard Law Review* 93 (1980): 518. Does the white self-interest principle have any validity? Criticalists point to President Lincoln's motivation for issuing the Emancipation Proclamation as a classic illustration of the white self-interest principle. Although Lincoln personally hated slavery and was, in fact, the first president to invite an African American (Frederick Douglass) to the White House, he issued the proclamation solely for military purposes, in other words, to save the Union rather than to save African Americans from slavery. Hence, the argument goes, Lincoln was willing to permit slavery, perhaps the worst form of human debasement and oppression ever seen on American soil, to continue if necessary to preserve the Union. As he wrote to newspaper editor Horace Greeley: "If I could save the Union without freeing any slave, I would do it." Derrick A. Bell, Jr., *Race, Racism and American Law* (New York: Aspen Law & Business, 2000), p. 28. In the same letter, Lincoln made it clear that: "I have stated my view of *official* duty; and I intend no modification of my oft-expressed *personal* wish that all men everywhere could be free." Ibid. at p. 29 (emphasis in original). See *Abraham Lincoln: Speeches and Writings 1859–1865: Speeches, Letters, and Miscellaneous Writings, Presidential Messages and Proclamations*, Don E. Fehrenbacher, ed. (New York: Literary Classics of the United States, 1989), p. 358. Of course, the strength of this illustration is somewhat undercut by the fact that the Union's purpose for fighting the Civil War had changed by the beginning of Lincoln's second term. Lincoln and many Union soldiers and civilians now saw the war's chief purpose as freeing the slaves. This was an avowed position. Indeed, many Union soldiers re-enlisted for that reason alone. They experienced a change of heart after seeing African Americans soldiers fight bravely. As James McPherson writes: "By the war's last year, the example of black soldiers fighting for Union as well as liberty had helped convince most white soldiers that they should fight for black liberty as well as Union. There were some

interest principle during the civil rights movement. White Americans, he declared, "don't know what morals are. They don't try to eliminate an evil because it's evil, or because it's illegal, or because it's immoral; they eliminate it only when it threatens their existence."[51]

c. Critical Feminist Theory

About the time race crits began to voice dissatisfaction with formal equal opportunity, feminist legal scholars, working under the rubric of Critical Feminist Theory (CFT), were happy to achieve even that level of legal protection. Women did not receive equal treatment under the Constitution until the early 1970s.[52] Victory for women came with the Supreme Court's 1971 decision in *Reed v. Reed*.[53] In *Reed*, the Supreme Court, for the first time, struck down a law that classified individuals on the basis of gender. The process of granting women equal legal rights was brought to fruition with a succession of subsequent Supreme Court cases handed down in the 1970s upholding the gender-blindness policy in a variety of contexts, and with the passage of Title IX of the Education Amendments of 1972, which proscribed

---

holdouts, to be sure....But these were distinctly minority views among Union soldiers by 1864. When Lincoln ran for reelection on a platform pledging a constitutional amendment to abolish slavery, he received almost 80% of the soldier vote—a pretty fair indication of army sentiment on slavery at the time."James M. McPherson, *For Cause and Comrades: Why Men Fought in the Civil War* (New York: Oxford University Press, 1997), pp. 128–29.

The white self-interest principle finds support in the work of non-criticalist scholars such as Philip A. Klinkner and Rogers M. Smith. They argue that significant racial progress occurs in our country only with the convergence of three circumstances: large-scale wars, which require extensive economic and military mobilization and, hence, African American assistance; an enemy whose repressive regime inspires American leaders to advocate inclusive, egalitarian values in order to justify the war; and domestic political organizations that are able to pressure American leaders to follow through on their rhetoric See Philip A. Klinkner and Rogers M. Smith, *The Unsteady March: The Rise and Decline of Racial Equality in America* (Chicago: University of Chicago Press, 1999), pp. 3–4.

51. Malcolm X, "The Ballot or the Bullet" (April 3, 1964) in *Malcolm X Speaks: Selected Speeches and Statements*, George Breitman, ed. (New York: Grove Weidenfeld, 1990), pp. 23, 40.

52. Equal treatment under statutory law was accorded to women as early as 1963 in the Equal Pay Act, 29 U.S.C. §206(d), and in 1964 in Title VII of the Civil Rights Act, 42 U.S.C. §2000e et seq. On the subject of sex equality, see generally Catharine A. MacKinnon, *Sex Equality* (New York: Foundation Press, 2001).

53. 404 U.S. 71 (1971).

sex discrimination in educational programs and activities that received federal funds.[54]

Thus, by the end of the 1970s, our civil rights laws operated under a regime of formal equal opportunity for persons of color and women alike. Although race crits were dissatisfied with formal equal opportunity and fem crits were not, the views of both groups largely converged by the end of the 1980s, with most fem crits moving closer to the critical view expressed by the majority of race crits. The dominant view in both camps was that formal equal opportunity was a hegemonic device that subserved the interests of insiders more than the interests of outsiders.

This shift in the criticalist perspective on formal equal opportunity was quite significant. It met that CRT and CFT would largely embrace the central idea of "difference." Most crits now believed that social transformation cannot be achieved through symmetrical legal rules, or, in other words, through a vision of "equality as sameness." Social transformation, the objective of an outsider jurisprudence, can only be engendered by "equality as difference," by acceptance of the fact that people of color and whites, and women and men are in reality asymmetrically situated in American society. "In order to treat some persons equally, we must treat them differently."[55]

This new awareness was not entirely self-generated. It was at least in part caused by a reaction to the CLS view on rights. Especially race but also fem crits reacted quite negatively to CLS's "trashing" of rights. And, in the process, both CRT and CFT sharpened their distinct voices.

d. The Rights Controversy

As we have seen, race and fem crits were most interested in deconstructing formal equal opportunity, the racial and gender component of law. CLS, on the other hand, generally ignored this aspect of law. Instead, they centered their analysis on rights in general, arguing that the very idea of rights should be rejected on the grounds that rights are "indeterminate," "inalienable," "unstable," "coopting," and, of course, hegemonic, "conceal[ing] and justify[ing]

---

54. Title IX is codified at 20. U.S.C. § 1681. For further discussion, see discussion of ACLU Women's Rights Project in Chapter 11, Section B1, infra.

55. *Regents of the University of California v. Bakke*, 438 U.S. 265, 407 (1978) (Blackmun, J., concurring in part and dissenting in part). See, e.g., Christine A. Littleton, "Reconstructing Sexual Equality," *California Law Review* 75 (1987): 1279, 1292. See generally, Roy L. Brooks, *Critical Procedure* (Durham: Carolina Academic Press, 1998), pp. 7–9 (sources cited therein).

unacceptable hierarchies of social power."[56] The indeterminacy claim was not entirely new. It traces back to legal realism,[57] the days of Blackstone,[58] and even Aristotle.[59] It is also reminiscent of Hegel's theory of ideas discussed earlier in this chapter.

CLS did more than merely assert the now-obvious claim of indeterminacy. It also attempted to explain why indeterminacy exists. Duncan Kennedy may be the leading CLS scholar on this point. In a famous law review article titled "The Structure of Blackstone's Commentaries,"[60] Kennedy argued that indeterminacy is a natural phenomenon of human consciousness. It arises from a fundamental tension or "contraction" that exists between the individual and the community. As Kennedy elaborates:

> [T]he goal of individual freedom is at the same time dependent on and incompatible with the communal coercive action that is necessary to achieve it. Others (family, friends, bureaucrats, cultural figures, the state) are necessary if we are to become persons at all— they provide us the stuff of our selves and protect us in crucial ways against destruction....But at the same time that it forms and protects us, the universe of others...threatens us with annihilation and urges upon us forms of fusion that are quite plainly bad rather than good....Numberless conformities, large and small abandonments of self to others are the price of what freedom we experience in society....Through our existence as members of collectives, we impose

---

56. Jerry L. Anderson, "Law School Enters the Matrix: Teaching Critical Legal Studies," *Journal of Legal Education* 54 (2004): 201, 201 (internal quotations omitted). See Brooks, "Racial Subordination Through Formal Equal Opportunity," supra note 36, at 984–87 (sources cited therein).

57. See discussion of Jerome Frank's rule-skepticism and fact-skepticism in Chapter 3, Section B2, supra.

58. See Introduction, Section B, supra.

59. See ibid. Recall in particular the discussion therein of John Selden's ridicule of equity: "One chancellor has a long foot, another a short foot. It is the same thing with the chancellor's conscience." The doctrine of causation provides a good illustration of indeterminacy on the law side. There is, CLS would argue, no necessary connection between cause and effect in the sense that a judge is able to say "Event A" is the proximate cause of "Event B." Causation is not something that can be measured and re-measured with the certainty of a carpenter's ruler. It is more akin to the chancellor's conscience in that it is a matter of the judge's belief as to how closely related apparent causes and their effects should be to justify a finding of liability. The fact that the judge's belief is merely a legal inference drawn from his own experience only adds more uncertainty to the doctrine of causation.

60. Duncan Kennedy, "The Structure of Blackstone Commentaries," *Buffalo Law Review* 28 (1979): 205.

on others and have imposed on us hierarchical structures of power, welfare, and access to enlightenment that are illegitimate.[61]

Indeterminancy makes law fertile ground for political infiltration, Kennedy argued. Ideological preferences (whether liberal or conservative) get translated into legal discourse. "Markers" exist in legal doctrine from which we can infer ideological bent. For example, "The rhetoric of self-reliance is conservative; that of sharing, liberal." Thus, Blackstone, Kennedy argued, had "an 'apologetic motive' in describing the English legal system."[62] Similarly, in contemporary American society, "legal discourse [is] a deliberate mystification, cloaking a capitalist ideological agenda in neutral terminology in order to mislead the masses about what [is] really going on."[63]

While sympathetic to CLS's oppositional stance to the existing legal order, race and fem crits severely criticized CLS for being "imperialistic" and even for "silencing" scholars of color or women scholars.[64] Richard Delgado, for example, even questioned the standing of white male liberals, many of whom were faithful soldiers in the civil rights movement, to raise racial issues that were meaningful to people of color:

[It] is possible to compile an *a priori* list of reasons why we might look with concern on a situation in which the scholarship about Group A is written by members of Group B. First, members of Group B may be ineffective advocates of the rights and interests of persons in Group A. They may lack information; more important, perhaps, they may lack passion, or that passion may be misdirected. B's scholarship may tend to be sentimental, diffusing passion in useless directions, or wasting time on unproductive breast-beating. Second, while the Bs might advocate effectively, they might advocate the wrong things. Their agenda may differ from that of the As; they may pull their punches with respect to remedies, especially where remedying A's situation entails uncomfortable consequences for B. Despite the

---

61. Ibid. at pp. 211–12.

62. Duncan Kennedy, *A Critique of Adjudication {fin de siècle}* (Cambridge: Harvard University Press, 1997), p. 54.

63. Ibid. at p. 55. For a critique of Kennedy and other leading CLS scholars, see Neil Duxbury, *Patterns of American Jurisprudence* (Oxford: Oxford University Press, 1997, first paperback with corrections), pp. 421–509.

64. See, e.g., Richard Delgado, "The Ethereal Scholars: Does Critical Legal Studies Have What Minorities Want?," *Harvard Civil Rights-Civil Liberties Law Review* 22 (1987): 301, 307; Harlan Dalton, "The Clouded Prism," *Harvard Civil Rights-Civil Liberties Law Review* 22 (1987): 335, 441.

best of intentions, Bs may have stereotypes embedded deep in their psyches that distort their thinking, causing them to balance interests in ways inimical to As. Finally, domination by members of Group B may paralyze members of Group A, causing the As to forget how to flex their legal muscles for themselves.[65]

Non-crit minority scholars, such as Randall Kennedy, pointed out in response that some CLS scholarship was very useful in the struggle for racial equality. For example, CLS scholar Alan Freeman (whom most crtis would probably classify as a race crit) has "articulated one of the most useful concepts we have for analyzing the jurisprudence of race relations—the distinction between the 'victim' and the 'perpetrator's' perspective."[66] Color did not matter.

But there was little doubt that CLS's critique and ultimate trashing of rights set it miles apart from race and fem crits. It could not be gainsaid, crits argued, that rights provided outsiders with tangible benefits. Without rights, there would have been no civil rights movement and no Title IX. Without rights, women could not protect themselves from male violence. Thus, outsiders *must* embrace rights as the only practical way to protect their interests. As historically disadvantaged groups, outsiders do not have the luxury to jettison rights. Outsiders are not as protected or as privileged in American society as the highly successful heterosexual white males (elites) who comprised CLS. Insiders may have no use for rights, but outsiders, because of their disadvantaged position in American institutions, must rely on rights to establish what Pat Williams referred to as "personhood." Outsiders, in a word, need rights to engender social transformation, "a transformation in the terms and conditions of power" in American society.[67]

Thus, CRT and CFT response to the CLS critique of rights was as much a self-defining moment as a criticism of CLS. It may be that CLS theorists mistakenly viewed outsider discourse on formal equal opportunity to be an organic attack on rights. In other words, CLS may have failed to understand that outsiders were criticizing formal equal opportunity not because the latter

---

65. Richard Delgado, "The Imperial Scholar: Reflections on a Review of Civil Rights Literature," *University of Pennsylvania Law Review* 132 (1984): 561, 567 (citations omitted).

66. Randall L. Kennedy, "Racial Critiques of Legal Academia," *Harvard Law Review* 102 (1989): 1745, 1786, citing Alan Freeman, "Legitimatizing Racial Discrimination Through Antidiscrimination Law," *Minnesota Law Review* 62 (1978): 1049.

67. Catharine A. MacKinnon, *Feminism Unmodified: Discourses on Life and Law* (Cambridge, Mass.: Harvard University Press, 1987), p. 23. See Patricia Williams, *Alchemy of Race and Rights* (Cambridge, Mass.: Harvard University Press, 1990).

thought rights (especially civil rights) were worthless, but because they thought that rights were important. CRT and CFT wanted *better*, not less, rights.

While the rights controversy may have played a role in the shift from sameness-equality (to which, it should be noted, some race and fem crits still subscribe) to difference-equality, and while this refocus was an important moment in CRT and CFT, another profound change in these critical theories was about to take place. This change was initiated by European or nonlegal critical theorists. Cultural-structuralism itself had come under attack, just as class-structuralism had previously been attacked by cultural-structuralism. (Hegel must have been smiling in his grave.) The challenge to structuralism would eventually result in a proliferation of outsider takes on the law—a kind of parsing of hegemony—from race crits, fem crits, and new crits.

3. The Postmodern Challenge

"The entire concept of hegemony," Litowitz notes, "underwent a radical challenge in the 1980s with the arrival of the intellectual movements of postmodernism and post-structuralism."[68] By the end of the 1980s, as Alan Hunt has observed, "Marx, Gramsci, Habermas and Freud ha[d] been replaced by Nietzsche, Derrida, and Foucalt."[69] Here, Ernst Laclau and Chantal Mouffe, whose work offered perhaps the "central postmodern engagement with Gramsci,"[70] should also be mentioned.[71]

Postmodernists, or poststructuralists, rejected the idea of a "single front" of domination—the insistence of a system-bound notion of exploitation—that characterized the concept of hegemony presented by structuralists (both class and cultural). Instead, postmodernists saw hegemony "diffused at mul-

---

68. Litowitz, "Gramsci, Hegemony, and the Law," supra note 15, at p. 533.

69. Alan Hunt, "The Big Fear: Law Confronts Postmodernism," *McGill Law Journal* 35 (1990): 507, 523.

70. Litowitz, "Gramsci, Hegemony, and the Law," supra note 15, at p. 535–36. Robert Bocock in his book *Hegemony* also points to Laclau and Mouffe's attack on essentialism in Gramsci's hegemony. See Robert Bocock, *Hegemony and Socialist Strategy: Towards a Radical Democratic Politics* (London: Verso, 1985), ch. 5.

71. See generally, Helen M. Stacy, *Postmodernism and Law: Jurisprudence in a Fragmenting World* (Burlington, VT: Ashgate Publishing Company, Ltd., 2001); Douglas E. Litowitz, *Postmodern Philosophy and Law*" (Lawrence: University Press of Kansas, 1997).

tiple sites (schools, the military, factories, universities)."[72] There is no hegemony of a single dominant class or culture. Hegemonic power is manifested in the creation and preservation of myriad social systems. Furthermore, hegemony typically operates through language or discourse by silencing alternative norms or narratives. Hence, the postmodernists "shifted the operative terminology" from class or cultural domination to hidden discourses; from a single hegemonic center to multiple hegemonies.[73]

In rejecting structuralism's "essentialism," the postmodernists, then, offered a more complex conceptualization of hegemony. There is no "hegemony," only "hegemonies." Domination "is constructed in a struggle of articulation between divergent forces, as each group forms its identity."[74] It is a struggle over norms—a series of cultural wars, if you will—that takes place in public and private institutions, and that proceed along lines of race, ethnicity, gender, class, language, art, and so forth. Finally, "there is no necessary connection between the marginalization experienced by various subaltern groups, so... [marginalization] can occur independently on several fronts along lines of gender, race, age, physical ability, and so on."[75]

With marginalization occurring on so many fronts, outsider groups have sought to "map out" hegemonies that relate to their particular time and place. As a consequence, the ranks of critical theorists began to swell after the 1980s to include more outsider groups and subgroups. Latinos, Asian Americans, and gays and lesbians are the latest crits to seek a voice at the table. Although homosexuals would, for the most part, settle for formalized equality, which persons of color and women have enjoyed since the 1970s, they, like other outsiders, claim a social experience that is unique yet also similar to the experiences of African Americans and women.[76] To that extent, all outsider experiences come under a single socio-legal umbrella; they merge into an analytical unit called "anti-objectivism" or "subordination." All claim through their systems of thought—e.g.,

---

72. Litowitz, "Gramsci, Hegemony, and the Law," supra note 15, at pp. 533–34.

73. See, e.g., Michael Foucault, *Madness and Civilization: A History of Insanity in the Age of Reason*, Richard Howard trans. (New York: Vintage Books, 1973); Jean François Lyotard, *Postmodern Condition : A Report on Knowledge*, Geoff Bennington and Brian Massumi, trans. (Minneapolis: University of Minnesota Press, 1984).

74. Litowitz, "Gramsci, Hegemony, and the Law," supra note 15, at p. 536.

75. Ibid.

76. See, e.g., Joyce Murdoch and Deb Price, *Courting Justice: Gay Men and Lesbians v. The Supreme Court* (New York: Basic Books, 2001); William N. Eskridge, Jr., *Gaylaw: Challenging the Apartheid of the Closet* (Cambridge, Mass.: Harvard University Press, 1999); Kenji Yoshino, "Assimilationist Bias in Equal Protection: The Visibility Presumption and the Case of 'Don't Ask, Don't Tell,'" *Yale Law Journal* 108 (1998): 485.

Critical Race Theory, Critical Feminist Theory, LatCrit Theory, Asian Crit Theory, and Queer Crit Theory—to experience socio-legal subordination, albeit in different ways.[77] A kind of structural-post-structuralism may be at work here.[78]

B. Anti-Objectivism

The central tenet in the outsider legal perspective is the characterization of American society and law as "racist," "sexist," and "homophobic." Derrick Bell, the most acclaimed crit and "father" of CRT, charges that:

> Black people will never gain full equality in this country. Even those herculean efforts we hail as successful will produce no more than temporary 'peaks of progress,' shortlived victories that slide into irrelevance as racial patterns adapt in ways that maintain white dominance. This is a hard-to-accept fact that all history verifies.[79]

Bell also writes about the "*ideological hegemony*' of white racism."[80] Professor Charles Lawrence argues that "[b]ecause racism is so deeply ingrained in our

---

77. As Frank Valdez suggests, there is a sense of solidarity among the groups resulting from their subordination. Yet, there is also an understanding that each group experiences subordination in a different way. See Francisco Valdez, "Theorizing Outcrit Theories: Coalitional Method and Comparative Jurisprudential Experience—Racecrits, Queercrits and Latcrits," *University of Miami Law Review* 53 (1999): 1265.

78. For a critique of postmodernism, see, e.g., Chapter 9, Section C2 & C4, infra (sources cited therein); Symposium—"The Future of Intersectionality and Critical Race Feminism," *Journal of Contemporary Legal Issues* 11 (2001): 667–936.

79. Derrick A. Bell, Jr., "Racial Realism," *Connecticut Law Review* 24 (1992): 363, 373. See Derrick A. Bell, Jr., *Faces at the Bottom of the Well: The Permanence of Racism* (New York: Basic Books, 1992).

80. Derrick A. Bell, Jr., *And We Are Not Saved: The Elusive Quest for Racial Justice* (New York: Basic Books, 1987), p. 156 (emphasis supplied). Thus, Bell describes the mission of the criticalist as "advancing a decidedly political project, that is, indicating the rule of law in the construction and maintenance of race based social domination and subordination.... Although the goal of critical race theory can be stated as altering the relationship between law and racial power, critical race commentators accept that race is permanently imbued with political content, and therefore is not, and cannot be, introduced as a neutral concept. In support of their thesis, CRTs point to the fact that almost a half-century after the formal rejection of de jure segregation and forma racial inequality [i.e., formal equal opportunity], basic assumptions and presuppositions about race continue to serve as the cornerstone of the contemporary social hierarchy. The goal of this text is to locate, deconstruct, and hopefully excavate those assumptions and presuppositions as they exist under

culture, it is likely to be transmitted by tacit understandings."[81] There is change from one era to another," Richard Delgado observes, "but the net quantum of racism remains exactly the same, obeying a melancholy Law of Racial Thermodynamics: Racism is neither created nor destroyed."[82] Racism is "a central ideological and political pillar upholding existing social conditions," Kimberlé Crenshaw asserts.[83] Catharine MacKinnon maintains that "the law sees and treats women the way men see and treat women. The liberal state coercively and authoritatively constitutes the social order in the interests of men as a gender, through its legitimizing norms, relation to society, and substantive policy."[84] And homophobia, or heterosexism, Marc Fajer argues, is deeply rooted in American society and American institutions, including the law.[85]

Criticalists, then, see in society an unmistakable slant or bias that favors insiders.[86] Dominant American cultural norms are not neutral as to matters of race, sex, and sexual orientation. This is not the natural state of the human condition; for, culture is constructed, as is the social reality it engenders. Thus, cultural norms that give shape to (or perhaps reflect) mainstream society and its institutions are neither universal nor objective—they are in fact *anti-objective*. They favor insiders and disfavor outsiders.[87]

---

law." Derrick A. Bell, Jr., *Teacher's Manual—Race, Racism, and American Law* 5th ed. (New York: Aspen Publishers, 2004), p. 7. See Section A2b, supra.

81. Charles Lawrence, "The Id, The Ego, and Equal Protection: Reckoning with Unconscious Racism," *Stanford Law Review* 39 (1987): 317, 324.

82. Richard Delgado, "When a Story is Just a Story: Does Voice Really Matter?," *Virginia Law Review* 76 (1990): 95, 106.

83. Kimberlé Crenshaw, "Race, Reform and Retrenchment: Transformation and Legitimation in Anti-Discrimination Law," *Harvard Law Review* 101 (1988): 1331, 1387.

84. Catharine A. MacKinnon, "Feminism, Marxism, Method, and the State: Toward Feminist Jurisprudence," *Signs* 8 (1984): 635, 644. See Littleton, "Reconstructing Sexual Equality," supra note 55, at p. 1279.

85. See Marc A. Fajer, "Can Two Real Men Eat Quiche Together? Storytelling, Gender-Role Stereotypes, and Legal Protection for Lesbians and Gay Men," *University of Miami Law Review* 46 (1992): 511, 611.

86. See generally, *Critical Race Theory: The Cutting Edge* 2d ed., Richard Delgado and Jean Stefancic, eds. (Philadelphia: Temple University Press, 2000), pp. xiii–xvii.

87. See Robin West, "Relativism, Objectivity, and Law," *Yale Law Journal* 99 (1990): 1473, 1487.

1. Three Levels of Anti-Objectivism

Anti-objectivism can be manifested in at least three mindsets, or, in other words, at three "levels."[88] It can take the form of overt expressions of antipathy toward an outsider group. This level of racism, sexism or heterosexism (Level 1) has received a good deal of attention from gays and lesbians but very little attention from other crits, perhaps because homosexuals are still fighting for equal rights and have been the victims of a large amount of violence.[89] Level 2 Anti-objectivism has received even less attention from crits. At this level, racism, sexism, and heterosexism operate "backstage." This is a term used by Professor Joe R. Feagin to describe a common phenomenon: insiders consciously, or strategically, keep their biases off the "frontstage" (i.e., out of the workplace, classroom, and other public places) but do not hesitate to display them in private (e.g., in the company of friends or family). The concern, of course, is that backstage bias is likely to appear on the frontstage cleverly disguised.[90] Finally, Level 3 Bias is the most difficult form of anti-objectivism to explain or comprehend. At this level, bias is frontstage but unconscious. That is, the perpetrator's bias operates in public (e.g., on college campuses in one-on-one encounters or through well-established institutional policies or procedures) but it is unacknowledged and uncontrolled.

Criticalists have devoted most of their time and attention to clarifying Level 3 Bias, unconscious bias. Some have tried to explain the processes by which it emerges, while others have sought to document its existence within individuals or institutions. Non-crit scholars have also contributed to this enterprise, and are often cited by crits. Before sampling the scholarship on Level 3 Bias, it might be useful to consider just how difficult it is for some to perceive unconscious bias.

---

88. These levels were suggested by Kevin O'Connor Moon, USD Law Class of '06, during the fall semester of 2004. Mr. Moon borrows from the three levels of judicial analysis presented in Chapter 7, supra.

89. See Chapter 9, Section B1, infra.

90. Professor Feagin's concept was presented at a conference honoring his scholarship, titled "Social Justice and Social Science," convened at the University of Illinois, April 13, 2004, and will appear in a forthcoming book. See Leslie Houts and Joe Feagin, *Backstage Racism* (forthcoming 2005).

2. Perceiving Level 3 Bias

Most criticalists would agree with the view that we live in a society that has moved beyond a time in which Level 1 Bias, intentional or purposeful bias, was the law of the land. "Colored only" restrooms and sections of public transportation, as well as public acceptance of the use of the "N" word have largely become relics of the past.[91] Today, we live in large part in a post-civil rights period of unconscious bias, as outline in the following report:

> As we look back over the years of the post-civil rights era, we see a positive trend in the self-reported racial attitudes of White Americans, especially in their attitudes toward African Americans. The demise of legalized racial segregation and discrimination was followed by a sharp decline in blatant, 'old-fashioned' racism which centered on the notion of biologically-based black racial inferiority. Today, national surveys show that white Americans overwhelmingly endorse the principles of racial equality and integration. This positive trend is also reflected in surveys of white college students, which show a steady decline in negative characterizations of blacks over the last 60 years. However, many researchers argue that while the fundamental norms with regard to race have changed, underlying negative attitudes toward African Americans and other minority groups persist, albeit in a new guise. While most whites no longer blatantly oppose the ideals of racial equality and integration, many show subtle and often *unconscious* biases toward members of minority ethnic groups. These newer forms of unintentional racial biases are exhibited by many whites who, on a conscious level, endorse egalitarian values and believe themselves to be nonprejudiced. These biases persist inconspicuously but can have grave effects on social perceptions, attitudes, and behaviors.[92]

Yet, how difficult is it to see unconscious bias? Consider the following story.

---

91. In some segments of the African American community today, the "N" word is used as a term of affection, see, e.g., Randall Kennedy, *Nigger* (New York: Pantheon Books, 2001), although most African Americans still reject its use altogether. See, e.g., David D. Kirkpatrick, "A Black Author Hurls *That* Word As a Challenge," New York Times, 12/1/01, p. A15.

92. Shana Levin, "Social Psychological Evidence on Race and Racism," Chapter 3, p. 2, in *A Report of the AERA Panel on Racial Dynamics in Colleges and Universities*, Mitchell Chang, Daria Witt, James Jones, Kenji Hakuta, eds. (Stanford, CA: Center for the Com-

A shop owner fired one of her employees for using a particular racial slur only a week after the employee had been told that the remark was offensive. Indeed, it was the shop owner herself who had heard the remark face-to-face on both occasions and who had issued the prior warning. In awarding unemployment benefits to the discharged employee under state law, the judge ruled that the discharged employee was entitled to such benefits because she did not intentionally use the racial slur. It was an "unconscious" slip of the tongue, according to the judge.[93]

If judges have a hard time comprehending overt expressions of unconscious bias, including their perniciousness, they will surely have a much more difficult time understanding subtle expressions of unconscious bias, which seem to be the more prevalent form of expression. This, indeed, is the challenge critical theorists face. In the absence of an overt expression of unconscious bias—which by itself would seem to amount to conscious bias save for the fact that the offending party truly does not *intend* to give offense—how does one establish unconscious bias?

3. Probing Level 3 Bias

Critical theorists have attempted to explain or establish the existence of unconscious bias in various ways. More than that, they have attempted to convey the understanding that the damage wrought by unconscious bias is just as great as (and sometimes greater than) the damage caused by conscious bias. Let us consider some of the ways in which criticalists have sought to convey this important information.

a. Psychology—Cognitive Schemes

Charles Lawrence has authored what many regard as the seminal criticalist work on unconscious bias. Focusing on racism, Lawrence argues that racial attitudes are hidden from view in the unconscious mind—the psyche:

> ...[M]ost of us are unaware of our racism. We do not recognize the ways in which our cultural experience has influenced our beliefs about race or the occasions on which those beliefs affect our actions.

---

parative Studies on Race and Ethnicity, 1999) (prepublication draft advance copy) (emphasis added).

93. See Jeff McDonald, "Shop Owner Fights Judge's Ruling in Ethnic Slur Case: Clerk Receiving Jobless Benefits," San Diego Union-Tribune, 9/17/01, p. B1.

In other words, a large part of the behavior that produces racial discrimination is influenced by unconscious racial motivation.

There are two explanations for the unconscious nature of our racially discriminatory beliefs and ideas. First, Freudian theory states that the human mind defends itself against the discomfort of guilt by denying or refusing to recognize those ideas, wishes, and beliefs that conflict with what the individual has learned is good or right. While our historical experience has made racism an integral part of our culture, our society has more recently embraced an ideal that rejects racism as immoral. When an individual experiences conflict between racist ideas and the societal ethic that condemns those ideas, the mind excludes his racism from consciousness.

Second, the theory of cognitive psychology states that the culture—including, for example, the media and an individual's parents, peers, and authority figures—transmits certain beliefs and preferences. Because these beliefs are so much a part of the culture, they are not experienced as explicit lessons. Instead, they seem part of the individual's rational ordering of her perceptions of the world. The individual is unaware, for example, that the ubiquitous presence of a cultural stereotype has influenced her perception that blacks are lazy or unintelligent. Because racism is so deeply ingrained in our culture, it is likely to be transmitted by tacit understandings: Even if a child is not told that blacks are inferior, he learns that lesson by observing the behavior of others. These tacit understandings, because they have never been articulated, are less likely to be experienced at a conscious level.[94]

Support for Lawrence's view comes from scholars outside the criticalist circle. Sounding the Freudian theme in Lawrence's argument, Joel Kovel, whose work actually predates Lawrence's, uses psychoanalytic theories to assert the "aversive racism" thesis. This thesis holds that consciously held egalitarian norms often stand in conflict with unacknowledged racial bias. Whites express this conflict when around racial minorities, not by open hostility, but by anxiety and discomfort.[95]

---

94. Lawrence, "The Id, The Ego, and Equal Protection: Reckoning with Unconscious Racism," supra note 81, at pp. 322–23.

95. Joel Kovel, *White Racism: A Psychohistory* (New York: Vintage Books, 1970), pp. 191–211. Lawrence, in fact, cites Kovel's work. See also, Paul L. Wachtel, *Race in the Mind of America: Breaking the Vicious Circle Between Blacks and Whites* (New York: Routledge, 1999).

Linda Hamilton Krieger supports the cognitive psychology theme in Lawrence's argument. Research shows, Krieger argues, that racial stereotyping is simply a method of categorizing our sensory perceptions, similar in structure and function to categorizing trees, rocks, and other natural objects. Racial stereotypes, then, are "cognitive mechanisms" that all persons, "not just 'prejudiced' ones, use to simplify the task of perceiving, processing, and retaining information about people in memory." These biases, Krieger continues, are "unintended." They "sneak up on" the individual—"distorting bit by bit the data upon which his decision[s] [are]...eventually based"—which is to say they are "*cognitive* rather than *motivational*." Racial stereotypes "operate absent intent to favor or disfavor members of a particular social group," they "operate beyond the reach of a...[person's] self-awareness."[96]

The cognitive dimension of unconscious bias can have deadly consequences for some outsiders, especially when dealing with the police. The famous case of Amadou Diallo illustrates the point. In 1999, four Bronx police officers, all of them white, fired 41 shots at close range at Amadou Diallo, a young African American, 19 of them finding their target. Several bullets hit the bottom of Diallo's feet as he lay dying in the doorway. Diallo was killed because the police officers "saw" a gun in his hand. The gun turned out to be a wallet Diallo was reaching for. Why did the police officers "see" a gun at such close range? Nothing in the personal histories of the police officers, all relatively inexperienced (which may be why more than half of the shots *missed*), suggests any of them harbored racial hatred. They were average white men who were "predisposed to look into a black face and see 'criminal.'"[97] Part of the risks of being black in a racist society is to always be perceived as a suspect, a threat. "Even black plain-clothes cops have been killed by their white fellow officers."[98] If one is black, one is likely to fit the criminal's profile. This much we know from the studies on race profiling.[99]

Focusing on women, Virginia Valian attempts to add further clarification to the cognitive bases of unconscious bias. She argues that disadvantage

---

96. Linda Hamilton Krieger, "Content of Our Categories: A Cognitive Bias Approach to Discrimination and Equal Employment Opportunity," *Stanford Law Review* 47 (1995): 1161, 1187–88.

97. William Raspberry, "Evidence Here That Race Still Matters," San Diego Union-Tribune, 3/4/00, p. B10.

98. Ibid.

99. On racial profiling, see, e.g., Roy L. Brooks, Gilbert Paul Carrasco, and Michael Selmi, *Civil Rights Litigation: Cases and Perspectives* 2d ed. (Durham: Carolina Academic Press, 2000), p. 695, "Top N.J. Cops Knew Minorities Targeted," San Diego Union-Tribune,10/13/00, p. A-7. For further discussion of the Diallo case; see, e.g., "New Yorkers' Attitudes Toward Cops Shifting," San Diego Union-Tribune, 3/5/00, p. A-12.

against women continues to exist in the professional work place as well as in other venues notwithstanding anti-discrimination laws or our political will to end such disadvantage. The reason, she argues, is because of "gender schemas." "Schemas are hypotheses that we use to interpret social events.... Gender schemes are hypotheses about what it means to be male or female, hypotheses that we all share, male and female alike."[100] "[I]mplicit gender schemes counter explicit intentions and unambiguous proscriptions."[101] Once they are invoked, gender schemas work to the disadvantage of women even in situations involving objective characteristics such as height. For example, in one experiment:

> ...the experimenters exploited the fact that our schemas include the information that men are on average taller than women. In this experiment, college students saw photographs of other students and estimated their heights in feet and inches. The photos always contained a reference item, such as a desk or a doorway, so that height could be accurately estimated.
>
> Unbeknownst to the students who were doing the estimating, the experimenters had matched the photographs so that for every photograph of a male student of a given height there was a female student of the same height. But the students were affected by their knowledge that men are on average taller than women. They judged the women as shorter than they really were, and the men as taller. The students' schemas distorted their judgments.
>
> In this experiment, as is typically the case, there were no differences in how male and female observers perceived the others. We all have unconscious hypotheses about males and females, and we all use those hypotheses in perceiving and evaluating others.[102]

In case after case, Valian demonstrates how gender schemas— from the assumption that women are less capable than men to the assumption that they are not interested in certain types of jobs—operate to deny recognition and advancement to women in social institutions. True, biological differences between men and women can sometimes explain sexual disadvantage. It is also true that women are frequently "active agents in the reproduction of their own

---

100. Virginia Valian, "The Cognitive Bases of Gender Bias," *Brooklyn Law Review* 65 (1999): 1037, 1044.

101. Marianne LaFrance, "The Schemas and Schemes in Sex Discrimination," *Brooklyn Law Review* 65 (1999) 1063, 1063.

102. Valian, "The Cognitive Bases of Gender Bias," supra note 100, at pp. 1045–46.

subordination. By being nice, by being communal, by being agreeable, and by providing emotional labor, women also lend support to a gendered occupational structure."[103] But, as Marianne LaFrance points out, "there is ample evidence to document the powerful influence exerted by gender schemas."[104]

Much of the bias towards gays and lesbians today is at Level 1.[105] There is, however, plenty of Level 3 Bias as well. For example, Frank Valdes and Marc Fajer argue that deeply ingrained social expectations regarding gender roles work to subordinate gays and lesbians as well as women. Fajer tells the story of a homosexual whose mother pays a visit to him and his lover for a few days. Upon leaving, the mother says to her son, "I don't quite understand…which of you does what?" The mother wanted to know who performs the wifely role of cook and cleaner. Heterosexuals' misunderstandings are so profound that they are in fact "pre-understandings," Fajer argues. These pre-understandings preclude heterosexuals from even envisioning how two men could function as a "household" or be "married."[106]

b. Sociology—Insider Privilege

Insider privilege is another conceptual device criticalists use to probe Level 3 Anti-Ojectivism. This is a sociological phenomenon in which unconscious racism, sexism, or heterosexism springs from the strategic choices white male heterosexuals make to preserve or exercise unfair or unearned social advantage. Like the cognitive explanation of unconscious bias, the charge of insider privilege is certainly not unique to critical theory. Noncrits have used the term to define racism. For example, George Fredrickson has stated that:

> Racism…can be defined as an ethnic group's assertion or maintenance of a privileged or protected status vis-a-vis members of another group or groups who are thought, because of defective ancestry, to possess a set of socially-relevant characteristics that disqualify them

---

103. LaFrance, "The Schemas and Schemes in Sex Discrimination," supra note 101, at p. 1071.

104. Ibid. at p. 1065 (sources cited therein).

105. See Chapter 9, Section B1, infra.

106. See Marc A. Fajer, "Can Two Real Men Eat Quiche Together? Storytelling, Gender-Role Stereotypes, and Legal Protection for Lesbians and Gay Men," *University of Miami Law Review* 46 (1992): 511, 611; Francisco Valdes, "Queers, Sissies, Dykes, and Tomboys: Deconstructing the Conflation of 'Sex,' 'Gender' and 'Sexual Orientation' in Euro-American Law and Society," *California Law Review* 83 (1995): 1.

from full membership in a community or citizenship in a nation-state.[107]

Thus, insider privilege is the retention of unfair cultural and socio-economic advantage by insiders. It is, as Robert C. Smith suggests, *"an implicit sense of group position"* that results in outsider subordination. Insider privilege, Smith continues, sends the message that insiders "will seek to defend their privilege no matter how they feel toward [outsiders]...."[108]

Focusing on "white privilege," Peggy McIntosh, in a famous passage, helps us to crystallize the concept of insider privilege:

> I have come to see white privilege as an *invisible package of unearned assets* which I can count on cashing in each day, but about which I was 'meant' to remain oblivious. White privilege is like an invisible weightless knapsack of special provisions, assurances, tools, maps, guides, codebooks, passports, visas, clothes, compass, emergency gear, and blank checks.[109]

McIntosh also equates white privilege with male and heterosexual privilege.[110] Along these lines, Cheryl Harris suggests that insider privilege operates in our culture as a property value premised on the right to exclude.[111]

Robert Jensen candidly describes insider privilege from an insider's view:

> When I seek admission to a university, apply for a job, or hunt for an apartment, I don't look threatening. Almost all of the people evaluating me for those things look like me—they are white. They see in me a reflection of themselves, and in a racist world that is an advantage. I smile. I am white. I am one of them. I am not dangerous. Even

---

107. George M. Fredrickson, "Reflections on the Comparative History and Sociology of Racism," p. 51, in *Racial Classification and History*, E. Nathaniel Gates ed. (New York: Garland Publications, 1997), p. 55.

108. Robert C. Smith, *Racism in the Post-Civil Rights Era* (Albany, N.Y.: State University of New York, 1995), p. 42 (emphasis added). See Mary Jackman and Marie Crane, "Some of My Best Friends Are Black....Interracial friendship and Whites' Racial Attitudes," *Public Opinion Quarterly* 50 (1985), p. 481.

109. Peggy McIntosh, "White Privilege and Male Privilege: A Personal Account of Coming to See Correspondences Through Work in Women's Studies," in *Critical White Studies: Looking Behind the Mirror*, Richard Delgado and Jean Stefancic, eds. (Philadelphia: Temple University Press, 1997), p. 291.

110. Ibid. at p. 297.

111. Cheryl Harris, "Whiteness as Property," *Harvard Law Review* 106 (1993): 1707.

when I voice critical opinions, I am cut some slack. After all, I'm white.[112]

One of the most impressive discussions of insider privilege in criticalist scholarship appears in Stephanie M. Wildman's book, *Privilege Revealed—How Invisible Preference Undermines America*. Wildman uses an interesting example, slightly modified here, to help us see the privileged identities in America. Let us assume a newspaper runs three headlines: (1) "Woman Elected Mayor"; (2) "Black Elected Tax Assessor"; and (3) "Family of 4 Wins Trip to Disneyland." Reading these headlines, the average American, whether insider or outsider, would assume that the new mayor was white, the new tax assessor was male, and the lucky family was heterosexual. "In each case we are demonstrating ingrained awareness of the norms that frame our perceptions."[113] In each case, an invisible yet unmistakable preference is revealed.

There is a default mechanism, Wildman argues, through which society categorizes our conceptual tools (words and ideas). Images are formed in our mind's eye, difficult to erase, that favor some and disfavor others. Those within the *circle of privilege*—whites, males, and heterosexuals—have a distinct social advantage over those who are not. Most people, however, live at the intersection of privilege and subordination, Wildman suggests. White women are privileged relative to African American women, but not with respect to white men. White homosexual men are privileged in relation to African American heterosexual men (particularly when the former choose to hide their sexual orientation), but not when situated against white heterosexual men (again, particularly if they choose not to hide their sexual orientation).

c. Institutional Policies or Practices

The claim of unconscious bias we have considered thus far rests upon the psychological or sociological dynamics of the individual. Yet, institutions can exhibit unconscious bias when human-created policies or practices disadvantaging outsiders have become part of the normal way in which the institution operates. Focusing on race, Ian F. Haney López argues "that group interaction generates racial institutions, and that such institutions influence

---

112. Race Relations: "Examining White Privilege and Whiteness Studies," wysiwyg://5/ http://racerelations.ab...actions/library/weekly/aa060200a.htm, 9/6/00.
113. Stephanie M. Wildman, *Privilege Revealed—How Invisible Preference Undermines America* (New York: New York University Press, 1996), pp. 80, 126–27. The quote is from Kathleen Hall Jamieson, *Beyond the Double Bind: Women and Leadership* (New York: Oxford University Press, 1995), p. 169.

individual behavior through widely shared cognitive processes."[114] By "racial institutions," López means "any understanding of race that has come to be so widely shared within a community that it operates as an unexamined cognitive resource for understanding one's self, others, and the-way-the-world-is."[115] Hence, "institutional racism" occurs, López argues, when institutional actions are influenced by racial stereotypes (i.e., "racial institutions") and have "the effect of enforcing a racial status hierarchy."[116] López largely concurs with Lawrence's observations that "we are all racists," stating: "In this country we are all constituted by and cognitively rely on racial institutions."[117]

To illustrate institutional racism, López discusses Los Angeles' system of selecting grand jurors that was in effect during 1968 and 1969. "The usual practice [was] for Superior Court judges to submit nominations of whomever they wish[ed] for prospective grand jurors."[118] This practice resulted in the near total exclusion of Mexican Americans from the grand juries. Although the dozens of judges questioned about this practice said they did not intend to discriminate against Mexican Americans, López argues that picking nominees on the basis of social acquaintances or nepotism exhibited institutional racism because it produced "racial status harms." The selection system was racist, in other words, because it had the effect of enforcing a racial status hierarchy.[119]

The tax code presents a more current illustration of institutional racism. Tax matters are traditionally evaluated from "the perspectives of horizontal equity (fairness as between similarly situated taxpayers), vertical equality (fairness as between income classes), economic efficiency, and simplicity or administrability."[120] As Karen B. Brown and Mary Louise Fellows have pointed out, little, if any, serious attention is ever given by the institutional players—

---

114. Ian F. Haney López,"Institutional Racism: Judicial Conduct and a New Theory of Racial Discrimination," *Yale Law Journal* 109 (2000): 1717, 1808.

115. Ibid.

116. Ibid. at pp. 1722, 1810.

117. Ibid. at pp. 1808–9.

118. Ibid. at p. 1731.

119. Ibid. at pp. 1731, 1808. "Under my definition, action influenced by racial institutions becomes "institutional racism" when those actions produce racial status harms." Ibid. at p. 1811.

120. Michael A. Livingston, Symposium: "Radical Scholars, Conservative Field: Putting 'Critical Tax Scholarship' in Perspective," *North Carolina Law Review* 76 (1998): 1791, 1792, citing William A. Klein & Joseph Bankman, *Federal Income Taxation* 11th ed. (New York: Aspen Law & Business, 1997), pp. 18–24.

Congress, the tax court, and tax scholars—to how the tax laws contribute to the subordination of outsiders.[121] Yet, Beverly Moran and William Whitford have demonstrated how tax laws governing the deduction for mortgage interest payments, the exclusion of certain gifts from taxation, the joint return marriage penalty, and other provisions in the tax code disadvantage African Americans.[122] These laws subordinate African Americans even when household income differences are taken into account, they argue. This is because African Americans tend to have fewer of the category of assets (such as stocks and home mortgages) that receive favorable treatment under these provisions of the tax code. African Americans on average have less inheritable wealth than whites due to a history of discrimination in employment markets.[123] In the decades before and after the Civil War, African Americans "were cheated out of their land or driven from it through intimidation, violence, and even murder."[124] They have also encountered more housing discrimination than whites over the years, which to this day affects their ability to obtain housing in more desirable neighborhoods.[125] Not surprisingly, then, African Americans have less mortgage interest payments to deduct.[126] Finally, African American husbands and wives "are more likely to have similar incomes at the time of marriage, resulting in the imposition of a relatively high marriage penalty."[127] Similar institutional bias can be shown against women and homosexuals.[128]

---

121. *Taxing America*, Karen B. Brown & Mary Louise Fellows, eds. (New York: New York University Press, 1996), p. 2.

122. See Beverly I. Moran and William Whitford, "A Black Critique of the Internal Revenue Code," *Wisconsin Law Review* 1996 (1996): 751.

123. See, e.g., Brooks, *Rethinking the American Race Problem*, supra note 42, at pp. 25–33, 51–64.

124. Todd Lewan and Dolores Barclay, "Oral History Found True: Hundreds of Blacks Were Cheated of Land," San Diego Union-Tribune, 12/2/01, p. A25 (discussing 18-month investigation by the Associated Press).

125. See, e.g., Roy L. Brooks, *Integration or Separation? A Strategy for Racial Equality* (Cambridge: Harvard University Press, 1996), pp. 51–68; Brooks, *Rethinking the American Race Problem*, supra note 42, at pp. 70–74. The denial of equal educational opportunity also plays a role in this discussion. See ibid. at pp. 74–83.

126. See Moran and Whitford, "A Black Critique of the Internal Revenue Code," supra note 122, at p. 759-800; Livingston, "Radical Scholars," supra note 120, at pp. 1807–8.

127. Livingston, "Radical Scholars," supra note 120, at p. 1807, citing Moran and Whitford, "A Black Critique of the Internal Revenue Code," supra note 122, at p. 800. Livingston's article defends criticalist analysis against criticisms made by non-crits.

128. See, e.g., Marjorie E. Kornhauser, "The Rhetoric of the Anti-Progressive Tax Movement: A Typical Male Reaction," *Michigan Law Review* 86 (1987): 465; Patricia A. Cain, "Same-Sex Couples and the Federal Tax Laws," *Law & Sexuality* 1 (1991): 97.

d. Transparency Phenomenon

Barbara Flagg offers yet another way to understand anti-objectivism both individually and institutionally. Her approach is centered on a concept she calls the "transparency phenomenon." This is "the tendency of whites not to think about whiteness."[129] In other words, "whiteness" functions through transparency for whites. It is invisible. It is seen by whites as normal, the way things are naturally. Whites do not think of their color as an asset because their color is not usually called to their attention. Again, for whites, "whiteness"—but not other colors—is transparent.

Flagg illustrates transparency through storytelling. The story she tells centers on an African American scientist who changed her name to Keisha Akbar and adopted speech and grooming patterns consistent with an African cultural perspective. Although she excelled at the technical aspects of her work, Ms. Akbar was denied a promotion to department head because her expression of African heritage was perceived as an inability or unwillingness to fit smoothly into the corporate culture. Flagg makes the point that the personal characteristics which disqualified Ms. Akbar from the management position "intersect seamlessly with her self-definition as a black woman."[130] Thus, Ms. Akbar's discrimination results from the transparency phenomenon, which escapes redress under Title VII, the federal employment discrimination law:

> White people externalize race. For most whites, most of the time, to think or speak about race is to think or speak about people of color, or perhaps, at times, to reflect on oneself (or other whites) in relation to people of color. But we tend not to think of ourselves or our racial cohort as racially distinctive. Whites' "consciousness" of whiteness is predominantly unconsciousness of whiteness. We perceive and interact with other whites as individuals who have no significant racial characteristics. In the same vein, the white person is unlikely to see or describe himself in racial terms, perhaps in part because his white peers do not regard him as racially distinctive. Whiteness is a transparent quality when whites interact with whites in the absence of people of color. Whiteness attains opacity, becomes apparent to the white mind, only in relation to, and contrast with, the "color" of nonwhites.

129. Barbara J. Flagg, *Was Blind, But Now I See: White Race Consciousness and the Law* (New York: New York University Press, 1998), p. 1.

130. Ibid., p. 87.

Just as whites tend to regard whiteness as racelessness, the transparency phenomenon also affects whites' decisionmaking; behaviors and characteristics associated with whites take on the same aura of race neutrality. Thus, white people frequently interpret norms adopted by a dominantly white culture as racially neutral, and so fail to recognize the ways in which those norms may be in fact covertly race-specific. Keisha would argue that she was not promoted because her personal style was found wanting when measured against a norm that was in fact transparently "white."

The manner in which... Keisha [was] treated violates the norm of colorblindness—the principle that race should not be taken into account in assessing the individual.... [T]he violation of the colorblindness norm takes the form of applying unconsciously white, and in that sense race-specific, criteria of decision. Thus, laws and policies designed to implement the colorblindness principle ought equally to disapprove the outcomes in [this case and the case where race-based decision making was more obvious].

... [Turning to Title VII for legal relief,] Keisha would have difficulty getting beyond the initial pleading stage because the form of discrimination she encountered cannot easily be addressed under either the disparate treatment or the current disparate impact model.[131]

C. Conclusion

Neither the traditional civil rights definition (which incorporates the element of antipathy) nor the economist's notion of rational discrimination (actors who engage in discrimination to maximize their interests)[132] fully captures the criticalist concepts of racism, sexism, and homophobia. From the criticalist point of

---

131. Barbara J. Flagg, "Fashioning A Title VII Remedy for Transparently White Subjective Decisionmaking," *Yale Law Journal* 104 (1995): 2009, 2013–14. For a discussion of the disparate treatment and disparate impact models of discrimination, see, e.g., *St. Mary's Honor Center v. Hicks*, 509 U.S. 502 (1995) (disparate treatment); *Ward's Cove Packing Co., Inc. v. Atonio*, 490 U.S. 642 (1989) (disparate impact).

132. For a more detailed discussion, see Ian F. Haney López, "Institutional Racism: Judicial Conduct and a New Theory of Racial Discrimination," supra note 114, at pp. 1761–69.

view, such bias consists of deeply ingrained mental states that operate at the conscious or unconscious level in persons and institutions. The problem, in short, is anti-objectivism, or subordination.

The structural feature of subordination is all-important. As john a. powell informs us: "Without characterizing oppression as structural, and without developing an agenda that is oriented toward destabilizing and disturbing this structure, any formal or individual progress will be largely rendered impotent."[133] This is as terse an explanation as one can find.

Critical theory is not, of course, beyond criticism. Like the traditional judicial theories discussed in Part 1, critical theory brings its own set of strengths and weaknesses to the table.[134] Many of these criticisms will emerge as we move through the remainder of the book. One of them can conveniently be mentioned here—to wit, critical theory offers little in the way of proposals for concrete social reform through law. Notwithstanding its desire for social transformation, critical theory provides no systematic program for achieving such an end.[135]

This failure to provide proposals for reform may be less a failure of critical theory than of critical theorists themselves. As we shall see in the next chapter, there are elements within critical theory that can be used to improve the human condition. As an added benefit, this discussion may resolve an internal criticism lodged by one of the pioneers of Critical Race Theory, Richard Delgado. This innovative and prolific theorist argues that CRT has, to its great detriment, been taken over by "idealists," who, influenced by the postmodernists, "work almost entirely in the realm of discourse." CRT, Delgado argues, needs to be reclaimed by the "realists" (or "materialists"), who hold "that while text, attitude, and intention may play important roles in our system of racial hierarchy, material factors such as profits and the labor market are even more

---

133. john a. powell, "An Agenda for the Post-Civil Rights Era," *University of San Francisco Law Review* 29 (1995): 889, 910.

134. For a collection of some of the criticisms of critical theory discussed in this book, see, e.g., *Critical Race Theory: The Cutting Edge* 2d ed., Richard Delgado and Jean Stefanic, eds. (Philadelphia: Temple University Press, 2000), pp. 553–90; Daniel A. Farber and Suzanna Sherry, *Beyond All Reason: The Radical Assault on Truth in American Law* (New York: Oxford University Press, 1997).

135. See, e.g., Bell, *Teacher's Manual*, supra note 80, at p. 7 (the job of Critical Race Theory is "to locate, deconstruct, and hopefully excavate those assumptions and presuppositions as they exist under law"). See also Litowitz, "Gramsci, Hegemony, and the Law," supra note 15, at p. 518 ("Gramsci's work provides important insights for understanding how the law sustains unequal power relations, but it offers scant direction for reforming the law"). Compare, Anderson, "Teaching Critical Legal Studies," supra note 56 (proposing ad hoc positive answers to identified subordination).

decisive in determining who falls where in the system."[136] Delgado's use of the term "realists"does not appear to refer to the "racial realists" or "feminist re-alists" who have abandoned the belief that "equality can be obtained through law,"[137] but, instead, seems reminiscent of an earlier discussion between Marx-ist idealists and economic determinists.[138] The remediation features of critical theory discussed in the next chapter—"reconstructive" and "internal cri-tique"—can perhaps yield the kinds of tangible legal benefits that emerged during the civil rights movement.[139]

---

136. Richard Delgado, "Crossroads and Blind Alleys: A Critical Examination of Recent Writing About Race," *Texas Law Review* 82 (2003): 121, 123–24. For a response to Del-gado's charge, see Kevin Johnson, "Roll Over Beethoven: 'A Critical Examination of Recent Writing about Race,'" *Texas Law Review* 82 (2004): 717.

137. Brooks, *Critical Procedure*, supra note 55, at pp. 4–5 (discussion the "realist" schol-arship of Robin Barnes, Robin West, and Derrick Bell).

138. See Section A1, supra.

139. As constructed in the next chapter, critical theory also mediates, to a lesser extent, the divide between structualist and postmodernist visions by moving these critical dis-courses into the "critical dimension" of theory, treating them as epistemologies of equal standing.

Chapter 9
Critical Theory: Operational Elements

Although there is little discussion among critical theorists about how law can be used to make concrete changes in social conditions, there are elements within critical theory that suggest such possibilities. Critical theory, in other words, is a complete theory. It has "a 'cognitive or explanatory dimension,' a 'constructive dimension,' and a 'critical dimension.' . . . The cognitive dimension . . . provides deconstructive analysis of law; the constructive dimension . . . facilitates reconstructive analysis; and the critical dimension is in the internal critique of the preferred equality rules. Of the three dimensions, reconstruction is the most difficult to formulate."[1] These elements lay the foundation for the construction of an outsider process of judicial decision making, called "critical process," presented in the next chapter; thus, transforming critical theory from a theory of legal criticism to a theory of judicial decision making.

A. Deconstruction and Reconstruction

The terms "deconstruction" and "reconstruction" carry different meanings depending upon the context in which they are used. For example, in the literary context, deconstruction most often denotes a theory of poststructuralism that criticizes the Western philosophical belief in "logocentrism," which Gloria Stephenson defines as "the concept of structure that depends on stabilizing, fixed, 'centers,' such as truth, God, consciousness, being, [and] essence,...and the inferior axiological oppositions, such as lie, Satan, nonconscious, nonbe-

---

1. Roy L. Brooks, Critical Procedure (Durham: Carolina Academic Press, 1998), pp. xxv–xxvi. As Harold Koh, dean of Yale Law School, explains: "The cognitive or explanatory dimension asks: when one looks at things [from an outsider or criticalist] perspective, does one see things that one does not see otherwise? Does this lens explain things for which one does not otherwise have a good explanation? Do practices that appear to be natural or invisible suddenly become visible and socially constructed? The constructive dimension asks: if [critical] theory does lead us to criticize [law], what reforms, if any, follow? The critical dimension asks: if we see the world in this new light through these [reconstructive measures], are we more or less happy with it? Are we more or less likely to criticize?" Ibid., quoting Harold H. Koh, "Two Cheers for Feminist Procedure," University of Cincinnati Law Review 61 (1993): 1201–2.

ing, [and] appearance...."[2] This concept of deconstruction is called "Derridean deconstruction," named after the French intellectual Jacques Derrida.[3]

In the context of law, deconstruction and reconstruction can be used to identify and remedy anti-objectivism, particularly in neutral settings. Deconstruction "can be seen as the breaking down of the walls of a building in order to see why it leans in one direction." Reconstruction "rebuilds the defective edifice into a palace of justice."[4] Thus, deconstruction and reconstruction work in tandem. Together, they constitute the "subordination question," a two-fold question which asks: Does a socio-legal arrangement (e.g., a case or specified legal doctrine) subordinate outsiders or a particular outsider group, and, if so, what can be done about it? *Asking the subordination question at every turn is what separates crits from non-crits.*

Precisely how are socio-legal arrangements deconstructed and reconstructed? The answer to this question depends upon the criticalist's particular vision of equality in American society. This vision is expressed through several equality models.

B. Equality Models

Criticalists are not a monolithic group. They have different views regarding the proper way to conceptualize equality as between outsiders and insiders. Some crits see the outsider/insider relationship as essentially *symmetrical*; that is, they envision a world in which outsiders and insiders are (and should be) symmetrically situated. Other crits define this relationship as essentially *asymmetrical*; that is, they see a world in which outsiders and insiders are (and should be) asymmetrically situated. Outsiders and insiders must be treated differently if they are to be treated equally. Thus, we have "sameness-equality" and "difference-equality" crits.

There is, however, further division within these groups. The sameness-equality crits are divided into two groups, or equality models: *assimilation* and *pluralism*.[5] The difference-equality crits have four equality models: *special*

---

2. Gloria Stephenson, "Deconstruction," in *Women's Studies Encyclopedia: Views from the Sciences*, vol. 1, Helen Tierney, ed. (New York: Peter Bedrock Books, 1991), p. 89.

3. Ibid. See also *A Handbook to Literature* 6th ed., C. Hugh Holman & William Harmon, eds. (New York: McMillan, 1992), pp. 128–29 (defining deconstruction).

4. Brooks, *Critical Procedure*, supra note 1, at p. 31.

5. Ibid.

rights; accommodation; empowerment; and *acceptance.*[6] Let us examine these
equality models with an eye toward their incorporation in a regime of judicial decision making.

1. Assimilation

Assimilation is the assertion that socio-legal arrangements should be constructed without regard to race, gender, or sexual orientation. They must be
neutral as to matters of race, gender, and sexual orientation. Although it
might appear that assimilation has nothing special to offer, that it is merely
routine civil rights, color-blind analysis, upon closer inspection one comes to
a different conclusion. To understand why assimilation belongs in critical theory, one need only compare it to the type of casual facially neutral decision
making found in civil rights law.

A good illustration of the latter is the case of *Bob Jones University v. United
States.*[7] The question before the Supreme Court was whether a religious university that engaged in racial discrimination could be denied federal tax-exempt status. Interracial dating and other forms of racial interaction were forbidden under the school's religious dogma. In an opinion written by Chief
Justice Warren Burger, the Supreme Court held that the government could
deny tax-exempt status to private schools that engaged in racial discrimination. Going from Point A to Point C, the Court vindicated the anti-discrimination policy over the freedom of religion value articulated in the Free Exercise Clause of the First Amendment. As Chief Justice Burger explained, "the
Government has a fundamental, overriding interest in eradicating discrimination in education [which] substantially outweighs whatever burden denial
of tax benefits places on petitioners' exercise of their religious beliefs."[8]

Although the Court reached the same result an assimilationist would reach
had she heard the case, the structure of the Court's reasoning is not assimilationist. It lacks *contextualization.* It does not explicitly rest the decision on a
relevant African American value. Proceeding under the assimilation model, a
judge begins by deconstructing the controlling law, the federal law denying
tax-exempt status to private schools engaged in racial discrimination. The
question is as follows: Viewed from the perspective of the relevant outsider
community—the African American community—is this law neutral on its
face as to matters of race? In other words, does the law validate the racial-neu-

---

6. Ibid.
7. *Bob Jones University v. United States,* 461 U.S. 574 (1983).
8. Ibid. at 604.

trality value that inheres in the African American community? One must answer this question in the affirmative. African Americans would certainly see the tax-exemption law as enforcing racial neutrality; a well-established value in the their community.[9] That value, an assimilationist would argue, trumps the freedom of religion value (also an African American value) because it has greater potential to counteract anti-objectivism and, as such, it has greater potential for social transformation. Notice that because the judge does *not* find subordination in the tax-exemption rule, she does not reach the reconstruction question. Her analysis naturally ends just short of that question.

Thus, unlike traditional judicial analysis (including traditional civil rights reasoning), assimilation, like all equality models, begins with an articulation of the outsider values at stake. A major objective of critical theory is to obtain judicial *validation* of outsider values. The judge's line of reasoning does not become enmeshed in abstract discussions of values. Instead, values are contextualized within the relevant outsider community. A community norm may be unique to this community or it may be held in common with other outsider communities or the larger American community. What matters to crits is that the judge locate this norm within the relevant outsider community. In this way the judiciary formally embraces a people whom the government has historically stigmatized and subordinated. (The reader unaware of outsider values may wish to consult the sources cited at the beginning of the next chapter.)

What sets assimilation apart from the other equality models is its special focus. All equality models have a limited focus based on their visions of equality. Assimilation's focus is limited to facially neutral values that inhere in outsider communities. The absence of such values in a socio-legal arrangement constitutes subordination. The attempt to redress such subordination with facially neutral laws constitutes reconstruction. Assimilationists believe outsiders are better served in the long run by facially neutral values and laws than by outsider-specific values and laws, which can stigmatize and, hence, undermine the claim of equality. This stance, intended to promote outsider values (albeit facially neutral) and outsider equality, is one reason assimilation is a bona fide plank in the critical theory platform.

Critical theory's rejection of "binary" analysis is yet another reason assimilation belongs in critical theory. Richard Delgado and others have argued that traditional civil rights analysis is binary: black v. white; women v. men; homosexual v. heterosexual; Latino v. white; Asian v. white. Binary thinking, Delgado argues, undercuts progress for all outsider groups, and it does so in

---

9. See generally Richard Kluger, *Simple Justice* (New York: Alfred A. Knopf, 1976).

several ways.[10] It often permits some outsiders to advance at the expense of others, pits outsiders against each other, encourages some outsiders to identify with insiders at the expense of other outsiders, clouds moral judgment, causes outsiders to unduly focus on their uniqueness, impairs the ability to generalize and learn from history, and prevents effective coalition-building among outsiders.[11] Delgado points to a number of historical events to support his position. He observes, for example, that rather than paying their former slaves for labor after the Civil War, southern plantation owners turned to Chinese laborers, and, as a result, in 1868 Congress ratified the Burlingame Treaty with China, which substantially increased the importation of Chinese laborers.[12] In similar fashion, Congress passed the Reconstruction Amendments to the Constitution (Thirteenth, Fourteenth, and Fifteenth Amendments), enlarging African American rights, while it simultaneously enacted laws (the Indian Appropriations Act and Dawes Act) restricting Native American rights.[13]

The rejection of binary bias argues strongly in favor of retaining assimilation in critical theory. Assimilation may not be very useful to outsider groups granted equal treatment under the law, such as African Americans and women,[14] but it is very useful to homosexuals who have yet to acquire such basic rights across the board. Federal civil rights laws do not, for the most part, reach gays and lesbians. Thus, it is legal under federal law to discriminate against homosexuals in employment, housing, and other major sectors of life. Legislation offering some protection for homosexuals has been pending in Congress for years.[15] On the other hand, Congress in short order passed the Defense of Marriage Act in response to the legalization of same-sex marriages in Hawaii in 1996.[16] This Act permits other states to deny full faith and credit to homosexual marriages, an unprecedented denial of comity. Although

10. See Richard Delgado, "Derrick Bell's Toolkit—Fit to Dismantle That Famous House?," *New York University Law Review* 75 (2000): 283.

11. See ibid. at pp. 291–306.

12. See ibid. at p. 294.

13. See ibid. at pp. 291–92.

14. See Chapter 8, Section A, supra.

15. See Employment Non-Discrimination Act of 1997, S.869 (protection from employment discrimination); Civil Rights Amendment Act of 1998, H.R.365 (protection from discrimination in several areas).

16. See *Baehr v. Miiko*, 1996 WL 694235 (Hawaii Cir. Ct.) (Hawaiian statute barring same-sex marriage violates equal protection clause of state constitution). The Defense of Marriage Act is codified as 1 U.S.C. §7(defining marriage as the union of one man and one woman), and Pub.L. 104-199, §2(a) 110 Stat. 2419, 28 U.S.C.A. §1738C (revoking full faith and credit for same-sex marriage states).

a ballot initiative stripping Hawaii's courts of jurisdiction over nuptials involving gays or lesbians passed in the November 1998 elections, the Defense of Marriage Act can still do damage. On July 1, 2000, the governor of Vermont signed into law a measure allowing homosexuals to form "civil unions" that would carry many of the benefits of marriage.[17]

The death of Matthew Shepard, the 21-year-old gay University of Wyoming college student who was tied to a fence, beaten, and left in a coma in the chill of an October night in 1998, is a vivid reminder of how homosexuals are regarded in American culture and society. As a New York Times editorial stated:

> There have been many other murders through the years. People were repelled in 1992 when a Navy enlisted man, Allen Schindler, was stomped to death in a men's room by two crewmates. Other young men have died horribly all around the country—slashed and dumped into the water off Staten Island, dropped through a manhole to drown in a Boston sewer, chased and stabbed to death in San Francisco, strangled and burned in Florida. The Southern Poverty Law Center, after studying F.B.I. statistics, has calculated that gay men and lesbians are six times as likely to be physically attacked as Jews or Hispanics in America, and twice as likely as African-Americans.[18]

The menace and hatred gays and lesbians still face in our communities is most strikingly revealed in a 1998 Time Magazine poll that concluded: "More than two-thirds of Americans believe an incident such as the beating death of a gay University of Wyoming student could happen in their own community."[19]

The Supreme Court did accord some protection to gays and lesbians in a 1996 case, *Evans v. Romer*.[20] In that case, the Court overturned a Colorado

---

17. See, e.g., Carey Goldberg, "First Gay Couples Join in Civil Unions: Cheers, Boos at Vermont Ceremonies," San Diego Union-Tribune, 7/2/00, at p. 1. Ross Sneyd, "Vermont House Passes Gay-Rights Legislation Allowing 'Civil Union,'" The News & Observer (Raleigh, N.C.), 3/17/00, at p. A10. On Hawaii's ballot initiative, see, e.g., Los Angeles Times, 11/4/98, at pp. A16, A31. See also David Orgon Coolidge, "Voters Finally Get A Say on Same-Sex Marriage," Wall Street Journal, 11/2/98, at p. A34; Van Deerlin, "Drawing the Battle Lines Anew on Same-Sex Marriage," San Diego Union-Tribune, 10/28/98, p. B-9.

18. "The Lesson of Matthew Shepard," The New York Times, 10/17/98 (internet). See generally Beth Loffreda, *Losing Matt Shepard: Life and Politics in the Aftermath of Anti-Gay Murder* (New York: Columbia University Press, 2000).

19. Steve Lopez, "To Be Young and Gay in Wyoming," 10/26/98, at 38.

20. 517 U.S. 620 (1996).

constitutional amendment that prohibited local governments within the state from passing laws outlawing discrimination against homosexuals. The Court, however, stopped short of giving gays and lesbians the same constitutional protection accorded to racial minorities and women. A few states and cities have extended equal legal treatment to homosexuals, but that is far weaker than federal protection. It is no wonder that, in 1998, 15 years after the Supreme Court's decision in *Bob Jones University*, this same university felt legally protected in threatening to arrest a gay alumnus if he set foot on campus. His transgression, quite simply, was the fact that he was gay. Obviously, there is much that assimilation can do for homosexuals.[21]

Why have homosexuals not been accorded constitutional protection similar to people of color and women? Kenji Yoshino observes that the talismanic classifications of race and sex give people of color and women a visibility factor and thus a peg on which formal equal opportunity can hang its hat. The absence of a visibility factor seems to be what disqualifies gays and lesbians from constitutional protection. Unlike other outsider groups, their differences are invisible and arguably mutable.[22] Does this explain the whole of "assimilationist bias" against homosexuals in the law? Do other factors, such as religion or antipathy, also play a role?

Although assimilationists are attentive to the social consequences of judicial decision making, they are not as result-oriented as other criticalists. Assimilationists seek equal treatment under the law, and let the chips fall where they may. In the long run, assimilationists argue, outsiders are best served by laws and judicial decision making that do not enshrine outsider or insider categories. Over time, this is the most effective way to counteract anti-objectivism, they believe.

Given this perspective, assimilationists must implicitly support judicial decisions that benefit insiders.[23] An example is the Supreme Court's decision in the same-sex sexual harassment case, *Oncale v. Sundowner Offshore Services, Inc.*[24] In that case, a straight white male employee brought a Title VII[25] action against a former employer alleging sexual harassment by fellow straight white

---

21. The Chronicle of Higher Education, 10/26/98 (internet news bulletin).

22. See Kenji Yoshino, "Assimilationist Bias in Equal Protection: The Visibility Presumption of 'Don't Ask, Don't Tell,'" *Yale Law Journal* 108 (1998): 485.

23. During the 1970s, the heyday of assimilationist crits, the ACLU Women's Rights Project successfully litigated a number of cases on behalf of men. See Chapter 11, Section B1, infra.

24. 523 U.S. 75 (1998).

25. 42 U.S.C. §§ 2000–2000e-17 (1994 & Supp. II 1997). Title VII is the nation's major employment discrimination statute.

male employees. Title VII prohibits work-related discrimination "because of... sex."[26] Both lower courts held that "Mr. Oncale, a male, has no cause of action under Title VII for harassment by male co-workers."[27] Reversing the court of appeals, the Supreme Court held that same-sex harassment is actionable under Title VII. The Court reasoned that "Title VII's prohibition of discrimination 'because of...sex' protects men as well as women," and that "nothing in Title VII necessarily bars a claim of discrimination 'because of...sex' merely because the plaintiff and the defendant (or the person charged with acting on behalf of the defendant) are of the same sex."[28] Although this is not assimilationist reasoning—there is no discussion of the subordination question and, hence, no attempt to contextualize the gender-neutrality value in the relevant outsider communities, women and homosexuals—an assimilationist would applaud the Court's gender-neutral judgment. More importantly, an assimilationist would not be upset by the fact that the Court's reasoning and judgment empowers insiders.[29]

Such generosity of thinking has made assimilationists the target of severe criticism from other criticalists. If one assumes a zero-sum game, these criticalists argue, empowering insiders necessarily disempowers outsiders. Assimilationists, of course, believe that outsider-specific laws may be more detrimental than beneficial to outsiders in the long run.

Many criticalists also argue that assimilation generates very little social transformation for most outsiders. There is virtually no promise of institutional restructuring to level the playing field, they argue. The passivity or reformist quality of assimilation has driven most criticalists to create stronger expressions of critical theory.

2. Pluralism

Like assimilation, pluralism is premised on the belief that outsiders and insiders should be symmetrically situated in American society. Both equality models also envision law playing an essential role in moving society towards this end. But while assimilationists believe the state should be neutral as to matters of race, sex, and sexual orientation, pluralists permit a certain amount of outsider accommodation as a necessary condition for social equality. Specifically, the pluralist picks some golden mean that can neutralize dif-

---

26. 28 U.S.C. § 2000e-2(a)(1).
27. 523 U.S. at 77.
28. Ibid. at 78–79.
29. See Brooks, *Critical Procedure*, supra note 1, at p. 14.

ferences arising from the uneven distribution of societal advantages and disadvantages between blacks and whites, women and men, homosexuals and
heterosexuals.[30] Consequently, the pluralist, unlike the more passive assimilationist, recognizes socioeconomic and cultural differences between outsiders and insiders and, most importantly, attempts to shape the law in such
a way as to neutralize such differences. The assimilationist ignores differences;
the pluralist neutralizes differences; the asymmetricalist, as we shall see,[31] ac-
cepts differences.

Pluralism favors outsiders no more or no less than it favors insiders. It is
"even-Steven." No group's life experiences, or values, are ignored or dis-
counted. The pluralist attempts to mediate identifiable differences—racial,
gender, sexual orientation, as the case may be—in arriving at a Solomon-like
result in the case.

Pluralism's attention to accommodation and accord gives it the appearance,
at first glance, of an alternative dispute resolution (ADR) device. Arbitration,
mediation, and other ADRs, purport to save time and money and reduce the
contentiousness and risks associated with full-blown litigation. To achieve
these benefits, arbitrators and mediators use flexible procedures (e.g., the rules
of procedure and evidence are relaxed) and sometimes resolve disputes by
merely splitting the difference between plaintiff and defendant.[32]

Pluralism, however, is not an ADR. In fact, critical theory rejects ADRs on
the ground that they subordinate outsiders.[33] Crits have argued, for example,
that mediation poses particular dangers for women because it stifles their authentic voice:

> ... [I]n our society many women are conditioned into an ethic of car-
> ing [and] connection. In addition, they are taught that their princi-
> pal role is that of homemaker and mother. In a face-to-face media-
> tion, they can easily accept too much responsibility for what went
> wrong. Feeling guilty that the other side is unhappy, they may give in
> when, had they been represented by a lawyer and gone to court, they
> might have won.

* * *

---

30. Ibid. at p. 15.

31. See Section B3,infra.

32. See, e.g., "Developments in the Law—The Paths of Civil Litigation," *Harvard Law
Review* 113 (2000): 1851–77. See generally, Laura J. Cooper, Dennis R. Nolan and Richard
A. Bales, *ADR in the Workplace: A Coursebook* (St. Paul: West Group, 2000).

33. See, e.g., Richard Delgado et al., "Fairness and Formality: Minimizing the Risk of Prejudice in Alternative Dispute Resolution," *Wisconsin Law Review* 1985 (1985): 1359, 1363–66.

...In-court adjudication of the formal variety is less apt to be infected with prejudice than the informal variety. In court, you have all those reminders—flags, the pomp, the judge sitting on high—that this is an occasion when the formal American values of equality, fairness, and so on, are to rule. In nonformal settings, fewer such reminders confront the participants. If one is a woman, a gay man, a black, or any other outsider, one should opt for as much formality as one can afford.[34]

Hence, it is the very informality of ADRs, usually touted as its virtue, that subordinates women.

There is nothing informal about pluralism. Pluralist rules of law are designed for the judicial process and not for ADR settings. Also, mediating differences between outsiders and insiders is much more difficult than splitting differences. Pluralist rules, as we shall see, are hard to fashion. Most importantly, pluralism and ADRs operate from different normative stances. Pluralism assumes anti-objectivism, ADRs do not. The latter proceeds from the same traditional legal perspective as regular litigation.

Pluralist rules are difficult to construct because they must neutralize differences between outsiders and insiders. One example of a pluralist rule is the Family and Medical Leave Act of 1992. This law gives public and private employees up to 12 weeks of unpaid leave per year for certain family and medical reasons (e.g., pregnancy and other "serious health conditions"), provided eligibility requirements are met.[35] The FMLA, as it is called, mediates differences between women and men in the workplace by giving expression to the sex-norming value of care and connection that inheres in women's culture. This value, which is discussed in greater detail in Chapter 11, validates women—their approach to life, their experiences—even as it helps insiders.

Pluralism, like assimilation, has been criticized by most crits on the ground that it offers a weak response to anti-objectivism and, consequently, engenders very little social transformation. To even the playing field in a socio-legal order so heavily slanted in favor of straight white males—to achieve measurable equality—requires less even-handed treatment of outsiders and insiders;

---

34. Richard Delgado, "Alternative Dispute Resolution, Conflict as Pathology: An Essay for Trina Grillo," *Minnesota Law Review* 91 (1997): 1391, 1396, 1398. See Trina Grillo, "The Mediation Alternative: Process Dangers for Women," *Yale Law Journal* 100 (1991): 1545. On the value of care or connection, see Chapter 11, Section C 1, infra.

35. See 29 U.S.C. § 2611 et seq.; 29 C.F.R. § 825 et seq.; *Kilcrease v. Coffee County, Ala.,* 951 F. Supp. 212 (M.D. Ala. 1996).

i.e., more preferential treatment of outsiders. Accordingly, most crits favor a stronger criticalist approach to law, to which we turn next.

3. SpecialRights/Accommodation/Empowerment/Acceptance

The asymmetrical equality models differ from the symmetrical models in their respective visions of equality; i.e., the ways in which they deconstruct and reconstruct law. Each of the former operates identically in their deconstructive modes but differently in their reconstructive modes. In their deconstructive modes, the asymmetrical equality models ask basically the same question: does the socio-legal arrangement under consideration adversely impact outsiders or an outsider group in such a way as to suggest "insiderism"? Does it, in other words, signal to the group Level 3 Bias (i.e., unconscious bias) as discussed in the last chapter?[36] Subordination, or anti-objectivism, is established, then, if a law or institutional practice negatively impacts outsiders and, at the same time, stereotypes, enhances or maintains insider privilege, enforces a racial hierarchy, and so on.

One can also establish insiderism by applying the "cultural meaning test." Developed by Charles Lawrence in the context of race, the cultural meaning test, in its widest application, allows an outsider to raise a rebuttable presumption of unlawful discrimination if she can show that her outsider group attaches cultural significance to an action or practice that adversely affects her or her outsider group. What does it mean in the African American culture, Lawrence asks, "to construct a barrier between all-white and all-black sections of Memphis?"[37] Likewise, what does it mean to women if a rule of law, neutral on its face, is applied in such a way as to require a woman to travel to New York to seek custody of her children and to obtain child support payments from her former husband rather than have him travel to California where she and the children reside?[38] And what does it mean to homosexuals when a college is able to publicly announce that it will arrest a gay alumnus if he steps foot on campus, simply because he is gay?[39]

The meanings outsiders would attach to these socio-legal arrangements are very different from what they would assign to, say, an employer's requirement

---

36. See Chapter 8, Section B, supra.

37. Charles Lawrence, "The Id, the Ego, and Equal Protections: Reckoning with Unconscious Racism," *Stanford Law Review* 39 (1987): 317, 355–81.

38. See the *Kulko* case discussed in Chapter 11, infra.

39. See the *Bob Jones University* case discussed in Section B1, supra.

that its truck drivers carry a valid driver's license. Even though such a requirement may disadvantage African American, female or homosexual employees who do not have valid driver's licenses, it does not raise a presumption of racism, sexism or heterosexism. What makes this a nonsubordinating situation is the fact that requiring a valid driver's license does not, in outsider communities, play to an outsider stereotype or otherwise reinforce insider status.

Hence, under the asymmetrical equality models, a law or institutional practice subordinates not because it adversely impacts outsiders, but because it does that *and* signals unconscious bias. Adverse impact that does not suggest insiderism, such as the driver's license requirement, is not actionable under the special rights, accommodation, empowerment, or acceptance equality models. This makes deconstruction under the asymmetrical equality models more than just an "effects test" whereby adverse impact alone—a discriminatory bottom line—is sufficient to trigger a violation of the law.[40]

Although Level 1 Bias (overt antipathy)[41] or Level 2 Bias (backstage antipathy)[42] can trigger insiderism, our focus here shall be on Level 3 Bias. In this way we avoid the near-impossible task of proving the defendant acted with a discriminatory purpose, which the plaintiff is required to do under some civil rights laws.[43]

Asymmetrical equality models differ primarily at the reconstruction end. They differ about difference. Each equality model has its own view as to the nature of the subordination at issue (including whether such debate is even worthwhile), and, hence, the reasons for going forward with reconstruction. The models take their names from these differences.

Special rights crits believe anti-objectivism should be redressed because it is ultimately predicated on the immutable group characteristics of outsiders—skin color, gender or sexual orientation. Outsider subordination may appear to reflect cultural differences (e.g., cultural preferences or interests) between outsiders and insiders, but it is actually rooted in biological differences. When a company excludes pregnancy from its disability benefits plan or refuses to

---

40. See generally Roy L. Brooks, Gilbert Paul Carrasco and Michael Selmi, *Civil Rights Litigation: Cases and Perspectives* 2d ed. (Durham: Carolina Academic Press) pp. 230–39, 482–556.

41. See Chapter 8, Section B1, supra.

42. See ibid.

43. See *Washington v. Davis*, 426 U.S. 229 (1976). See generally, Roy L. Brooks, *Rethinking the American Race Problem* (Berkeley: University of California Press, 1990), pp. 11, 94–97, 104, 161–62 (education law); 53 (employment law); and 11, 83–87, 90, 103, 158 (housing law).

grant pregnancy leave and reinstatement after childbirth, the argument continues, that is biologically based discrimination; it is not culturally based.[44]
Likewise, African American underrepresentation in corporate America[45] may
appear to result from cultural differences between blacks and whites—e.g., the
alleged lack of African American interest in such jobs—but in fact is rooted
in immutable differences between them. Skin color explains the dearth of
African American executives. Subordination based on immutable group characteristics is unfair and unreasonable, to say the least, and should be eradicated through reconstruction.

An accommodationist, like a special rights crit, is interested in the cause
of subordination. Is the disadvantage facing outsiders ultimately the result of
immutable group characteristics, as the special rights crit maintains, or is it
the result of something else? Could it be socioeconomic? Could it be culture?
Thus, an accommodationist, unlike a special rights crit, acknowledges the
possibility that some forms of subordination may be due not to immutable
group characteristics but to class, cultural, or hard-to-classify differences.[46]
For example, the low percentage of African Americans in high-level corporate positions may be due to a supply problem rather than to immutable
group barriers operating against African Americans within corporate America. It is therefore more accurate to justify and characterize reconstruction as
a vehicle for eradicating class subordination rather than racial subordination.[47]

Empowerment, the third asymmetrical equality model, asserts that white
heterosexual maleness is the root of outsider subordination, and that the need
to end such hegemony is reason enough for reconstruction. This view of subordination is closely associated with Catharine MacKinnon. She, like Simone
de Beauvoir, asserts that "one is not born, one rather becomes a woman."[48]
Women are socialized into submissive, sexual beings by a male-dominated society, MacKinnon argues. What we ordinarily take to be women's sexuality is,

---

44. See, e.g., Brooks, *Critical Procedure*, supra note 1, at pp. 16–17 (sources cited
therein).

45. See Andrew Hacker, *Two Nations: Black and White, Separate, Hostile, Unequal* (New
York: Ballantine Books, 1995), pp. 107–33.

46. See Brooks, *Critical Procedure*, supra note 1, at pp. 17–18, 35.

47. At a more refined level, accommodation posits that subordination based on immutable group characteristics should be redressed by preferential treatment (more about
which in due course) while all other forms of outsider subordination should be remedied
by pluralist reconstructive measures. See Brooks, *Critical Procedure*, supra note 1, at pp.
35, 57.

48. Simone de Beauvoir, *The Second Sex* (New York: Knopf, 1974), p. 249.

in fact, a product of male domination. It is not an authentic manifestation of women's sexuality.[49]

Implicit in this critique is the idea that differences as to race, gender, and sexual orientation that give rise to subordination are socially constructed. This feature of empowerment is supported by the scholarship of Ian Haney López, who argues that "despite the prevalent belief in biological races, overwhelming evidence proves that race is not biological."[50] Indeed, law is one of the social forces that gives meaning to racial categories. For example, the "one-drop" rule mandated that any person with at least one drop of "negro" blood was deemed to be black.[51] Similarly, Frank Valdez argues that heterosexism is inextricably intertwined with sexual or gender subordination, in other words, male domination. Heterosexism is really about preserving traditional categories of "maleness" and "femininity" under which women are dependent on men, particularly in marriage and family. The lesbian couple and "effeminate" male pose a threat to the established order, Valdez and others argue.[52]

Acceptance, the last asymmetrical equality model, breaks ranks with special rights, accommodation, and empowerment. The acceptance equality model posits that the debate about difference gets one nowhere, that the only thing that really matters is the subordination itself. Whether it is biological in nature, cultural or class-based, or the expression of white heterosexual male hegemony, in the end subordination is subordination. No one can deny that subordination presents a negative set of circumstances for outsiders; so let's just deal with that. In this sense, acceptance attempts to provide a pragmatic reason for reconstruction.[53]

---

49. See Catharine A. MacKinnon, "Feminism, Marxism, Method, and the State: An Agenda for Theory," *Signs: Journal of Women in Culture & Society* 7 (1982): 515, 530–31.

50. Ian F. Haney López, "The Social Construction of Race: Some Observations on Illusion, Fabrication, and Choice," *Harvard Civil Rights-Civil Liberties Law Review* 29 (1994) 1.

51. Ibid. at p.6. See generally Ian F. Haney López, *White by Law: The Legal Construction of Race* (New York: New York University Press, 1996).

52. See Chapter 8, Section B3a, supra. See also Francisco Valdez, "Queers, Sissies, Dykes, and Tomboys: Deconstructing the Conflation of 'Sex,' 'Gender,' and 'Sexual Orientation' in Euro-American Law and Society," *California Law Review* 83 (1995): 1; Sylvia A. Law, "Homosexuality and the Social Meaning of Gender," *Wisconsin Law Review* 1998 (1988): 187; Mary Ann Case, "Disaggregating Gender from Sex and Sexual Orientation: The Effeminate Man in the Law and Feminist Jurisprudence," *Yale Law Journal* 105 (1995): 1. In social construction discourse, "sex" is a biological concept and "gender" is a socially constructed term. See Valdez, "Queers, Sissies, Dykes, and Tomboys," p. 21.

53. See Christine Littleton, "Reconstructing Sexual Equality," *California Law Review* 75 (1987): 1279, 1296–97.

Given these different characterizations of the reconstructive mission, what type of reconstructive measures do asymmetricalist crits favor? Special rights, accommodation, and empowerment crits each believe the grant of outsider preferences (affirmative action) is the most effective way to achieve successful reconstruction.[54] For this reason, they can be called the "preference equality models." Acceptance, on the other hand, asserts that the best way to redress subordination consistent with its particular take on the problem is to create culturally coded outsider and insider complements; in other words, distinctly outsider choices equally accessible to *both* outsiders and insiders.[55] Thus, under the acceptance model, once one uncovers subordination, she then proceeds to formulate remedial policies reflective of outsider values. Although specifically designed to help outsiders (culturally coded for outsiders), the new law can be used for the benefit of insiders as well. " 'Acceptance' means 'includes [straight] white men.' "[56] Civil rights laws, designed for outsiders but opened to all, are prime examples of acceptance rules.

Although acceptance and pluralism operate differently in their respective deconstructive modes, they are functionally indistinguishable in their reconstructive styles. True, pluralist rules seek the golden mean while acceptance rules consciously attempt to favor outsiders. But both sets of reconstructive rules are accessible to insiders. As a practical matter, both have the effect of neutralizing differences between outsiders and insiders. Thus, acceptance and pluralism can be viewed as reconstructive twins.

C. Criticalist Epistemologies

In addition to deconstruction, reconstruction, and the equality models, another operational element in critical theory that may be useful for judicial theory is the criticalist way of knowing. There are in fact four theories of knowing, or epistemologies, criticalists employ in their reasoning: (1) "rational/ empirical"; (2) "standpoint" (or what might be called "experiential/essential-

---

54. See Charles Lawrence, Symposium: Race and Remedy in a Multicultural Society: Forward: "Race, Multiculturalism, and the Jurisprudence of Transformation," *Stanford Law Review* 47 (1995): 819, 824 (arguing for a view of equality in which equality is defined as a "substantive societal condition"). See generally Charles Lawrence and Mari Matsuda, *We Won't Go Back: Making the Case for Affirmative Action* (New York: Houghton Mifflin Co., 1997).

55. Brooks, *Critical Procedure*, supra note 1, at p. 21.

56. Ibid.

ism"); (3) postmodern (or what might be called "experiential/anti-essential-ism"); and (4) "positionality."[57] Like the equality models, the epistemologies demonstrate the diversity of critical thought. Indeed, as we consider these epistemologies seriatim, notice how they interact, playing off each other's perceived deficiencies.

1. Rational/Empirical

Critical theory is often criticized on the ground that its underlying mode of thinking is irrational. The rational/empirical position shows this to be a canard. Rational/empiricists support their positions with inductive and deductive arguments and empirical evidence. Such reasoning is amply represented in criticalist discourse.

Criticalists frequently use analyses that appeal to abstract reasoning, and often push empirical points. They parse through the language of cases, statutes, and legal doctrine, drawing factual distinctions along the way.[58] Criticalists resort to rational argument and empirical validation when challenging assumptions about outsiders that underpin extant rules of law or public policies. For example, in challenging an employer's policy of denying disability benefits to pregnant women, criticalists have sought to demonstrate that the employer's policy was irrational given the similarities between pregnancy and the covered disabilities.[59] The rational/empirical mode of thinking can also be found in criticalist self-examination. As Katherine Bartlett observes:

> Faced with state laws designed to address the disadvantages experienced by pregnant women in the workplace, some feminists argued that such 'special treatment' for pregnant women reinforces stereotypes about women and should be rejected under the equality principle. Other feminists argued that pregnancy affects only women and that lack of accommodation for it will prevent women from achieving equality in the workplace. Each side of the debate defended a dif-

---

57. Katherine T. Bartlett, "Feminist Legal Methods," *Harvard Law Review* 103 (1990): 829, 868, 872, 877, 880.

58. See, e.g., Derrick Bell, *Race, Racism, and American Law* 1st ed., 2d ed., 3d ed. (Boston: Little, Brown and Company, 1973, 1980, 1992) (criticizing and distinguishing dozens of cases as irrational or empirically unsound). The 4th edition was published by Aspen Law and Business in 2000. See also Richard Delgado, "The Imperial Scholar: Reflections on a Review of Civil Rights Literature," *University of Pennsylvania Law Review* 132 (1984): 561, 566–67 (drawing logical analogies between legal doctrines).

59. Bartlett, "Feminist Legal Methods," supra note 57, at p. 869.

ferent concept of equality, but the underlying argument focused upon which is the most rational, empirically sound and legally supportable interpretation of equality.[60]

There is little doubt, then, that at least some of the time criticalists are rational/empiricists.

Criticalists do not, however, abandon their belief in anti-objectivism when they are in the rational/empirical mode. This, indeed, distinguishes criticalist from non-crits who engage in traditional legal analysis, which is routinely rational/ empirical. For critical theorists, rational/empirical epistemology "assumes that law is not objective, but that identifying and correcting its mistaken assumptions can make it more objective."[61]

Yet, it is true that most crits do not believe the rational/empirical epistemology can, by itself, lead to effective redress of outsider subordination. They argue that the rational/empirical approach to truth and knowledge cannot reach, for example, "the deeper gendered nature of law."[62] Hence, criticalists will not limit themselves to the rational/empirical mode of legal analysis because they believe it can only lead to "reformism"; it has little transformative value.

2. Standpoint

While the rational/empirical epistemology challenges only the factual accuracy of legal propositions, the remaining epistemologies challenge the functional value of such propositions. Standpoint epistemology, in particular, looks at life from the victim's or outsider's perspective. It relocates the source of knowledge from the perpetrator to the victim, from the oppressor to the oppressed. Thus, standpoint epistemology identifies the outsider's status "as that of victim, and then privileges that status by claiming that it gives access to understanding about oppression that others cannot have."[63]

It is this view of identity, most particularly racial identity, that informs Derrick Bell's indictment of then-Supreme Court nominee Clarence Thomas (who

---

60. Ibid. (citations omitted).
61. Ibid. at p. 869.
62. Ibid. at pp. 870–71.
63. Ibid. at p. 872. It is argued that women's subordinate status in our society leaves them "with a motivation for finding out what is wrong, for criticizing accepted interpretations of reality and for developing new and less distorted ways of understanding the world." Ibid. (quoting Andrea Jaggar, *Feminist Politics and Human Nature* (Totowa, N.J.: Roman and Allanheld, 1983), p. 370).

opposed affirmative action and held other conservative beliefs) on the ground that "he doesn't think like a black."[64] Bell also contended that "[r]ace can [be an important factor] in filing a teaching position intended to interpret...the impact of racial discrimination on the law and lawyering."[65] An authentic black representative, Lani Guinier says, is one who is "politically, psychologically, and culturally black."[66] Standpoint epistemology also sustains Richard Delgado's argument that "it is possible to compile an *a priori* list of reasons why we might look with concern on a situation in which the scholarship about group A [outsiders] is written by members of group B [insiders]."[67] And when Mari Matsuda maintains that "those who have experienced discrimination speak with a special voice to which we should listen,"[68] that "the victims of racial oppression have distinct normative insights,"[69] and that "[t]hose who are oppressed in the present world can speak most eloquently of a better one,"[70] she is proceeding from the standpoint theory of knowledge.

Standpoint epistemology contains several elements of essentialism that require elaboration. One of the most important is the assertion of "authenticity," the notion that people of color, women, and homosexuals have a distinct nature, that each has an authentic self. Women, for example, have a true na-

---

64. Wall Street Journal, 9/5/91, at p. A15, col 3.

65. Derrick Bell, "A Question of Credentials," *Harvard Law Record*, 9/17/82, at p. 14.

66. Lani Guinier, "The Triumph of Tokenism: The Voting Rights Act and the Theory of Black Electoral Success," *Michigan Law Review* 89 (1991): 1077, 1103.

67. Delgado, "Imperial Scholar," supra note 58, at p. 567. The reasons are:
First, members of group B may be ineffective advocates of the rights and interests of persons in group A. They may lack information; more important, perhaps, they may lack passion, or that passion may be misdirected. B's scholarship may tend to be sentimental, diffusing passion in useless directions, or wasting time on unproductive breast-beating. Second, while the B's might advocate effectively, they might advocate the wrong things. Their agenda may differ from that of the A's, they may pull their punches with respect to remedies, especially where remedying A's situation entails uncomfortable consequences for B. Despite the best of intentions, B's may have stereotypes embedded deep in their psyches that distort their thinking, causing them to balance interests in ways inimical to A's. Finally, domination by members of group B may paralyze members of group A, causing the A's to forge how to flex their legal muscles for themselves.
Ibid. (Citations omitted).

68. Mari Matsuda, "Looking to the Bottom: Critical Legal Studies and Reparations," *Harvard Civil Rights-Civil Liberties Law Review* 22 (1987): 323, 324.

69. Ibid. at p. 326.

70. Ibid. at p. 346. See also, Derrick Bell, *Faces From the Bottom of the Well: The Permanence of Racism* (New York: Basic Books, 1992).

ture that transcends differences in race, color, class, and sexual orientation.[71] For instance, Robin West argues that what she calls the "separation thesis"—which claims that human beings are individuals first "and *then* we form relationships and engage in co-operative arrangements with others"[72]—describes men's nature but not women's nature. "Indeed," she asserts, "perhaps the central insight of feminist theory of the last decade has been that women are 'essentially connected,' not 'essentially separate,' from the rest of human life, both materially, through pregnancy, intercourse, and breast-feeding, and existentially through moral and practical life."[73]

The assertion of racial authenticity is best understood against the historical backdrop of slavery, although it is certainly not limited to the African American experience. Most plantations had two classes of slaves: "field Negroes" and "house Negroes." The latter were deemed by whites to be a cut above the former in terms of intelligence, trustworthiness, and physical appearance. Authenticity asserts that one (most African Americans would say the "field Negro") but not the other is representative of the true African American slave experience or slave identity.[74]

Perhaps less a clash between the ideal and the real than a struggle between two realities, the authentic self is constantly in conflict with the anti-self. The former creates the latter; they are antithetical selves. Author Susan Cheever describes a version of this conflict—the anti-woman conflict—in an essay on the British supermodel Twiggy, who became famous so fast that when she was first asked for an interview upon her arrival at Kennedy Airport in March 1967, she did not even know what an interview was:

> Twiggy was the anti-woman: she had no breasts, she wore white lipstick, her nails were bitten, her shoulders were bony and her hair was cut like a boy's. She was the negative image of everything a

---

71. Such essentialism is espoused by Professor MacKinnon, see, e.g., Catharine MacKinnon, *Feminism Unmodified* (Cambridge, Mass.: Harvard University Press, 1987), pp. 88, 91, 160, 195, and Professor Robin West, see, e.g., Robin West, "Jurisprudence and Gender," *University of Chicago Law Review* 55 (1988): 1, 4.

72. West, "Jurisprudence and Gender," supra note 71, at p. 2. Professor West asserts that this commitment to "the priority of plurality over unity…underlies virtually all of our legal theory." Ibid. (citations omitted).

73. Ibid. at p. 3.

74. See generally Michael E. Dyson, *Race Rules: Navigating the Color Line* (Reading, Mass.: Addison-Wesley Publishing Company, 1996). Professor Michael E. Dyson argues that the extraordinary hatred for O.J. Simpson exhibited by many whites may arise from a sense that O.J., the safe, raceless "house Negro," betrayed white society's "race rules."

woman was supposed to look like. She was so skinny it was hard to tell she was a woman at all. Instead of a shirtwaist, she wore a skirt no bigger than a proper lady's pocket handkerchief. Instead of standing as if she were balancing a book on her head, she was knock-kneed and coltishly awkward. She was everything unfeminine in a way that seemed, mysteriously, totally girlish. The power of her appeal redefined femininity. Though she was only a 91-pound teen-ager, she cast a gargantuan shadow over the image of the American housewife—a lovable species that would soon become extinct.[75]

In addition to authenticity, standpoint epistemology makes an essentialist claim concerning the accessibility of knowledge. Whites cannot intellectually or emotionally access the nonwhite frame of mind, men cannot access the woman's point of view, and heterosexuals cannot get into the homosexual's mindset. Like the authenticity assertion, the accessibility assertion goes back a long way. A good example comes, again, from the African American experience. In correspondence between the African American historians Carter G. Woodson and Charles Wesley in 1927, Wesley argued that white historians could not report the history of African Americans as "successfully" as African American historians, because "the one who feels the pinch can tell the story of the joy or pain more convincingly and truthfully than another."[76] Woodson himself agreed with this view, believing that "men of other races cannot function efficiently [in black society] because they do not think black."[77] African American literary figure William Pickens wrote in 1922 that "it is not simply that the white story teller will not do full justice to the humanity of the black race; he *cannot*."[78]

Some criticalists (and noncriticalists[79]) are uncomfortable with "vulgar essentialism"—the reduction of truth and knowledge to skin color, gender, or sexual preference—embodied in standpoint epistemology. Truth and knowl-

---

75. Susan Cheever, "Twiggy: A Stick Figure," New York Times Magazine, 11/24/96, at p. 74.

76. August Meier and Elliott Rudwick, *Black History and the Historical Profession, 1915–1980* (Urbana: University of Illinois Press, 1986), p. 289.

77. Ibid.

78. *The Black Aesthetic*, Addison Gayle, Jr., ed. (Garden City, N.Y.: Doubleday, 1972), p. xvii (emphasis in original).

79. Legal scholars who do not identify with critical theorists are also uncomfortable with racial and gender essentialism. The most famous criticism from this camp is Randall Kennedy, "Racial Critiques of Legal Academia," *Harvard Law Review* 102 (1989): 1745. For a response to Kennedy, see, e.g., Richard Delgado, "Mindset and Metaphor," *Harvard Law Review* 103 (1990): 1872 (sources cited therein).

edge for them do not inhere in such socially constructed identities. Whether one is an "African American" or "white," for example, is strictly a matter of social, historical, and ideological forces."[80] Biologically, there is only one race—the human race—which shares the same set of genes. Knowledge and emotion must, therefore, be seen as commodities capable of being accessed across race, gender, and sexual orientation divisions. Thus, Pearl S. Buck, a white missionary's daughter raised in China during the first third of the twentieth century, was able to think and write across class and racial lines in such books as *The Good Earth* for which she eventually won the Nobel Prize in Literature in 1938.[81]

Essentialism, then, is problematic even for some critical theorists. Several concerns are raised. First, it overstates differences. Second, in so doing, it obscures factors other than race, sex, and sexual preference that may provide more powerful explanations of subordination.[82] Third, essentialism "project[s] the meaning speakers give to their own experiences onto the experiences of others."[83] Fourth, essentialism engenders a "rhetoric of opposition," an adversarial we/they politics between outsiders and insiders.[84] Finally, it is argued that essentialism makes a claim of epistemic advantage—that the oppressed have not only different ways of knowing, but also better ways of knowing; i.e., that "the oppressed may make better biologists, physicists, and philosophers than their oppressors."[85] Christina Hoff Sommers writes that, "if they were right, the most disadvantaged groups would produce the best scientists. In fact, the oppressed and socially marginalized often have little access to the information and education needed to excel in science, which on the whole puts them at a serious 'epistemic *dis*advantage.'"[86] But is this a fair criticism? Are the crits not making a different claim—to wit, outsiders have superior knowledge about the conditions under which *they* live and what it will take to ameliorate *these* conditions because of their proximity to the action?

---

80. Bartlett, "Feminist Legal Methods," supra note 57, at p. 878. See Section C3, infra.

81. See Peter Conn, *Pearl S. Buck: A Cultural Biography* (New York: Cambridge University Press, 1996).

82. Bartlett, "Feminist Legal Methods," supra note 57, at p. 874. See generally Angela P. Harris, "Race and Essentialism in Feminist Legal Theory," *Standford Law Review* 42 (1990): 581.

83. Bartlett, "Feminist Legal Methods," supra note 57, at p. 876.

84. Ibid. For a racial criticism of gender essentialism see, e.g., Harris, "Race and Essentialism," supra note 82.

85. Christina Hoff Sommers, *Who Stole Feminism: How Women Have Betrayed Women* (New York: Simon and Schuster, 1994), p. 74.

86. Ibid. at p. 75 (quoting Professor Susan Haack).

For all the criticisms of standpoint epistemology, two points seem sustainable. First, it is simply bad form for an insider to assume the *leadership* role in the public articulation of outsider positions. This type of public display not only undercuts the outsider claim for equality but, in a real sense, inhibits the growth and development of outsider leadership. When a male is presented as the leader or spokesperson for women, what does that say publicly about the ability of women to speak for themselves or to govern their own affairs? Leadership is a precondition for empowerment.

Second, there have been more than a few occasions, as Bell and Delgado point out, when insiders have not been effective advocates for outsiders. Whether for lack of empathy, awareness or exposure to the outsider culture, insider representation has often been maladroit and even incompetent. Cross-representation among outsider groups is similarly problematic. How many African Americans know the homosexual value system? How many white homosexuals know the African American value system? The reference to sources on outsider values cited at the beginning of the next chapter is not just for insiders.

3. Postmodernism

Because of the perceived shortcomings in standpoint epistemology, some criticalists organize their knowledge around postmodernism, sometimes referred to as "poststructuralism" or "anti-essentialism."[87] Rooted in a rejection of the Enlightenment's twofold claim that objective (or, more precisely, common) truth exists and can be discovered through reason, postmodernism embraces multiple "truths." These truths arise from different forms of cultural understanding. That they may conflict on occasion is not cause for alarm; it is, postmodernists claim, reason for celebration.

Postmodern epistemology, therefore, can be viewed as a sustained criticism of standpoint epistemology. It "posits that the realities experienced by the subject are not in any way transcendent or representational, but rather particular and fluctuating, constituted within a complex set of social contexts. Within

---

87. Postmodernism and poststructuralism refer to theories of interpretation in which meaning is viewed as "a cultural construction mediated by arrangements of language or symbolic form. What distinguishes post-structuralism [and postmodernism] from other interpretive schools is the premise that these arrangements are unstable and contradictory, and that readers create rather than simply discover meaning." Deborah L. Rhode, "Feminist Critical Theories," *Stanford Law Review* 42 (1990): 617, 620 n.8. See also Richard K. Sherwin, *When Law Goes Pop: The Vanishing Line Between Law and Popular Culture* (Chicago: University of Chicago Press, 2000); David Kennedy, "Critical Theory, Structuralism and Contemporary Legal Scholarship," *New England Law Review* 21 (1986): 209.

this position, being human, [African American,] female, [or homosexual] is strictly a matter of social, historical, and cultural construction."[88] And, by extension, one must conclude that law, legal analysis, and the criteria for legitimacy and validity in law are social constructs rather than representational givens.[89]

Patricia Williams is one of the most important postmodern, anti-essentialist criticalists. Her legal analysis is intensively contextualized and subjective, so much so that it can properly be described as "personal." Indeed, when she tells a story, she not only uses allegory, like Derrick Bell,[90] but, unlike Bell, she also uses dreams,[91] other personal experiences,[92] and the personal experiences of others.[93]

The postmodernist claim is not only that we are "situated," that what we know about the world is shaped by the moment—by our culture, sensibility, background, race, sex, sexual orientation, and more—but also that we cannot transcend our situation. Brian Leiter calls this the "Flesh & Blood argument": "Since, as knowers, we cannot escape our human situation—we cannot transcend, as it were, our flesh and blood (not to mention our race, our gender, our class, etc.)—we can never have objective knowledge of the world."[94]

Postmodernism has garnered both encomium and sharp criticism. Its critique of essentialism may be its most powerful feature. Anti-essentialism is particularly attractive to those outsiders "[w]hose experiences affirm that rules and principles asserted as universal truths reflect particular, contingent realities that reinforce their subordination."[95]

But what some see as intellectual and moral suppleness, others see as identity politics and moral relativism. Postmodern claims are undermined by the absence of any sense of objective validity or universal truths. Each intersectionality, or subgroup (e.g., black women, poor Asian lesbians, and, disabled white men) as well as each group (e.g., the house slave, the field

---

88. Bartlett, "Feminist Legal Methods," supra note 57, at pp. 877–78 (citations omitted).

89. Ibid. at p. 878.

90. See Derrick Bell, *And We Are Not Saved* (New York: Basic Books, 1979); Patricia Williams, *Alchemy of Race and Rights* (Cambridge, Mass.: Harvard University Press, 1991), p. viii.

91. Williams, *Alchemy of Race and Rights*, supra note 90, at p. 209.

92. See, e.g., ibid. at pp. 55–56, 80–97, 146–48, 202–13.

93. See e.g., ibid. at pp. 12–13, 56–58, 136–38, 191–94, 217–19.

94. Brian Leiter, "Rethinking Legal Realism: Toward A Naturalized Jurisprudence," *Texas Law Review* 76 (1997): 267, 315 (citing Stanley Fish, *Doing What Comes Naturally* (Durham: Duke University Press, 1989): 1, 5–6).

95. Bartlett, "Feminist Legal Methods," supra note 57, at p. 879.

slave, and even Twiggy) presents equally legitimate claims of reality and, hence, truth. Postmodern epistemology "questions the possibility of knowledge, including knowledge about categories of people such as women."[96] This places postmodern criticalists in a peculiar if not impossible situation. As Bartlett, agreeing with Deborah Rhode, observes: "[criticalists] influenced by postmodernism are 'left in the awkward position of maintaining that [outsider] oppression exists while challenging the capacity to document it.'"[97]

The denial of universal truths creates yet another serious problem. If each group's or subgroup's claim to truth, knowledge or moral rectitude is deserving of equal status or respect, how is one to arbitrate among competing claims? Does it all come down to a battle of perspectives, a question of identity politics? The major shortcoming of postmodernism is not, as some have argued, its insistence that one's citizenship cannot be recreated, a damaging message for the young.[98] Rather, it is that postmodernism may take us deep into the world of Thrasymachus wherein truth, knowledge, morality, and, ultimately, justice "mean[] what is for the interest of the stronger, ruling party."[99]

Finally, the inference postmodernists draw from our situatedness—namely, that we cannot transcend our situatedness—may be false. "Even if," as Brian Leiter observes, "we are situated—as no one denies—it may still be possible to have objective knowledge of a strongly objective world."[100] The challenge for those who take this counterposition, however, is, as Leiter recognizes, to demonstrate precisely "how we overcome the limits of our situation."[101] A white male may be able to intellectually access the experience of an African American woman; but can he emotionally access that experience, especially if the element of class is thrown in?

---

96. Ibid. at p. 877. See also Frances E. Macia-Lees, Patricia Sharpe & Colleen Ballerino Cohen, "The Postmodernist Turn in Anthropology: Cautions from a Feminist Perspective," *Signs* 15 (1989): 7, 27 ("in deconstructing categories of meaning, we deconstruct not only patriarchal definitions of 'womanhood' and 'truth' but also the very categories of our own analysis—'women' and 'feminism' and 'oppression'").

97. Ibid. (citing Rhode, "Feminist Critical Theories," p. 620). See generally Daniel A. Farber and Suzanna Sherry, *Beyond All Reason: The Radical Assault on Truth in American Law* (New York: Oxford University Press, 1997).

98. See Jeffrey Hart, *Smiling Through the Cultural Catastrophe* (New Haven: Yale University Press, 2001).

99. *The Republic of Plato*, F. M. Cornford, trans. (New York: Oxford University Press, 1945), p. 15.

100. Leiter, "Rethinking Legal Realism," supra note 94, at p. 315.

101. Ibid.

4. Positionality

"Individuals cannot separate where they stand in the web of reality from what they perceive."[102] That statement, Joe Kincheloe and Shirley Steinberg assert, "lays the foundation for the concept of 'positionality' [in] contemporary critical social and educational theory."[103] One must move beyond positionality's foundation, however, to see what is truly unique about this epistemology.

Positionality attempts to deal with the problem of arbitrariness associated with postmodernism and standpoint epistemologies. It does so by "acknowledg[ing] the existence of empirical truths, values and knowledge...."[104] But, somewhat reminiscent of postmodernism, positionality also asserts that empirical truth, values, and knowledge are "contingent" in the sense that commitment and action based upon them are "subject to further critical evaluation and revision... [as] [e]xperience interacts with an individual's current perceptions to reveal new understandings...."[105] Because of the possibility of further evaluation and revision of commitment and action, it can be said that truth, values, and knowledge are imperfect, internal, contingent, evolving, and, hence, necessarily incomplete.

These features of positionality draw it closer to the standpoint and post-modern epistemologies than to the rational/empirical epistemology. Like standpoint epistemology, positionality "retains a concept of knowledge based on experience," and like postmodern epistemology, it "rejects the perfectibility, externality, or objectivity of truth."[106] Conflicts cannot be resolved, as rational/empirical epistemology would have us believe, by reference to some *a priori*, "external pre-social standard of truth." As Bartlett elaborates:

> From the positional stance, any resolutions that emerge are the products of human struggles about what social realities are better than others. Realities are deemed better not by comparison to some external, 'discovered' moral truths or 'essential' human characteristics, but by internal truths that make the most sense of experienced, social existence. Thus, social truths will emerge from social relation-

---

102. Joe L. Kincheloe and Shirley R. Steinberg, "Addressing the Crisis of Whiteness: Reconfiguring White Identity in a Pedagogy of Whiteness," in *White Reign: Deploying Whiteness in America*, Joe L. Kincheloe, Shirley R. Steinberg, Nelson M. Rodriguez & Ronald E. Chennault, eds. (New York: St. Martin's Griffin, 1998), p. 3.

103. Ibid.

104. Bartlett, "Feminist Legal Methods," supra note 57, at p. 880.

105. Ibid.

106. Ibid.

ships and what, after critical examination, they tell social beings about what they want themselves, and their social world, to be.[107]

How can positionality acknowledge the contingency of truth while at the same time posit the existence of empirical truths? It does so by asserting that empirical truth is discovered through a continuous process of self-reflection and questioning. Thus, there are empirical truths, but they are partial and situated. Meaning arises from particular involvement and relationships. Differently situated, one person may have access to truths that another person may not. Incorporating other viewpoints in our thinking will overcome our limited perspectives and, thereby, yield new truths.

This process of considering and weighing the opinions of others will eventually lead to what can be called "hypertruths," or what Bartlett calls "permanent truths." These are truths that are shown to be increasingly fixed or final, but that are not objective, *a priori* or pre-social. They are, nonetheless, truths by which we may judge the world around us. The inherent wrongness of murder and racial bias, and the love one has for one's children are examples of hypertruths.[108]

The foundational elements of positionality—the necessary contingency of truths and the deontological need to self-criticize—are themselves no more than hypertruths. They are not claims of objective, *a priori* or pre-social truth, rising above the contingency or situatedness of truth. This is all the more reason our truths must not be taken too uncritically or defended "too harshly and dogmatically."[109] This type of thinking makes it difficult to understand positionality's basis for claiming to be more determinate than postmodernism.

Positionality's concept of truth is somewhat Millian. John Stuart Mill saw truth as conditional, as a transitory state in which we accept one proposition over another based upon information available at the moment. Because it is always possible that a proposition might be proven false with the gathering of additional information, truth ultimately remains beyond our reach. Thus, in reality, we do not labor with truth in hand; we only labor under an estimation of where the truth might lie. Truth (even a hypertruth) is in a state of becoming, never a state of being.[110]

---

107. Ibid. at p. 884.

108. Ibid. at p. 883. But even these truths must not be taken too uncritically or defended "too harshly and dogmatically." Ibid. at pp. 883–84.

109. Ibid. at pp. 883–84.

110. See, John Stuart Mill, *On Liberty*, Elizabeth Rappaport, ed. (Indianapolis: Hackett, 1978), pp. 16–18. See also Isaiah Berlin, *Four Essays on Liberty* (New York: Oxford University Press, 1969), p. 188 ("[Mill assumed] that human knowledge was in principle never

Can the elements of critical theory identified and clarified in this chapter be used to transform critical theory from a theory of legal criticism into a theory of judicial decision making? This is the question to which we turn in Section B of this part of the book.

---

complete, and always fallible."). Yet, Mill did suggest that "whole truth" was attainable, although unlikely. See Mill, *On Liberty*, at p. 116.

CRITICAL PROCESS

The chapters in this section of Part 2 attempt to transform critical theory from a theory of legal criticism, its current state, into a theory of judicial decision making. Critical theory thereby becomes "critical process." The latter is an attempt to do justice where justice is not being done for outsiders under the traditional regime of judicial decision making. This endeavor can entail judicial activism at its highest level, and, thus, raises an important question of institutional legitimacy. The answer to that complex question is to be found, at least in part, in the policy method.[1]

Critical process can be conceptualized as an extension of the policy method. The judge is permitted (indeed, has a duty) to formulate policy. Policy-formulation is, however, limited to outsider norms. Whether dealing with the written or unwritten law, the judge is constrained by the community expectation of outsiders—*reasoned elaboration from existing outsider arrangements.* The criticalist judge discovers or vindicates outsider policies. Policy-discovery and policy-vindication turn to policy-making, however, when the criticalist judge imposes outsider norms on the larger society or on a particular insider community before the people therein are ready to accept them.[2] To this extent, critical process is methodologically similar to legal realism, although substantively distinct.[3]

Though critical process fits within the general framework of the policy method, it is more difficult to locate within the traditional levels of judicial analysis.[4] Policy-oriented, critical process is certainly not Level 1/judicial positivism. However, neither is it Level 2/judicial pragmatism, because it envisions policy-making, nor is it Level 3/judicial nominalism, because the judge is constrained by the expectations of the relevant outsider community. The judge

---

1. See Chapter 10, Section D, infra.
2. For an explanation of the judicial policy-foundation function, see Introduction, Section C.
3. See Chapter 3, supra.
4. See Chapter 7, supra, for a discussion of the levels of traditional judicial analysis.

looks outside herself for guidance in formulating policies. In short, the criti-calist judge operates somewhere between Levels 2 and 3; perhaps Level 2½.

Within these broad frameworks—the policy method and levels of judicial analysis—critical process incorporates and synthesizes the mission and oper-ational elements of critical theory. Though counteracting anti-objectivism re-mains the central goal,[5] the six equality models[6] are merged into three—"sym-metrical model" (equality as sameness); "asymmetrical model" (equality as difference); and "hybrid model" (equality as a combination of sameness and difference). Each model entails deconstruction and reconstruction,[7] the latter of which is subjected to the internal critique.[8] The structure of critical process can be outlined as follows:

Critical Process
> Point A: Issue
> Point B: Reasoning
>> (1) The Subordination Question (Deconstruction and Reconstruction)
>>> (a) Symmetrical Model (Equality as Sameness)
>>> (b) Asymmetrical Model (Equality as Difference)
>>> (c) Hybrid Model (Equality as Sameness and Difference)
>> (2) Followed by Internal Critique
>>> (a) Rational/Empirical
>>> (b) Standpoint
>>> (c) Postmodern
>>> (d) Positionality
> Point C: Judgment

In addition to explaining and illustrating critical process, the chapters in this section of Part 2 will also deal with some of the major issues facing an outsider-oriented process of judicial decision making. Some criticisms re-garding critical process are external while others are internal, coming from criticalists themselves. Both sets of questions help us assess the legitimacy of the latest, but undoubtedly not the last, theory of judicial decision making.

---

5. See Chapter 8, supra.
6. See Chapter 9, Section B, supra.
7. See Chapter 9, Section A, supra.
8. See Chapter 9, Section C, supra.

Chapter 10
Structure of Critical Process

Critical process prescribes a judicial process in which the judge moves from Point A to Point C by reasoned elaboration from existing outsider norms, and does not hesitate to impose such norms on the larger society. Judicial decision making is disciplined by the validation of outsider values. This line of judicial reasoning unfolds through two stages—the "subordination question" (deconstruction and reconstruction) and the "internal critique"—employed by three equality models—"symmetrical," "asymmetrical," and "hybrid."

A. From Legal Criticism to Judicial Theory

This chapter creates and applies a process of judicial decision making called "critical process." Critical process combines the operational elements of critical theory discussed in the last chapter with the traditional structure of judicial decision making broached in the Introduction and illustrated in Part 1. Most importantly, critical process is driven by outsider values. It is an attempt to ferret out and redress subordination in socio-legal arrangements. This feature of critical process—its consequentialism—places it within the policy method. In this sense, critical process can be viewed as the latest expression of the policy method.[1]

Given critical process' commitment to outsider values, some knowledge of outsider community norms is necessary for a correct understanding and an informed implementation of critical process. This observation applies to insiders who are unfamiliar with a particular outsider culture and to outsiders who are unaware of other outsider cultures. For starters, the uninitiated might wish to peruse books or articles dealing with outsider cultures; e.g., *The African American Book of Values*;[2] *Still Unequal: The Shameful Truth About Women and Justice in America*;[3] *Gaylaw: Challenging the Apartheid of the Closet*;[4] "Latina/o Ethnicities";[5] and "Toward An Asian American Legal Scholarship."[6]

---

1. See Part 1, Section B, supra.

2. *The African American Book of Values*, Steven Barboza, ed. (New York: Doubleday, 1998).

3. Lorraine Dusky, *Still Unequal: The Shameful Truth About Women and Justice in America* (New York: Crown, 1996).

4. William N. Eskridge, Jr., *Gaylaw: Challenging the Apartheid of the Closet* (Cambridge: Harvard University Press, 1999).

5. Francisco Valdes, Forward: "Latina/o Ethnicities, Critical Race Theory, and Post-

One faces a special challenge in attempting to mold critical theory into a process of judicial decision making. The difficulty is to devise the means by which a judge can uncover and redress subordination, or anti-objectivism, in a judicially recognizable manner. Critical process must be able to determine what counts as "lawful" and "unlawful" behavior while, at the same time, effectively redressing subordination. The judge must be able to move from Point A to Point C in such a way as to remain faithful to the judicial function as well as to the mission of critical theory. This calls for the imposition of certain constraints on judicial reasoning under the criticalist model, primarily at Point B.

B. Limitations on Process

Point B under critical process must begin not with a rule of law, as in traditional process, but with a question, the *subordination question*. This is a two-fold inquiry that asks: (1) whether a socio-legal arrangement (e.g., a case or specific legal doctrine or practice) subordinates (i.e., devalues or ignores altogether) important outsider norms (community expectations, values or concerns that ultimately bear upon an outsider's chances for worldly success and personal happiness); and, if so, (2) what can be done to redress the identified subordination—what can be done to bring about social transformation?[7] The first part of the subordination question calls for deconstruction, and the second part calls for reconstruction.[8] Thus, in moving from Point A to Point C, the judge will deconstruct the socio-legal arrangement under consideration to reveal the ways in which it does or, equally important, does not invalidate or undercut outsider norms. If subordination is uncovered, the judge will construe extant law or create new law as a reconstructive response to the identified subordination. Raising the subordination question enables the judge to uncover anti-objectivism, if any, in a socio-legal arrangement that might otherwise go unnoticed, especially in facially neutral arrangements.

As the judge unearths subordination through deconstruction and fashions a reconstructive measure to redress the identified subordination, she must ex-

---

Identity Politics in Postmodern Legal Culture: From Practices to Possibilities," *La Raza Law Journal* 9 (1996): 1.

6. Robert S. Chang, "Toward An Asian American Legal Scholarship: Critical Race Theory, Post-Structuralism, and Narrative Space," *California Law Review* 81 (1993): 1241.

7. See Chapter 9, Sections A & B, supra. See generally Roy L. Brooks, *Rethinking the American Race Problem* (Berkeley: University of California Press, 1990), pp. 9, 14–22.

8. See Chapter 9, Section A, supra.

ercise restraint. Critical process cannot be used as a vehicle for the judge to vent her personal sense of justice in a given case. Many criticalists are uncomfortable with unbridled judicial discretion or with loose rules of law. They fear that these arrangements can provide an easy pretext for subordination, allowing racism, sexism, and homophobia to go unchecked.[9] Given this concern, three additional structural limitations seem appropriate and even necessary.

First, the judge, an adherent of the policy method, must limit policy-formulation to the outsider community. The mission of critical theory—its war against anti-objectivism—surely warrants this limitation.[10] Thus, the criticalist judge is free to discover or vindicate outsider norms, giving preference to those norms that offer the greatest potential for counteracting anti-objectivism. Naturally, policy-making, which in this context must mean the imposition of outsider norms on the larger society or on a particular insider community, is permitted.[11]

Second, deconstruction and reconstruction must proceed through the prism of a particular equality model. The equality models not only give structure to critical analysis but also add intellectual diversity to such analysis.[12] For purposes of judicial analysis, the six equality models discussed in Chapter 9 can be synthesized into the following three working equality models: *symmetrical* (which is essentially assimilation);[13] *asymmetrical* (which brings together under a single conceptual umbrella the preference equality models, special rights, accommodation in its special rights mode, and empowerment);[14] and *hybrid* (which incorporates acceptance as well as the reconstructive side of pluralism).[15]

The third structural limitation on judicial decision making is the *internal critique*. Every reconstructive measure, whether symmetrical, asymmetrical or hybrid, must pass through the criticalist epistemologies discussed in Chapter 9.[16] Such additional criticalist analysis adds even more intellectual diversity to critical process, including viewpoints that, by happenstance rather than

---

9. See, e.g., Patricia Williams, "Alchemical Notes: Reconstructing Ideals from Deconstructed Rights," *Harvard Civil Rights-Civil Liberties Law Review* 22 (1987): 401, 406–8; Mari Matsuda, "Public Responses to Racist Speech: Considering the Victims' Story," *Michigan Law Review* 87 (1989): 2320, 2325.

10. See Chapter 8, supra.

11. See Introduction, Section C, supra, for a more detailed discussion.

12. See Chapter 9, Section B, supra.

13. See Chapter 9, Section B1, supra.

14. See Chapter 9, Section B3, supra.

15. See Chapter 9, Sections B2 & B3, supra.

16. See Chapter 9, Section C, supra.

by design, might resonate with insiders. More importantly, the internal critique further contextualizes the reconstructive (or preferred equality) rule. This important point is developed further in the discussion of Step 2 of critical process, which appears next.

C. Two-Step Process

With the above limitations in mind, critical process can be structured as a two-step process of judicial analysis. Step 1 asks the subordination question. Step 2 applies the internal critique.

Step 1 (Subordination Question). The judge asks the subordination question—to wit, does the socio-legal arrangement (a case or specific legal doctrine) *sub judice* subordinate outsiders or an outsider group (deconstruction) and, if so, how can such subordination be effectively redressed (reconstruction)? If a judge does not find subordination, she must still contextualize. She must explain how the matter under consideration validates relevant outsider values.[17] In this way law formally and unambiguously embraces outsider norms. Judicial acceptance of outsider norms is, indeed, the central mission of critical process.

Applying the *symmetrical equality model*,[18] the judge finds subordination if the matter under consideration is insider- or outsider-conscious. Thus, subordination exists if a socio-legal arrangement involves an explicit outsider/insider classification or otherwise fails to validate or enforce the value of neutrality that inheres in all outsider communities. Such subordination is more likely to arise in cases involving homosexuals than in cases involving other outsiders.[19] Having found subordination, the judge then prescribes a facially neutral law to redress the identified subordination.

Proceeding under the more complex *asymmetrical equality model*,[20] the judge deconstructs by asking whether the law or legal problem under consideration adversely affects outsiders or an outsider group in such a way as to suggest insiderism—mainly unconscious bias or insider privilege. Note the two elements of this test: (1) subordinating effects and (2) subordinating state of mind.[21] The latter element, insiderism, can be determined in several ways.

---

17. Application of the symmetrical equality model to the *Kulko* case, see Chapter 11, Section B1, infra, illustrates this point.

18. See Section A1, supra.

19. See Chapter 9, Section B1, supra.

20. See Section A1, supra.

21. See Chapter 9, Section B3, supra.

One way is by applying the cultural meaning test discussed in Chapter 9.[22] This test asks, for example, what does it mean in the African American community when a politician campaigning for office airs the infamous Willie Horton TV commercial[23] or runs a newspaper advertisement featuring a white woman who tells her neighbor she pulled her son out of public school because of drugs, violence, and a "bit more diversity than he could handle"?[24] What does it mean to women when the law partner in charge of a meeting assigns the lone female lawyer in attendance to lead the coffee detail, or refers to her as "sweetie"? What does it mean to the homosexual community when the local school board sponsors a "family values" week at the local high schools? And finally, what does it mean to African Americans when a white college student says he plans to attend the University of California at Santa Barbara "because it's the UC with the most white kids."[25] The cultural meaning test probes Level 3 Bias, unconscious bias.[26]

In addition to the cultural meaning test, insiderism can be established by answering two other questions. The first asks whether the matter under consideration reek of stereotyping? The second question asks whether the matter under consideration enforces insider privilege? Does it enhance white, male, or heterosexual privilege or, conversely, harm outsider status? Does it support an implicit sense of group position? These questions probe Level 3 Bias.[27]

The insiderism element can sometimes be established by simply determining whether the matter under consideration validates relevant outsider values. If the matter involves an institutional practice (e.g., a corporation's hiring process) or a prior judicial ruling, insiderism would be established if important outsider norms were unconsciously ignored or consciously devalued. Invidious intent is quite beside the point.[28]

To establish subordination in any of these ways, the plaintiff may have to produce evidence in a pretrial hearing probative of relevant outsider norms. The judge could, for example, ask the plaintiff to submit testimony or affi-

---

22. See ibid.

23. Aired during the 1988 Presidential Election campaign by Republican candidate George Bush, this controversial political ad presented a young African American male, named Willie Horton, as the face of crime in America.

24. Laura Meckler, "Ad Takes Swipe at 'Diversity,'" San Diego Union-Tribune, 9/19/00, p. A9.

25. Sandy Banks, "When Racial Bias Emerges, Despite Our Best Efforts," Los Angeles Times, 9/19/00, Part E (Southern California Living), p. 1.

26. For a discussion of unconscious bias, see Chapter 8, Section B3, supra.

27. See ibid.

28. See Chapter 8, Section B, supra; Chapter 9, Section B3, supra.

davits from community leaders, such as ministers, educators, politicians and community activists. The defendant would, of course, be permitted to submit countervailing evidence.

If the plaintiff is successful in proving insiderism, the case moves to reconstruction. Here, the asymmetricalist judge will typically prescribe rules that grant preferences to outsiders adversely affected by insiderism. Affirmative action, as mentioned in Chapter 9, is a favorite remedy of most critical theorists.[29]

Using the *hybrid equality model*,[30] the judge applies the asymmetrical rule of deconstruction. In response to identified subordination, the judge, however, fashions a reconstructive rule that is equally accessible to insiders. Hence, the hybrid equality model is asymmetrical in its deconstruction mode and symmetrical-like on its reconstructive side. In other words, while the hybrid equality model mimics asymmetrical deconstruction, it does not entirely repeat symmetrical reconstruction. Unlike the latter, hybrid equality rules can be outsider-conscious. An example would be proportional representation rules. Hybrid equality rules can also be culturally coded in favor of outsiders, such as "parental" leave rules, which tend to help working mothers more than working fathers. Offering insiders equal access to reconstructive rules is what gives the hybrid equality model its symmetricality.

Step 2 (Internal Critique). Whether proceeding under the symmetrical, asymmetrical or hybrid model, the judge runs each preferred equality rule through the criticalist epistemologies. Specifically, the judge asks herself the following questions in succession: Does the rule make sense because it is logical or empirical (rational/empirical)?[31] Does the rule make sense because it is narrowly tailored to validate the experiences of the relevant essential, or "typical," outsider— the authentic self as opposed to the anti-self (standpoint)?[32] Does the rule make sense because it validates relevant intersectional experiences or identities of outsiders (postmodernism)?[33] and Does the rule make sense because it validates a hypertruth (positionality)?[34]

As more fully discussed earlier in Chapter 9,[35] these modes of thinking give various criticalist spins to the proposed equality rules generated by the equality models. They provide different internal takes on a criticalist response or

---

29. See Chapter 9, Section B3, supra.
30. See Section A1, supra.
31. See Chapter 9, Section C1, supra.
32. See Chapter 9, Section C2, supra. See also Chapter 12, Section B2, infra.
33. See Chapter 9, Section C3, supra.
34. See Chapter 9, Section C4, supra.
35. See Chapter 9, Section C, supra.

solution to a legal problem involving subordination. Engaging the internal critique is much like Plato and his students sitting around a table each offering a different perspective on the meaning of a just society. Here, of course, the preferred equality rule is the topic of discussion.

But the rewards of the discussion are more than just philosophical. Indeed, there is much to be said for delving deeper into the process. Pushing forward to the internal critique permits the judge to further contextualize her reasoning. She does so by dealing directly with normative positions that were merely suggestive in Step 1, particularly in the reconstructive process. This is the time for the judge to formally consider criticalist ways of knowing that murmur or perhaps even rumble beneath the surface of the equality models. One of three things can happen to the holding (the reconstructive measure, or preferred equality rule) as a result of this excursion, each of which appreciably improves the judicial process. First, the proposed holding could be sustained but with richer supporting analysis. Second, it could be modified to take account of additional considerations. Third, it could be jettisoned in light of overwhelming outsider concerns.[36]

In applying this two-step process, the three equality models—symmetrical, asymmetrical, and hybrid—should be viewed as three different judicial approaches to cases. Thus, there could be as many as three different criticalist takes on a single legal problem. Rather than trying to reconcile these equality models (or judicial mindsets), which probably could not be done, we must simply accept the diversity of judicial decision making under critical process.

D. Institutional Legitimacy

Is judicial decision making based on outsider norms a legitimate exercise of the judicial function? This is a complex question that calls for a great deal of reflection and debate. In grappling with this question, one must necessarily incorporate structural deficiencies in traditional decision making schemes.[37] The following discussion is merely suggestive of some of the salient considerations that should be addressed.

The most important argument against the institutional legitimacy of critical process is that it conflicts with our traditional notions about judicial decision making. Unelected and, hence, unaccountable to the people, judges

---

36. See Chapter 11, Section B, infra, for illustrations.
37. See Part 2, Section A, supra; Chapter 8, supra. See also Chapter 12, infra.

proceeding under critical process will at times be called upon to impose outsider norms on insiders before the latter are prepared to accept them. This makes a mockery of "democratic restraint."[38] There is little respect for our democratic ideal, which is to say, criticalist judges have no mandate on which to legislate policy. Such an undemocratic assumption of power by judges cannot be tolerated in a liberal democratic society like ours.[39]

In response, it could be argued that policy-making under critical process is legitimate in those areas wherein the legislature is able to step in with corrective legislation; namely, common law and statutory cases. Conceding the wrongness of such policy-making, this argument relies on the legislature to step in and make changes to common law rules and statutory interpretations it dislikes.[40]

This argument is a weak response to the legitimacy question. First, it has limited range; it has no application to constitutional cases. In the realm of the Constitution, the Supreme Court has the last word.[41] Thus, the argument would exclude critical process from constitutional cases, relegating it only to those areas in which the legislature exercises veto power. Second, the argument is vulnerable to a powerful response, which goes as follows. The idea that critical process can proceed in common law and statutory cases because the legislature can intervene therein with corrective legislation "embrace[s] the general proposition that a wrong may be done if it can be undone." Like the Supreme Court, we should refuse to accept this proposition.[42] But perhaps the most serious flaw with the corrective legislation argument is that it concedes too much—namely, that criticalist policy-making is wrong, that it is democratically deficient. This, in fact, may not be true.

There are several reasons or theories that suggest judicial decision making under critical process may not be wrong. These theories support the institutional legitimacy of an outsider-oriented judicial process. The first theory concerns the notion of equality, which proceeds as follows. Judges should be permitted to use their institutional powers to redress social inequality visited upon historically disadvantaged groups, or to at least prevent such inequality from widening. This argument (the ideal of equality) has deep roots in American society. It extends back to our Founding Fathers, inspiring John Adams to write: "The doctrine of human equality is founded entirely in the Christian

---

38. See discussion in Introduction, Section C2, supra.
39. See ibid.
40. See Introduction, Section C2, infra, for relevant discussion of Judge Posner's views on the legitimacy question.
41. See *Marbury v. Madison*, 5 U.S. (1 Cranch), 137 (1803).
42. *Stanley v. Illinois*, 405 U.S. 645, 647 (1971).

doctrine that we are all children of the same Father, all accountable to Him for our conduct to one another, all equally bound to respect each other's self love."[43] Of course, criticalists, like our Founding Fathers,[44] have different notions of equality. They defined equality in different ways.[45] But this should not matter, because the equality argument advanced here is not one of absolute, or egalitarian, equality.[46] Rather, it is an argument for equality in response to identified subordination; in other words, group-specific, socially constructed deprivation.[47]

It may also be possible to support the legitimacy of critical process on the basis of a different level of equality; namely, juridical equality. Deficiencies in traditional process—its disregard of outsider norms (avowed in the case of homosexuals and more unconscious in the case of people of color and women[48])—suggest that judicial decision making is not neutral as to matters of race, sex or sexual orientation. These deficiencies are *structural*. They deny outsiders juridical equality, the very equality (along with political equality) guaranteed as a basic right in all liberal democratic societies.[49] Through the systemic internalization of outsider norms, critical process guarantees outsider equality within the judicial process.

A final theory rests outsider-oriented policy-making on an important exception to the principle of democratic restraint discussed earlier. This exception permits judges to act in extraordinary ways where there has been a failure of the democratic ideal. The civil rights cases are classic examples. *Brown v. Board of Education* and its progeny[50] imposed the equality norm on a dem-

---

43. David McCullough, *John Adams* (New York: Simon & Schuster, 2001), p. 619.

44. Adams, for example, believed that all men were "born equally free and independent," whereas most educated Americans, following the Declaration of Independence, believed that all men were "born free and equal." Ibid. p. 224. Of course, woman were conspicuously absent from either formulation, and slaves were completely disregarded—virtually invisible.

45. See Section A2, supra.

46. See discussion in Preface, Section B note 9, supra.

47. See Section C, supra, & Chapters 8 & 9, supra. See also discussion of welfare liberalism in Preface, Section B, supra.

48. See Part 2, Section A, supra, & Chapters 8 & 9, supra. People of color and women are virtually invisible in traditional process, not unlike their treatment in the earliest formulations of equality in our society. See note 44, supra.

49. See discussion in Preface, Section B note 9, supra.

50. 347 U.S. 483 (1954). See, e.g., *Brown v. Board of Education*, 349 U.S. 294 (1955) (ordering the desegregation of public schools "with all deliberate speed"); *Cooper v. Aaron*, 358 U.S. 1 (1958) (holding that the governor and legislature of Arkansas were bound by the holding in the Brown cases, despite violent white opposition to such rulings); *Green v. County School Board of New Kent County, Virginia*, 391 U.S. 430, 441 (1968) (school board's

ocratically deficient southern community. In the wake of *Brown*, southern federal judges (men like Richard Taylor Rives, John R. Brown, Elbert P. Tuttle, Frank M. Johnson, John Minor Wisdom, and J. Skelly Wright, all judges on the Fifth Circuit) persistently imposed the democratic ideal on their friends and neighbors who were unwilling to accept racial change.[51] This was judicial activism at its highest level—a commandeering of power by unelected judges—but it was not undemocratic. It was judicial action taken in the name of democracy. The judges acted in furtherance of the democratic ideal. Their policy-making made our society and our government more democratic, especially in the south.[52]

Hence, when the criticalist judge acts consistent with the democratic ideal—America's foundational norm—she is acting within the powers of her office.[53] She proceeds under democratic authority when she lifts the burden of subordination from the lives of historically subordinated people. When subordination is a *badge or condition* of citizenship, it nullifies that minimum of liberties deemed necessary to enable citizens to freely exercise their political rights. Constrained by the inertia of cultural or social traditions that work in favor of insiders, subordinated people—people of color, women, and homosexuals—are denied an effective voice in their own governance.

Whether the existence of subordination establishes democratic deficiency automatically or whether democratic deficiency needs to be established on a case-by-case basis is a question that can only be answered after we have had an opportunity to work with critical process over a period of time. As we work through the cases, the conditions constitutive of democratic deficiency, including the relevancy of democratic recourse in other organs of government, will become more clear.

"freedom of choice" desegregation plan "cannot be accepted as a sufficient step to 'effectuate a transition' to a unitary system" mandated by *Brown*).

51. See generally Jack Bass, *Unlikely Heroes* (New York: Simon and Schuster, 1981).

52. See John Hart Ely, *Democracy and Distrust: A Theory of Judicial Review* (Cambridge: Harvard University Press, 1980).

53. By "democracy" I mean both procedural and substantive democracy. See Introduction, Section C2, supra. The quest-for-justice argument can, perhaps, sustain policy-making in individual cases (i.e., on an ad hoc basis) but not the type of persistent, broad policy-making critical process seems to require. See ibid.

Chapter 11
In re *Kulko v. Superior Court*

To further our understanding of critical process, we shall apply it to a routine legal problem. Like most legal problems, the one we shall analyze is facially neutral; it is not explicitly conscious of race, sex, or sexual orientation. The problem involves civil litigation.

A. Facts

One of the most important doctrines in civil litigation is the doctrine of personal jurisdiction. This doctrine locates the proper place for trying a civil (i.e., private or non-criminal) lawsuit. When the parties live in different states, the judge must decide whether the lawsuit should be tried in the state wherein the plaintiff resides or in a different state, such as the state wherein the defendant resides. *Kulko v. Superior Court*[1] is a famous personal jurisdiction case. The opinion was written by Justice Thurgood Marshall, one of the most liberal justices ever to sit on the Supreme Court. Although an old case, it presents a modern problem, and is still good law.[2]

The primary facts of the case are as follows. Mrs. Sharon Kulko Horn lived with her two children in California. Her former husband, Mr. Ezra Kulko lived in New York and had been to California on only two occasions, the last time being in 1960, for a total of four days. Mrs. Kulko sued her former husband in a California court in 1976 to, among other things, obtain full custody of their children and to increase Mr. Kulko's child-support payments. Under the doctrine of personal jurisdiction, a civil court can order a defendant to appear before it and answer the complaint only if, *inter alia*, "minimum contacts" exist between the defendant and the state wherein the court is located. There is no bright-line test for determining when "minimum contacts" have been established.[3] Essentially, the term means that there must be a sufficient connection or relationship between the defendant (Mr. Kulko) and the forum state (California) such that the defendant should reasonably anticipate that he

---

1. 436 U.S. 84 (1978).
2. See, e.g., *Burnham v. Superior Court of California*, 495 U.S. 604 (1990).
3. See, e.g., *International Shoe Co. v. State of Washington*, 326 U.S. 310 (1945); *World-Wide Volkswagen Corp. v. Woodson*, 444 U.S. 286 (1980); *Burger King v. Rudzewicz*, 471 U.S. 462 (1985).

could be amenable to a lawsuit in the forum state.[4] The Supreme Court ultimately ruled that Mr. Kulko could not be forced to litigate in California because of the absence of "minimum contacts." As Mr. Kulko had only been in the state on two brief occasions in the distant past and had no business ties to the state, there was no sufficient connection or relationship between him and the state. "The cause of action herein asserted arises, not from the defendant's commercial transactions in interstate commerce, but rather from his personal, domestic relations," Justice Marshall observed.[5]

Let us consider how three criticalist judges each proceeding under a different equality model—symmetrical, asymmetrical, and hybrid—might decide *Kulko*. The elements of each equality model (subordination question and internal critique) unfold linearly like all judicial decision making, beginning with Point A (the dispositive issue of the case) proceeding to Point B (the reasoning) and ending at Point C (the judgment or decision). Not unlike traditional process, Point B is the most important point in the process. This is where the subordination question and the internal critique take place.[6]

B. Symmetrical Equality Model

Approaching the case from the symmetrical equality model, a judge would have little to say, except to contextualize the Court's reasoning. Point A frames the dispositive issue of the case: Whether a state court can exercise *in personam* jurisdiction over a nonresident parent in a child custody and support case? With the framing of the issue, the criticalist judge moves to Point B.

1. Subordination Question

Point B begins by asking whether, from the woman's perspective, the law governing the case—the minimum contacts rule as construed by the Court in *Kulko*—involves an explicit outsider/insider classification or otherwise fails to validate or enforce the value of gender-blind treatment inherent in the woman's culture. In other words, is the minimum contacts rule gender-conscious? Clearly, the answer is an emphatic no. Women would certainly find minimum contacts to be a facially neutral doctrine, as it clearly is. The gov-

---

4. See, e.g., *World-Wide Volkswagen Corp. v. Woodson*, 444 U.S. 286, 297 (1980).

5. 436 U.S. at 97.

6. For a discussion of the various points in traditional judicial reasoning, see Introduction, Section A, supra. See also the outline of critical process in Part 2, Section B (Critical Process), supra.

erning law promotes gender neutrality. However, the criticalist judge cannot simply leave the matter at that. She must now go forward and contextualize the relevant value—gender neutrality—in the relevant outsider community—women. In this way, law embraces and validates outsider norms.[7]

The gender-neutrality norm is an important feature of the women's culture. It is a value for which women have fought long and hard to assert and defend, especially through litigation. For example, the ACLU Women's Rights Project initiated litigation to overturn state and federal laws that discriminated against women. Justice Ginsburg, who at the time was a law professor, argued many of the Project's cases before the Supreme Court. The Project's efforts resulted in a number of victories for women—e.g., the invalidation of an Idaho statute that gave men a preference over women in estate administration[8]—and victories for men—e.g., the overturning of a provision in the Social Security Act that awarded child-in-care benefits to mothers but not to fathers.[9] Although the Project litigated on behalf of men—indeed most of the major constitutional sex discrimination cases filed during the 1970s were brought on behalf of male plaintiffs[10]—women were seen as the ultimate victors, because the Supreme Court in each of these cases vindicated the gender-neutrality policy. So contextualized, the Supreme Court's reasoning in *Kulko* is further validation of this well-established woman's norm.

Given the absence of a finding of subordination, reconstruction is unnecessary. In other words, if there is no subordination, there is no need for reconstruction. Thus, in the absence of a finding of subordination, the symmetricalist judge follows the governing law—*Kulko*'s construction and application of minimum contacts—and simply explains why the governing law does not subordinate. The judge demonstrates the absence of subordination through reasoned elaboration from existing outsider arrangements, in this case from the gender-neutrality norm many women embrace.

2. Internal Critique

The internal critique is an essential feature of critical process. Its purpose is to facilitate debate and discussion from outsider reference points, which, in

---

7. See Chapter 10, Section C, supra.

8. *Reed v. Reed*, 404 U.S. 71 (1971). See, e.g., *Frontiero v. Richardson*, 411 U.S. 677 (1973) (federal law that afforded male military officers housing and medical benefits covering their wives cannot deny such benefits to husbands of female military officers).

9. *Weinberger v. Wiesenfeld*, 420 U.S. 636 (1975).

10. See, e.g., David Cole, "Strategies of Difference: Litigating for Women's Rights in a Man's World," *Law & Inequality: A Journal of Theory and Practice* 2 (1984): 33, 53–92.

turn, "briefs" the judge on the full range of outsider voices. Some of these voices cross paths with insider impulses. But the purpose here is not to explore insider points of view, which find ample expression in traditional process, but, rather, to attempt to discover how outsiders, with all their intellectual diversity, view the matter. In this way the internal critique further contextualizes the reconstructive measure.[11]

Where, as here, subordination is not established, the internal critique is easy—it does not take place. Because of the absence of subordination, there is no reconstruction; and if there is no reconstruction, there is no internal critique. The internal critique is suspended in this particular instance. There is simply no need to employ it, as there is no preferred equality rule to critique. The judge could, of course, apply the internal critique to the *Kulko* holding if she wanted to, but she is not required to do so.

We now arrive at Point C. Judgment is rendered in favor of the defendant, which, of course, sustains the Supreme Court's judgment.

C. Asymmetrical Equality Model

Once again, we start at the beginning of judicial decision making—Point A. Point A under the asymmetrical equality model is the same as it is under the symmetrical equality model. The difference is at Point B, the judge's reasoning, which in critical process consists of the subordination question and the internal critique.[12]

1. Subordination Question

A judge proceeding under the asymmetrical equality model would deconstruct *Kulko* by asking whether the minimum contacts doctrine as construed and applied in *Kulko* adversely impacts women (the relevant outsider group) in such a way as to suggest insiderism. The answer would have to be yes, both in terms of invalidating an important women's value and in terms of creating a gender status harm.[13]

Some fem crits maintain that there is such a differential in the biology or experiences of men and women that the sexes perceive themselves and their worlds

---

11. Further discussion, see Chapter 10, Sections B & C, supra.

12. For a discussion of the various points in traditional judicial reasoning, see Introduction, Section A, supra. See also the outline of critical process in Part 2, Section B (Critical Process), supra.

13. See Chapter 10, Section C, supra.

differently. For example, the male tendency, it is argued, is to dominate and conquer while the female tendency is to nest and nurture. More than women, men value independence and view the world and relationships in terms of status. More than men, women value caring and connection, and express vulnerability.[14] Carrie Menkel-Meadow discusses psychological studies that demonstrate "women experience themselves through connections and relationships to others while men see themselves as separately identified individuals.... [W]omen express vulnerability instead of strength, responsiveness instead of independence."[15]

Any theory that imputes distinct qualities, attitudes, or duties to outsiders and insiders is bound to be criticized as stereotypical and wrong. But any resolution of the uniqueness issue is tentative at best. For example, the value of care and connection certainly suggests that mothering can best be performed by women. Indeed, the British child psychologist Penelope Leach believes that mothers and fathers are neither the same nor equal in the caring of babies and young children.[16] Dr. Daniel Levinson, on the other hand, cites research that tends to show that male and female roles in child care are functions of "gender splitting," by which he means the practice in all societies of assigning certain child-nurturing tasks to women and others to men. Levinson goes on to argue that the lives and personalities of men and women are converging as societies move forward.[17]

In response to the claim of gender stereotyping, many criticalists would probably agree with Robin West's assertion that:

> There is surely no way to know with any certainty whether women have a privileged access to a way of life that is more nurturing, more caring, more natural, more loving, and thereby more moral than the lives which both men and women presently pursue in the public sphere, including the legal sphere of legal practice, theory, and ped-

---

14. See Deborah Tanner, *You Just Don't Understand: Women and Men in Conversation* (New York: Ballantine Books, 1990), p. 26. See generally Anne Moir and David Jessel, *Brain Sex: The Real Difference Between Men and Women* (New York: Dell Publishing, 1991).

15. Carrie Menkel-Meadow, "Portia in a Different Voice: Speculations on a Woman's Lawyering Process," *Berkeley Women's Law Journal* 1 (1985): 39, 49. Psychologists believe that "these differences are the result of a childrearing system which is based on mothering, so that growing up is a process of identification and connection for a girl and separation and individuation for a boy." Ibid.

16. See Roy L. Brooks, *Critical Procedure* (Durham: Carolina Academic Press, 1998), p. 9.

17. See Daniel J. Levinson (with Judy D. Levinson), *The Seasons of a Woman's Life* (New York: Knopf, 1996).

agogy. But it does seem that whether by reason of sociological role, psychological upbringing or biology, women are closer to such a life....[18]

Regardless of the merits of the debate, it is clear that the value of care and connection is claimed by many women.

Assuming, then, that the value is a legitimate women's value, it could be argued that the Supreme Court's reasoning in *Kulko* is "sexist" because it subordinates women. It does so by giving little or no respect to an applicable women's value—the value of care and connection. The Supreme Court indicates quite clearly that minimum contacts recognizes "commercial" ties as valid forum contacts, but not "personal" ones. This reasoning totally ignores the male litigant's continuing care and connection to his children; i.e., the father-child relationship. A child is not merely a "minimum contact" but a *meaningful* contact.

It could also be argued that the Supreme Court's reasoning in *Kulko* is "sexist" in another way. The Court's application of the minimum contacts rule adversely affects women in child custody and support cases in such a way as to augment or protect, in the eyes of women, male status or privilege. Women get custody of children in 90% of divorce cases involving minor children, and more than 50% of all divorced fathers do not meet their child support or spousal maintenance obligations.[19] By placing the burden of travel on women in these cases, the Court empowers divorced dads and simultaneously subordinates divorced moms. The Court's ruling makes it easier for divorced men to evade their responsibilities to divorced women as well as their children.

Turning to reconstruction, the second phase of Step 1, a judge proceeding under the asymmetrical equality model would typically favor some form of affirmative action.[20] Perhaps the following preferred equality rule would be acceptable to an asymmetrical judge: the state in which the female plaintiff resides is the proper place for trial in child custody and support cases. Thus, if the female plaintiff resides in California and the male defendant resides in New York, the trial will be held in California.

---

18. Robin West, "Feminism, Critical Social Theory and Law" *University of Chicago Legal Forum* 1989 (1989): 59, 83. See also Deborah L. Rhode, "Feminist Critical Theories," *Stanford Law Review* 42 (1990): 617, 624.

19. See, e.g., Deborah Rhode, *Justice and Gender* (Cambridge: Harvard University Press, 1989), p. 151.

20. See Chapter 9, Section B3, supra.

2. Internal Critique

Moving to Step 2, the internal critique, the judge could support as well as reject the female-plaintiff-residency jurisdictional rule. Wearing the rational/empirical epistemological hat,[21] the judge could support the rule based on the following logic: (1) the relative lack of flexibility and wealth, plus other diurnal burdens the custodial parent shoulders make travel to litigate lawsuits difficult; (2) as mentioned earlier, women get child custody in 90% of divorce cases; (3) ergo, women are less able to travel to litigate child custody and support matters, at least in 90% of such cases, and, therefore, should not have to do so. Men are better able to travel to litigate these cases than women.

Arguing against the asymmetrical rule, a rational/empirical minded judge might press the point that the rule, by portraying women as hapless victims in need of special treatment, reinforces female stereotyping and, thus, undercuts the claim for gender equality. The rule hurts women in at least two specific ways: it undermines women's equality by portraying them in a negative light; and it may spark a backlash, especially when men see rich women taking advantage of the rule. A logical response to this argument could be that if judges reject the female-plaintiff-residency rule, all doubt will be removed: women litigants will indeed be hapless victims in child custody and support cases. Responding to the last argument in his on-going internal debate, the judge might offer the following slippery-slope, line-drawing argument: if an exception is carved out for women with children in domestic relations cases, what's to stop courts from making exceptions for other groups in other cases? This type of argument might also resonate with insiders. If so, it is not by design; for, the primary purpose of the internal critique is to advance arguments (opposing or not) that are meaningful to outsiders.[22] In rebuttal, the judge might argue that we draw the line at outsider status; outsiders get the exceptions, insiders do not. A rejoinder to that argument might be that we risk balkanizing the rules governing civil litigation if exceptions are made for outsiders. Yet, on the other hand, litigation rules are riddled with exceptions; there is, in fact, little uniformity here.[23] This internal Socratic discourse could continue for perhaps several more rounds. Whether rational/empirical considerations suggest that the female-plaintiff-residency rule is, on balance, a good rule for women is a conclusion the reader will have to draw on her own, proceeding from the women's perspective, of course.

---

21. See Chapter 9, Section C1, supra.
22. See Chapters 8, 9 & 10, Section B, supra.
23. Brooks, *Critical Procedure*, supra note 16, at pp. 54–55.

The slippery-slope argument provides a standpoint crit with a convenient place to enter the judge's inner discussion.[24] She has a ready response to the line-drawing argument—namely the authentic woman. As suggested in the rationalist discourse above, the typical woman in child custody and support cases is the divorced or separated woman with full or partial legal custody of her children. The divorced or separated father infrequently has full legal custody of his children. Women and children are inextricably bound together in such cases. Hence, the authentic woman in these cases is one who has legal custody of her children.

In furthering his understanding of the authentic outsider in this case, the asymmetricalist judge would take notice of the history and tradition of mothers with children in divorce cases. Despite "equal" or "equitable" property distribution laws, "wives have in practice received neither equality nor equity. In the vast majority of cases, women end up with far greater caretaking responsibilities and far fewer resources to discharge them."[25] Hence, judges may be responsible in no small measure for the sad state of divorced women in American society. Indeed, one scholar, Deborah Rhode, argues that judges tend to forget that the parental responsibilities of single women necessarily remove them from the labor market or force them into low-wage jobs. Also, she notes that many judges still have skewed attitudes about divorced women, viewing them as indolent and alimony-grubbing. "All too often," Rhode writes, "legal and legislative decision making has been skewed by assumptions about 'alimony drones,' the mythical legions of women living in a 'perpetual state of secured indolence' who become a drain upon society and a menace to themselves."[26]

Looking at law through the eyes of a standpoint crit, the judge understands that rules of law not only decide concrete disputes, but they also affirm or disaffirm, value or devalue life experiences. Rules shape the ways in which we understand our world and the behaviors and attitudes of people in it. To quote Benjamin Young, "inherent in a [rule of law] grounded in history and tradition is the choice of which history and whose tradition."[27]

Standpoint crits seek to validate the history and tradition of the essential or typical woman in child custody and support cases—the divorced or separated woman with full or partial legal custody of her children. Clearly, the fe-

---

24. See Chapter 9, Section C2, supra.

25. Rhode, "Feminist Critical Theories," supra note 18, at p. 617.

26. See Rhode, *Justice and Gender*, supra note 19, at p. 150.

27. L. Benjamin Young, Jr., "Justice Scalia's History and Tradition: The Chief Nightmare in Professor Tribe's Anxiety Closet," *Virginia Law Review* 78 (1992): 581, 596.

male-plaintiff-residency jurisdictional rule is not narrowly tailored to validate the experiences of this woman. Other women come within the reach of the rule; most obviously divorced or separated women without legal custody of their children. This group includes those who have previously relinquished legal custody of their children and now seek to regain custody (perhaps the anti-woman in this situation). The rule overextends itself by attempting to serve these "nonessential" interests. Consequently, the rule makes no sense from the standpoint perspective. Broad rules of law are simply not as potent as situation-specific rules in validating essential outsider norms.

Making no distinction between an authentic self and other selves, let alone an anti-self, postmodernism is more generous in deciding who is to benefit from a preferred equality rule.[28] A judge who sees life through postmodern consciousness would probably find the female-plaintiff-residency jurisdictional rule appealing, because the rule is broad enough to reach all relevant intersectionalities. All divorced or separated women, whether with or without legal custody of their children, are protected by the rule.[29] Thus, the female-plaintiff-residency jurisdictional rule makes postmodernist sense because it validates not only Mrs. Kulko's jurisdictional interest in child custody and support cases, but, equally important, the "seasons" in a woman's life; not all seasons, just those in the relevant socio-legal arrangement—child custody and support cases.

An inner discussion based on positionality would consider a variety of arguments, including ones already mentioned, in determining whether the preference given to female plaintiffs in child custody and support cases vindicates a hypertruth.[30] One important consideration is the fact that divorced and separated women with children seeking child custody and support could gain a measure of social and economic equality as well as litigation equality if personal jurisdiction law was slanted in their favor. Although these positions might suggest the presence of a hypertruth—to wit, gender equality—it is equally true that some custodial fathers are less able to travel than some noncustodial mothers. Is that fair to the father or the child? The fact that some custodial fathers might be disadvantaged by the preference creates a hypertruth conflict. One hypertruth (economic fairness) rubs against another hypertruth (gender equality). The judge will now have to decide which hypertruth serves women best. If it is economic fairness, the jurisdictional rule fails

---

28. See Chapter 9, Section C 3, *supra.*

29. Single women who never married would not be litigants in child custody and support cases, unless, of course, out-of-wedlock children are involved.

30. See Chapter 9, Section C 4, *supra.*

under positionality. If it is gender equality, it passes muster under positionality. Again, the reader is left to draw his own conclusion.

It should be noted that the foregoing internal critique is not intended to be definitive. The goal here is to simply illustrate the type of internal analysis that might occur under critical process when operated asymmetrically. A judge proceeding in this fashion now has a deeper understanding of the preferred equality rule. Taking into account information generated under all the epistemologies, the judge may wish to modify, abandon or retain the female-plaintiff-residency rule.[31]

Assuming the asymmetrical rule is retained unmodified, the holding of the case (which is where Point B ends[32]) might be stated as follows: The proper place for trial in child custody and support cases is the state in which the female party-plaintiff resides. *In personam* jurisdiction exercised therein is constitutionally sufficient.[33]

As the forum state in the *case sub judice* is the state in which the female party plaintiff resides, the exercise of *in personam* jurisdiction therein is proper. Judgment (Point C) is therefore rendered in plaintiff's favor. The Supreme Court's judgment is reversed.

D. Hybrid Equality Model

Moving to the hybrid equality model,[34] the judge proceeds directly to Point B. Again, the dispositive issue (Point A) does not change.

1. Subordination Question

Deconstruction under the hybrid equality model is the same as it is under the asymmetrical equality model. Thus, since gender subordination is found under the asymmetrical equality model, it is also established under the hybrid equality model. The difference between these equality models comes in their respective reconstructive modes.[35]

A hybrid equality rule, whether culturally coded in favor of outsiders, outsider-conscious or anything else, must be equally available to insiders.[36] Ac-

---

31. See Chapter 10, Section C, supra.
32. See Introduction, Section A, supra.
33. See sources cited in note 3, supra.
34. See Chapter 10, Section C, supra.
35. See ibid.; Chapter 9, Section B3, supra.
36. See Chapter 10, Section C, supra.

cordingly, a judge proceeding under the hybrid equality model might announce the following preferred equality rule: the state with which the child has the closest personal connections shall be the proper place for trial in child custody and support cases.[37] The word "child" is culturally coded to include mothers. Children are closely associated with mothers in the American culture. To a large extent, the daily experiences of children are the life experiences of mothers.[38] A male litigant, however, can certainly benefit from the child-centered jurisdictional rule if he lives in a state with which the child has the closest personal ties.

2. Internal Critique

Moving to the internal critique, Step 2 in critical process, a rational/empirical-minded judge might see strengths and weaknesses in the child-centered jurisdictional rule. On the one hand, the rule makes sense for several reasons. For example, it appears to neutralize the difference between the father and mother. A child, after all, is the "golden mean" between father and mother. Also, the parent most responsible for the child's care and support should not bear the additional cost of litigating in a far-away place to establish or enforce rights involving child custody and support.

On the other hand, the rule mediates differences between father and mother only in form, not in substance. If mothers get custody of minor children in 90% of divorce cases, as noted earlier,[39] then the child-centered jurisdictional rule actually favors mothers in 90% of divorce cases involving minor children. Thus, to the extent that rules which seek the golden mean appeal to an outsider's rational or perhaps intuitive sense of fairness, the hybrid preferred equality rule flunks that test. It does not, as an empirical matter, take a middle position as between fathers and mothers.

The fate of the hybrid equality rule under the rational/empirical epistemology turns on which of the rational/empirical arguments serves women best. If, for example, the judge determines that it is not in the best interest of women to have a jurisdictional rule whose rationality cannot be established on the basis of purported even-handed application, then the hybrid preferred

---

37. This rule is similar to the Uniform Child Custody Jurisdiction Act, which has been adopted in all 50 states. See Uniform Child Custody Jurisdiction Act §3, 9 U.L.A. 143; Cal. Civ. Code §§5150–5174. The Act, however, has been interpreted as governing only subject matter jurisdiction. Barbara Ann Atwood, "Child Custody Jurisdiction and Territoriality," *Ohio State Law Journal* 52 (1991): 369, 374–75.

38. See Section C 2, supra.

39. See ibid.

equality rule makes little sense. But if the rule can be justified on some other rational basis (e.g., the custodial parent should not assume additional child-rearing expenses), then the rule is acceptable under the rational/empirical epistemology.

The judge might reach a more definite conclusion based on standpoint epistemology. Discussion under the asymmetrical model established the essential woman in child custody and support cases as the divorced or separated woman with full or partial legal custody of her children. This being so, the child-centered jurisdictional rule makes no sense. It is hardly narrowly tailored to validate the experiences or expectations of the typical female litigant in these cases. The rule is centered on children, not on divorced or separated women with legal custody of their children. True, the rule could possibly reach the essential woman, but there is no guarantee that it will. The decision in a sense is taken out of the hands of the woman and placed in the hands of the child. Divorced or separated women with legal custody of their children will not get a favorable jurisdictional ruling if the child has closer personal ties to the father's forum state.

Seen in a postmodernist light, the hybrid equality rule is also a disappointment. It empowers women only on a conditional basis: they must have significant custody of their children. But what about divorced mothers who do not have full custody of their children? What if both parents share custody, as in the case of the Kulkos? If a child spends half her time with both parents, or if the significant occasions during the year—such as birthdays, holidays, and vacations—are spent with the father, there is nothing in the child-centered jurisdictional rule that would prevent a judge from concluding that the child's "closest *personal* connections" are with the father's state. The impotency of the hybrid rule is clearly revealed by the fact that Mrs. Kulko may not win the procedural issue if it is decided under the hybrid equality rule.

Thinking about the hybrid rule from a postmodernist perspective, then, the criticalist judge would view the child-centered jurisdictional rule as dangerously naive. The rule does not validate the experiences of women intersectionally. In particular, it is not broad enough to reach the relevant intersectional experiences of women with children in custody and support cases. The child-centered jurisdictional rule only helps divorced or separated women with children whose personal connections are strongest to the state in which they (the women) reside. It does not bring in other relevant subgroups of women, such as women who do not have full or other significant custody of their children.

Positionality is the final criticalist epistemology to consider. Proceeding from this reference point, the judge might find not a little but a lot of wisdom in the hybrid equality rule. The rule, at bottom, is about children, the love and responsibility parents have (or should have) for their children. The love of one's child is a hypertruth in multicultural America. Ergo, any rule of law that validates children makes perfect sense to the positionality mindset. The child-centered jurisdictional rule is acceptable, in short, because it vindicates a hypertruth. This consideration alone may be sufficient to sustain the hybrid equality rule. It depends on how the criticalist judge balances the relevant competing interests.

Assuming the hybrid rule is retained without modification, Point B might end with the following holding: where the forum state in a child custody and support case is the state in which the child in question maintains the closest personal ties or relations, a state court therein may exercise valid *in personam* jurisdiction. As the current record does not contain sufficient facts to sustain a ruling under this holding—e.g., there is no specific finding as to whether the children continue to maintain any ties with their father in New York and, if so, how often and under what circumstances[40]—the Supreme Court's judgment must be reversed and the case remanded for further consideration not inconsistent with this hybrid opinion. Thus, Point C reverses and remands the case.

---

40. Although the children in this case resided with their father in New York during the school year and with their mother in California during major holidays and summer vacations as required by the separation agreement and divorce decree, both lived in California with their mother full time at the time of the lawsuit. There are no facts indicating whether the children continue to maintain any contacts, ties, or relations with their father's home state. See 436 U.S. at 87–88.

Chapter 12
In re *Brown v. Board of Education*

There is no better way to highlight the power and uniqueness of critical process than to apply it to *Brown v. Board of Education*.[1] As we see in Part 1, *Brown*'s decision prohibiting states from operating racially segregated public schools is thoroughly embraced by most of the traditional processes. With the exception of Scalian textualism, whose originalism and minimalism preclude the type of national judicial authority boldly on display in *Brown*,[2] each model reads its own judicial philosophy into the Court's reasoning. Legal formalism sees in *Brown* a syllogism tethered to the holding in *Plessy v. Ferguson*.[3] Legal realism justifies *Brown*'s judgment on grounds of policymaking, the imposition of the progressive policy of equal educational opportunity.[4] Sociological jurisprudence attempts to frame *Brown* as a policy-vindication case, a case in which the Court gives effect to the progressive and morally correct policy of equal educational opportunity articulated nationwide through the Fourteenth Amendment.[5] Legal process sees in the Court's reasoning the exercise of institutional duty, which entails not only the vindication of constitutional policies in the public's interest but also a judicial indisposition to respect the undemocratic nature of the segregation statutes.[6]

It should come as no surprise that critical process also embraces *Brown*'s decision to overturn state segregation laws in the areas of public primary and secondary education. These Jim Crow laws, laws that mandate separate but equal, are the most visible signs of anti-objectivism we have ever seen, except, of course, for slavery itself. The road on which each equality model—symmetrical, asymmetrical, and hybrid—travels to reach the judgment in *Brown* is, however, very different from the path taken by any of the traditional models sustaining *Brown*. There is more disdain than acceptance or reverence for *Brown*'s reasoning, whether characterized as syllogistic, policy-vindication, policy-discovery or policy-making. In each instance, a conscious

---

1. 347 U.S. 483 (1954).
2. See Chapter 2, Section D, supra.
3. 163 U.S. 537 (1896). See Chapter 1, Section D, supra.
4. See Chapter 3, Section C2, supra.
5. See Chapter 4, Section D3, supra.
6. See Chapter 5, Section C3, supra.

attempt is made to *contextualize* legal analysis in the country's history of racial subordination. Contextualization, a necessity in critical process,[7] leads to holdings that seek to do more about the lingering damage of prior subordinating regimes than either *Brown*'s holding or its rationale could ever hope to accomplish.[8]

A. Back to 1954

Returning now to May 17, 1954, three additional Supreme Court justices, each a criticalist, render separate opinions concurring in the Court's judgment (Point C) in favor of the Negro plaintiffs, as African Americans were referred to back then. Justice Stencil Savage, a symmetricalist, goes first, followed by Justice Leemon Snyder, an asymmetricalist, and then Justice Bialecki Kim, a hybrid crit. Note again that the elements of each equality model (subordination question and internal critique) unfold linearly like all judicial decision making. Each opinion begins with Point A (the dispositive issue of the case) proceeding to Point B (the reasoning) and ending at Point C (the judgment or decision). Point B is the most important point in the process, just as it is in traditional process. This is where the subordination question and the internal critique are addressed.[9]

B. Symmetrical Equality Model

JUSTICE STENCIL SAVAGE, CONCURRING:

The question before this Court (Point A) is presented in Chief Justice Earl Warren's majority opinion as follows: "Does [*de jure*] segregation of children in public schools solely on the basis of race, even though the physical facilities and other 'tangible' factors may be equal, deprive the children of the minority

---

7. See Chapter 10, Section C, supra.

8. For an interesting discussion of the capacity for contextualization, see Christopher Shea, "White Men Can't Contextualize," *Linguafranca: The Review of Academic Life*, September 2001, p. 44.

9. For a discussion of the various points in traditional judicial reasoning, see Introduction, Section A, supra. See also the outline of critical process in Part 2, Section B (Critical Process), supra.

group equal educational opportunities?"[10] I believe we must approach this question by asking another question (Point B): the subordination question.

1. Subordination Question

The majority does not raise the subordination question because it does not see racism as an ingrained feature of our society. I, however, concur in the assumption underlying Justices Snyder's and Kim's concurring opinions, which is that racism is a structural problem in our society. Racism is not American society run amok. Racism is normal science in American society.[11]

Although I concur in the anti-objectivist assumption of Justices Snyder and Kim, I do not concur in their framing of the subordination question. For me, the question is whether, from the Negro point of view, the Jim Crow doctrine is racially neutral on its face—does it validate or enforce the Negro value of color-blind treatment—and, if not, what should be done to redress such subordination? The first part of the question calls for deconstruction, the second part calls for reconstruction.[12]

Clearly, the separate-but-equal doctrine in the context of public education is not facially neutral. It is not color-blind. It is, instead, color-conscious, explicitly directing that white and Negro students be treated in a manner that takes cognizance of their skin color. The term "separate" means not only "different racial treatment" but also "negative racial treatment"—specifically racial segregation. This is how most Negroes see it, even the many in the South, almost a majority, who prefer racial separation (voluntary racial isolation for self-support) to either racial integration (racial mixing) or, of course, racial segregation (involuntary racial isolation that subordinates and stigmatizes).[13]

---

10. 347 U.S. at 492.

11. See Chapter 8, Section B, supra.

12. See Chapter 10, Section C, supra.

13. Stephan and Abigail Thernstrom correctly note that about 47% of the blacks represented by the plaintiff class in *Brown* (southern plus older and less educated than their northern counterparts) had strong reservations about the Court's decision. See Stephan Thernstrom and Abigail Thernstrom, *America in Black and White: One Nation, Indivisible* (New York: Simon & Schuster, 1997), pp. 103–4. They fail to note, however, that the opposition was mainly to the integrative rather than the desegregative implications of the case. In other words, there is an important distinction, as noted in the accompanying text, between integration and desegregation, and between segregation and separation. See, e.g., Roy L. Brooks, *Integration or Separation? A Strategy for Racial Equality* (Cambridge: Harvard University Press, 1996), p. 7; Roy L. Brooks, *Rethinking the American Race Problem* (Berkeley: University of California Press, 1990), p. 30. See also W. E. B. DuBois, "Does the Negro Need Separate Schools?" *Journal of Negro Education* 4 (July 1935): 328–35 (no

There is also ample proof visible to all Americans that racial segregation is the referent for the term "separate-but-equal."[14] "Jim Crow" means racial segregation in all American communities, certainly in the Negro community. The separate-but-equal doctrine in the context of public education is, in short, facially slanted in favor of one race over another, whites over Negroes. That is a per se violation of the symmetrical equality norm not only enshrined in the Fourteenth Amendment's Equal Protection Clause, but also (and more importantly) in the Negro community.[15]

The majority's failure to provide an appropriate remedy, or holding, for the identified subordination is the more significant reason for this concurrence. I find two substantial deficiencies in the majority's holding, both of which arise from the absence of contextualism. First, after ruling that "[s]eparate educational facilities are inherently unequal,"[16] the majority fails to provide the plaintiffs with any relief. No rules for desegregating public schools are announced. The decrees to which the plaintiffs are immediately entitled are, instead, put off until further argument: "In order that we may have the full assistance of the parties in formulating decrees, the cases will be restored to the docket."[17]

Second, the holding, such as it is, fails to make an appropriate cultural acknowledgment. There is no attempt by the majority to situate its holding within the Negro value system. Indeed, rather than embracing Negro norms, rather than validating a positive, empowering image of the Negro, the majority's opinion reeks of racial stigmatization. I shall elaborate on this important point during the internal critique of my reconstructive measure, to which I now turn.

---

longer an integrationist, DuBois argues that sending black students to hostile white schools causes more harm than good to these students).

14. See, e.g., *McLaurin v. Oklahoma State Regents*, 339 U.S. 637 (1950); *Sweatt v. Painter*, 339 U.S. 629 (1950); *Sipuel v. Oklahoma*, 332 U.S. 631 (1948); *Missouri ex rel. Gaines v. Canada*, 305 U.S. 337 (1938). See also, Derrick Bell, "Brown v. Board of Education: Forty-Five Years After the Fact," *Ohio Northern University Law Review* 26 (2000): 171, 174.

15. See cases cited in note 14, supra.

16. 347 U.S. at 494.

17. Ibid. One year later and after further oral arguments, the Court ordered desegregation to proceed "with all deliberate speed." *Brown v. Board of Education*, 349 U.S. 294 (1955), commonly known as "*Brown* II." "This method did not further the hopeful message set forth in *Brown* I, however, but instead served as an invitation to delay desegregation efforts rather than implement them immediately." Roy L. Brooks, Gilbert Paul Carrasco and Michel Selmi, *Civil Rights Litigation: Cases and Perspectives*, 2d edition (Durham: Carolina Academic Press, 2000), pp. 91–91.

As I see it, the only appropriate holding in this case is a race-neutral one; that is, a symmetrical equality rule which is self-consciously attuned to the values of Negro Americans. Accordingly, I would rule that, in furtherance of the Negro value of racial neutrality, all children, regardless of race, must be given equal access to all public schools within their school districts, and that these districts must themselves be formed in a race-neutral manner. Guided by this simple freedom-of-choice rule, school districts will be able to desegregate their schools immediately and without regard to race.

2. *Internal Critique*

Although the freedom-of-choice rule seems to provide adequate relief to Negro children, we cannot be certain until it is tested (i.e., further contextualized) against several outsider-oriented standards; specifically, rational/empirical, standpoint, postmodern, and positionality.[18] When evaluated pursuant to the rational/empirical epistemology, this reconstructive measure looks pretty solid. Freedom-of-choice desegregates public schools without undercutting Negro equality. This preferred equality rule, in other words, eschews the majority's jurisprudence, which is "based upon a theory of [Negro] inferiority."[19] The majority's principal ruling—"Separate educational facilities are inherently unequal"—stigmatizes Negro children by suggesting they need to capture a white child in order to obtain a quality education. The main problem with the Negro schools, as the record in this case clearly indicates, is not that they are racially isolated, but rather that they are denied adequate books, chairs, desks, funding and other educational resources.[20] The majority's reasoning will come back to haunt Negroes for years.

Given its avoidance of racial stereotyping, the freedom-of-choice rule is a better desegregation rule than Justice Snyder's asymmetrical rule, infra. As Justice Snyder's own internal critique acknowledges, her preferred equality rule stereotypes Negroes by providing them with special treatment. There are no racial preferences in the freedom-of-choice rule, nor is there anything else in the rule that would stereotype Negroes as hapless victims in need of special treatment.

I do recognize, however, that *de facto* segregation by geography or personal preference can creep in under a freedom-of-choice desegregation regime. Where Negroes and whites reside in racial isolation, school districts can eas-

---

18. See Chapter 10, Section C, supra.

19. Brooks, *Integration or Separation*, supra note 13, at p. 17 (quoting Justice Clarence Thomas).

20. See ibid. at pp. 9–10.

ily remain segregated even when redrawn without regard to race. Also, Negroes and whites may exhibit a preference for one-race schools within the same redrawn school district.[21]

Under these circumstances, forced racial integration may well be the only way to achieve desegregation in fact. But that would entail race-consciousness, and, hence, a violation of our color-blind Constitution.[22] That, I simply cannot abide. "The difficulty of overcoming [segregation] is as nothing compared with the difficulty of eradicating from our society the source of [segregation], which is the tendency—fatal to a nation such as ours—to classify and judge men and women on the basis of their country of origin or the color of their skin. A solution to the first problem that aggravates the second is no solution at all."[23] The use of governmental powers to make race-based decisions is "illegal, immoral, unconstitutional, inherently wrong, and destructive of democratic society."[24]

What I fear most is that the majority's reasoning will undermine the color-blind principle in the cause of integration. Race-conscious school redistricting and pupil reassignment will come to be legitimate desegregation methods wherever de facto school segregation occurs. The majority's holding—"Separate educational facilities are inherently unequal"—will give plaintiffs a constitutional right to attend not the school of their choice but an integrated school.[25]

The freedom-of-choice rule is, in my view, sustainable under standpoint scrutiny. The rule is narrowly tailored to give desegregative relief to the essential outsider in this case—the Negro child who attends a segregated pub-

---

21. See note 13, supra.

22. "Our Constitution is color-blind, and neither knows nor tolerates classes among citizens." *Plessy v. Ferguson*, 163 U.S. 537, 559 (1896) (Harlan, J., dissenting); accord, *Ex parte Virginia*, 100 U.S. 339, 345 (1880); 2 J. Story, Commentaries on the Constitution § 1961, p. 677 (T. Cooley ed. 1873); T. Cooley, Constitutional Limitations 439 (2d ed. 1871).

23. *City of Richmond v. Croson*, 488 U.S. 469, 520–21 (1989) (Scalia, J., concurring).

24. Alexander Bickel, *The Morality of Consent* (New Haven: Yale University Press, 1975), p. 133.

25. See, e.g., *United States v. Hall*, 472 F.2d 261, 265 (5th Cir. 1972) (finding in *Brown* and its progeny "a constitutional right to attend an integrated school"). Implementing *Brown*'s desegregation mandate in later years "with all deliberate speed," *Brown v. Board of Education*, 349 U.S. 294 (1955) (*Brown* II), the Supreme Court has upheld the use of racial balancing, or quotas, in pupil and teacher assignments, see *Swann v. Charlotte-Mecklenburg Board of Education*, 402 U.S. 1, 22–31 (1971), and has rejected a freedom-of-choice plan under which not a single white student chose the Negro high school, and only 15% of the Negro high school students chose the white high school. See *Green v. County Board of Education of New Kent County, Virginia*, 391 U.S. 430 (1968). For a general discussion of the supremacy of racial integration over racial separation in the Court's civil rights' jurisprudence, see *Integration or Separation*, supra note 13.

lic school and wants out. This person is "essential," or "authentic," in that he is politically, psychologically, and culturally representative of the Negro at this time and place,[26] and is relevant—the "relevant essential outsider"—because he fits within the contours of the factual pattern in the lawsuits consolidated in this case.[27] The case before us is essentially about this particular category of Negro outsiders. It does not deal with Negro children who attend integrated public schools or private secular or religious segregated schools. None of these children would have standing to bring the case sub judice. The Negro children in each of the consolidated lawsuits in the case are forced to attend public schools that are racially segregated.

Other Negroes relevant to the case do not come within the reach of the freedom-of-choice rule. Most importantly, the Negro child who attends a segregated public school and sees nothing wrong with that does not benefit from this rule. This person (perhaps the anti-self, commonly referred to in the culture as an "Uncle Tom" or "Oreo") dislikes the idea that Negro children should be allowed to attend the public school of their choice if that means they have a right to attend an integrated public school, which, of course, is precisely what the freedom-of-choice rule allows.

Admittedly, the freedom-of-choice rule raises significant postmodern concerns. These concerns go beyond the failure of the rule to satisfy the anti-self, which, as an intersectionality, presents a legitimate postmodern claim.[28] The major problem is this: the rule does not provide relief beyond desegregation, and, hence, it does not address the needs of all relevant intersectionalities. Most importantly, it does not resolve the problem of unequal educational funding, which, along with segregation, is a major concern for most of the relevant intersectionalities (e.g., Negro children from poor or working-class families). This is a serious problem because it can prevent Negro public schools, largely left intact under a freedom-of-choice regime, from providing their students with equal educational opportunity. *Underfunded schools are inherently unequal.*

The underfunding problem arises from the manner in which public schools are traditionally funded. Public school funding comes mostly from local property taxes, which favor wealthy communities or school districts. Federal funding accounts for only about 6% of the public school budget.[29]

---

26. See, e.g., Lani Guinier, "The Triumph of Tokenism: The Voting Rights Act and the Theory of Black Electoral Success," *Michigan Law Review* 89 (1991): 1077, 1103.

27. Compare similar discussion of "relevant essential outsider" in Chapter 11, Section C2, supra.

28. See Chapter 9, Section C3, supra.

29. See Brooks, *Integration or Separation*, supra note 13, at p. 215.

The freedom-of-choice rule, quite obviously, does not do much for Negro children living in poor communities. Their choices are rather limited to poor school districts.

Although race-conscious redistricting, which places poor Negro and wealthy white schools in the same school districts, can resolve the equal funding problem, I find it to be an unacceptable solution. It violates the color-blind principle and, hence, the Constitution as I would construe it. Racial redistricting can create a host of practical problems as well. Negro and white schools may be too far apart to form rational district boundaries. Also, interdistrict busing could entail long daily rides for Negro and white children alike. This could prove costly, not to mention the toll it would take on the children themselves.

There is a more prudent way to resolve the equal funding problem. The district courts can order state officials to collect local property taxes into a state educational fund for redistribution on a per student, need-only basis. Schools running relatively expensive remedial educational programs would receive more public funds on a weighted per pupil basis than other schools. These added funds are needed to adequately meet the educational needs of poor students. If Negro children receive disproportionately more state funding, as they likely will, it shall be on the basis of their needs, rather than their race. As many states use a "revenue equity system" of funding, which seeks to reduce the differences in school revenues on a per student basis, rather than a "taxpayer equity" system, which attempts to reduce variation in taxpayer burden, they will not find it too difficult to switch to this more equitable revenue system.[30]

Issuing school funding orders is well within the district courts' remedial powers. It is incidental to the constitutional right to attend a desegregated school announced today. Negro children trapped in low-tax school districts are no less "segregated" than Negro children forced to attend one-race schools in wealthier school districts. Neither situation allows for the exercise of choice, which is the essence of the equal-protection right I see in the Constitution. District courts have equitable powers to order states to adopt a fair school funding system. Justice demands this much in this case.[31]

---

30. For a discussion of school financing systems, see, e.g., ibid. at pp. 215–17.

31. In *San Antonio Independent School District v. Rodriguez*, 411 U.S. 1 (1973), a divided Supreme Court held the state funding of schools based on property taxes did not violate the Equal Protection Clause because the funding scheme is rationally related to a legitimate state interest, namely, local control of school districts. However, in *Missouri v. Jenkins*, 495 U.S. 33 (1990), the Supreme Court held that the district court can, under certain circumstances, compel local authorities to levy taxes in excess of statutory limits to fund school desegregation.

The freedom-of-choice rule is sustainable under the positionality standard. Liberty, a hypertruth in the American culture, is clearly enhanced by the rule. For the first time in the history of our nation, Negro children will have equal access to public schools in their own school districts, North and South, East and West. With liberty comes another hypertruth—human dignity. The latter hypertruth carries great weight in this case because a correct reading of the psychological studies referenced in footnote 11 of the majority's opinion highlights the damaging effect segregation can have on the hearts and minds of Negro children in the absence of such mediating institutions as the Negro church and family.[32]

Some might argue that the freedom-of-choice reconstructive rule undermines the racial integration and quality education hypertruths. It is, of course, debatable whether integration even qualifies as a hypertruth not only in the South but also in the North. Despite the "American Creed," segregation is widely practiced by custom in the North and by law in the South. Our decision today in the companion case, *Bolling v. Sharpe*,[33] overturning school desegregation statutes in the District of Columbia, as well as the case *sub judice*, demonstrates broad rejection of racial integration in our culture. Describing his first visit to the North not long ago, one southern newspaper editor writes: "Proudly cosmopolitan New York was in most respects more thoroughly segregated than any Southern city; with the exception of a small coterie of intellectuals, musicians, and entertainers, there was little traffic between the white world and the black enclave in upper Manhattan called Harlem."[34]

Also, many Negroes see nothing special in integration.[35] They are proudly supportive of their own institutions, especially the Negro Church and Negro schools. For Negroes, the problem with segregation is not the absence of integration, but the denial of equal resources.[36] Nonetheless, for purposes of discussion, I shall assume that integration is a hypertruth in the American culture.

While it is true that integration is not a sure bet under a freedom-of-choice regime, it is also true that integration is not entirely foreclosed. Negroes and

---

32. See Brooks, *Integration or Separation*, supra note 13, at pp. 216–24, for a discussion of *Brown*'s flawed reading of the social science data. See also Chapter 4, Section D, supra.

33. 347 U.S. 497 (1954).

34. Harry S. Ashmore, *Hearts and Minds: The Anatomy of Racism from Roosevelt to Reagan* (New York: McGraw-Hill, 1982), p. 37 (the reference is to the Ashmore's visit to New York in the 1930s).

35. See note 13, supra.

36. See ibid.

white children are free to choose an integrated educational experience. Nothing is forced; not separation, not integration. Were this Court to force integration, not only would we violate our color-blind Constitution, but we would also diminish the quality of the integrated experience. Negro children would not be accepted or, if accepted, it would only be on a less-than-equal basis. This makes for unhealthy and potentially explosive racial mixing.

The quality education argument is also problematic because it can be read in two different ways. A "quality education" can be defined as an integrated education. So defined, the argument suggests that a Negro child needs to sit next to a white child in order to obtain a quality education. I do not believe the highest court in the land should be making that type of argument. A quality education can also be defined as a resource-rich education, in which case no stigma attaches. So defined, I would readily agree with the argument that the freedom-of-choice rule, standing alone, does little to promote the quality education hypertruth. Freedom-of-choice is of little practical value in the face of structural inequality. That is reason enough for me to modify the reconstructive measure to include an equitable school funding requirement.

Accordingly, I would hold (Point B) that the Fourteenth Amendment's Equal Protection Clause gives every child, regardless of race, the right to attend any public school within his or her school district and, further, requires state officials to collect local property taxes into a state educational fund for redistribution on a per student, need-only basis. To this extent, I join in the judgment (Point C) of the case.

C. Asymmetrical Equality Model

JUSTICE LEEMON SNYDER, CONCURRING

This Court issues today a holding that is long overdue: "The Fourteenth Amendment forbids states to use their governmental powers to bar children on racial grounds from attending schools where there is state participation through any arrangement, management, funds or property."[37] While I join in the majority's decision (Point C) to overturn state school segregation statutes, I do not believe the holding goes far enough to protect the rights of Negro children. As Justice Savage points out in her concurring opinion, supra, the Court gives the states no guidance in moving from a dual to a unitary public school system, and fails to contextualize its holding in Negro norms. While

---

37. *Cooper v. Aaron*, 358 U.S. 1, 4 (1958) (restating *Brown*'s holding).

Justice Savage's freedom-of-choice and equitable-school-funding holdings offer some guidance in desegregating the public schools, they do not go as far as I believe the Constitution mandates. For these reasons, I write separately.

1. Subordination Question

Like Justice Savage, I approach the issue of the case—the constitutionality of school segregation statutes—with the subordination question. I frame the deconstruction part of the question not as a question of facial neutrality, however, but as an inquiry into insiderism. Does the separate-but-equal doctrine suggest Level 3 Bias, unconscious bias? Does it stereotype or enforce insider privilege? Does it ignore or discount relevant outsider values? Each question is probative of insiderism,[38] and each question must be answered with an emphatic yes.

The conscious bias (let alone unconscious bias) in the Jim Crow statutes at issue in this case is too obvious to miss. Like other such laws, the school segregation statutes are predicated on a belief in the natural inferiority of the Negro. That belief was succinctly stated in the *Encyclopedia Brittanica* not long after these statutes were enacted: "The negro would appear to stand on a lower evolutionary plane than the white man, and to be more closely related to the highest anthropoids."[39]

This finding of overt bias more than meets the unconscious-bias requirement. Yet, there is also direct proof of unconscious bias in the record. Applying the cultural meaning test, the separate-but-equal doctrine carries definite meaning in the Negro community. As the majority points out in its opinion:

> To separate negro children from others of a similar age and qualifications solely because of their race generates a feeling of inferiority as to their status in the community that may affect their hearts and minds in a way unlikely ever to be undone....
>
> Segregation of white and colored children in public schools has a detrimental effect upon the colored children. The impact is greater when it has the sanction of the law; for the policy of separating the races is usually interpreted as denoting the inferiority of the negro group. A sense of inferiority affects the motivation of a child to learn.[40]

---

38. See Chapter 10, Section C, supra; Chapter 9, Section B3, supra; Chapter 8, Section B3, supra.

39. This passage is taken from the 1910 edition and is quoted in Ashmore, *Hearts and Minds,* supra note 34, at p. 44.

40. 347 U.S. at 494.

There is no mistake that school segregation statutes also protect insider privilege and, simultaneously, harm outsider status. The NAACP lawyers in this case have documented substantial racial inequality in school buildings, per pupil expenditures for textbooks and equipment, and teacher salaries throughout the Jim Crow states, even among Negro and white schools in the same school district. "[T]he typical black teacher labored in a poorly equipped classroom, taught larger classes for fewer days per year, and earned less doing it than did her white counterpart."[41] Southern states frequently allocate 2 to 3 times more money per pupil to white students than to Negro students.[42] Testifying during the trial phase of *Briggs v. Elliot*,[43] one of the cases consolidated for decision in this case, as to the condition of the African American schools in Clarendon County, South Carolina, Matthew Whitehead stated:

> The total value of the buildings, grounds, and furnishings of the two white schools that accommodated 276 children was four times as high as the total for the three Negro schools that accommodated a total of 808 students. The white schools were constructed of brick and stucco; there was one teacher for each 28 children; at the colored schools, there was one teacher for each 47 children. At the white high school, there was only one class with an enrollment as high as 24; at the Scott's Branch high school for Negroes, classes ranged from 33 to 47. Besides the courses offered at both schools, the curriculum at the white high school included biology, typing, and bookkeeping; at the black high school, only agriculture and home economics were offered. There was no running water at one of the two outlying colored grade schools and no electricity at the other one. There were indoor flush toilets at both white schools but no flush toilets, indoors or outdoors, at any of the Negro schools—only outhouses, and not nearly enough of them.[44]

School segregation statutes, in short, support an explicit, let alone implicit, sense of group position for white children. This is insiderism, pure and simple.

---

41. Robert A. Margo, *Race and Schooling in the South, 1880–1950: An Economic History* (Chicago: University of Chicago Press, 1990), p. 56. See also, Thurgood Marshall, "Teacher Salary Cases" in *The Negro Handbook* 1946–1947, Florence Murray, ed. (New York: A.A. Wynn, 1947), pp. 40–50.

42. Walter G. Stephan, "Blacks and Brown: The Effects of School Desegregation on Black Students" (prepared for the United State Department of Education, National Institute of Education, 1983), p. 3 (sources cited therein).

43. 98 F. Supp. 529 (1951).

44. Richard Kluger, *Simple Justice* (New York: Knopf, 1976), p. 332.

It, therefore, goes without saying that the separate-but-equal doctrine ignores or discounts relevant outsider values. In the context of public education, this doctrine discounts the value of equal educational opportunity Negroes hold so dearly.[45] Extending as far back as the pre-Revolutionary War era, Negroes have fought for equal educational opportunity. Many slaves risked punishment and even death to learn to read and write in violation of southern law. Today's ruling is the culmination of the NAACP's nearly three-decades-long effort to constitutionalize the Negro norm of educational equality.[46]

Having found racial subordination in the school segregation statutes, this Court must, in addition to overturning the statutes, give the local school boards guidance in moving from a dual school system to a unitary one. Otherwise, school boards are free to choose desegregative means that can in fact lead to segregative results. Such is the case with Justice Savage's freedom-of-choice holding. At a minimum, vestigial pockets of segregation will be found in nearly every school district in the country under her reconstructive measure.

The best way to redress the subordination identified above is through the following two-part reconstructive model. First, schools must be racially mixed wherever feasible. This might include inter-district pupil reassignments involving contiguous school districts. Second, the special funding requirement in the symmetrical reconstruction measure should apply only to Negro schools (i.e., de facto segregated schools) demonstrating financial need, provided that such special funding should not last longer than 10 years.

2. Internal Critique

This two-prong reconstructive rule can be justified on several grounds. Both prongs can withstand scrutiny under the rational/empirical test. While racial mixing may require mandatory busing of pupils (not just out-busing of Negroes, but also in-busing of whites) and thereby set off a reign of white backlash, a racially integrated student body can also be achieved through less coercive measures. For example, magnet schools can attract pupils of both races.

---

45. Richard Kluger tells the story of the struggle for equal educational opportunity in his award-winning book, *Simple Justice,* supra note 44.

46. See, e.g., Brooks, *Integration or Separation?,* supra note 13, pp. 5–7. On the compelling story of slaves who risked punishment and death to learn, see generally, Janet Duitsman Cornelius, *When I Can Read My Title Clear: Literacy, Slavery and Religion in the Antebellum South* (Columbia: University of South Caroline Press, 1991). See generally Kluger, *Simple Justice,* supra note 44.

Forced integration is not, however, an irrational act even given white (or Negro) resistance. Negro and white children must learn to live together. The future of our nation depends on the strength of our diversity. What Justice Harlan said in his lone dissent in *Plessy v. Ferguson*[47] nearly fifty years ago applies with perhaps greater force today: "The destinies of the two races, in this country, are indissolubly linked together."[48] I note also that the government's amicus curiae brief refers to Secretary of State Dean Acheson's report stating that "racial discrimination in the United States remains a source of constant embarrassment to this Government in the day-to-day conduct of its foreign relations; and it jeopardizes the effective maintenance of our moral leadership of the free and democratic nations of the world."[49] Permitting a large number of our schools to remain segregated in appearance after today's decision raises a strong suspicion of continuing racial discrimination and, thereby, undercuts "our moral leadership of the free and democratic nations of the world."[50]

Special funding for Negro schools during the next 10 years makes a great deal of sense as well. Some Negro schools will not be integrated because of geographic restrictions. We cannot expect these schools or even those schools that become partially integrated to provide an "equal" education without repairing the damage caused by decades of underfunding. The racial deficit must be made up if true equality is ever to be established; otherwise, there will always be a built-in racial differential between Negro and white schools even in the same school districts. Limiting funding to a ten-year period and only to those Negro schools that demonstrate student need places rational parameters around this important desegregation requirement.

Racial integration and special funding are rationally related to the majority's reading of the Fourteenth Amendment's Equal Protection Clause. This Court reads the Clause as a constitutional requirement for desegregation in the field of education. Racial integration and special funding are absolutely necessary to remove the vestiges of segregation from primary and secondary schools. Without these ingredients, schools will in fact remain segregated, both in their student bodies and in their financial resources. This will make a mockery of the constitutional mandate for school desegregation.

Conservative Negroes would argue against special funding of Negro schools on the ground that it is contrary to the Negro's interests. The fear is that such

---

47. 163 U.S. 537 (1896).

48. Ibid at p. 560 (Harlan, J., dissenting).

49. Bell, "Brown v. Board of Education," supra note 14, at pp. 179–80 (citing Brief for the United States as Amicus Curiae).

50. Ibid., at p. 180.

special funding could put Negroes on the slippery slope of preferential treatment. Once on that slope, the Negro may never attain the values of hard work and discipline necessary for success that whites and certain ethnic groups have acquired over the years.[51] The problem with this argument is that it transforms the racial stereotypes underpinning segregation into "positive social norms." Culture, thereby, replaces race as the acceptable means of subordination. The subordinating norm, although no longer explicitly couched in the now-discredited ideology of white supremacy, is still operative.[52]

There is an old Negro saying that "two wrongs don't make a right." This expression which, of course, is not exclusive to Negroes, was often invoked by older Negroes as an injunction against acts of violence younger Negroes were planning against whites in retaliation for racial injustice. Some might argue that race-consciousness associated with the integration plan and racial entitlement sanctioned by the special funding plan violate this Negro norm. Assuming *arguendo* that the asymmetrical reconstruction plan constitutes a wrong, to argue that it breaches the multiple-wrongs injunction misses the point of the command. "Two wrongs don't make a right" presupposes the second wrong is of equal or greater evil than the first wrong.[53] "If I am forgetful and permit one child to stay up a few minutes past her bedtime, I might permit the other child to do the same."[54] Similarly, the state's execution of a serial killer invokes a lesser wrong than the 50 killings for which the murderer was executed. Gunning down Hitler in cold blood is a lesser wrong than exterminating six million Jews. Likewise, race-conscious decisions or even racial preferences that bring about racial inclusion (as in the case of the asymmetrical reconstructive plan) entail a lesser wrong (again, assuming, for the sake of argument, that a wrong has been committed) than race-conscious decisions or racial discrimination designed to exclude, subordinate or stigmatize (as in the case of the school segregation statutes). Wrongs cannot be judged in a vacuum. The purpose for which action is taken cannot be ignored when assessing the justice or the injustice of the action; otherwise, how could we ever explain justifiable wrongs, such as wrongs committed in self-defense?

Racial integration and special financing of Negro schools also make sense from the standpoint perspective. The factual pattern of the consolidated cases

---

51. See, e.g., Thomas Sowell, *The Quest for Cosmic Justice* (New York: Free Press, 1999).

52. See, e.g., Kimberle W. Crenshaw, "Race, Reform, and Retrenchment: Transformation and Legitimation in Antidiscrimination Law," *Harvard Law Review* 101 (1988): 1331.

53. See Kenneth W. Simons, "The Logic of Equality Norms," *Boston University Law Review* 80 (2000): 693, 763.

54. Ibid. at pp. 763–64.

certainly support Justice Savage's finding that the essential outsider in this case is the Negro child who is forced to attend a segregated public school. This pupil would benefit directly and exclusively from the asymmetrical desegregation plan advanced in this opinion. Some will be part of a racially mixed student body. They will learn, as will their white classmates, "human nature in all its phases, with all its emotions, passions and feelings, loves and hates, its hopes and fears, its impulses and sensibilities."[55] Other authentic Negro students may not be part of an integrated educational experience, and may not learn as much about "the secret springs of human nature" as perhaps they should. But they will at least have been given adequate financial resources and, hence, the opportunity to obtain a quality education in terms of the "Three Rs." Though this is not the highest quality education possible—for in a racially diverse society the highest quality education must of necessity take place within a racially diverse setting—it is far better (more "equal") than an underfunded education.

Taking Judge Savage's findings as to the relevant intersectionalities, the asymmetrical desegregation plan largely makes sense when judged against the postmodern standard. It provides relief to all the relevant intersectionalities, most of whom suffer from *both* school segregation and school underfunding. Negro schools that are segregated but not underfunded with respect to the students' needs will receive adequate relief, but they will not receive a financial windfall. They are entitled to desegregation—the removal of government-sanctioned subordination and stigmatization, no small matter—but not special funding. The asymmetrical rule does not, of course, reach the anti-self (the Negro child who wants to attend a segregated public school) and to that extent could be rejected under postmodern scrutiny.

Finally, racially integrated public schools and adequately funded Negro public schools promote several hypertruths. Racial equality is certainly one such hypertruth. The two-prong asymmetrical desegregation plan will give Negroes the opportunity to obtain a quality education, which all Americans, regardless of color, value. Liberty will also be achieved as Negroes will no longer be limited by law to one-race, mostly dilapidated schools. The removal of racial shackles in public education lays the groundwork for the eradication of segregation in other areas as well, such as, housing, employment, and public accommodations. This will simply add to the human dignity hypertruth (particularly racial esteem and self-esteem) unleashed through school desegregation. True, the racial harmony hypertruth may be threatened by forced integration or, for that matter, any integration. On the

---

55. *Board of Education of Ottawa v. Tinnon*, 26 Kan. 1, 19 (1881).

other hand, we know from experience that there is no racial harmony in keeping the races apart. As Justice Harlan noted in his dissent in *Plessy v. Ferguson*:[56]

> What can more certainly arouse race hate, what more certainly create and perpetuate a feeling of distrust between these races, than state enactments, which, in fact, proceed on the ground that colored citizens are so inferior and degraded that they cannot be allowed to sit in public coaches occupied by white citizens?[57]

In any event, we cannot allow violence or the threat of violence to nullify constitutional rights.

Based upon this internal critique, I see no need to modify the preferred equality rule announced earlier.

Accordingly, I would hold (Point B)that all public schools shall be immediately desegregated and that such desegregation shall be accomplished through racially integrated student bodies where physically feasible, including inter-district pupil reassignments. In addition, similar to the funding portion of the symmetrical holding, Negro public schools must receive additional funding on a needs-only basis for 10 years beginning with the 1954–55 school year.

I join in the judgment (Point C)to this extent.

D. Hybrid Equality Model

JUSTICE BIALECKI KIM, CONCURRING

1. Subordination Question

While I completely concur in Justice Snyder's deconstruction of the separate-but-equal doctrine in the context of public schools, I write separately to offer a reconstructive scheme that is more open to white children than Justice Snyder's asymmetrical holding.

I would adopt as a matter of law the following three-phase desegregation plan offered by a highly respected critical theorist, Derrick Bell:

> *Phase I.* Equalization. Effective immediately on receipt of this court's mandate, school officials of the respondent school districts must: 1) ascertain through standardized tests and other appropriate

---

56. 163 U.S. 537 (1896).
57. Ibid. at p. 560 (Harlan J., dissenting).

measures the academic standing of each school district as compared to nationwide norms for school systems of comparable size and financial resources. This data will be published and made available to all patrons of the district. 2) All schools within the district must be equalized in physical facilities, teacher training, experience, and salary with the goal of each district, as a whole, measuring up to national norms within three years.

Phase II. Representation. The battle cry of those who fought and died to bring this country into existence was "Taxation Without Representation Is Tyranny." Effective relief in segregated school districts requires no less than the immediate restructuring of school boards and other policy-making bodies to insure that those formally excluded from representation have persons selected by them in accordance with the percentage of their children in the school system. This restructuring must take effect no later than the start of the 1955–56 school year.

Phase III. Access. Effective with the 1955–56 school year, any child seeking courses or instruction not provided in the school in which he or she is assigned may transfer without regard to race to a school where the course of instruction is provided.

To effectuate the efficient implementation of these orders, federal district judges are instructed to set up three-person monitoring committees with the Negro and white communities each selecting a monitor and those two agreeing on a third. The monitoring committees will work through with the school officials and the boards the necessary plans and procedures enabling the school districts' compliance. The district courts will give compliance oversight priority attention and will address firmly any actions intended to subvert or hinder the compliance program.[58]

2. Internal Critique

Before it can ripen into a holding, this three-phase reconstructive measure must be tested and further contextualized through the internal critique.

Rationally and empirically, this three-phase desegregation process makes sense, on balance. Phase I is a rational ruling, because there has been no direct testing of academic performance in either the Negro or white schools in connection with this or any other school desegregation case. There has only

---

58. Bell, "Brown v. Board of Education," supra note 14, at pp. 180–81.

been an assumption, based on gross inequality in facilities and per pupil spending for Negro and white schools, of low Negro achievement. As one expert has said, "'little or no data existed on the relative achievement levels of [Negro] and whites in segregated schools,' social scientists have had to hypothesize the existence of low academic achievement in segregated [Negro] schools by comparing school facilities and per pupil expenditures of these schools with those of white schools."[59] Phase I seeks to establish a rational and empirically validated baseline from which progress toward academic equality can be measured school by school, year by year.

Skipping Phase II for the moment, Phase III (course access) also meets the rational/empirical standard. It empowers Negro children, as well as white children, to overcome curricular limitations in their schools by transferring to schools that offer desired or needed courses. This will also encourage school districts to deploy their limited resources more efficiently. Some schools might become science academies and others writing academies, all equally accessible to students regardless of race.

Turning now to Phase II, I am quite aware that this portion of the desegregation plan, which calls for racial representation on school boards and the like (including monitoring committees mandated in the final portion of the plan), is problematic from a rational/empirical point of view. Some would argue that it stigmatizes Negroes and also continues the color-conscious focus on education introduced under the now-illegal school segregation statutes. See, supra, Savage, J., concurring. But it cannot be gainsaid that the very legitimacy of school desegregation in this new era of racial diversity brought into existence today by the decision in this case depends on the anterior decision to use race in the construction of racially inclusive school boards. Our democracy's legitimacy is undermined when policy-making bodies maintain the appearance of prior subordinating regimes. The vestiges of Jim Crow and slavery must be eliminated "root and branch."

Not only the legitimacy, but also the effectiveness of the entire desegregation enterprise depends on proportional representation. School boards will be responsible for supervising the campaign to desegregate public schools. Indeed, this approach seems more appropriate than having courts dictate specific methods of desegregation, which might foreclose local experimentation. School boards will need to draw upon the knowledge and skills of the entire community if they are to be effective. This means, in particular, that Negro

---

59. Brooks, *Integration or Separation*, supra note 13, at pp. 8–9 (quoting Walter Stephan).

community leaders—who are in the best position to protect the educational interests of Negro children—must be included in the decision-making process.

We must next determine whether the hybrid reconstruction model passes scrutiny under the standpoint test. It could be argued that proportional representation, in many ways the heart of the hybrid desegregation plan, founders on the shoals of either standpoint or postmodernist test, that it cannot survive scrutiny under both tests simultaneously. Because this argument relates to both tests, I shall address them together.

To set up the argument, I shall refer to the following story told by Harold Cruse, a rising star among Negro intellectuals:

> In 1940, as one of my first acts in the pursuit of becoming a more 'social' being, I joined a YMCA amateur drama group in Harlem. I wanted to learn about theater so I became a stage technician—meaning a handyman for all backstage chores. But the first thing about this drama group that struck me as highly curious was the fact that all the members were overwhelmingly in favor of doing white plays with Negro casts. I wondered why and very naively expressed my sentiments about it. The replies that I got clearly indicated that these amateur actors were not very favorable to the play about Negro life, although they would not plainly say so. Despite the fact that this question of identity was first presented to me within the context of the program of a small, insignificant amateur drama group, its implications ranged far beyond. A theater group, no matter how small, must have an audience. What did the audience at the Harlem YMCA really think about the group's productions?[60]

The "identity question," as Cruse calls it, is an important question in the Negro community. Leaders within the community have staked out different positions on the identity question. On the one hand, some argue that racial kinship is the primary basis for Negro identity. More than class, gender, occupation, citizenship or even religion, race defines the Negro, which is to say his first commitment, attachment, and loyalty belongs (or should belong) to his race. Whether Negro or white, we are all prisoners to the legacy of slavery and Jim Crow, both in terms of the present-day psychology of race and in terms of the present-day socio-economics of race—the unjust enrichment

---

60. Harold Cruse, *The Crisis of the Negro Intellectual: From Its Origins to the Present* (N.Y. William Morrow & Co., 1967), p. 3.

today's whites enjoy from slavery and government-sanctioned racial oppression.[61]

This argument leads to the view that Phase II should require the Negro representative to be authentic; that is, to be politically, psychologically, and culturally Negro.[62] The Negro representative must be one who is sensitive to educational matters of vital importance to Negroes *and* is willing to zealously represent those concerns at school board meetings. Certainly he cannot be the Negro anti-self (Uncle Tom), but nor can the Negro representative, like the Negro cast Cruse encountered in 1940, be of a mind to mimic whites; otherwise what good is he to the Negro community? Doesn't that defeat the democratic intent behind Phase II?

The identity question is not this simple; for it also has a definite postmodern dimension. Negro leaders have questioned the utility of race as a descriptive, analytical or prescriptive concept in the Negro community. Indeed, some Negroes have attempted to create an identity as an individual rather than as a Negro or colored person. In *Invisible Man* (1947), for example, Ralph Ellison, the famous Negro author, argued for an identity independent of race, one that rejects the stereotypical view of Negroes put forth by white racists. Ellison was raised in Oklahoma where "the frontier spirit…had fostered in him a sense of human possibility that he considered the very essence of American democracy."[63] Likewise, Ellison rejected the mindset of Bigger Thomas, the young Negro male character created by the famous Negro author Richard Wright in *Native Son* (1940), who was driven to murder by his own suffering as a victim of a racist society. "Bigger Thomas murders a white girl because the racist society has so imbued him with a fear of being found alone with a white female that his own instinct for survival leads him to kill her, virtually by reflex. Racism so determines Bigger's self that his will is irrelevant."[64]

The individualized/postmodern view of Negro identity would suggest that Phase II should perhaps not mandate proportional representation at all. Proportional representation is nothing more than racial essentialism, which oversimplifies African American identity and deprives African Americans of their

---

61. For an excellent discussion of white unjust enrichment, see Joe R. Feagin, *Racist America: Roots, Current Realities, and Future Reparations* (N.Y.: Routledge, 2000).

62. See, e.g., Lani Guinier, "The Triumph of Tokenism: The Voting Rights Act and the Theory of Black Electoral Success," *Michigan Law Review* 89 (1991): 1077, 1103.

63. *The Norton Anthology: African American Literature*, Henry Louis Gates, Jr. & Nellie Y. McKay, gen. eds. (N.Y.: W. W. Norton and Company, 1997), p. 1515.

64. Shelby Steele, "The Content of His Character," *The New Republic*, March 1, 1999, at p. 31.

agency. It teaches Negro children the wrong lesson: give up your aspirations and, instead, become driven by "Bigger Thomas-style determinism into self-destruction."[65] Furthermore, if Negro identity is so individualistic, so personal, how can it be represented fairly or accurately? A white person can just as effectively represent Negroes as any Negro can, because we are all, at bottom, flesh and blood. We have the same basic wants and needs, fears and passions.

Hence, the proportional representation rule cannot survive under both the standpoint and postmodern tests. It is sustainable under one but not the other. The tests cannot be reconciled in this case.[66] That is the argument, an interesting one at that, but one that I believe badly misses the mark.

The proper question for application of the standpoint and postmodern tests is not whether the tests can be reconciled in the actual selection of a particular school board member, but rather whether the *selection process*—proportional representation—can satisfy the standpoint and postmodern tests. The clear answer to this question is yes. Negro communities can use proportional representation to select whomever they desire as their representatives. There is nothing in proportional representation, or, for that matter, any other part of the hybrid equality rule, that favors or prejudices a particular Negro mindset. The person(s) voted to the school board can go as the representative(s) of the essential Negro child or as the representative(s) of any other intersectionality. He (or they) can even go as the anti-self. It is up to the Negroes making the selections.

On the other hand, I understand the argument that standpoint review requires more than just the mere opportunity to select an authentic representative to the school board. Standpoint epistemology, the argument goes, requires that the essential outsider must in fact be selected; for only she has correct knowledge of the Negro children's interest, and only she can zealously represent that interest. In this sense, the proposed hybrid holding cannot pass muster under standpoint scrutiny. Given the conflict between standpoint and postmodern epistemologies, positionality's position on the matter takes on added weight.

The propriety of the hybrid desegregation model can be firmly established by positionality. Phases I to III validate at least two hypertruths: equal educational opportunity and democratic decision making. Equal educational opportunity is promoted by the requirement in Phase I that "[a]ll schools within

---

65. Ibid, at p. 32.

66. Usually they cannot be reconciled because the standpoint test rejects the anti-self while the postmodern test regards the anti-self as a legitimate intersectionality. See Justice Savage's Internal Critique, supra.

the district must be equalized in physical facilities, teacher training, experience, and salary," by the additional requirement therein for testing in all schools, and by the equal access command in Phase III. The democratic ideal is effectuated through proportional representation, Phase II. Like Phrases I and III, Phase II is applicable to Negroes and whites alike.

These values—equal educational opportunity and democracy—are so accepted in our society by all races that they must be viewed as hypertruths. They are so ingrained in the American culture that they have been enshrined in our Constitution. Equal protection under the Fourteenth Amendment, as interpreted by the Court today, supports equal educational opportunity and, necessarily, democratic decision making in school governance. Equal educational opportunity means nothing without the right to participate in the decision-making process shaping one's education.

Accordingly, I believe the hybrid three-phase reconstruction rule should be taken as the holding (Point B)of this case. My support for the judgment (Point C) goes no further than that.

Epilogue

Jurisprudence attempts to explain the process by which a judge arrives at a decision in a case as well as specify the sources upon which the judge calls for assistance. Both elements of jurisprudence—process and sources—are connected to the judge's social setting. There is, indeed, a symbiotic relationship between judicial analysis and social context. That is precisely why the traditional process—legal formalism, Scalian textualism, legal realism, sociological jurisprudence, and legal process—may be insufficient for modern American society.

Our society is more heterogeneous today than at any other time in its history. Demands on insiders to share power have become the norm rather than the exception. Yet, none of the traditional jurisprudential models is able to absorb these social forces. Too often judges, when moving from Point A to Point C, subordinate rather than validate outsider norms. Outsider norms are often "invisible," to borrow from Ralph Ellison, to the naked insider eye. What is needed, then, is a jurisprudence that teaches judges how to be cognizant of relevant outsider norms, and, thus, avoid juridical subordination.

Critical theory may be that vehicle. What most criticalists desire more than anything else is an America free of subordination. They want a society in which the terms and conditions of power are transformed to permit more inclusion of outsiders. Criticalists see law as playing a vital role in engendering "social transformation."

Critical process is an attempt to make this happen. It is an attempt to move critical theory from the realm of protest to the realm of judicial theory. Just as Holmes, Pound, Llewellyn, Hart and Sacks have sought to conform jurisprudence to the social settings of their era—the twentieth century—so too must contemporary legal scholars attempt to conform law and legal analysis to today's social needs—the needs of the twenty-first century. Change in law and legal method is nothing new. "The difference from age to age," as Cardozo has said, "is not so much in the recognition of the need that law shall conform itself to an end. It is rather in the nature of the end to which there has been need to conform."[1] Using formalism as an example, Cardozo observed that "[t]here have been periods when uniformity, even rigidity, the elimination of the personal element, were felt to be the paramount needs."[2]

The question is whether critical process is the appropriate vehicle for bringing jurisprudence into the new millennium. Critical process is not sufficiently broad to carry the load by itself—it does not apply in the absence of a finding of subordination. It will therefore have to be joined with traditional process to form a unified process of judicial decision making. Another problem that needs to be addressed is the concept of "outsider." Is it too narrow to reach all those who should be reached (such as the poor and disabled)? Or does it sweep too broadly, lumping under a single conceptual umbrella groups with very different subordination experiences (such as white homosexuals and African American young men)? Should the outsider concept be disaggregated in the twenty-first century? These and other issues will arise as scholars continue to modernize jurisprudence.

1. Benjamin N. Cardozo, The Nature of the Judicial Process (New Haven: Yale University Press, 1921), p. 116.

2. Ibid.

INDEX

285–87, 293–95, 299–300; critical
process, 260, 262–64, 268; criticalist
sense, 226; *Kulko v. Superior Court,*
270–71, 272–74, 278–79
Substantive due process, 49, 50, 51,
57–58
Summers, Robert, 94–95, 95n30
Supreme Court: Fuller Court, 46;
Jacksonian Era, 42; Lochner Court,
18, 37–38, 39; nominees'
qualifications, 16n59; pragmatism
and justices, 172; Rehnquist Court,
18; Warren Court, 18, 18n62, 147
Supreme Court decisions: *Alden v.
Maine,* 18n64, 59n117, 179n42,
188n3; *Allgeyer v. Louisiana,* 51–52;
Block v. Hirsh, 56; *Bob Jones
University v. United States,* 231; *Boys
Markets, Inc. v. Retail Clerks Union,
Local 770,* 141n40; *Brown v. Board of
Education,* xlii, xliii, 22, 25, 55,
76–77, 89, 102–8, 124–25, 130–31,
147–49, 189, 189n10, 267–68,
267n50, 283–305, 288n25; *Bunting
v. Oregon,* 56; *Bush v. Gore,* 11–12,
11–12n39, 19n70, 37n3, 177n32,
178, 178n36–39, 179n40–42;
Caterpillar Inc. v. Lewis, 33, 79, 81;
*Charles River Bridge v. Warren
Bridge,* 42–43, 46, 58; *Chevron
U.S.A., Inc. v. Natural Resources
Defense Council,* 83; *Cooper v.
Aaron,* 267n50; *Coy v. Iowa,* 73n58;
Dred Scott v. Sandford, 37n3; *Evans
v. Romer,* 234–35; *Farwell v. Boston
& Worcester R.R. Corp.,* 99–101,
101n61; *Frontiero v. Richardson,*
271n8; *German Alliance Ins. Co. v.
Lewis,* 56, 123; *Green v. County
School Board of New Kent County,
Virginia,* 267n50, 288n25; *Griswold
v. Connecticut,* 20–21; *Grutter v.*

Bollinger, 21n79; *Helvering v.
Hallock,* 141n40; *Holy Trinity
Church v. United States,* 68, 77;
Kulko v. Superior Court, 269–81;
Lochner v. N.Y., 37n3, 45, 53–54,
56, 92–93, 102; *Maryland v. Craig,*
72n53; *Missouri v. Jenkins,* 290n31;
Montana v. Egelhoff, 80, 80n96;
Moragne v. States Marine Lines,
140–41, 142; *Muller v. Oregon,*
54–55, 56, 128; *National
Endowment for the Arts v. Finley,*
73n57; *National Labor Relations
Board v. Fruit and Vegetable Packers
and Warehousemen, Local 760,* 144;
*Oncale v. Sundowner Offshore
Services, Inc.,* 235–36; *Plessy v.
Ferguson,* 77, 104–5, 296, 299;
*Pollock v. Farmers Loan and Trust
Co.,* 52; *Printz v. United States,* 73;
Reed v. Reed, 204, 271n8; *Robinson
v. Shell Oil Co.,* 81–83; *Rochin v.
California,* 146–47; *Roe v. Wade,*
20–21; *San Antonio Independent
School District v. Rodriguez,* 290n31;
*Santa Clara County v. Southern
Pacific Railroad,* 38, 48; *Shelley v.
Kraemer,* 89, 97; *Slaughterhouse
Cases,* 38n6, 51; *Smith v. United
States,* 66–67; *St. Mary's Honor
Center v. Hicks,* 225n131; *Swann v.
Charlotte-Mecklenburg Board of
Education,* 288n25; *United States v.
Lopez,* 18n64, 59n117, 179n42,
188n3; *United States v. Microsoft
Corp.,* 58–59, 58n112; *United States
v. Morrison,* 59, 179n42, 188; *Ward's
Cove Packing Co., Inc. v. Atonio,*
225n131
Syllogisms: in legal formalism, 39, 46,
47–51, 56; validity of, 57